Cambridge Monographs and Texts in Applied Psycholinguistics

**Advances in applied psycholinguistics, Volume 2**
**Reading, writing, and language learning**

Cambridge Monographs and Texts in Applied Psycholinguistics

*General Editor:* Sheldon Rosenberg

# Advances in applied psycholinguistics, Volume 2

## Reading, writing, and language learning

*Edited by*

SHELDON ROSENBERG

University of Illinois at Chicago

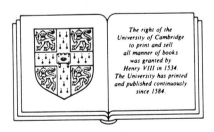

The right of the
University of Cambridge
to print and sell
all manner of books
was granted by
Henry VIII in 1534.
The University has printed
and published continuously
since 1584.

CAMBRIDGE UNIVERSITY PRESS

*Cambridge*

*New York    New Rochelle    Melbourne    Sydney*

Published by the Press Syndicate of the University of Cambridge
The Pitt Building, Trumpington Street, Cambridge CB2 1RP
32 East 57th Street, New York, NY 10022, USA
10 Stamford Road, Oakleigh, Melbourne 3166, Australia

© Cambridge University Press 1987

First published 1987

Printed in the United States of America

*Library of Congress Cataloging-in-Publication Data*
Advances in applied psycholinguistics.

(Cambridge monographs and texts in applied
psycholinguistics)
Published also in 2 v.
Includes index.

1. Psycholinguistics.   2. Language acquisition.
3. Language disorders.   4. Reading.   5. Writing.
I. Rosenberg, Sheldon.   II. Series.
P37.A33 1987   401'.9      87–10285

Advances in applied psycholinguistics.

(Cambridge monographs and texts in applied
psycholinguistics)
Published also in 1 v.

Includes indexes.

Contents: v. 1. Disorders of first-language
development – v. 2. Reading, writing, and language
learning.

1. Psycholinguistics.   2. Language acquisition.
3. Language disorders.   4. Reading.   5. Writing.
I. Rosenberg, Sheldon.   II. Series.
P37.A33 1987b   401'.9      87–13258

*British Library Cataloguing in Publication Data*
Advances in applied psycholinguistics –

(Cambridge monographs and texts in applied
psycholinguistics).

1. Psycholinguistics
I. Rosenberg, Sheldon
401'.9      BF455

ISBN 0 521 30027 4 hard covers (combined set)
ISBN 0 521 31732 0 v.1 : paperback
ISBN 0 521 31733 9 v.2 : paperback

# Contents

*To*
LEONARD D. ERON
*colleague extraordinaire*

# Preface

The present volume, *Advances in applied psycholinguistics: reading, writing, and language learning,* and its companion volume, *Advances in applied psycholinguistics: disorders of first-language development,* are part of the series entitled Cambridge Monographs and Texts in Applied Psycholinguistics, which began with the publication in 1983 of Ann M. Peters's *The units of language acquisition.* The general aim of this series is to bring together work from all of the subfields of applied psycholinguistics by authors who approach applied problems from the vantage point of basic research and theory in psycholinguistics and related areas of cognitive psychology. The aim of the present *Advances* was to make available high-level up-to-date reviews of research, theory, and practice in the two major areas of applied psycholinguistics: (1) disorders of first-language development and (2) reading, writing, and language learning, with each review focusing, wherever possible, on the published and ongoing work of its author or authors. Thus, the *Advances* should help researchers, teachers, students, and practitioners in the many areas of applied psycholinguistics – from fields such as psychology, speech–hearing–language sciences and pathology, applied linguistics, educational psychology, special education, neurology, psychiatry, foreign-language teaching, and English composition – keep abreast of major developments in their areas of interest.

Although the present chapters underwent editorial review for style, organization, and accuracy of content, the content, scope, and organization of a given manuscript have ultimately been left to its author or authors.

It is significant that the present volume contains three chapters dealing with what has clearly become a frontier issue in applied psycholinguistics, namely, writing. I refer to the chapter by Scardamalia and Bereiter, which highlights the possible role of writing in the development of knowledge, to the latest contribution of Hayes et al. to the cognitive, information-processing theory of writing processes, and to Perfetti and McCutchen's proposals concerning the role of linguistic abilities in reading and writing. Contrasting approaches to the origin and treatment of reading disorders are presented by Vellutino and Scanlon and by Blanton,

Semmel, and Rhodes. The latter summarize work on the reading of mentally retarded individuals that has emphasized the role of cognitive strategies, whereas
the former champion a largely linguistic approach to the understanding and treatment of reading disorders in otherwise normal school children. Finally, current
research and theory in the field of language learning are well represented by Hatch
and Hawkins and by Hakuta, Ferdman, and Diaz. Hakuta et al., for example, discuss research that is believed to be consistent with the claim that bilingualism facilitates cognitive functioning.

Sheldon Rosenberg

Chicago, Illinois

# Contributors

**Carl Bereiter** Centre for Applied Cognitive Science, Ontario Institute for Studies in Education, 252 Bloor Street West, Toronto, Ontario M5S 1V6, Canada

**Linda P. Blanton** Department of Language, Reading, and Exceptionalities, Appalachian State University, Duncan Hall, Boone, North Carolina 28608

**Linda Carey** Department of English, Carnegie Mellon University, Schenley Park, Pittsburgh, Pennsylvania 15213

**Rafael M. Diaz** Department of Psychology, University of New Mexico, Albuquerque, New Mexico 87106

**Bernardo M. Ferdman** Departments of Psychology and Latin American and Caribbean Studies, State University of New York at Albany, Albany, New York 12222

**Linda Flower** Department of English, Carnegie Mellon University, Schenley Park, Pittsburgh, Pennsylvania 15213

**Kenji Hakuta** Department of Psychology, Yale University, P.O. Box 11A Yale Station, New Haven, Connecticut 06520-7447

**Evelyn Hatch** English as a Second Language, Department of English, University of California, Los Angeles, California 90024

**Barbara Hawkins** English as a Second Language, Department of English, University of California, Los Angeles, California 90024

**John R. Hayes** Department of Psychology, Carnegie Mellon University, Schenley Park, Pittsburgh, Pennsylvania 15213

**Deborah McCutchen** Department of Psychology, University of Colorado, Muenzinger Psychology Building, Campus Box 345, Boulder, Colorado 80309

**Charles A. Perfetti** Learning Research and Development Center, University of Pittsburgh, 3939 O'Hara Street, Pittsburgh, Pennsylvania 15260

**Sharyn S. Rhodes** Loyola College, 4501 North Charles Street, Baltimore, Maryland 21210-2699

**Donna M. Scanlon**  Child Research and Study Center, State University of New York at Albany, Husted Hall, Downtown Campus, Albany, New York 12222

**Marlene Scardamalia**  Centre for Applied Cognitive Science, Ontario Institute for Studies in Education, 252 Bloor Street West, Toronto, Ontario M5S 1V6, Canada

**Karen A. Schriver**  Communication Design Center, Carnegie Mellon University, Schenley Park, Pittsburgh, Pennsylvania 15213

**Melvin I. Semmel**  Program in Special Education, University of California, Santa Barbara, California 93102

**James F. Stratman**  Graduate School of Industrial Administration, Carnegie Mellon University, Schenley Park, Pittsburgh, Pennsylvania 15213

**Frank R. Vellutino**  Child Research and Study Center, State University of New York at Albany, Husted Hall, Downtown Campus, Albany, New York 12222

# 1    Linguistic coding and reading ability

*Frank R. Vellutino and Donna M. Scanlon*

## Seminal research

Reading disorder in young children is undoubtedly associated with a variety of etiologies, both constitutional and environmental, but the source(s) of such disorder in the population of poor readers that has been most extensively studied over the years would seem to be more circumscribed. We refer here to those children who encounter significant difficulties in learning to read, especially in learning to identify individual words, despite average, above-average, or even superior intelligence and despite apparently normal functioning in other domains. Such terms as *specific reading disability* and *dyslexia* have often been used to refer to impaired readers of this description, and it has often been assumed that their learning difficulties stem from neurological disorder that causes dysfunction in one of the basic cognitive abilities that are prerequisites for acquiring skill in word identification. Hypotheses offered to explain word identification problems in these children have implicated foundational abilities that are germane to reading – specifically, visual perception, visual memory, and linguistic coding – as well as foundational processes that are involved in all learning and therefore are *not* specific to reading – in particular, cross-modal transfer, association learning, serial memory, and, more recently, what has been termed rule learning.

We tested each of these hypotheses in laboratory studies of comparably selected samples of severely impaired readers who were normal in all other respects and who were selected in accord with intellectual and exclusionary criteria typically employed in the literature (Vellutino, 1979). Thus, our poor readers were, on average, below the 10th percentile on an oral reading test, had average or above-

The studies reported in this chapter were supported in part by grants from the National Institute of Child Health and Human Development (RO1HD09658) and Recording for the Blind, Inc. The authors wish to express their sincere appreciation to the students, teachers, and administrators from schools in the Albany, New York, area who participated in this research. We also wish to thank the many people who helped with data collection and analysis, especially Linda Rupert and Mark Prockton. Many thanks also go to Melinda Taylor and Judy Moran for typing and editing this chapter.

1

average intelligence, and were free of uncorrected sensory problems, extreme physical, neurological, emotional, behavioral, and sociocultural deficits, and frequent absences from school. The normal readers were randomly selected from the children remaining in the same grade and school from which poor readers were selected after the poor readers had been identified. In order to qualify for the sample, normal readers had to be reading at or above the 50th percentile for their grade placement and had to meet the same intellectual and exclusionary criteria applied to the poor readers.

Most of the subjects were monolingual children who attended schools located in middle- to upper-middle-class neighborhoods. Moreover, they were not clinic cases. Poor- and normal-reader groups were also equated for sex ratios, with boys outnumbering girls by ratios ranging between 3 : 1 and 6 : 1. Age levels studied ranged from 7 through 15 (grades 2 through 8), but in most of our studies we stratified our samples at grades 2 and 6, which corresponds to ages 7 to 8 and 11 to 12, respectively. With our particular selection criteria, this procedure contrasts poor- and normal-reader groups matched for age and grade as well as poor- and normal-reader groups (second-grade normal and sixth-grade poor readers) matched for reading ability.

We elected to study severely impaired poor readers, because we expected that any hypothesized process disorder that might potentially be documented by our research would more likely be found in these children than in poor readers who were only mildly or moderately impaired. Thus, if given disorders were not supported by our research with these more severely impaired subjects, they could more readily be ruled out.

### Perceptual deficit theories

Our seminal investigations evaluated the widespread belief that reading disability is caused by atypical neurological development leading to deficiencies in visual perception and/or visual memory. The strong version of the hypothesis was articulated by Orton (1925). He suggested that, because of the failure to establish hemispheric dominance for language, poor readers are subject to anomalies in visual perception such as letter and word reversals (e.g., "seeing" *was* as *saw*) that make it difficult for them to learn to read and spell. A weaker version of the visual-deficit explanation of reading disability was proposed by Hermann (1959), who hypothesized that poor readers have difficulty with orienting and (left to right) sequencing of letters in words because of genetically endowed tendencies toward spatial and directional confusion.

In a series of studies using a variety of visual memory paradigms, we found no support for either the strong or the weak version of the visual-deficit explanation of reading disability. Our results suggested, instead, that the orientation and sequencing difficulties observed in poor readers' attempts at letter and word identification are likely due to dysfunction in linguistic coding and lexical retrieval, rather than to dysfunction in visual–spatial processing. Thus, in two separate studies (Vellutino, Smith, Steger, & Kaman, 1975; Vellutino, Steger, & Kandel, 1972) poor readers performed as well as normal readers in "reading out" and copying the letters in visually similar words after brief tachistoscopic presentation of these words. However, they did not perform as well as normal readers in naming the same words as wholes on subsequent (tachistoscopic) presentations. In other words, poor readers could correctly orient and sequence the letters in such words as *was, bad,* and *loin* from visual memory, despite the fact that they could not name them correctly. This finding suggested that so-called reversal errors are manifestations of dysfunction in verbal mediation and that the child who makes them is *not* impaired by visual–spatial confusion.

The inference was reinforced by a subsequent series of studies (Vellutino, Pruzek, Steger, & Meshoulam, 1973; Vellutino, Steger, DeSetto, & Phillips, 1975; Vellutino, Steger, Kaman, & DeSetto, 1975) in which poor and normal readers were found to be equivalent in visual recall and recognition of letters and words written in Hebrew, an orthography that was unfamiliar to them. They did not, however, perform as well as control-group children who were learning to read and write Hebrew. Moreover, the poor and normal readers who were unfamiliar with Hebrew manifested virtually identical scanning tendencies in left–right sequencing of the Hebrew letters and words. The scanning tendencies of these subjects, however, were directly opposite to the scanning tendencies of subjects who were familiar with Hebrew, those in the latter group ordering the stimuli from right to left. These results were interpreted to mean that, when poor readers have difficulty maintaining a left to right progression in reading connected text, it is a consequence of their reading problems rather than a basic cause of these problems.

### Cross-modal transfer and association learning

The possibility that reading difficulties in the children we elected to study might be attributed to linguistic coding and lexical processing deficits was given even greater impetus by the results of another series of experiments conducted in our laboratory evaluating both the cross-modal-transfer and associative-learning-deficit explanations of reading disability.

The most popular variation of the cross-modal-transfer theory of reading disability (often called the intersensory deficit theory) was articulated by Birch (1962). According to this point of view, many poor readers are encumbered by the inability to associate and integrate representations stored in different cognitive systems (e.g., the visual and auditory modalities) but may have no difficulty in associating and integrating representations *within* these systems. Initial documentation of this theory was provided by Birch and Belmont (1964), who found that many poor readers in their sample could not match auditorily presented rhythmic (Morse code–like) patterns with their visual counterparts. These and similar findings were replicated in subsequent investigations by other researchers (see Vellutino, 1979, for a comprehensive review), but Blank and her associates (Blank & Bridger, 1964, 1966; Blank, Weider, & Bridger, 1968) later observed pattern-matching difficulties in poor readers when stimuli were presented within as well as across the auditory and visual modalities. They also found that the poor readers were less proficient than the normal readers in using verbal coding devices and rehearsal strategies to help them store and retrieve these patterns from short-term memory. They therefore rejected Birch's cross-modal-transfer theory and suggested, instead, that verbal coding deficits may be common to both the pattern-matching and the word identification problems encountered by poor readers.

In order to evaluate these alternatives more fully, we contrasted comparably selected samples of severely impaired and normal readers on measures of nonverbal and verbal paired-associates learning that controlled both for short-term-memory constraints and for previous learning (Vellutino, Steger, Harding, & Phillips, 1975; Vellutino, Steger, & Pruzek, 1973). The nonverbal tasks involved learning within and between given modalities. The *within*-modalities tasks presented subjects either with simple visual forms as stimulus and response associates or with environmental sounds as stimuli and easily imitated vocalizations (e.g., coughing or humming) as responses. The *between*-modalities task used simple visual forms as stimuli and nonverbal vocalizations as responses.

The verbal learning tasks consisted of two between-modalities subtests that, respectively, simulated object naming and whole-word learning. These subtests were always presented in the same order, with the object-naming tasks being given first. Object naming required that subjects associate a novel cartoon figure with a consonant–vowel–consonant nonsense word presented auditorily. The whole-word learning task was given shortly after and used novel script as stimuli and the same nonsense words presented under the object-naming condition as responses. The novel characters did *not* correspond invariantly to the phonemes in the nonsense words.

The important findings in these studies were that the poor readers performed as well as the normal readers on both the within- and between-modalities nonverbal learning tasks and did not perform as well as the normal readers on the simulated object-naming and whole-word learning tasks. Moreover, on both of these tasks, poor readers produced more semantic substitution errors than did normal readers, whereas the normal readers produced more phonetic substitutions. These findings suggest that the poor readers were attuned more to the semantic than to the phonetic associates activated by the nonsense words, whereas the normal readers were more evenly attuned to both phonetic and semantic associates.

Our results were at once contrary to the cross-modal-transfer and associative-learning theories of reading disability and strongly supportive of the verbal-deficit explanation of this disorder. In addition, they suggested that poor readers have less facility than normal readers in coding the phonological attributes of spoken words. Still more support for the verbal-deficit hypothesis emerged in subsequent studies in which we evaluated a second variation of the cross-modal-transfer theory of reading disability that was suggested by research conducted by Sperry (1964) and his associates (Gazzaniga, Bogen, & Sperry, 1965). These investigators provided direct evidence for the possibility that the corpus callosum (midbrain connective tissue) is responsible for the transmission of information between the two hemispheres of the brain by demonstrating that adult patients whose brains were surgically bifurcated at the corpus callosum could visually reproduce but could not name printed words when visual hemifield presentations of these words stimulated the right hemisphere. However, they could name as well as copy these same words when such presentations stimulated the left hemisphere. Moreover, the results were consistent with previous clinical studies (Geschwind & Fusillo, 1966) wherein naming difficulties were observed in stroke victims who had incurred damage to the corpus callosum. Extrapolating from the combined data sets, we hypothesized that word identification problems in poor readers could be due to dysfunction in interhemispheric transmission. This hypothesis seemed plausible in view of other studies (Denckla & Rudel, 1976a, 1976b), which demonstrated not only that poor readers were much slower than normal readers in rapid naming of common objects and colors, but also that they appeared to be "subtly dysphasic" in naming these items, as manifested in frequent circumlocutions, substitutions, and hesitations.

In three separate investigations, we tested the hypothesis using the visual hemifield presentation technique of Sperry (1964). In two of these investigations the subjects were presented with paired-associates learning tasks using Chinese idiographs as stimuli and common English words as responses (Vellutino, Bentley, & Phillips, 1978; Vellutino, Scanlon, & Bentley, 1983). The idiographs appeared randomly in the left, central, and right visual fields, but a given stimulus always appeared in the same visual field. Random presentations to the central field served to stabilize eye fixations. We reasoned that, if poor readers' difficulties with word identification and other visual–verbal learning tasks are caused by dysfunction in hemispheric transmission, these children should perform below their normal reading peers on the paired-associates tasks when visual stimuli are presented to the left visual field (right hemisphere) but as well as the normal readers when visual stimuli are presented to the right visual field (left hemisphere). However, contrary to the hypothesis, poor readers performed below the normal readers on all visual field presentations. We therefore concluded that reader group differences on the learning tasks were likely due to group differences in verbal processing and not to group differences in interhemispheric transmission.

This conclusion was buttressed by the third study we conducted using a less complex task that evaluated speed of interhemispheric transmission (Vellutino et al., 1983). The technique employed was that described by Filbey and Gazzaniga

(1969). Poor and normal readers were given right- and left-field presentations of a simple dot stimulus and were asked to respond "yes" only if a dot had appeared in either field and "no" if no dot appeared. Contrary to the interhemispheric transmission notion, within-group latencies were no greater for left- than for right-visual-field presentations, although the poor readers generally responded more slowly than did the normal readers.

### Pattern analysis and rule learning

The foregoing studies strongly support a linguistic-coding-deficit explanation of reading disability. Adding to this evidence are the results of another study from our laboratory, which evaluated the possibility that poor readers' difficulties in word identification are occasioned by deficiencies in pattern analysis and rule learning. Such skill is especially important in detecting the grapheme–phoneme invariance embedded in the orthography and in synthesizing such invariance in the form of symbol–sound correspondence rules that can be used to facilitate code acquisition. The impetus for our study came initially from Rabinovitch (1959), who conjectured that poor readers may have difficulties in the detection of grapheme–phoneme invariance because of a more general deficit in conceptual learning (see Morrison & Manis, 1982, for a more recent version of this theory).

In the study addressing the question (Vellutino, Harding, Phillips, & Steger, 1975), poor and normal readers (grades 4, 5, and 6) were randomly assigned to one of two experimental conditions that involved the learning of paired associates containing invariant units. In a visual–verbal learning condition, subjects were presented with novel digraphs as visual stimuli and bisyllabic nonsense words as responses. The two designs in a given digraph were in one-to-one correspondence with respective syllables in a given nonsense word. In a visual–visual condition, the paired associates were two sets of novel digraphs, and each of the designs comprising the digraphs in the stimulus sets corresponded invariantly with respective designs comprising the digraphs in the response sets. Each condition consisted of an initial learning subtest on which the subjects were first exposed to the paired associates and a transfer learning subtest on which invariant units were permuted to form "new" stimulus and response pairs. On both subtests (and under both conditions), the subjects were informed of which units were in one-to-one correspondence; their task was to learn these relationships on the initial learning subtest and generalize them to aid learning on the transfer subtest.

The results of this study provided *no* support for the rule-learning hypothesis. That is, poor readers performed below the level of normal readers under the visual–verbal condition, but not under the visual–visual condition. Moreover, when performance on the initial learning subtest of the visual–verbal condition was used as a covariate, reader group differences on the transfer subtest were eliminated. The combined results suggest that poor readers may have difficulty in abstracting invariance in learning visual–verbal associates, not because of basic deficiencies in pattern analysis and rule learning, but because of basic deficiencies in processing the verbal components of these associates (see Vellutino & Scanlon, 1982, and Morrison & Manis, 1982, for more comprehensive discussions of this issue).

To summarize, our seminal experiments evaluating process dysfunction theories of reading disability provided no support for those implicating deficits in foundation abilities that are involved in all learning and thus not specific to reading, in particular cross-modal transfer, serial memory, associative learning, and rule learning. Nor did they provide any support for etiological theories implicating dysfunction in visual–spatial ability, which is a foundation ability that *is* specifically involved in reading. In contrast, our investigations provided consistent evidence that poor readers are encumbered by deficiencies and/or inefficiencies in processing verbally coded information. Especially impressive are the findings of those studies that systematically contrasted comparably selected reader groups on measures of verbal and nonverbal learning wherein group differences were obtained on visual–verbal learning tasks, but not on nonverbal learning tasks that involved both intermodal and intramodal associates. This pattern of results provided us with two alternative explanations of reader group differences on word identification and other visual–verbal learning tasks. The first, which from our data seemed highly likely, is that poor readers may be especially encumbered in remembering the verbal response components they encounter on such learning tasks. Our surmise here was that, because of more basic difficulties in accessing name codes, these children may find it especially difficult to use language to code information and may therefore have difficulty in acquiring relationships that necessitate their doing so.

The second alternative is that poor readers may be encumbered by a more circumscribed deficit in cross-referencing and integrating visual and verbal associates, implying that they would have difficulty in learning only when asked to pair such associates. We therefore designed a series of studies that more directly evaluated these alternatives. These investigations made use of a variety of experimental paradigms that contrasted poor and normal readers on the degree to which they are attuned to and make functional use of linguistic and nonlinguistic representations of the featural attributes of printed and spoken words in encoding the information contained in these stimuli and in learning to discriminate and remember them. We reasoned that if poor readers' difficulties in word identification and other visual–verbal learning tasks are due primarily to deficiencies in processing the verbal components of such tasks, these deficiencies should be manifested on verbal memory tasks that do *not* involve the processing of visual associates, as well as on learning tasks that involve the integration of both visual and verbal associates. However, if poor readers' difficulties are due to a more circumscribed deficit in visual–verbal integration, they should perform below the level of normal readers only 'on tasks of the latter type.

The main body of this chapter is devoted to a discussion of studies conducted in our laboratory evaluating these hypotheses. However, to appreciate the logic behind these studies fully, it will be necessary to define more clearly what we mean by the term *linguistic coding*.

## Linguistic and nonlinguistic codes

### Definition

Words in the lexicon are complex mental representations that symbolize concepts, entities, attributes, and ideas taken from one's experiences that are coded in units of language. Linguistic codes are, themselves, complex representations of the physical properties that define those words and of the "rules" that constrain their use. Thus, all words have both substantive and structural components that we assume are qualitatively and functionally distinct.

The substantive components of a single word can be conceptualized as a collection of memory codes that signify the meanings embodied in that word, both denotative and connotative. These have been termed *semantic codes*. During the course of lexical development, semantic codes become increasingly elaborated, more highly differentiated, and better integrated and come to exist in a complex network of hierarchically ordered associates that are connected to various degrees. It seems probable that a child with a more highly differentiated and more highly elaborated inventory of semantic codes, as manifested in a rich fund of world knowledge and a rich vocabulary, is better able to make functional use of semantic or meaning-based strategies in storing and retrieving spoken and written words than a child with a less highly differentiated and less highly elaborated inventory of semantic codes.

The structural components of a single word can also be conceptualized as a collection of memory codes, but these refer to the formal properties of the word that define it as a morphological unit in language. The formal properties of spoken words are defined by coded representations of their *phonological* and *syntactic* attributes, or what, in the basic sense, can be called their "purely linguistic" properties. The formal properties of written words are defined, as well, by coded representations of their *graphic* and *orthographic* attributes, or what can be called their nonlinguistic properties.

Phonological codes are highly abstract representations of the basic sound units defining given words. Such representations have elsewhere been termed *systematic phonemes* (Chomsky & Halle, 1968) and are functional in that they allow one to recognize given words in the language, despite surface or allophonic variations arising from differences in the pronunciation of those words. The term *phonological codes* also refers to a system of "rules" that set constraints on and generate particular orderings of phones and phonemes in the language. In addition to a rich fund of semantic information, children's ability to store and retrieve spoken and written words would seem to depend on their ability to assign phonological codes to a word's substantive and visual properties, as well as on their ability to activate and access those codes at will. It would seem, in addition, that phonological coding ability could greatly influence lexical or vocabulary development and thus semantic development in general. Availability of and access to phonological representations of given words are undoubtedly an important prerequisite to learning to spell those words orally and, more basically, to segmenting them into functionally distinct units, syllabically and phonemically.

*Syntactic codes* are also highly abstract representations, which can be conceived of as grammatical "rules" that set constraints on the order and use of words in sentences and thus define the functional as well as the formal properties of those words. The term is generic and at once refers to representations that allow us to (1) comprehend sentences characterized by different syntactic structures; (2) generate grammatically well formed sentences; (3) distinguish, categorize, and make use of form class differences in words (e.g., nouns vs. verbs); and (4) distinguish, categorize, and make use of inflectional differences in words (e.g., *ed* vs. *ing*). There seems little doubt that a child who is able to represent grammatical distinctions among sentences will be better able to encode and comprehend those sentences than a child who has difficulty in representing such distinctions. Similarly, a child who is able to distinguish form class differences in words and who is sensitive to the shades of meaning and structural differences associated with inflectional changes in given words is better equipped to store and retrieve these words from memory than a child who has difficulties making such distinctions.

*Graphic codes* are representations of the unique visual patterns formed by the particular arrangement of letters defining a given word and the visual patterns formed by the letters themselves.

*Orthographic codes* are representations of the structural attributes of words in the writing system, in the form of rules that constrain the spatial ordering of the graphemes or characters used in that system. In order to learn to identify and spell printed words, beginning readers must store representations of the unique graphic features of those words along with representations of their constituent letters. They must also store representations of the orthographic features that these words have in common with other words, if they are to acquire any degree of fluency in word identification.

### Qualitative and functional properties

The qualitative and functional properties of the linguistic and nonlinguistic codes we have just described correspond to distinct, though complementary, responsibilities assigned to each of these representations in processing spoken and written language for different purposes. Thus, in the fluent reader, semantic and syntactic codes are activated and, no doubt, are in primary attendance when he or she is *listening* to connected text for meaning. Moreover, there is good reason to believe (Perfetti & Lesgold, 1979; Perfetti & McCutchen, 1982) that, under these circumstances, phonological codes are maintained long enough to allow sentences in the text to be fully processed, the inference here being that the sound attributes of words are especially important for maintaining information in temporary storage for higher-order encoding. When one is *reading* connected text for meaning, graphic and orthographic codes may also be activated for lexical access, but semantic and syntactic codes would again be in focal attention. However, it is an open question whether, in fluent readers, activation of phonological codes is necessary for printed word identification. There is, however, some evidence that they are activated postlexically, again to maintain verbatim information in short-term memory long enough to allow sentences to be fully processed (Perfetti & McCutchen, 1982).

When the learner's task also requires verbatim memory of spoken or written words (e.g., when it involves recall of factual information, names, or randomly presented words on a list to be learned), a good deal more attention would be deployed to phonological and/or graphic and orthographic attributes. These attributes would, of course, be in focal attention when the task requires structural analysis and attendance to structural detail, as in proofreading connected text for spelling and punctuation errors. The point to be emphasized in connection with these illustrations is that the fluent reader is presumed to have acquired a full inventory of linguistic and nonlinguistic codes that are activated automatically in the processing of spoken and written words and, depending on the learner's purpose, are accessed selectively and economically.

The situation is quite different for beginning readers, who, at the outset, are attuned primarily to the substantive or meaning component of language and who have not acquired much explicit information about its structural properties (Gibson, 1971). At this stage of language development, distinctions between substantive and structural codes tend to be made implicitly, and it will take some time before the child begins to engage in the type of "metalinguistic" analysis that will make the units and structures of spoken language explicit. Learning to read is an enterprise that, increasingly, promotes this type of analysis (Ehri, 1980), but there is evidence of a wide range of individual differences in what has been called "linguistic awareness" even in children who have not been exposed to formal instruction in reading (Bradley & Bryant, 1983; Fox & Routh, 1980; Liberman, Shankweiler, Fischer, & Carter, 1974).

Similarly, the beginning reader, by definition, does not have a full inventory of graphic and orthographic codes, and it will take some time to acquire such an inventory. However, we suggest that there is an intrinsic but asymmetric relation between the linguistic and nonlinguistic components of printed words, such that the ability to identify these stimuli, and thus to learn to read, is directly tied to one's ability to make functional use of their semantic, syntactic, and phonological attributes in differentiating and coding their graphic and orthographic attributes. Reading is primarily a linguistic skill, insofar as learners are required to code particular visual units in their natural language and decode those units to that language. Moreover, it is the linguistic attributes of printed words, not their visual attributes, that invest them with meaning and substance. It follows that language is the dominant system in learning to read, and the ability to associate the linguistic with the nonlinguistic components of printed words would seem to be the primary determinant of the way in which their nonlinguistic components are analyzed and ultimately represented.

## Strategies for word identification

To concretize these points, consider the alternative means by which the beginning reader may learn to identify printed words. Partly because attendance to meaning is the dominant processing mode for all children (Biemiller, 1970; Vellutino, Scanlon, DeSetto, & Pruzek, 1981; Weber, 1970) and partly because of the way in which most reading programs initiate learning, the typical approach to word identification, at the outset, is to rotely associate whole words with names that code meaningful concepts. If the words initially presented to the child represent highly familiar concepts and thereby permit ready access to their associated names, and if the printed forms of these words are highly distinct, a whole-word, meaning-based approach to identification will be functional and the child will be able to acquire a reasonably good corpus of words that can be identified with dispatch.

In an orthography based on an alphabet, however, words are characterized by a high degree of structural redundancy, and because of such redundancy, the beginner is soon confronted with a large number of words characterized by a great deal of visual similarity (e.g., *cat/rat; was/saw; lion/loin*). Thus, if, for whatever reason, the child uses only a whole-word approach to word identification, he or she will tend to make a large number of discrimination errors and will ultimately have difficulty in acquiring any degree of fluency in word identification. Moreover, a likely consequence of total reliance on a whole-word strategy of identification is the failure to detect the graphophonemic invariance contained in the orthography, which, of course, precludes the acquisition of alphabetic mapping rules. Detection and functional use of such invariance provide the child with a means of avoiding such errors, in the form of letter sounds that mediate to a correct response (e.g., /s/ in *saw*).

A second likely consequence of an exclusive whole-word approach to word identification would be the failure to distinguish between root and bound morphemes. For example, as just noted, there are many subword units that occur with high frequency, which is especially true of inflectional morphemes (e.g., *ing, ed, tion*) that change grammatical properties, such as tense, number, and case. The failure to make such distinctions in learning to identify printed words would be especially probable in the case of children who are inaccurate in making them in spoken language. The implication, in such instances, is that syntactic and phonological development are, for some reason, impeded in such children, the end result being that they fail to acquire morphophonemic rules governing the use of inflectional morphemes at an age-appropriate level. Exclusive reliance on whole-word processing would compound this problem.

In underscoring the hazards inherent in using only a wholistic meaning-based approach to word identification, we allude to the second way in which words may be identified by beginning readers, specifically through the use of grapheme–phoneme correspondence or alphabetic mapping rules. This approach typically involves the use of letter–sound associates that the child synthesizes to recover the names of given words and thereby their meanings. It is often called the "phonologically mediated" or indirect approach to word identification, and it has a great deal of utility for identifying words that conform to alphabetic mapping rules, what some (Baron, 1979) have called "regular" words. Because a sizable number of words in the language have this property, the use of such rules allows the learner to synthesize a large amount of visual information and thereby reduce the load on visual memory.

However, grapheme–phoneme correspondence rules do not work very well with words that do not conform to alphabetic mapping rules, often called "exception" words (e.g., *break* vs. *beak*). Moreover, total reliance on a letter–sound or phonetic decoding method of identifying printed words is hazardous in that it may lead to an inordinately piecemeal approach to identification, thereby limiting the child's ability to acquire an adequate corpus of whole words that can be rapidly identified on sight, a limitation that, itself, will impair the child's ability to acquire any degree of fluency in word identification.

A third strategy for identifying at least some words in written English, one that is intermediate between the whole-word and grapheme–phoneme rule approach, is the use of analogies. Many subword units can be identified through analogy with familiar words containing these units, as exemplified by rhyming words such as *boy, toy, joy* or by words containing inflectional morphemes that have invariant sound properties: go*ing*, com*ing*; bak*ed*, walk*ed*. Obviously, this strategy also helps reduce the load on visual memory.

A fourth way in which printed words may, on occasion, be identified is to infer the word's identity from a given sentence context. For example, in the incomplete sentence "The cat _____ black," the verbs *is* and *was* are among the few words that would be grammatically acceptable, and one would need only a partial cue (i.e., *i* or *w*) to "guess" accurately. However, despite suggestions to the contrary (Goodman, 1973; Smith, 1973), this method is highly unreliable and, by itself, would not lead to very much facility in word identification (see Gough, Alford, & Holley-Wilcox, 1981, for an excellent discussion of this point). If, however, the child has sufficient syntactic development to make accurate judgments as to the grammaticality of sentences he or she is asked to read, he or she will be able to use sentence contexts to provide corrective feedback when word identification errors make a given sentence ungrammatical. Such ability indirectly enhances facility in word identification and therefore complements other approaches to identification.

It should be apparent that sole reliance on any one of these strategies in learning to identify printed words would greatly reduce the probability that the beginner would become conversant with the multiple attributes of given words, and he or she would therefore have difficulty in acquiring a full inventory of graphic and orthographic representations endowed with the linguistic associates required to make them functional in word identification. It should also be apparent that these respective strategies may be complementary, insofar as each provides the child with qualitatively different representations of printed words (and their constituents) that may be used as alternative vehicles for word identification. As these representations are cross-referenced and integrated, performance becomes increasingly stable and the process eventuates in automatic retrieval of name codes and meanings on presentation of words as wholes.

Finally, it would seem that the particular graphic and orthographic representations of printed words that are incorporated by the beginner are determined, in large measure, by the processing strategies employed in word identification and, further, that these strategies, themselves, are determined by the child's familiarity with the linguistic attributes of those words and by his or her ability to use each of these attributes in coding their graphic and orthographic counterparts. This is what we meant when we said earlier that the ability to learn to read is directly tied and, in fact, constrained by linguistic coding ability.

## The linguistic-coding-deficit explanation of reading disability

With the foregoing conceptualizations in mind, we can be more explicit about the linguistic-coding-deficit theory of reading disability put forth earlier. As we indicated, our conceptualization of the probable causes of reading disability in otherwise normal children is based on the assumption that their reading impairment, defined herein as pervasive deficits in word identification, is due in large measure to difficulties they encounter in using language to code information. Either because of constitutional factors, characterized by neurological damage, maturational delay, and/or limited genetic endowment, or because of inadequate environmental stimulation, these children seem to be linguistically less sophisticated than normal readers at the same age and grade level and have difficulty in acquiring and/or accessing units and structures in one or more of the domains of language. As a result, they are less proficient than normal readers in storing and retrieving coded representations of particular linguistic units and may therefore have difficulty in some aspect of word identification.

In keeping with the distinction we made earlier between substantive and structural codes, we suggest that children who are deficient in lexical (vocabulary) development, and semantic development generally, will be especially deficient in learning to identify words as wholes, in this instance, because of probable deficiencies in using semantic codes for lexical access. In contrast, children who are deficient in phonological development and thus in phonological coding would be expected to encounter difficulties in metalinguistic analysis and thus in acquiring phoneme awareness. Such children should therefore have difficulty in learning to map alphabetic symbols to sound. Phonological deficits should also lead to significant difficulties in learning to associate names and meanings with their visual counterparts.

Finally, we expect that children who are characterized by basic deficiencies in syntactic development would also be characterized by basic deficiencies in the semantic and phonological domains of language given the pervasive and deleterious effects on the acquisition of linguistic subskills that would result from language comprehension problems. These children should be the most seriously impaired readers, and their difficulties in word identification should be manifested by difficulties in both whole-word learning and alphabetic mapping.

If we grant, for the moment, the validity of our speculations, certain testable hypotheses logically emerge. For one thing, it might be expected that linguistic codes, especially those we have called purely linguistic, would be a good deal more salient for normal readers than for poor readers, as manifested by differential sensitivity in the two groups to the substantive versus the structural attributes of printed and spoken words. It might also be anticipated that sensitivity to structural or purely linguistic codes would be somewhat greater in older than in younger poor readers, given increased experience in the older children of the type that promotes such sensitivity, for example, the metalinguistic analysis typically facilitated by school learning and by reading itself (Ehri, 1980). However, given the cumulative deficits in syntactic and semantic development that would, inevitably, be associated with long-standing reading disorder, it would seem likely that poor readers would fall increasingly behind normal readers in both of these domains.

Second, the differences one would expect between poor and normal readers in performance on learning and memory tasks that rely heavily on linguistic coding ability should be apparent in the processing of spoken as well as printed words and should therefore be manifested by qualitative and quantitative differences in encoding both types of stimuli.

Third, if it is true that children who are severely impaired in word identification (as manifested by deficiencies in both whole-word learning and alphabetic mapping) are likely impaired in the phonological, syntactic, and semantic domains of language, these same children should be less proficient than normally developing readers on measures evaluating development in each of these domains.

Finally, if it is true that deficiencies in word identification may be caused either by inadequacies in storing and retrieving name codes or by inadequacies in phoneme segmentation leading to deficiencies in alphabetic mapping, training in either or both of these skills should have a salutary effect on word identification.

In the following sections, we discuss several studies from our laboratory that tested these hypotheses employing a variety of experimental paradigms that both directly and indirectly evaluated phonological, syntactic, and semantic coding processes in poor and normal readers. The subjects in all of the experiments described were poor and normal readers selected in accord with the criteria outlined earlier.

## Studies evaluating reader group differences in linguistic versus semantic coding ability

### *Phonetic decoding*

Perhaps the most reliable body of evidence in support of our linguistic-coding-deficit explanation of reading disability inheres in our consistent finding of significant differences between poor and normal readers in phonetic decoding [1] ability, as manifested by measures of pseudoword decoding. Pseudoword decoding is, of course, the critical test in evaluating one's knowledge of phonic generalizations and grapheme–phoneme correspondence rules, and it is fair to say that a child who has age-appropriate facility in pseudoword decoding is less apt to have difficulties in learning to identify printed words than a child who does not have age-appropriate ability in pseudoword decoding. It would also seem that a child who does have age-appropriate facility in pseudoword decoding can be credited with having adequate ability in linguistic coding in the sense in which we have used this term. Indeed, it is partly because of the consistency with which we and others (Firth, 1972; Perfetti & Hogaboam, 1975) have found poor readers to be deficient in pseudoword decoding that we have been prompted to speculate that severely disabled readers are basically impaired in their ability to code information linguistically. Our own studies are especially significant in this regard because we have, in all instances, compared poor and normal readers on a test of pseudoword decoding after they have been selected as subjects for our research. In other words, we have always used pseudoword decoding as a dependent measure rather than as a selection criterion.

To concretize these points, Table 1 presents results for poor and normal readers (grades 2 through 6), who had been given a pseudoword decoding test (Bryant, 1963) in conjunction with their involvement in a series of studies conducted over

Table 1. *Measures of intelligence, oral reading accuracy, and pseudoword decoding for randomly selected samples of poor and normal readers (N = 20/group).*

| Grade | Reader group | Verbal IQ | Performance IQ | Full-scale IQ | Oral reading[a] | Phonic skills[b] |
|-------|-------------|-----------|----------------|---------------|-----------------|-------------------|
| 2 | Poor χ̄ | 105.50 | 105.90 | 106.15 | 0.36 | 2.75 |
|   | SD | 10.90 | 9.99 | 9.69 | 0.65 | 3.04 |
|   | Normal χ̄ | 113.50 | 110.65 | 113.35 | 3.46 | 17.50 |
|   | SD | 8.79 | 11.23 | 8.49 | 0.56 | 6.50 |
| 3 | Poor χ̄ | 100.10 | 100.75 | 100.50 | 1.77 | 4.85 |
|   | SD | 11.72 | 9.63 | 9.81 | 0.62 | 4.22 |
|   | Normal χ̄ | 101.55 | 105.15 | 103.50 | 4.32 | 19.05 |
|   | SD | 10.44 | 11.44 | 9.41 | 0.60 | 6.79 |
| 4 | Poor χ̄ | 103.35 | 105.00 | 104.60 | 2.49 | 9.05 |
|   | SD | 13.79 | 11.15 | 11.64 | 0.76 | 3.94 |
|   | Normal χ̄ | 106.90 | 109.25 | 108.85 | 5.26 | 22.65 |
|   | SD | 9.43 | 7.58 | 7.06 | 1.15 | 6.49 |
| 5 | Poor χ̄ | 97.05 | 97.85 | 97.20 | 3.11 | 12.65 |
|   | SD | 8.91 | 8.10 | 7.59 | 0.70 | 4.48 |
|   | Normal χ̄ | 106.55 | 104.95 | 106.30 | 6.04 | 27.05 |
|   | SD | 8.71 | 11.88 | 8.34 | 1.37 | 4.07 |
| 6 | Poor χ̄ | 94.50 | 103.25 | 98.75 | 3.44 | 14.30 |
|   | SD | 9.39 | 14.41 | 10.44 | 0.90 | 5.25 |
|   | Normal χ̄ | 106.30 | 100.80 | 104.00 | 7.37 | 25.45 |
|   | SD | 8.62 | 11.62 | 9.56 | 1.84 | 4.84 |

*Note*: Subjects were employed in studies conducted by Vellutino and associates between 1971 and 1976. Intelligence was in all instances measured by the Wechsler Intelligence Scale for Children (Wechsler, 1949). Oral reading was measured by the Gilmore Oral Reading Test (Gilmore & Gilmore, 1968). The test of phonic skills is an experimental measure and has no published norms.
[a] Grade equivalents.
[b] Raw scores (total possible, 35).
*Source*: Vellutino (1979). Copyright MIT Press. Used with permission.

a 10-year period evaluating different theories of reading disability (Vellutino, 1979). All subjects were selected for our research on the basis of their performance on an oral reading test (Gilmore & Gilmore, 1968) and the exclusionary criteria mentioned earlier. The data presented were yielded by subsamples (*N* = 20) randomly selected from much larger samples of the poor and normal readers we have been studying.

It can be seen that, at every grade level with no exceptions, the poor readers performed significantly below the normal readers on the pseudoword decoding (phonic skills) test. Moreover, if one compares reader groups matched for oral reading ability, in this case the second-grade normal and sixth-grade poor readers, it will be seen that the sixth-grade poor readers performed no better than the second-grade normal readers on the pseudoword test. In contrast, the reader groups at the upper grade levels are closer together on this test than are those at the lower grade levels, consistent with our suggestion that poor and normal readers in the upper grades would be in closer approximation in linguistic coding ability than would poor and normal readers in the lower grades. Although these results were generated by the seminal studies initially conducted in our laboratory, the same patterns have been observed in studies conducted more recently including those to be reported in this chapter.

These findings are impressive. For one thing, they provide clear-cut and highly reliable documentation that children who are extremely impaired in their ability to identify printed words they encounter in connected text are also severely impaired in phonetic decoding ability. Such impairment, of course, is consistent with the view that deficiencies in phonological coding are a major source of poor readers' difficulties in word identification and reading in general. Moreover, they are entirely consistent with our suggestion that severely impaired readers have particular difficulty in using the purely linguistic or structural attributes of words in spoken language as vehicles for coding the visual attributes of words in written language. We turn now to studies that more directly evaluated this suggestion.

### *Differential sensitivity to the meaning and structural attributes of printed words*

If deficiencies in phonetic decoding are an indication that poor readers are significantly impaired in their ability to code the visual attributes of printed words phonologically, then, in processing printed words, these children should be typically more attuned to the semantic than to the structural components of the words and should be particularly insensitive to their phonological components. If it is also true that older poor readers are more attuned to linguistic codes than are younger poor readers, the older poor readers should be more sensitive than the younger poor readers to the phonological attributes of printed words.

These hypotheses were tested in three separate but related investigations using categorization tasks involving words that could be grouped according to given featural attributes. In the first study (Vellutino et al., 1981), we tested poor and normal readers in grades 1 through 6, as well as randomly selected ninth graders and college students. Subjects in each group were presented 16 sets of words (six per set) that could be categorized either on the basis of similarities in meaning or on the basis of similarities in orthographic or phonological structure (e.g., *duck, moose, goat; caboose, truck, boat* – meaning; *duck, truck; goat, boat; moose, caboose* – structure).[2] The words in each set were randomly displayed, and subjects were simply asked to group together the words they thought belonged together. Scoring was based only on those words in respective stimulus sets that a subject could correctly identify, and the subject's ability to identify words on the

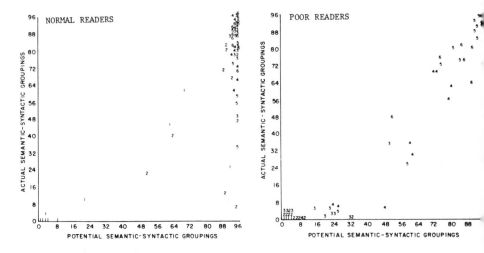

Figure 1. Scatter plots depicting the relation between the number of items potentially available for semantic-syntactic categorization and the number of items actually categorized on the basis of semantic-syntactic principles for poor and normal readers in grades 1 through 6. From Vellutino, Scanlon, DeSetto, & Pruzek, 1981. Copyright by Springer-Verlag. Used with permission.

entire list was tested after the experiment proper. The critical measure on which the groups were compared was the proportion of words that were actually categorized on the basis of meaning, relative to the number of words in a set that could have been categorized on this basis. Meaning and structural categorizations were therefore reciprocals of one another.

Figure 1 presents scatter diagrams depicting the results of this study for poor and normal readers in grades 1 through 6. It can be seen that meaning was the dominant processing mode for most subjects. More important for the present purposes is the fact that normal readers at the lower grades (between first and fourth) demonstrated greater variability in their use of meaning and structural categories than did normal readers at the upper grades. Especially impressive is the fact that a sizable number of normal readers at each of the lower grade levels made extensive use of structural categories, some even making primary use of these categories. In contrast, sixth-grade subjects categorized these stimulus sets almost exclusively on the basis of meaning. This was true also of ninth graders and college sophomores (data not shown).

Poor readers were somewhat less variable than normal readers and seemed to be generally more inclined to categorize the words they could read on the basis of meaning than to categorize them on the basis of structure. This is indicated by the fact that fewer poor readers were high on the axis depicting number of words potentially available for categorization on the basis of meaning and low on the axis

Table 2. *Percentages of the total number of structural classifications based on higher-order orthographic principles*

| Grade | Poor readers | | | Normal readers | | |
|---|---|---|---|---|---|---|
| | $\overline{x}$ | SD | $N^a$ | $\overline{x}$ | SD | $N$ |
| 1[b] | — | — | — | 66 | 14 | 10 |
| 1 | 58 | 19 | 10 | 66 | 23 | 20 |
| 2 | 71 | 20 | 19 | 92 | 16 | 18 |
| 3 | 77 | 15 | 19 | 100 | 0 | 17 |
| 4 | 85 | 17 | 19 | 99 | 2 | 18 |
| 5 | 93 | 11 | 11 | 99 | 6 | 17 |
| 6 | 100 | 0 | 7 | 100 | 0 | 6 |
| 9[b] | — | — | — | 100 | 0 | 9 |
| College | — | — | — | 95 | 14 | 6 |

*Note*: "Higher-order orthographic principles," in this instance, refers to the use of spelling patterns (e.g., *duck, truck*) rather than individual letters (e.g., *truck, goat*) as the basis for classification when the words in a given set were classified according to similarity of structure rather than similarity of meaning.
[a]$N$ equals the number of subjects producing this type of classification.
[b]Tested at the beginning of the year; all others tested at the end of the year.
*Source*: Data from Vellutino, Scanlon, DeSetto, & Pruzek (1981). Copyright 1981 by Springer-Verlag. Used with permission.

depicting number of words that were actually categorized on this basis. In fact, the correlation between these two variables was stronger in poor readers ($r = .96$, $p < .001$) than in normal readers ($r = .80$, $p < .001$, for one-tailed tests).

Another indication that poor readers are less sensitive than normal readers to the structural attributes of printed words is provided by the types of orthographic and phonological principles used by these two groups when they did categorize stimulus words on the basis of structural attributes. Whereas the normal readers' categorizations were typically based on the higher-order orthographic and phonological principles built into the stimulus sets, the categorizations of poor readers at the same grade level were more often based on idiosyncratic principles. This was especially true of the poor readers in the lower grades. For example, the poor readers were as likely to put *goat* and *truck* together as to put *goat* and *boat* together, because they all contain the letter *t*. These results are presented in Table 2, where it can be seen that, by no later than second and third grade, those normal readers who continued to utilize structural categories were attuned almost exclusively to higher-order structure. However, this was not true for poor readers until fifth and sixth grade.

It should also be clear from the data that the older poor readers were much more sensitive than the younger poor readers to the orthographic and phonological regularities in the stimulus words, as we predicted. Also striking is the fact that normal and poor readers matched for reading ability (second-grade normal readers and sixth-grade poor readers) showed comparable degrees of sensitivity to higher-order structure. However, it is significant that a much larger number of subjects in the (younger) normal reader groups utilized structural categories. This finding suggests that the younger normal readers were more attuned to word structures than were the older poor readers, quite likely because they were disposed more to structural analysis than were the older poor readers. If so, it might also be inferred that the older poor readers were more reliant on word meanings than word structures as vehicles for word identification.

These data are consistent with our suggestion that poor readers are generally more attuned to the meanings than to the structural attributes of printed words and less attuned to structural attributes than are normal readers. They can also be taken as evidence that normal readers are especially sensitive to the internal structures of words during the period of development, when they can be presumed to be heavily invested in code acquisition. Additional support for these inferences is provided by a second study (Vellutino & Scanlon, 1986) in which we attempted to replicate our findings.

In this study, we evaluated poor and normal readers in the second, fourth, and sixth grades, as well as a randomly selected group of first graders. However, to reduce the complexity of the categorization task, we used a forced-choice procedure involving three-word stimulus sets containing word pairs that could be grouped either on the basis of similarities in meaning or on the basis of similarities in orthographic or phonological structure (e.g., *room, goose, duck*). We also made an attempt to construct triads composed of words that were more easily identified than those employed in the previous study.

The results of the second study essentially replicated those of the first (graphs not shown). Normal readers were again found to be more variable than poor readers in their use of meaning categories, especially so at the lower grade levels. Moreover, the correlation between words actually categorized on the basis of meaning and words potentially available for such categorization was much higher in the poor readers than the normal readers (poor readers: $r = .90, p < .001$; normal readers: $r = .22; p < .05$; two-tailed tests). When we combined our randomly selected first-grade group with the normal reader groups above first grade, however, the correlation between these two variables was significantly increased ($r = .89, p < .001$). We can therefore be reasonably certain of the reliability of group trends.

The first two investigations compared poor and normal readers on sensitivity to semantic versus orthographic or phonological attributes of printed words, but the third study we conducted evaluated differential sensitivity to orthographic as opposed to phonological attributes of these stimuli (Vellutino & Scanlon, 1986). This study also employed a forced-choice procedure involving printed word triads, but in this instance two of the three words in a set could be categorized on the

Table 3. *Percentage of items actually categorized on the basis of phonological similarity to those potentially available for such categorization*

| Grade 4 poor | | Grade 4 normal | |
|---|---|---|---|
| x̄ | 9.93 | x̄ | 44.93 |
| SD | 21.68 | SD | 32.90 |
| Grade 6 poor | | Grade 6 normal | |
| x̄ | 24.33 | x̄ | 44.33 |
| SD | 36.01 | SD | 38.89 |

*Note*: An item was counted as being available for sorting on the basis of phonological principles if the child was able to read all three words in the set.

basis of either orthographic or phonological similarity (e.g., *said, paid, made*). However, in all sets, similarity in meaning was avoided.

The subjects were poor and normal readers in the fourth and sixth grades, and the dependent measure was the proportion of word sets categorized on the basis of phonological similarity. Again, proportions were based only on those words in a given set that a particular subject had identified correctly. These results are presented in Table 3.

The data accord with our suggestion that poor readers are generally less sensitive to the phonological attributes of printed words than are normal readers. It can be seen that the normal readers at both grade levels categorized a much larger proportion of the words they could identify on the basis of similarity in sound than did the poor readers at these grade levels. Indeed, the normal readers used both orthographic and phonological categories in approximately equal measure, whereas poor readers made primary use of orthographic categories.

Also noteworthy is the fact that the sixth-grade poor readers made greater use of phonological attributes than did the fourth-grade poor readers, which, of course, is consistent with our suggestion that older poor readers are more sensitive to the linguistic attributes of printed words than are younger poor readers.

It is clear from these data that, even when poor readers are forced to attend to the structural characteristics of printed words, they are more attentive to their orthographic than to their phonological properties. The results are therefore in keeping with the linguistic coding hypothesis put forward earlier. Moreover, insofar as older poor readers appear to be more sensitive to structural codes than younger poor readers, our data support the developmental hypothesis advanced.

To summarize, comparisons of poor and normal readers at different age and grade levels on measures of phonetic decoding indicate that poor readers are much less proficient than normal readers in using alphabetic mapping rules to identify printed words, and these findings strongly suggest that poor readers are significantly impaired in their ability to code visual information phonologically. This possibility is reinforced by the results of studies evaluating differential sensitivity to the meaning and structural attributes of printed words, in which it was found that poor readers are a good deal more sensitive to word meanings than to word structures and are especially insensitive to the phonological attributes of these stimuli. The data are therefore quite convergent and are entirely consistent with the linguistic coding explanation of reading disability. In the next section, we report the results of a study contrasting poor and normal readers on the ways in which they encode the meaning and structural attributes of spoken words.

### Differential sensitivity to the meaning and structural attributes of spoken words

If poor readers are relatively insensitive to the phonological attributes of printed words and more sensitive to their meanings, as seems indicated by the results discussed thus far, and if this difference is an outgrowth of basic deficiencies in their ability to code information linguistically, a similar pattern ought to be evidenced in the processing of spoken words. The study to be described evaluated this possibility and was essentially an extension of a previous study conducted by Byrne and Shea (1979), who used a continuous recognition procedure originally described by Felzen and Anisfeld (1970). In the Byrne and Shea (1979) investigation, second-grade poor and normal readers were given repeated presentations of antecedent words followed by distractor words that either were similar to the antecedents in meaning or rhymed with the antecedents. These stimuli were randomly comingled with control words that were matched with distractors on all but the meaning and rhyming dimensions. The subject's task was simply to indicate whether a given word presented had been encountered before. The critical measure on this task was the number of false positive errors (saying "old" to words not encountered before) made in response to each different type of distractor word. A sizable number of false positive errors on semantically similar distractors (relative to control words) presumably indicates sensitivity to word meanings, whereas a sizable number of false positives on rhyming distractors indicates sensitivity to their sound properties.

Consistent with the linguistic-coding-deficit notion, Byrne and Shea (1979) found that poor readers made relatively few false positive errors on distractors that rhymed with antecedent words but a sizable number of false positives on distractors that were similar in meaning to the antecedents. In contrast, normal readers made a sizable number of errors of both types. The combined results suggest that the poor readers were more attuned to the meanings of the stimulus words than to their phonological attributes, whereas the normal readers were more evenly attuned to both sets of attributes.

In the study we conducted (Vellutino, Scanlon, & Greenberg, in preparation), there were three experimental conditions, and all subjects were exposed to each in counterbalanced order. The results of two of those conditions are especially relevant here. In Condition A, subjects were presented with three types of distractor words: those that were phonologically (P) similar to antecedents, in this case rhyming words (e.g., *train* vs. *cane*); those that were semantically (S) similar to antecedents (e.g., *train* vs. *car*); and those that were both phonologically and semantically (PS) similar to antecedents (e.g., *train* vs. *plane*). This condition was similar to that used by Byrne and Shea (1979), except that these investigators did not employ distractors that were *both* semantically and phonologically similar to the antecedents. Moreover, our study included sixth- as well as second-grade poor and normal readers, whereas Byrne and Shea's study included only second-grade reader groups. Our intent was to evaluate the reliability of Byrne and Shea's findings with second graders, as well as extend their findings to reader groups at the sixth-grade level. We were also interested in further evaluating our developmental hypothesis and reasoned, in accord with this hypothesis, that the sixth-grade poor readers should demonstrate greater sensitivity to the rhyming words than the second-grade poor readers.

The second condition more directly evaluated sensitivity to phonological versus syntactic and grammatical attributes of spoken words and eliminated semantic similarity between antecedent and distractor words. This condition was specifically designed to compare poor and normal readers on sensitivity to inflectional morphemes, and antecedent words therefore consisted of root and bound morphemes (e.g., *boy* + *s* = *boys*). In order to evaluate differential encoding of the phonological and morphological attributes of the antecedents, three sets of distractors were developed. One set consisted of words that were phonologically (P) similar to antecedent words, insofar as they rhymed with the antecedents but did not contain root and bound morphemes (e.g., *boys* vs. *noise*). A second set (S) consisted of words characterized by root and bound morpheme structure, but the root morphemes were phonologically dissimilar to antecedents, whereas the bound morphemes were identical to those contained in the antecedents (e.g., *boys* vs. *dogs*). A third set (PS) of distractors consisted of words that also contained root and bound morphemes, but in this set the root morphemes rhymed with their counterparts in the antecedent words, and the bound morphemes were identical to those in respective antecedents (e.g., *boys* vs. *joys*).

Table 4 presents the group means and standard deviations for total recognition accuracy scores under each of the experimental conditions. As is apparent, the normal readers at each grade level recognized substantially more words than did the poor readers at those grade levels ($p < .05$). This, of course, indicates that short-term memory encoding was considerably better among the normal than among the poor readers. If it is true that processing in short-term memory is especially dependent on facility in coding information phonologically, as suggested by a number of researchers (Baddley & Hitch, 1974; Kleiman, 1975; Perfetti & McCutchen, 1982), these results can be taken as additional support for our suggestion that poor readers are deficient in linguistic coding ability.

Noteworthy here is the fact that, under both conditions, the magnitude of the mean differences between age-matched reader groups is larger at the second- than

Table 4. *Percentage of correct responses in overall accuracy of identifying "old" and "new" words in a continuous recognition task*

|  | Condition A | Condition B |
|---|---|---|
| *Grade 2 poor* | | |
| x̄ | 78.03 | 75.97 |
| SD | 10.07 | 11.49 |
| *Grade 2 normal* | | |
| x̄ | 88.47 | 87.87 |
| SD | 5.64 | 6.11 |
| *Grade 6 poor* | | |
| x̄ | 85.11 | 84.47 |
| SD | 8.24 | 8.11 |
| *Grade 6 normal* | | |
| x̄ | 90.70 | 90.37 |
| SD | 4.08 | 5.79 |

at the sixth-grade level, consistent with our developmental hypothesis. Also consistent with this hypothesis is the fact that second-grade normal and sixth-grade poor readers, who, as we said, were matched for reading ability, are comparable in recognition accuracy. In fact, the younger normal readers are even somewhat above the older poor readers on this measure. This finding suggests that poor readers take considerably longer than normally developing readers to achieve the same level of competence in short-term memory encoding.

Turning now to the false positive data, Figure 2 presents results for group contrasts on featural encoding of the stimulus words. The graphs depict the means of the difference scores, computed by subtracting the number of false positive errors made on control words associated with each distractor type from the number of false positive errors made on each of the three distractor types for each respective reader group at each grade level.

With regard to the second-grade contrasts, it can be seen that the normal readers were disrupted more by the rhyming words than were the poor readers, as manifested by significantly greater difference means ($p < .05$) for distractors that were phonologically similar to antecedents as well as for those that were both phonologically and semantically similar to antecedents. In contrast, the difference means for the semantic distractors were comparable in the two groups. These results essentially replicate Byrne and Shea's (1979) findings, and the combined data sets provide rather strong support for the suggestion that poor readers are less sensitive than normal readers to the phonological attributes of spoken words.

However, contrasts at the sixth-grade level produced a different pattern of results. Although the normal readers appeared to be somewhat more inclined than the poor readers to make false positive errors on the rhyming distractors, this dif-

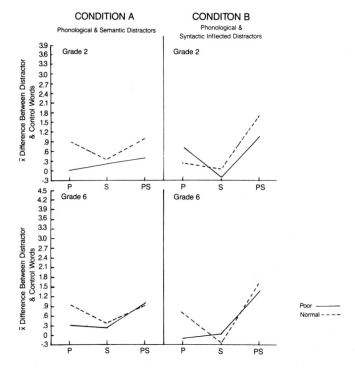

Figure 2. Graphs depicting the incidence of false positive responses on various distractor types (relative to control words associated with each distractor type) for poor — and normal --- readers at two grade levels under two stimulus conditions. [Study conducted by F. R. Vellutino, D. M. Scanlon, & S. N. Greenberg (in preparation) and reported in D. Gray & J. Kavanagh (Eds.), *Biobehavioral measures of dyslexia.* (in press). Parkton, MD: York Press. Used with permission.]

ference was not statistically significant. Moreover, the two groups did not differ substantially in proportion of false positive errors, either on the semantic distractors or on the phonological and semantic distractors. These results are consistent with our suggestion that older poor readers may be more sensitive to phonological codes than are younger poor readers and perhaps closer to normal readers on this dimension.

Figure 2 also presents results for Condition B, which compares poor and normal readers on differential sensitivity to the phonological versus the syntactic attributes of spoken words. The first thing to note is that neither the poor nor the normal reader groups made many false positive errors (relative to control words) on the S-type distractors, which, it will be recalled, were similar to the antecedents only insofar as both had identical inflectional morphemes. Thus, words that differ in meaning and overall sound structure appear to be readily discriminated, even if they carry the same inflectional morphemes.

The second finding of note is that overall differences *between* reader groups on the P- and PS-type distractors are not large. In contrast, *within*-group differences on these distractors are substantial, and the pattern of differences varies. At the second-grade level, the proportion of false positive errors on the P distractors is negligible in normal readers and is even somewhat lower than that made by the poor readers on these stimuli, although these differences were not statistically significant. In contrast, the proportion of false positives made by the normal readers on the PS distractors is significantly greater than the proportion made on the P distractors. In the poor readers, however, the difference between these two types of distractors is not statistically significant.

Here, again, we find a different pattern of results at the sixth-grade level, where the difference between the P and PS distractors is statistically significant in the poor readers as well as in the normal readers. However, in this instance, the difference between the P distractors and control words is somewhat greater in the normal readers.

It is important to note in connection with these findings that, except for the second-grade poor readers, the relative number of false positive errors on the P distractors is lower under Condition B than under Condition A. Since the P-type distractors were rhyming words under both conditions, we in effect have discrepant findings that require some explanation. As it turns out, the explanation is theoretically interesting.

To be more specific, it will be recalled that the antecedent words used in Condition B were all composed of root and bound morphemes, but none of the antecedents in Condition A had this structure. Moreover, neither of the P distractor sets used in Conditions A and B were composed of root and bound morphemes. This presents the possibility that in all groups, save for the second-grade poor readers, subjects in Condition B were inclined to encode root and bound morphemes separately (i.e., *boy* + *s*), giving semiautonomous status to the two structures. This strategy would account not only for the pattern of differences observed under Condition B, but also for the fact that all but the second-grade poor readers made fewer false positive errors on P distractors under this condition than under Condition A. This disparity is especially apparent among the second-grade normal readers, who in all other instances demonstrated a comparatively strong tendency toward false positives on phonologically similar distractors.

The fact that the second-grade poor readers were not substantially different in the number of false positives they made on the P- and PS-type distractors is consistent with the possibility that they were not as sensitive as their normal-reader counterparts to the linguistic differences between distractors and antecedents and, in particular, their morphological differences. Given that similarity in meaning was not a factor manipulated in Condition B, it is not surprising that the second-grade poor readers were somewhat more sensitive to the phonological attributes of the words presented under this condition than to the phonological attributes of those presented under Condition A, where similarity in meaning was a factor that may have influenced performance.[3]

Byrne and Shea (1979) obtained similar results in the study we discussed earlier. In a second phase of their study, the same subjects used in the first phase were given nonsense words as antecedents and rhyming and nonrhyming nonsense words as distractors. Under these circumstances, poor readers made proportionately more false positive errors on rhyming distractors than they had during the first phase of the experiment, when real words were the stimuli, suggesting that poor readers may be more sensitive to the phonological attributes of words when their meanings are not available. Nevertheless, the present findings provide strong evidence that, under normal circumstances, young poor readers are a good deal less sensitive to the phonological and morphological attributes of spoken words than are normal readers at the same age and grade level.

The sixth-grade poor readers, in contrast, appear to be much more attuned than the second-grade poor readers to both the phonological and the morphological attributes of spoken words and are closer to their normal-reading peers in coding these linguistic attributes. Indeed, as is evident in Figure 2, the sixth-grade poor readers made no more false positive errors than did the sixth-grade normal readers on P-type distractors (relative to control words) and, like the normal readers, made significantly more false positives on PS- than on P-type distractors. It is therefore clear that the older poor readers were at least as sensitive as the older normal readers to the structural properties of the antecedent and distractor words.

We should note, however, an alternative explanation for the observed pattern of differences under Condition B, specifically, that the second- and sixth-grade normal readers and the sixth-grade poor readers may have been better able than the second-grade poor readers to encode the spellings of antecedents and distractors rather than inflectional differences between these stimulus sets. This, of course, is an entirely plausible explanation of observed results, but it does not rule out the possibility that root and bound morphemes were encoded separately by the more discriminating subjects. That is, given the likelihood that young children are taught to distinguish between root and bound morphemes in learning to spell inflected and noninflected words, it is conceivable that some children relied heavily on knowledge of spelling differences in distinguishing between antecedents and phonological-type distractors. This, however, does not eliminate the possibility that a distinction was made between inflected and noninflected units in doing so. It therefore seems reasonable to infer that the second- and sixth-grade normal readers and the sixth-grade poor readers encoded the morphological as well as the phonological attributes of the distractors presented under Condition B, whereas the second-grade poor readers encoded only the phonological attributes of these stimuli.

Additional support for the linguistic coding hypothesis under consideration is provided by the overall similarity between the second-grade normal and the sixth-grade poor readers (who, it will be recalled, were matched for reading ability) in the number and type of false positive errors they made under the two experimental conditions. This pattern parallels the results on the total number of recognition errors made by these two groups (Table 4), and the combined data add more weight to our suggestion that subjects at the same level of reading ability are comparable in linguistic coding ability. In fact, the results discussed to this point are consistent with the possibility that proficiency in linguistic coding ability sets upper limits on reading ability.

To summarize, the fact that the second- and sixth-grade normal readers and the sixth-grade poor readers were disrupted more by distractor words that were phonologically and syntactically similar to antecedent words than by distractors that were only phonologically similar to the antecedents suggests that subjects in these groups were a good deal more sensitive to the more abstract components of language than were the second-grade poor readers, who manifested no appreciable tendency to be disrupted more by the PS than by the P distractors. These findings are consistent with the possibility that the coding difficulties observed in many poor readers, and, in particular, poor readers at younger age levels, not only are a manifestation of a limited ability to represent the phonological or surface features of language but reflect significant impairment in representing its syntactic and grammatical features. In the next three sections, we discuss research that adds substance to this possibility.

### Inflectional morphology in productive language

If poor readers are less proficient than normal readers in coding the phonological and syntactic components of language, and if it is true that such deficiencies are manifested by relative insensitivity to inflectional morphemes in spoken language, it is reasonable to expect that poor readers would also be less proficient than normal readers in using inflectional morphemes in productive language. The results of a study recently completed in our laboratory confirmed this expectation (Vellutino & Scanlon, in preparation).

In this study poor and normal readers in the second and sixth grades were given the Wug Test constructed some years ago by Berko (1958). This test evaluates a child's generative use of morphophonemic rules by requiring that he or she inflect nonsense word analogs of words in given form classes (e.g., "Here is a *wug*. Now there are two of them. There are two *(wugs)*"). The particular structures evaluated include formation of plurals, tenses, possessives, derivatives, imperatives, superlatives, compounds, and agentives. Thus, the test is rather comprehensive and provides a reasonably accurate estimate of the child's generative use of inflections.

Table 5 presents the means and standard deviations for the number of correct responses for second- and sixth-grade reader groups on this test. As is apparent,

Table 5. *Percentage of correct responses on a test measuring the ability to apply morphological markers generatively*

|  | Poor | Normal |
|---|---|---|
| *Grade 2* |  |  |
| X̄ | 59.09 | 79.85 |
| SD | 23.58 | 18.12 |
| N | 16 | 14 |
| *Grade 6* |  |  |
| X̄ | 68.64 | 87.88 |
| SD | 19.54 | 6.61 |
| N | 18 | 17 |

*Note*: The test was that of Berko (1958).

the means for the poor readers are significantly below those for the normal readers at both grade levels. In addition, the sixth-grade poor-reader groups performed substantially below the second-grade normal-reader groups on this test, the combined results suggesting that poor readers have not acquired the same level of linguistic sophistication as their normal-reading peers. Moreover, because the second-grade normal readers were matched with the sixth-grade poor readers on oral reading ability, it seems reasonable to infer that observed differences between age-matched reader groups are likely associated with basic language deficits and are not simply the result of reading problems.

It is interesting that these results deviate somewhat from those obtained under Condition B in the experiment reported in the preceding section, in which the sixth-grade poor readers demonstrated at least as much sensitivity to morphological markers as both the age-matched and reading-ability-matched normal-reading groups. Ability to use morphological markers productively and generatively, however, is no doubt a later acquisition, and it is apparent from the present results that poor readers take longer than normal readers to achieve the same level of sophistication in the use of inflectional morphemes.

In our opinion, these results, coupled with the results reported in the preceding section, provide strong support for our suggestion that the poor readers we have been studying are impeded by linguistic coding deficits. Indeed, age-appropriate use of inflectional morphemes is one of the most reliable indicators of normal language development insofar as it "reflects the fact that a child has begun to internalize the more abstract and fine-grained system of rules necessary for understanding and producing grammatically sophisticated language. Correct use of inflections requires the coordination of semantic, syntactic and phonological information and thus implies an intimate acquaintance with the comprehension and production rules characteristic of those linguistic subsystems" (Vellutino, 1979,

p. 279). A child who acquires such facility within the normal time frame can be credited with normal language development. In contrast, a child who lags behind his or her peers in acquiring such facility cannot be credited with normal language development. Insofar as deficiencies in the sensitivity and use of inflectional morphemes reflect deficiencies in coding the structural and formal components of language, they should be found to coexist with impairment in the domains of language that rely heavily on such coding.[4] Additional support for this possibility is provided by studies we conducted evaluating other types of syntactic development in poor and normal readers.

### Syntactic competence

In this study (Vellutino & Scanlon, in preparation), second- and sixth-grade reader groups were presented with several different measures of syntactic competence using sentences varying in both degree of syntactic complexity and length. The competence measures consisted of tasks evaluating (1) ability to judge whether sentences were grammatical or nongrammatical, (2) ability to comprehend sentences as measured by response to comprehension questions, and (3) ability to recall sentences verbatim. Each of these tasks presumably evaluated the extent to which the subjects had incorporated reliable representations of given syntactic structures that enabled them to process sentences meaningfully. However, each task evaluated such "knowledge" in a slightly different way and some were more demanding than others. Thus, the grammaticality judgments task assessed one's ability to distinguish between grammatically well formed and ill formed sentences and involved more metalinguistic analysis than did the other two tasks. It was therefore a more direct measure of linguistic maturity than were the other measures. The sentence comprehension task assessed the ability to derive the correct meanings from the different types of sentences, whereas the sentence recall task assessed the ability to utilize syntactic and grammatical constraints to organize and order word sequences for storage in short-term memory. It also allowed us to evaluate the degree to which the subject was able to store sentences having different syntactic properties in short-term memory, such ability being an important component of sentence comprehension.

Syntactic complexity was inherent in the types of sentences used and was based on normative data reported by Quigley, Steinkamp, Power, and Jones (1978). These included simple active declarative sentences, infinitivals, participial complements, passives, that complements, and relative clause constructions. For each sentence type, subjects were given two items at each of four lengths: 9, 11, 13, and 15 words. A computer program randomly selected items for each subject; thus, each received a different set of items ($n = 48$ items).

To increase the probability that these tasks relied more heavily on syntactic competence than on vocabulary development, the words used to construct given sentences were limited to those that appear at or below the second-grade reader level, based on normative data collected by Harris and Jacobson (1982).

Because we were also interested in evaluating the relation between short-term memory and syntactic competence, *one* sentence of each type and length was randomly selected by the computer ($n = 24$), and the words comprising each sentence were randomly permuted. This procedure created a set of scrambled word strings, the lengths of which directly paralleled the lengths of grammatically ordered parent sentences. To approximate presentation rates of the words in grammatically ordered sentences; an attempt was made to administer the words in the scrambled word strings in sentence rather than listlike fashion, varying prosody and intonation in presenting each array. Finally, the order of presentation of the different measures was randomized for each subject.

Table 6 presents the results for preliminary analyses, both on the syntax measures (collapsed across sentence types) and on the word recall task. Also presented are the results of a more brief test ($n = 16$ items) of sentence comprehension constructed by Menyuk,[5] which we used to cross-validate our own comprehension measure.

The first thing to note is that poor readers at both grade levels performed below their normal-reading peers on all measures. However, the magnitudes of respective group differences vary with the particular task. On the grammaticality judgments task, group differences tend to be larger on the nongrammatical than on the grammatical sentences and, in fact, achieve statistical significance only on the nongrammatical sentences. Obviously, the nongrammatical sentences were more discriminating than the grammatical sentences, which is quite likely due to the fact that they were also more difficult and prompted greater variability than did the grammatical sentences.

A similar pattern can be observed among the sentence comprehension measures, insofar as group differences are larger on the Menyuk test than on the test we constructed. However, the Menyuk test includes a heavier concentration of complex and embedded sentences than does our comprehension test. Yet when we compared respective reader groups only on the more difficult sentence constructions of the types that appear in greater number on the Menyuk test (e.g., relative clauses and other types of embedded sentences, data not shown), group differences were comparable to those obtained on the latter test. These results, in combination, indicate that, although poor readers are *not* grossly deficient with respect to syntactic competence, they may often be less proficient than normal readers in processing more complex syntactic constructions, suggesting that they are not as linguistically sophisticated as normal readers. These impressions are reinforced by results on the sentence recall test.

As is evident, poor readers at both grade levels performed substantially below the normal readers at these levels, but group differences were larger on the more complex sentences, especially that complements and relative clauses (data not

Table 6. *Percentages of correct responses on a variety of measures of syntactic comprehension*

| | Judgments of grammaticality | | Sentence comprehension | | | Sentence recall | Scrambled sentences |
| | Grammatical | Nongrammatical | Vellutino & Scanlon | Menyuk[a] | | | |
|---|---|---|---|---|---|---|---|
| *Grade 2 poor* | | | | | | | |
| X̄ | 83.33 | 60.21 | 84.43 | 60.19 | | 21.05 | 38.93 |
| SD | 10.12 | 19.38 | 8.05 | 14.19 | | 5.55 | 7.54 |
| *Grade 2 normal* | | | | | | | |
| X̄ | 87.92 | 79.17 | 89.47 | 70.75 | | 37.17 | 47.44 |
| SD | 10.38 | 13.04 | 7.23 | 9.88 | | 13.84 | 9.18 |
| *Grade 6 poor* | | | | | | | |
| X̄ | 88.83 | 80.29 | 88.27 | 69.63 | | 32.68 | 47.86 |
| SD | 8.08 | 9.62 | 6.49 | 11.13 | | 15.21 | 8.46 |
| *Grade 6 normal* | | | | | | | |
| X̄ | 95.42 | 90.79 | 95.06 | 79.24 | | 54.17 | 56.49 |
| SD | 4.79 | 8.29 | 3.55 | 9.56 | | 10.83 | 6.65 |

*Note:* $N$'s range between 19 and 22 subjects per group.
[a] Unpublished test developed by Paula Menyuk, Boston University.

shown). The sentence recall task, however, was much more difficult for all subjects than was either the grammaticality judgments or sentence comprehension task. A likely explanation for this disparity is that performance on sentence recall relied more heavily on short-term memory than did performance on the other two tasks. This raises the question of the extent to which reader group differences on the syntax measures were influenced by group differences in short-term memory. This is an important question in light of the fact that we also observed large reader group differences on the scrambled sentences task (Table 6). In order to answer this question, we conducted covariance analyses on each of these measures, using performance on the scrambled sentences task as the covariate. For present purposes, it will be sufficient to point out that, at the second-grade level, reader group differences on the sentence comprehension measures were eliminated after the effects of the covariate were removed, but group differences on the nongrammatical sentences and sentence recall tasks remained significant. However, at the sixth-grade level, group differences on all measures remained significant after covariance analysis, although they were reduced substantially.

We tentatively conclude from the foregoing that disparities that may be observed between poor and normal readers in processing sentences of various degrees of syntactic complexity are due, in part, to reader group differences in encoding and comprehending the syntactic properties of these sentences and, in part, to reader group differences in short-term-memory storage. It also seems clear from the data that, in the second-grade group, differences between poor and normal readers on measures of short-term memory accounted for more of the variance on the syntactic measures than did group differences in syntactic ability, a pattern that was especially evident among the comprehension measures. However, at the sixth-grade level, group differences remained statistically significant for all measures after the effects of the covariate were removed. Thus, at this level, differences between poor and normal readers in syntactic competence apparently carried as much weight as or more weight than reader group differences in short-term memory in determining performance differences on tasks requiring facility in processing syntactic structures, sentence comprehension tasks in particular.

Finally, consistent with all other developmental contrasts discussed to this point, the second-grade normal readers performed at least as well as the sixth-grade poor readers on all measures. Since the two groups were matched for reading ability, these and similar results could be interpreted to mean that the second-grade normal and sixth-grade poor readers had achieved approximately the same level of language development as a result of the limitations placed on such development by their reading ability. The results could also be interpreted to mean, however, that their language development placed upper limits on their reading ability. Morever, when combined with findings such as those obtained on the test of inflectional morphology, where the second-grade normal readers performed better than the sixth-grade poor readers, the latter alternative would seem more viable.

In sum, the results for several different measures of syntactic competence indicate that poor readers representing a wide age–grade range, though they do not appear to be grossly deficient, are not as adept as normally developing readers in encoding the syntactic properties of sentences characterized by different degrees of syntactic complexity and in comprehending those sentences generally. The data suggest, in addition, that poor readers are not as adept as normal readers at short-term-memory encoding of sentence constituents and that this failing may also contribute to observed group differences in sentence processing. When combined with results on the continuous recognition and categorization tasks, these findings add weight to our contention that poor readers are not as sensitive as normal readers to the structural or purely linguistic attributes of spoken and written words, consistent with our linguistic coding explanation of reading disability. In the next section, we discuss results of research contrasting poor and normal readers in vocabulary development, and it will be seen that a slightly different pattern of results emerges for such measures.

### Reading ability and vocabulary development

In keeping with the distinction we made earlier between purely linguistic and semantic codes, it is necessary to address the question of how linguistic coding deficits might affect development in the semantic domain of language. A reasonable expectation is that such deficits will have a deleterious effect on vocabulary development, and semantic development in general. That is, if it is true that poor readers have difficulty in coding information linguistically, they should also have difficulty in using language to code world knowledge, and such difficulty should be reflected in below-average vocabulary development.

However, in view of the fact that world knowledge is coded in language long before children are exposed to reading as a formal enterprise, we would expect that observed differences between poor and normal readers on measures of vocabulary would be smaller at younger than at older age levels. That is, given the cumulative deficiencies in vocabulary and acquired knowledge, generally, that are an inevitable consequence of long-standing reading disorder, reader group differences on vocabulary and vocabulary-related tasks should be greater at more advanced age and grade levels than at those closer to the beginning stages of reading acquisition. This, of course, is the converse of the developmental hypothesis advanced earlier, which suggests that differences between poor and normal readers, on measures evaluating word identification, pseudoword decoding, spelling, and other tasks that depend heavily on facility in the use of structural codes, should be greater in beginning readers than in those at more advanced age and grade levels.

Curiously, vocabulary and other aspects of semantic development have not been extensively studied in relation to reading disability in young children (see Vellutino, 1979). However, because we have typically employed the Wechsler Intelligence Scale for Children (Wechsler, 1949, 1974) to estimate intelligence in the poor and normal readers we have been studying, we have collected considerable data that allow us to compare these groups on a measure of productive vocabulary as well as on a measure of verbal concept development, specifically the Vocabulary and Similarities subtests of the Verbal scale. In addition, we have recently completed a study contrasting poor and normal readers on different measures of intelligence, and we therefore tested some of the same subjects on the Peabody Picture Vocabulary Test (Dunn, 1965), which is a measure of receptive vocabulary. These data were collected in conjunction with studies conducted in our laboratory from 1979 to 1982. All subjects were selected on the basis of the oral reading and exclusionary criteria mentioned earlier and had to obtain an IQ of 90 or above on either the Verbal or the Performance scales of the WISC-R (Wechsler, 1974).

Table 7 presents results on these measures for poor and normal readers in the second and sixth grades. Also presented are the grade equivalents yielded by the oral reading test used for sample selection (Gilmore & Gilmore, 1968) and the raw scores on the pseudoword decoding test of phonics skills discussed earlier (Bryant, 1963). In addition, results on these measures are presented for reader groups at both grade levels, matched respectively on WISC-R Verbal and Performance IQ.[6]

Focusing initially on the data for the unmatched groups, we note that subjects in each reader group fall within the normal range on both scales of the WISC-R, although the poor readers are somewhat below the normal readers on both scales. This is to be expected given that subjects for the normal reader groups are, by definition, sampled from a range of intellectual abilities that is a good deal broader than that for poor readers.

In addition, reader group differences on these scales are somewhat larger on the Verbal than on the Performance scale. Furthermore group differences on the Verbal scale are considerably larger at the sixth- than at the second-grade level. (Reference to Table 1 indicates that the same patterns emerged in contrasts of poor and normal readers administered the WISC in selecting subjects for the seminal studies we discussed earlier.) To the extent that the Verbal scale measures some aspects of lexical and semantic development, these results can be taken as support for our development hypothesis. More direct support for this hypothesis is provided by results on the Vocabulary and Similarities subtests and on the Peabody Picture Vocabulary Test.

As is evident in Table 7, poor readers at both grade levels are substantially below the normal readers on all three of these measures. Moreover, group differences are larger at the sixth- than at the second-grade level. In fact, poor readers in second grade are within the average range on each, whereas their normal-reading coun-

Table 7. IQ, reading achievement, and phonetic decoding ability for poor and normal readers at two grade levels

| | WISC-R Verbal IQ | WISC-R Performance IQ | WISC-R Similarities | WISC-R Vocabulary | Peabody Picture Vocabulary Test[a,b] | Gilmore Oral Reading Test[c,d] | Bryant Test of Phonic Skills[d,e] |
|---|---|---|---|---|---|---|---|
| *Grade 2 poor* | | | | | | | |
| All subjects (n = 50) | | | | | | | |
| X̄ | 99.00 | 102.40 | 9.88 | 10.48 | 111.06 | 0.92 | 6.57 |
| SD | 9.92 | 10.20 | 2.06 | 2.53 | 14.44 | 0.59 | 3.49 |
| (%ile) | (48) | (56) | (48) | (56) | (64) | nc | nc |
| VIQ-Matched (n = 25) | | | | | | | |
| X̄ | 104.56 | 103.12 | 10.36 | 11.60 | na | 1.05 | 7.16 |
| SD | 9.48 | 9.85 | 1.55 | 2.59 | | 0.55 | 3.08 |
| (%ile) | (62) | (58) | (55) | (70) | | nc | nc |
| PIQ-Matched (n = 35) | | | | | | | |
| X̄ | 98.74 | 106.14 | 9.79 | 10.60 | na | 0.96 | 6.60 |
| SD | 10.05 | 7.98 | 2.01 | 2.59 | | 0.58 | 3.63 |
| (%ile) | (47) | (66) | (47) | (58) | | nc | nc |
| *Grade 2 normal* | | | | | | | |
| All subjects (n = 55) | | | | | | | |
| X̄ | 111.62 | 110.42 | 12.84 | 12.98 | 116.21 | 3.87 | 22.15 |
| SD | 11.61 | 10.81 | 2.40 | 3.06 | 13.15 | 0.91 | 6.27 |
| (%ile) | (78) | (76) | (83) | (84) | (86) | nc | nc |
| VIQ-Matched (n = 25) | | | | | | | |
| X̄ | 105.16 | 108.72 | 11.96 | 11.00 | na | 3.59 | 21.04 |
| SD | 8.59 | 11.97 | 2.35 | 2.40 | | 0.91 | 5.54 |
| (%ile) | (63) | (72) | (74) | (63) | | nc | nc |
| PIQ-Matched (n = 35) | | | | | | | |
| X̄ | 110.03 | 105.91 | 12.60 | 12.54 | na | 3.87 | 21.49 |
| SD | 10.40 | 7.96 | 2.43 | 2.68 | | 0.94 | 6.50 |
| (%ile) | (75) | (65) | (80) | (80) | | nc | nc |

| | | | | | | | |
|---|---|---|---|---|---|---|---|
| **Grade 6 poor** | | | | | | | |
| All subjects (n = 56) | | | | | | | |
| X̄ | 94.43 | 97.57 | 9.64 | 8.44 | 97.92 | 3.50 | 21.27 |
| SD | 10.02 | 8.43 | 2.46 | 1.90 | 14.03 | 0.76 | 5.93 |
| (%ile) | (36) | (44) | (45) | (29) | (45) | nc | nc |
| VIQ-Matched (n = 22) | | | | | | | |
| X̄ | 102.36 | 99.32 | 10.91 | 9.50 | na | 3.35 | 21.59 |
| SD | 7.76 | 7.94 | 2.39 | 1.47 | | 0.87 | 5.50 |
| (%ile) | (56) | (48) | (62) | (44) | | nc | nc |
| PIQ-Matched (n = 26) | | | | | | | |
| X̄ | 94.19 | 100.44 | 9.81 | 8.30 | na | 3.53 | 21.62 |
| SD | 11.18 | 7.77 | 2.82 | 1.90 | | 0.72 | 5.25 |
| (%ile) | (35) | (51) | (48) | (29) | | nc | nc |
| **Grade 6 normal** | | | | | | | |
| All subjects (n = 54) | | | | | | | |
| X̄ | 112.67 | 108.11 | 12.91 | 11.70 | 117.64 | 8.62 | 30.47 |
| SD | 13.27 | 12.41 | 2.76 | 2.15 | 15.55 | 1.03 | 3.31 |
| (%ile) | (80) | (71) | (83) | (72) | (96) | nc | nc |
| VIQ-Matched (n = 22) | | | | | | | |
| X̄ | 102.36 | 101.77 | 11.64 | 10.27 | na | 8.26 | 29.27 |
| SD | 7.82 | 10.29 | 2.70 | 1.16 | | 1.15 | 3.22 |
| (%ile) | (56) | (55) | (71) | (53) | | nc | nc |
| PIQ-Matched (n = 26) | | | | | | | |
| X̄ | 107.73 | 100.12 | 11.81 | 11.11 | na | 8.56 | 30.52 |
| SD | 11.57 | 7.69 | 2.55 | 1.95 | | 1.11 | 3.34 |
| (%ile) | (70) | (50) | (73) | (64) | | nc | nc |

[a] IQ scores. This test was administered to only a subset of the subjects, resulting in the following sizes: grade 2 poor, n = 18; grade 2 normal, n = 29; grade 6 poor, n = 25; grade 6 normal, n = 28.

[b] na, Data not available due to relatively small n's in the "all subjects" group receiving the PPVT and to a substantial proportion of subjects being used in both the Verbal- and Performance-matched (VIQ- and PIQ-matched) groups, which would have resulted in means for the VIQ-matched and PIQ-matched groups that had a high degree of overlap in data points.

[c] Grade equivalent score.

[d] nc, Percentiles were not calculated because the necessary information for doing so is not provided in the test manual.

[e] Total correct out of 35.

terparts are above average on each. In contrast, sixth-grade poor readers fall below the 50th percentile on all three measures and especially on the WISC Vocabulary subtest.

More impressive, however, is the fact that these patterns are maintained at both grade levels when poor and normal readers are matched on WISC-R Performance IQ.[7] Indeed, matching on Performance IQ provides a reasonably good estimate of subtest scores that emerged in these two groups when subjects were not deliberately matched on either the Verbal or Performance IQ. This is true for all subtest scores, and not only for the Vocabulary and Similarities subtests (data not shown). These findings are, of course, consistent with the more general observation that the poor readers we have been studying tend to be closer to normally developing readers on the nonverbal type of skills measured by the Performance scale of the WISC than on those measured by the Verbal scale. If the IQ on the Performance scale is used as an estimate of "general intelligence," as seems legitimate, it can be safely concluded that vocabulary and verbal concept development and thus semantic development in general are, in most severely impaired readers, substantially below that of normal readers, even when these subjects have comparable levels of intellectual ability. It can also be concluded that the disparities between these two groups in vocabulary, verbal concept, and semantic development become exaggerated over time, quite likely because of prolonged reading disability in the impaired readers.

Our data indicate, however, that there are a substantial number of severely impaired readers among those we have been studying who closely approximate normal readers in vocabulary and verbal concept development. Reference to Table 7 indicates that the poor and normal readers matched for Verbal IQ are much closer to normal readers on the Vocabulary and Similarities subtests of the WISC-R than are those subjects in the other two groups. But even in these groups, the poor readers at both grade levels are yet below the normal readers on the Similarities subtest and, at the sixth grade level, on the Vocabulary subtest as well. This is not surprising, given that these subtests measure vocabulary and verbal concept development more directly than do any of the other subtests included in the Verbal scale. Also of interest in this connection is the fact that matching these groups for Verbal IQ does not change their relative standing very much on Performance IQ. The latter finding is yet another indication that poor readers tend to be closer to their normal reading peers in nonverbal than in verbal abilities.

Perhaps the most impressive support for the developmental hypothesis of concern herein, and for the more general distinction we make between linguistic and semantic coding, comes from reader group contrasts on the pseudoword decoding test relative to contrasts of the same subjects on the measures of vocabulary and semantic development we have just discussed. Table 7 indicates that the means for respective reader groups on the pseudoword decoding test do not vary substantially as a function of the IQ matching procedures. More specifically, within a reader group at a given grade level, the means on the pseudoword test for the various IQ groupings are similar to one another and to the unmatched (all subjects) group. It is also important to note that the magnitudes of the reader group differences on the pseudoword decoding test do not differ appreciably from those obtained in our seminal studies (see Table 1) and that subjects matched for reading ability (i.e., second-grade normal and sixth-grade poor readers) performed at approximately the same level on this test, as was the case in the seminal studies. This pattern is evident in the groups matched respectively on Verbal and Performance IQ as well as in the unmatched groups.

These results suggest that regardless of variability that might be observed on measures such as the WISC-R subscales and the Peabody Picture Vocabulary Test, each of which relies heavily on lexical and semantic development, poor and normal readers tend to maintain their relative standing on measures, such as the pseudoword decoding test, that rely more heavily on linguistic (phonological) coding ability. They also suggest that the latter measures may be better estimates of word identification and oral reading ability than are tests such as the Verbal subtests of the WISC-R and the Peabody Picture Vocabulary Test that evaluate semantic coding ability. Reinforcing this suggestion is the fact that our youngest poor readers, who were severely impaired in both oral reading and phonetic decoding, performed at an average level on the Vocabulary and Similarities subtests. In contrast, our oldest poor readers, though still significantly impaired in oral reading ability, had made considerable progress in phonetic decoding ability but at the same time performed below average on these measures and especially on the Vocabulary subtest. The data thus provide additional support for the linguistic-coding-deficit explanation of reading disability we have put forth and are entirely consistent with our suggestion that older poor readers would be more significantly impaired than younger poor readers on measures of vocabulary and semantic development.

Finally, the fact that poor readers who were matched with normal readers on Verbal IQ performed well below the normal readers on the pseudoword decoding task (which, it will be recalled, was *not* used for sample selection) suggests that there may be a substantial number of children who become poor readers despite basically adequate semantic development, that is, to the extent that the Verbal subtests of the WISC-R measure such development. This generalization would appear to be especially applicable to children at the beginning stages of reading acquisition, who were found to be extremely deficient in phonetic decoding and oral reading ability despite the attainment of at least an average level of vocabulary and verbal concept development. This is not to suggest that adequate development in the latter areas is unimportant for acquiring skill in reading, but rather to suggest that, by itself, such development is not sufficient for acquiring such skill. As we suggested earlier, it seems reasonable to expect that beginning readers with a meager vocabulary and poor semantic development in general would be impaired in learning to identify printed words and would have particular difficulty in learning to identify words as wholes. Such children may or may not have the means for learning to identify words phonetically. If not, they are likely to have extreme difficulty with word identification and should be among the most severely impaired poor readers. If they do have such means, they should be able to acquire some degree of facility in word identification, though probably not to the same level of sophistication as children with adequate development in all domains of language. The severely impaired readers we have studied tend to be impaired in all linguistic domains, but the results we have just reviewed suggest that there may be a subgroup of these children who are selectively impaired in phonetic decoding. This, of course, is an open question that will require additional research.

In sum, reader group contrasts on measures of vocabulary and verbal concept attainment suggest that poor readers at the beginning stages of reading acquisition, although generally not as well developed as normal readers, tend to be less deficient in these areas than older poor readers who have had long-standing reading disability. The data suggest, as well, that poor readers at the lower grade levels are especially deficient in phonetic decoding ability and improve somewhat with experience in reading. In the next section, we discuss research that further validates our conceptualizations through reader group contrasts on measures of verbal memory that rely differentially on one's ability to encode the structural and meaning attributes of spoken words.

### Linguistic coding and semantic memory

Additional support for the developmental hypothesis we have advanced comes from the results of another study conducted in our laboratory evaluating semantic memory in poor and normal readers (Vellutino & Scanlon, 1985). In yet another test of the linguistic-coding-deficit explanation of reading disability, reader groups in grades 2 and 6 were contrasted on free recall of concrete and abstract words. Previous research conducted by Paivio and his associates (Paivio, 1971; Paivio & Begg, 1971a, 1971b) has provided compelling evidence that abstract words are more difficult to recall than are concrete words, not only because they are less imbued with referential imagery but also because they are linguistically more complex.

Some abstract words derive their meanings primarily from their relationship with other words (e.g., functor words such as *is, but, their*), while others are derivatives from concrete words or other abstract words (e.g., *judge–justice–judicial*). Many abstract words also require a functional knowledge of complex syntactic rules for comprehension and correct usage, as with morphological prefixing and suffixing (judicial–prejudicial; judge–judgement). Abstract words are consequently more diffuse and less easily discriminated than are concrete words and facility in encoding and retrieving such words would seem to imply a high degree of linguistic sophistication. (Vellutino & Scanlon, 1982, p. 232)

In accord with this logic, we reasoned that, if poor readers are less proficient than normal readers in using linguistic (phonological and syntactic) codes to store and retrieve information, they should perform significantly below normal readers on recall of abstract words, since these stimuli make greater demands on one's linguistic abilities. However, on the basis of previous studies conducted in our laboratory, which demonstrated that poor readers are comparable to normal readers in visual processing abilities (Vellutino, 1979), we expected that poor readers would be as well equipped as normal readers to utilize imagery in memory encoding and would therefore be closer to normal readers on recall of concrete words.

Two separate experiments were conducted to evaluate these hypotheses. In the first, reader groups at both grade levels were given random presentations of concrete and abstract words that were equated for both referential and connotative meaning.[8] In the second, independent samples from both groups were given the same words in homogeneous blocks counterbalanced for order of presentation. These data are presented in Figure 3.

As is apparent, poor readers at each grade level performed below normal readers with both concrete and abstract words. However, the hypothesized interaction between reading ability and word type was evident only at the second-grade level. As predicted, the poor readers in second grade were well below the normal readers in recall of abstract words but were closer to normal readers in recall of concrete words. In contrast, the poor readers in sixth grade were as far below the normal readers on recall of the concrete words as they were on recall of the abstract words.

However, these grade-level disparities might be better understood in the context of the developmental hypothesis advanced earlier. Thus, it may be inferred that the second-grade poor readers had more difficulty than their normal-reading peers in remembering the abstract words because they were not as proficient in utilizing the phonological and syntactic attributes of these words to aid recall, although closer to the normal readers in encoding their semantic or substantive attributes. However, the linguistic coding aspect of the developmental hypothesis cannot be as readily applied as an explanation of reader group differences at the sixth-grade level because it does not adequately account for the fact that these subjects performed well below the level of the sixth-grade normal readers with the concrete as well as with the abstract words. Yet if we consider the likelihood that the older poor readers had a more poorly developed vocabulary than the older normal readers and a less elaborate semantic network generally (no doubt because of long-standing reading disorder, as we said earlier), the performance patterns observed at the sixth-grade level become coherent. Thus, the poor readers did not perform as well as the normal readers in recall of both the concrete and abstract words, because the normal readers were generally better equipped than the poor readers to assimilate all of the words presented on the free-recall task to structures in long-term memory, regardless of the linguistic properties of those words. Put another way, the normal readers were more facile than the poor readers in encoding the semantic attributes of the words on the list to aid recall. This is not to suggest that the sixth-grade poor readers were as effective as their normal reading peers in en-

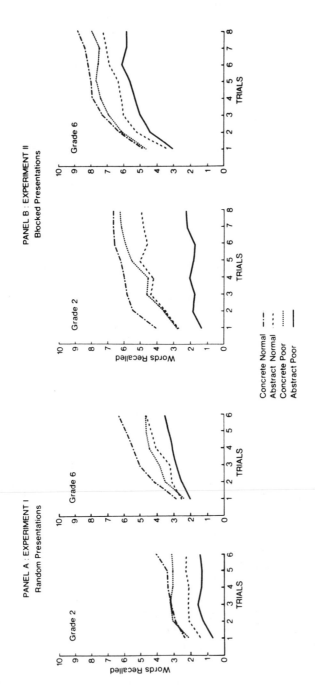

PANEL A : EXPERIMENT I
Random Presentations

PANEL B : EXPERIMENT II
Blocked Presentations

Concrete Normal
Abstract Normal
Concrete Poor
Abstract Poor

Figure 3. Graphs depicting the number of words recalled per trial by second- and sixth-grade poor and normal readers required to freely recall lists of concrete and abstract words under randomized (Panel A) and blocked (Panel B) presentation conditions. (From Vellutino & Scanlon, 1985. Copyright 1985 by Academic Press. Used with permission.)

coding the linguistic (phonological and syntactic) attributes of the word stimuli, but rather that linguistic coding deficits were compounded by semantic coding deficits at the sixth-grade level and may have contributed less to reader group differences at this level than did semantic coding deficits.

Additional support for this interpretation is provided by the results of a qualitative analysis of the different types of intrusion errors made by subjects in each reader group. In order to gain insight into the encoding strategies employed by our subjects, we made a frequency count of errors that were prompted either by the meaning or by the structural components of particular word stimuli. Accordingly, substitution errors such as *prince* for *queen* or *thinking* for *thought* were taken as an indication that subjects were more attuned to the semantic than to the phonological and syntactic attributes (respectively) of stimulus words. In contrast, such errors as *fought* for *thought* and *though* for *thought* were believed to reflect a subject's tendency to be respectively more attuned to their phonological and orthographic attributes than to their semantic attributes.

Consistent with the hypothesis, second-grade poor readers made more meaning- than structural-type errors, whereas the normal readers made an approximately equal number of errors of both types. In contrast, poor readers at the sixth-grade level made as large a proportion of stuctural-type errors as the sixth-grade normal readers, whereas the sixth-grade normal readers made a slightly larger proportion of meaning errors than did the sixth-grade poor readers.

These results complement those of studies reported in the previous sections and provide additional documentation for both the linguistic coding and developmental hypotheses put forward in these sections. However, all of the findings discussed thus far are correlational and therefore constitute only indirect support for these hypotheses. The final investigation we shall discuss provides more direct support for a causal relation between linguistic coding deficit and reading disability.

### *Phonological coding, phonemic awareness, and code acquisition*

This investigation (Vellutino & Scanlon, in press) had several objectives. One major purpose was to evaluate Liberman and Shankweiler's (1979) contention that the difficulties encountered by poor readers in word identification are caused by deficiency in phonemic segmentation ability ("phonemic awareness") associated with more basic ineptitude in phonological coding. This hypothesis is consistent with the linguistic coding hypothesis we have suggested, the only difference being the role we have assigned to possible deficits in the syntactic component of language as a factor contributing to reading disability.

A second purpose was to evaluate whether hypothesized deficits in phonological coding are also causally related to observed differences between poor and normal readers in learning to associate names with object referents. This question was prompted by the more basic question of whether reader group differences on word identification and other visual–verbal learning tasks are the result of dysfunction in storing and/or retrieving the verbal counterparts of such tasks or the result of a more specific deficit in visual–verbal integration. If poor readers were found to be deficient on verbal memory tasks designed to evaluate phonological coding ability, as well as on paired-associates learning tasks that (respectively) simulated name acquisition and word identification, their difficulties with visual–verbal learning tasks could be attributed to more basic difficulties in learning the verbal response components used as associates on such tasks.

In order to answer these questions, we compared poor and normal readers in the second and sixth grades on measures of verbal response learning as well as on code acquisition tasks with or without training in phonemic segmentation. Code acquisition tasks simulated the type of transfer learning involved in beginning reading, for example, when a child learns new words such as *cat, fat, ran,* and *pan* that contain grapheme–phoneme invariants and generalizes these invariants in the learning of new words such as *can, fan, rat, pat,* and so forth.

Approximately 1 week before initiation of the experiment proper, all subjects were administered a test of phonemic segmentation ability similar to that used by other researchers (Bradley & Bryant, 1983; Fox & Routh, 1980; Liberman et al., 1974). This test was given both to evaluate the reliability of previous findings and to ensure that poor readers in our samples were deficient in this ability. Subjects in each group were then randomly assigned to one of five treatment conditions. In one condition – phonemic segmentation training (PST) – subjects received five or six consecutive days of training (½ hr/day) in phonemic analysis. This consisted initially of several exercises involving auditory and visual analysis of phoneme-sized units in real words and pseudowords. These exercises were followed by extensive practice in learning to detect grapheme–phoneme invariance in novel trigraphs paired with consonant–vowel–consonant nonsense syllables (Figure 4). The purpose of phonemic segmentation training was to foster an analytic attitude that would encourage subjects to search for and utilize grapheme–phoneme units in learning to associate letter strings with their verbal responses.

After a hiatus of no more than 2 days, subjects were given the code acquisition training subtest, which consisted of 20 paired-associates learning trials involving novel trigraphs and nonsense syllables (*gov, goz, vab, zab*) characterized by grapheme–phoneme correspondence (Figure 4). These stimuli were completely different from any of the stimuli presented during the segmentation training program. The subjects could not therefore transfer grapheme–phoneme relations acquired during phonemic segmentation training to the learning of the associates presented on the code acquisition subtests.

On the following day these subjects were given the code acquisition transfer subtest, which consisted of 20 more paired-associates trials involving trigraphs and nonsense syllables that were reversed derivatives of the paired associates used on the training subtest (*vog, zog, bav, baz*). However, grapheme–phoneme correspondence was maintained. It is important to note that, on both the training and

A. <u>Stimuli Used in the Coding Portion of the Phonemic Segmentation Training Program</u>

B. <u>Stimuli Used in the Picture-Syllable Portion of the Response Acquisition Treatment</u>

C. <u>Stimuli Used in the Training and Transfer Subtests of Code Acquisition</u>

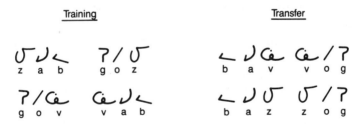

Figure 4. Stimuli employed in the study evaluating reading and coding ability. (From Vellutino & Scanlon, in press.)

transfer subtests of code acquisition, the paired associates were presented as wholes, and the subjects were *not* encouraged to "sound out" the graphemes in each of the trigraphs. Our intent was to evaluate the degree to which the subjects had acquired an implicit disposition to search for invariant relations that could be applied in discriminating words as wholes, rather than have them learn individual letter sounds that they might attempt to synthesize piecemeal.

In a second condition – response acquisition (RA) – the subjects were presented with 20 trials involving free recall of the same nonsense syllables that were to be used on the code acquisition training subtest, both to facilitate prior learning of these stimuli and for purposes of reader group comparison. This task served as our operational measure of phonological coding ability. After a 5-min break, subjects were given 15 paired-associates learning trials in which the same nonsense syllables were paired with novel cartoon-like animal pictures (Figure 4) in an effort to simulate the process whereby names and meanings are attached to syllables in the language. This task served as a measure of the child's ability to learn the names of objects and therefore allowed group contrasts to be made on visual–verbal association learning, when objects rather than printed characters were the visual stimuli. In addition, by conferring meaning on the stimuli used as verbal responses on the training subtest of code acquisition, we were able to compare poor and normal readers on a task that simulated a whole-word or meaning-based approach to initial word identification. On the two consecutive days following administration of the picture–syllable learning task, subjects in the RA condition were given the same code acquisition subtests given to subjects in the PST condition using the same presentation procedures.

In a third condition (PSTRA), the subjects received both segmentation training and response acquisition training before presentation of the code acquisition subtests. The fourth and fifth conditions were control conditions. In one – the C-1 condition – the subjects were presented with both the training and transfer subtests of code acquisition but were given no segmentation training and no prior exposure to the stimuli used in code acquisition. In the other – the C-2 condition – the subjects received only the transfer subtest of code acquisition.

Finally, after exposure to given treatments, all subjects were administered an alternative form of the test of phonemic segmentation ability administered before the experiment proper.

The important findings were as follows. Poor readers, at both grade levels, performed below the normal readers at these grade levels on the pre- and postexperimental test of phonemic segmentation ability, verifying that our poor readers were deficient in this ability (Table 8). Poor readers at both grade levels also performed below the level of their normal reading counterparts on both the free-recall and picture–syllable subtests of response acquisition (Figures 5 and 6), as well as on the training and transfer subtests of code acquisition (Figures 7 and 8). Moreover, performance on both the response acquisition subtests and the phonemic segmentation tests was highly correlated with performance on the code acquisition subtests (Tables 9 and 10).

With regard to the effects of the treatment conditions, phonemic segmentation training had a positive effect on performance on both the training and transfer subtests of code acquisition, but the effects of this training were especially evident on the transfer subtest (Figure 8). In fact, subjects who received only segmentation training, that is, those in the PST condition, learned the paired associates on the

Table 8. *Percentage of correct responses on pre- and post-treatment measures of phonemic segmentation ability*

| | Grade 2 poor | | Grade 2 normal | | Grade 6 poor | | Grade 6 normal | |
|---|---|---|---|---|---|---|---|---|
| Condition | Pre | Post | Pre | Post | Pre | Post | Pre | Post |
| *PSTRA* | | | | | | | | |
| $\bar{\text{X}}$ | 43.46 | 53.21 | 63.21 | 76.05 | 57.78 | 75.55 | 76.05 | 88.27 |
| SD | 10.98 | 10.64 | 14.31 | 15.26 | 18.00 | 11.23 | 14.22 | 6.05 |
| *PST* | | | | | | | | |
| $\bar{\text{X}}$ | 46.05 | 54.81 | 57.65 | 69.75 | 62.35 | 76.79 | 70.99 | 85.55 |
| SD | 6.71 | 10.54 | 18.77 | 18.72 | 14.66 | 11.69 | 15.96 | 8.32 |
| *RA* | | | | | | | | |
| $\bar{\text{X}}$ | 45.31 | 45.43 | 57.41 | 60.00 | 60.25 | 61.23 | 75.43 | 80.74 |
| SD | 8.28 | 9.72 | 15.53 | 13.03 | 11.48 | 16.38 | 12.59 | 16.00 |
| *C-1* | | | | | | | | |
| $\bar{\text{X}}$ | 41.98 | 44.81 | 56.54 | 64.32 | 59.26 | 65.80 | 75.55 | 86.19 |
| SD | 7.69 | 6.31 | 15.82 | 13.74 | 14.24 | 12.40 | 15.27 | 10.28 |
| *C-2* | | | | | | | | |
| $\bar{\text{X}}$ | 45.19 | 51.73 | 54.32 | 63.58 | 59.51 | 63.58 | 73.21 | 78.27 |
| SD | 11.26 | 12.07 | 12.80 | 13.58 | 11.88 | 13.35 | 12.02 | 12.93 |

*Source*: Vellutino and Scanlon (in press).

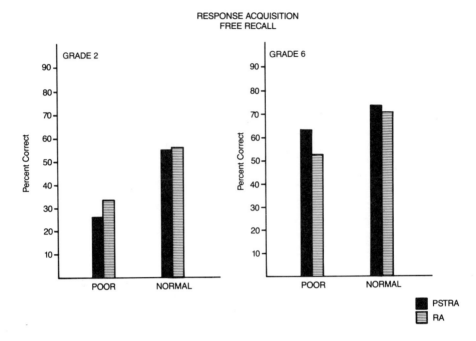

Figure 5. Percentage of correct responses for second- and sixth-grade poor and normal readers in free recall of nonsense syllables in the study evaluating reading and coding ability. (From Vellutino & Scanlon, in press.)

training subtests more slowly at the outset than did the subjects who received only response training, that is, those in the RA condition, who, from all indications, utilized a whole-word strategy in learning to name the pseudowords presented on this subtest. However, the subjects in the PST condition ultimately caught up with and surpassed the subjects in the RA condition and maintained their advantage over the subjects in this condition on the transfer task. In addition, segmentation training had a positive effect on performance on the postexperimental test of phonemic segmentation ability. However, it had no apparent effect on free recall of nonsense syllables, which was our operational measure of phonological coding ability.

Response acquisition training, in contrast, had a positive effect on performance on the initial training subtest of code acquisition, and subjects who received this training (RA and PSTRA groups) performed better on the first few trials of this subtest than did subjects who did not receive this training. However, response training alone (RA condition) had a deleterious effect on the transfer subtest of code acquisition, quite likely because of proactive interference occasioned by response learning. It seems likely that subjects who received only response training were at risk for making generalization errors on the transfer subtest, not only be-

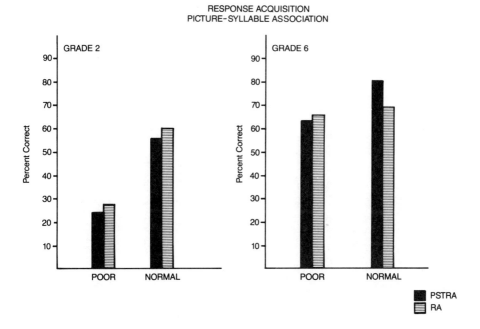

Figure 6. Percentage of correct responses for second- and sixth-grade poor and normal readers in picture–syllable association learning in the study evaluating reading and coding ability. (From Vellutino & Scanlon, in press.)

cause the stimuli used on this subtest were (visually) similar to those used on the training subtest, given that they were reversed derivatives of the training stimuli, but also because response training encouraged them to process the pseudowords globally rather than analytically. Thus, unlike subjects in the groups that received segmentation training (PST and PSTRA), they were not apt to detect fine-grained differences in the pseudowords and, therefore, made a large number of generalization errors. A striking illustration of this pattern is the fact that subjects in both the RA and the C-1 groups, none of whom received segmentation training, made many more reversal errors on the transfer subtest than did subjects who received segmentation training (Figure 9). This is significant given the fact that reversal errors are often interpreted as manifestations of dysfunction in visual perception (Hermann, 1959; Orton, 1925). The present findings suggest that such errors may be more parsimoniously explained as a consequence of global processing strategies associated with the failure to make use of the alphabetic principle in word identification.

It should be clear from the foregoing that both segmentation and response training had both positive and negative effects on performance, depending on the stage of learning. Thus, response training facilitated more rapid initial learning than did

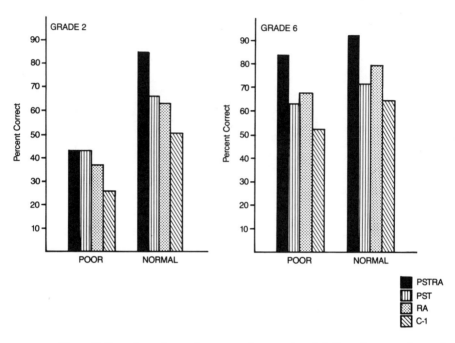

Figure 7. Percentage of correct responses for second- and sixth-grade poor and normal readers on the training subtest of code acquisition in the study evaluating reading and coding ability. (From Vellutino & Scanlon, in press.)

segmentation training but had a deleterious effect on transfer learning. In contrast, segmentation training had a beneficial effect on transfer learning but fostered slow initial learning. It is therefore significant that subjects in the PSTRA group, who received both segmentation and response training, in general performed better than subjects in all other groups, suggesting that they enjoyed the advantages of wholistic/meaning-based and analytic strategies in both initial learning and transfer learning while suffering none of their disadvantages. In fact, qualitative analyses of error patterns suggest that the PSTRA group subjects used more flexible processing strategies than did the PST, RA, and C-1 group subjects, insofar as they utilized what appeared to be a whole-word, meaning-based approach on the training subtest of code acquisition and a more analytic approach on the transfer subtest. The second-grade poor readers in the PSTRA condition were the only subjects who did not manifest this pattern of results, to the extent that they did not maintain their advantage over PST subjects beyond the second trial block of code acquisition training and performed no better than these subjects on code acquisi-

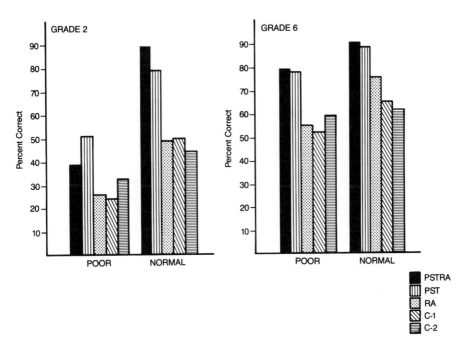

Figure 8. Percentage of correct responses for second- and sixth-grade poor and normal readers on the transfer subtest of code acquisition in the study evaluating reading and coding ability. (From Vellutino & Scanlon, in press.)

tion transfer. However, this appeared to be due to the fact that the second-grade poor readers in the PSTRA condition, had extreme difficulty in remembering the nonsense syllables used as verbal responses on the code acquisition subtest, as did the second-grade poor readers in the RA condition.

It is interesting to note, in connection with our developmental hypothesis, that the magnitudes of reader group differences on all of the dependent measures used in this study were much greater at the second- than at the sixth-grade level. At the same time, there was a striking similarity between reading-ability-matched poor and normal readers (second-grade normal and sixth-grade poor readers) on each of these measures. These results are, of course, consistent with our repeated observation that younger and older children matched for reading ability perform at the same level on tasks evaluating sensitivity to and facility with linguistic codes.

There are several important conclusions to be drawn from this study relative to both the linguistic coding and the developmental hypotheses of central concern in this chapter. First, the results in general provide strong support for our suggestion

Table 9. *Correlations between response acquisition and code acquisition measures*

| | Grade 2 poor | | | Grade 2 normal | | |
|---|---|---|---|---|---|---|
| | Picture–syllable association | Code acquisition | | Picture–syllable association | Code acquisition | |
| Test | | Training | Transfer | | Training | Transfer |
| *PSTRA* | | | | | | |
| Free recall | .545* | .551* | .040 | .624* | .382 | .264 |
| Picture–syllable association | — | .252 | .403 | — | .505* | .479 |
| *RA* | | | | | | |
| Free recall | .855** | .542* | −.108 | .552* | .576* | .441 |
| Picture–syllable association | — | .557* | −.009 | — | .675** | .700** |

| | Grade 6 poor | | | Grade 6 normal | | |
|---|---|---|---|---|---|---|
| | Picture–syllable association | Code acquisition | | Picture–syllable association | Code acquisition | |
| Test | | Training | Transfer | | Training | Transfer |
| *PSTRA* | | | | | | |
| Free recall | .513* | −.215 | −.291 | .827** | .199 | .530* |
| Picture–syllable association | — | .511* | .093 | — | .443 | .212 |
| *RA* | | | | | | |
| Free recall | .487 | .631* | .343 | .631* | .653** | .484 |
| Picture–syllable association | — | .796** | .739** | — | .820** | .372 |

*Significant at .05 level.
**Significant at .01 level (two-tailed tests).
*Source*: Vellutino and Scanlon (in press).

Table 10. *Correlations of pre- and posttreatment tests of phonemic segmentation ability with code acquisition scores*

| | Grade 2 poor | | Grade 2 normal | | Grade 6 poor | | Grade 6 normal | |
| --- | --- | --- | --- | --- | --- | --- | --- | --- |
| Condition | Training | Transfer | Training | Transfer | Training | Transfer | Training | Transfer |
| *Pretest* | | | | | | | | |
| PSTRA and PST | −.24 | .28 | .40* | .65** | −.01 | .34 | .18 | .37* |
| RA and C-1 | .05 | .09 | .24 | .12 | .30 | .58** | .45* | .52** |
| *Posttest* | | | | | | | | |
| PSTRA and PST | .32 | .38* | .50** | .69** | .08 | .44* | .34 | .42* |
| RA and C-1 | −.15 | −.17 | .36* | .24 | .12 | .35 | .10 | .13 |

*Note:* $N = 30$ for each correlation.
\* Significant at .05 level.
\*\*Significant at .01 level (two-tailed tests).
*Source:* Vellutino and Scanlon (in press).

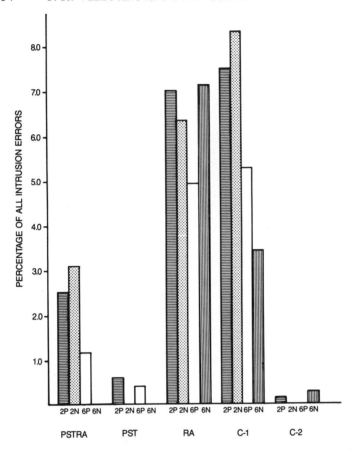

Figure 9. Percentage of word reversal errors occurring on the transfer subtest of the code acquisition task in the study evaluating reading and coding ability. (From Vellutino & Scanlon, in press.)

that poor readers of the type we have been studying – that is, severely impaired children who are apparently normal in other areas of cognitive development – are encumbered by basic and rather pervasive deficits in processing phonological information. These deficits were particularly apparent on the measures evaluating phonemic segmentation ability and on the free-recall test, which served as our operational measure of phonological coding ability.

Second, there is little doubt that reader group differences in phonological coding ability are intrinsically and causally related to differences in visual–verbal association learning. This may be inferred from the fact that, at both grade levels, poor readers performed below the level of normal readers on free recall of nonsense syllables and from the fact that these groups differed, as well, on both the picture–syllable test and the code acquisition subtests. However, when performance on the free-recall test was statistically controlled, reader group differences on both the picture–syllable and code acquisition subtests were greatly reduced or eliminated. In addition, the results on the free-recall and picture–syllable subtests were highly correlated with results on the code acquisition subtests. The data are therefore highly convergent and lead us to conclude that previously observed differences between poor and normal readers on word identification and other visual–verbal integration tasks (Vellutino, Steger, Harding, & Phillips, 1975) are due primarily to group differences in learning the verbal response components of these tasks or, in other terms, to dysfunction in lexical storage and retrieval rather than to more specific dysfunction in integrating the lexical with the visual components of printed words.

It is also clear from the present findings that previously observed differences between poor and normal readers on tests of phonemic segmentation ability (Bradley & Bryant, 1983; Fox & Routh, 1980; Liberman et al., 1974) are directly and causally related to group differences in alphabetic mapping and code acquisition. This conclusion is supported by the fact that subjects in all groups who received phonemic segmentation training performed significantly better on the code acquisition tasks than did subjects who did not receive this training. Thus, it can be comfortably inferred that sensitivity to the phonological attributes of spoken and written words in general, and the ability to grasp the phonemic segmentation principle in particular, are basic prerequisites for success in alphabetic mapping and word identification. Reinforcing this inference is the fact that performance on the test of phonemic segmentation ability was found to be positively and significantly correlated with performance on the code acquisition subtests. Especially impressive is the fact that the correlations between these variables were greater when the transfer subtest was the dependent measure, these results suggesting that skill in phoneme analysis may be especially important for the type of transfer learning involved in identifying alphabetically "regular" words (e.g., *cat, fat, ran, can*).

It also seems reasonable to conclude from our findings that, despite their deficiencies in phonological processing, poor readers are able to profit from training that sensitizes them to the grapheme–phoneme correspondences in printed words and, furthermore, that such ability is functional in word identification. Although it is true that poor readers who received segmentation training did not perform as well as normal readers who also received the training, they were able to perform as well as or better than normal readers in the control groups that did not receive segmentation training. In light of the fact that the phonemic segmentation training program was a greatly condensed and simulated version of more extensive training in phonemic analysis of the type that might take place in the natural setting, these findings are impressive and speak for the utility of such training as an important component of remedial instruction.

This conclusion is provided additional support by a review paper by Jorm and Share (1983). After surveying a large number of studies evaluating different instructional approaches to beginning reading, they concluded that code-oriented programs are "superior" to programs that emphasize the "look say" or whole-word method of initial instruction. Although our findings do not necessarily warrant this conclusion, they are consistent with the idea that phonics instruction is an important component of both initial reading and remedial reading programs.

Another conclusion that can be drawn from our results is that the ability to store and readily retrieve the names and meanings associated with printed words is also an important determinant of skill in word identification. Indeed, our data suggest that name code retrieval and alphabetic mapping are complementary subskills that are both important prerequisites for success in word identification. The data also suggest that dysfunction in both of these areas is related to more basic deficits in one's ability to store and retrieve phonological representations of spoken and printed words. Such deficiency appears to be characteristic of the severely impaired readers we have been studying as is amply documented in the present study. Indeed, of all the results we have discussed thus far, the data from this study constitute the strongest and most direct evidence in support of our linguistic coding explanation of reading disability.

If, however, it is true that such children are characterized by basic deficits in storing and retrieving phonological representations, as manifested by difficulties in both name retrieval and alphabetic mapping, it would appear to be imperative to make heavy use of meaning and semantic context in teaching them word identification skills, to help compensate for such difficulties. Here we underscore the utility of both wholistic or meaning-based and analytic strategies of word identification, the complementary use of which not only is intuitively sound but, more important, is supported by our data.

Finally, the present results provide additional support for our developmental hypothesis. That reader groups at the second-grade level were much more disparate than those at the sixth-grade level on all of the dependent measures used in this study constitutes strong evidence for our suggestion that young poor readers are especially encumbered by deficiencies in using phonological codes to store and retrieve information. The fact that the sixth-grade poor readers more closely approximated the sixth-grade normal readers on all of these measures is consistent with our suggestion that older poor readers are closer to their normal reading counterparts in phonological coding ability. These findings are, of course, in contrast to results of reader group comparisons on measures of lexical and semantic memory, where group differences at older age levels were as great as or greater than they were at younger grade levels.

### Relative proportions of variance accounted for by reader group membership on linguistic coding measures

One question that naturally arises in the study of generic disorders such as reading disability is whether there is reliable overlap in the distribution of scores on any criterial measure contrasting poor and normal readers for purposes of construct validation. Maximum overlap of these groups on any given variable of interest is tantamount to group equivalence on that variable and indicates that individual rather than group differences largely account for distributional properties. In contrast, minimum overlap coincides with group rather than individual differences on the variable of interest, and it is this circumstance that is most desirable in testing hypotheses concerned with criterial attributes that define disabled readers.

The question of distributional overlap is especially important in the development of criteria for defining etiologically distinct subgroups of poor readers whose difficulties in reading, theoretically, issue from qualitatively different origins. Though all agree that reading disability is not caused by a single factor, the nature and origin of specific causes of the disorder are hotly debated (Vellutino, 1979; Vellutino & Scanlon, 1982). It is therefore encumbent upon investigators to be keenly aware of the extent to which the measures they use for construct validation accurately identify given subjects as poor or normal readers. In other words, in evaluating the importance of results from reader group contrasts on measures designed to test specific etiological hypotheses, investigators should take account of the proportion of variance on given measures that can and cannot be attributed to reader group differences. The greater the amount of variance found to be attributed to group differences, the lower is the degree of distributional overlap between poor and normal readers on those measures and vice versa.

In the present context, the major question that must be addressed is, What proportion of the variance on respective measures of linguistic coding ability is accounted for by reader group membership? Of particular interest are the different patterns that might emerge on the various measures of phonological, syntactic, and semantic coding ability we have discussed in this chapter. A useful index of the variance estimates we seek is omega squared, or $\omega^2$ (Keppel, 1973), which is essentially a correlation ratio that indicates the proportion of the total variability attributed to group or treatment effects. Thus, it is analogous to the coefficient of determination ($R^2$) except for the fact that it is based on the variability created by group rather than individual differences. Because it takes account of sample size, it provides a less biased estimate of the strength of group effects than does the $F$ ratio, which, of course, can be brought to any level of significance with a large enough sample. In fact, $\omega^2$ is *larger* in experiments with smaller sample sizes when the $F$ ratios in these experiments are of comparable magnitudes (see Keppel, 1973, for a good discussion of the pros and cons of using $\omega^2$).

In order to provide estimates of the magnitude of reader group difference on measures of linguistic coding ability, $\omega^2$ estimates were computed for several of the tests of phonological, syntactic, and semantic coding discussed earlier (Keppel, 1973). These results appear in Figure 10, where it can be seen that, for the most part, observed patterns conform closely to the pattern of results presented in this chapter. Thus, at the second-grade level, reader group membership accounted

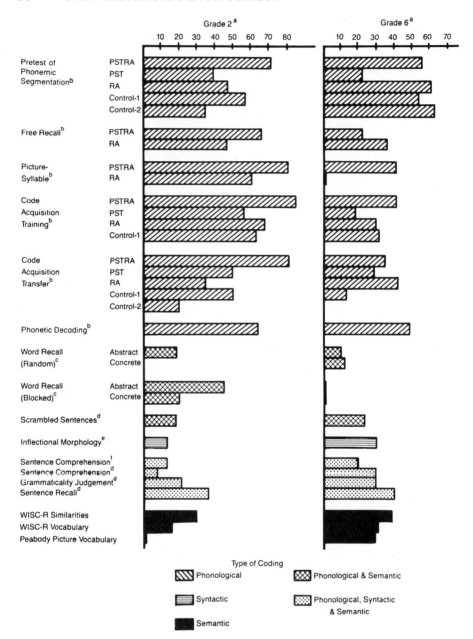

Figure 10. The $\omega^2$ estimates for the proportion of variance accounted for by reader group membership on tasks requiring the processing of phonological, syntactic, and semantic codes. (a) In all cases, estimates are based on $F$ ratios computed without the use of a covariate. (b) Estimates based on data reported in Vellutino & Scanlon (in press). (c) Estimates based on data reported in Vellutino & Scanlon (1985). (d) Test constructed by F. R. Vellutino and D. M. Scanlon. (e) Estimates based on data yet to be published. (f) Test constructed by P. Menyuk.

for more of the variance on measures that relied more directly on phonological coding ability than on measures that relied more directly on syntactic coding ability and the smallest proportion on measures that relied more directly on semantic coding ability. However, at the sixth-grade level, reader group membership accounted for less of the variance on the measures of phonological coding ability than it did at the second-grade level, whereas group membership accounted for slightly more of the variance on the syntactic coding measures than it did at the second-grade level and a good deal more of the variance on semantic coding measures than it did at this level. In fact, it appears that for sixth-grade contrasts, reader group membership accounted for comparable proportions of the variance in all three domains of language, that is, in terms of the range of $\omega^2$ estimates on respective measures in these domains. On tasks that, to a greater or lesser extent, depend on coding ability in more than one domain and less directly on coding ability in one or the other, an analogous pattern of results emerges. For example, on free recall of concrete and abstract words, reader group membership accounted for a good deal more of the variance on abstract words than on concrete words, but this was true only at the second-grade level. At the sixth-grade level, group membership accounted for comparable proportions of variance on the two types of words. In contrast, on the tasks evaluating sentence recall and recall of scrambled sentences, reader group membership accounted for comparable proportions of the variance at both grade levels. However, this similarity may be misleading since reader group differences on these tasks are probably attributable to ability differences in the use of given linguistic codes at each grade level. What is more apparent is that, at both grade levels, the sentence recall task discriminated the groups more than did the scrambled sentences task, no doubt because the former involved syntactic coding and was, therefore, linguistically more complex.

There are several points to be made in light of these results. First, the data are entirely consistent with both the linguistic coding and developmental characterizations of reading disability discussed throughout this chapter. Second, they serve to refine and qualify these characterizations. Thus, it is clear that most of the severely impaired readers we have studied, especially those in the early grades, were characterized by deficiencies in their ability to code and encode information phonologically and phonetically. The data also indicate either that a much smaller proportion of these subjects were characterized by pronounced deficiencies in syntactic and/or semantic coding ability, in addition to their phonological coding deficiencies, or that most were characterized by ineptitude in syntactic and semantic coding that tended to be less pronounced than their ineptitude in phonological coding. These possibilities are not mutually exclusive, and it is, in fact, likely that our poor-reader samples consisted of some children whose reading problems were caused by generalized language deficiencies and others whose problems were caused by more specific language deficiencies. In any event, the data provide strong support for the idea that phonological coding deficit is a common attribute among severely impaired readers, such as those we have typically studied, and may well be the leading cause of reading disability in these children.

The third point we wish to make is concerned with the developmental differences noted in the results. It is clear that either the extent (in terms of the number of children affected) or the magnitude of basic phonological coding deficits is substantially reduced in older poor readers, whereas the extent and/or magnitude of syntactic and semantic coding deficits increases in this population. The increased overlap in the distributions of reader group scores yielded by sixth-grade contrasts on phonological processing measures could be due either to the fact that phonological coding ability is characterized by some "upper limit" that both groups were approaching or to reduced difficulty levels of the phonological processing tasks for older children. Ruling out the latter explanation is the fact that there was ample ceiling on most of these tasks, depending, of course, on the treatments to which given groups were exposed. Favoring the former is the fact that the second-grade normal readers typically performed as well as or better than the sixth-grade poor readers on the phonological coding tasks and often approximated the level of performance achieved by the sixth-grade normal readers.

The decreased overlap in the distributions of these scores on measures of syntactic and semantic coding ability is no doubt due, in part, to experiential deficiencies caused by long-standing reading disorder in the sixth-grade poor readers, but this possibility is more strongly indicated by results on the semantic coding measures. That is, given that the sizes of the $\omega^2$ estimates on the syntax measures did not change dramatically from second to sixth grade, it might reasonably be inferred that the variance estimates yielded by these contrasts accurately define the range within which to approximate the amount of variance in syntactic competence due to reader group membership. Additional research will be needed to determine if this is the case. However, we are more confident that the data provide reasonably accurate estimates of the amount of variance that may be due to reader group membership on measures of semantic coding ability and especially on those that directly measure this ability, for example, tests of vocabulary development.

Finally, the present results suggest that the number of severely impaired readers whose difficulties in beginning reading are *not* caused by linguistic coding deficits would be very small in comparison with the number who are encumbered by such deficits. The most impressive bit of evidence in support of this generalization is provided by results of second-grade contrasts on the code acquisition subtests for subjects exposed to both phonemic segmentation and response acquisition training (PSTRA groups). Under these conditions, reader group membership respectively accounted for 85 and 81% of the variance on the training and transfer subtests. Given the small amount of residual variance that might be attributed to error of measurement and the like, these results suggest that almost all of the normal readers in this sample profited much more than almost all of the poor readers in the sample from the combined training they received in their attempts to learn to identify the analogs of printed words used as stimuli in this experiment. We presume that this was because the normal readers were inherently better equipped than the poor readers to represent, activate, and access the phonological and phonetic codes corresponding to the verbal counterparts of these stimuli. If this presumption is correct, and our findings suggest that it is, the generalization would seem to hold.

One other point should be made here. It should be understood that there is no generally accepted standard for attaching significance to $\omega^2$ estimates of any given size. This means that the interpretation of a particular estimate must take place within a theoretical context, which is to suggest that a small estimate may have as much significance as a large estimate in refining a particular theory. In the present instance, the large discrepancy between the sizes of the variance estimates yielded by the phonological coding measures compared with those yielded by the syntactic and semantic coding measures suggests, as we said earlier, that although most severely impaired readers suffer from rather pronounced deficiencies in phonological processing, deficiencies in syntactic and semantic processing may be neither as pronounced nor as pervasive in this population. This finding could have theoretical significance, with respect to both the etiology of reading disability and the nature of the word identification process itself. It may have etiological significance insofar as it provides additional insight into the different types of linguistic coding deficits that may encumber beginning readers. On the one hand, it is clear that not all poor readers are characterized by semantic and syntactic coding deficits at the outset but may well acquire such deficits as a result of protracted reading disorder. On the other hand, the fact that most of them are characterized by deficiencies in phonological coding provides a clue as to the word identification process insofar as it suggests that the ability to code and decode printed words phonetically may be a critical and rather basic subskill for word identification and that children who have difficulty in acquiring this skill will also have difficulty in learning to read. Thus, it is the relations between and among the variance estimates that are instructive rather than the sizes of these estimates.

## Synthesis

In this chapter, we have attempted to trace the history of our study of the etiology of reading disability, from the seminal investigations we have conducted up to the present. Our analysis of the problem and of competing etiological hypotheses has been primarily data based, but our inquiry has been guided by certain theoretical and logical considerations that have helped to shape our own tentative explanation of the disorder.

Both traditional and contemporary conceptualizations of reading disability implicate dysfunctions in visual perception, cross-modal transfer, serial memory, association learning, and rule learning as root causes of the problem, but we questioned each of these conceptualizations on empirical grounds. They can be questioned on theoretical and logical grounds as well. Of all of these hypotheses, the visual-deficit notion has the most face validity and has certainly been the most popular. This is not surprising. That is, given that the beginning reader is required to negotiate a rather complex symbol system characterized by a high degree of visual similarity, it would be expected that a child with limited ability to internalize visual information would have difficulty in mastering the system. However, as with any orthography based on an alphabet, there is a great deal of redundancy that can be put to good advantage once the child becomes conversant with the "rules" for doing so. This necessitates a functional knowledge of orthographic, graphophonemic, and morphophonemic invariance, which in turn is dependent on the ability to code information phonologically. If phonological coding ability is intact and if the child has acquired the metalinguistic abilities necessary for analyzing and synthesizing letter strings (e.g., "phoneme awareness"), he or she should have little difficulty in learning to map alphabetic symbols to sound, and the load on visual memory should be minimal. If, however, phonological coding ability is deficient, the child should be encumbered in alphabetic mapping, the load on visual memory should be extraordinary, and discrimination errors should abound.

In short, we believe that reading is an enterprise that can tolerate a wide range of individual differences in visual processing ability, provided that the learner acquires the grapheme–phoneme correspondence rules that would minimize the demands made on the visual system, and this in turn depends on linguistic coding ability. By logical extension, we should look for deficiencies in linguistic coding ability when visual memory problems seem to be the ostensible cause of reading disability.

Of the other explanations of reading disability that our research has provided reason to question, the cross-modal-deficit theory ranks second only to the perceptual-deficit theory in popularity. However, it, along with the association-learning and rule-learning-deficit theories, can be rejected on logical grounds. It will suffice to point out in support of the argument that it is difficult to imagine how a child who is truly deficient in any of these areas can possibly score in at least the average range on an intelligence test. Yet a basic defining characteristic of reading-disabled children, for both research and clinical purposes, is average or above-average intelligence. Thus, the etiological and the definitional characterizations of such children are incompatible.

The serial-memory-deficit explanation of reading disability also has some face validity, given the sequential property of the spoken and written language, but this explanation can be questioned on theoretical grounds. Serial-deficit hypotheses, by definition, postulate that the brain is equipped with an "ordering mechanism" – a neurological entity, if you will – that is responsible for generating rules and algorithms for putting an inherently ordered array of elements in their proper sequence. This, to us, seems highly unlikely. More likely is the possibility that different representational systems are organized and constrained by algorithms that are particular to and govern those systems and that the brain stores and uses each set of algorithms autonomously. Thus, we suppose that the syntactic rules for ordering spoken words are substantially different from the phonological rules that order the phones and phonemes that comprise those words as well as the alphabetic characters that represent them in their written form. Each of these rules is quite different from those that one uses to recognize or hum a melody or from those that order the numerical concepts used to represent quantities. We believe, therefore, that the sequential-deficit theories of reading disability that have been advanced in the literature will prove to be untenable.

In making reference to the functional role assigned to the phonological and syntactic components of spoken language in coding and ordering written language, we allude to the explanation of reading disability to which we are partial. It seems likely that difficulties in learning to read emanate from deficiencies and ineptitude in one or more of the domains of language. Indeed, reading is primarily a linguistic skill, and it is the components and units of language and the information coded in language that give printed words their meanings and functional valences and determine the strategies one uses for learning to identify them.

However, we have evolved a developmental hypothesis incorporating the idea that the nature of the language deficits that lead to difficulties in reading changes along the age or grade continuum. In brief, we suggest that poor readers who are closer to the beginning stages of skills acquisition are especially encumbered by ineptitude in utilizing the phonological and/or syntactic components of language – what we have termed their purely linguistic attributes – to code, store, and retrieve information. In contrast, there is reason to believe that, either because of maturation that might have taken place or because of experience of the type that promotes metalinguistic analysis (e.g., instruction in reading and spelling; exposure to formal language), deficiencies in structural coding, especially phonological coding, are not as pronounced in older poor readers as they are in younger poor readers. Yet because of the cumulative deficits in lexical development that would inevitably accrue as a result of long-standing reading disorder, older poor readers may be encumbered as much or more by deficiencies in semantic coding as by deficiencies in structural coding and would be differentiated from older normal readers on tasks that rely more heavily on semantic coding.

Thus, in studies more recently conducted in our laboratory, we have observed that young poor readers are less sensitive than young normal readers to the phonological and syntactic components of spoken and written words and are less proficient than normal readers in using these codes to store and retrieve these stimuli. We have also observed that reader groups at the younger age levels more closely approximate one another in their sensitivity to the semantic components of language and are somewhat closer together on tasks that directly measure and rely on semantic and lexical development for successful performance (e.g., lexical memory, vocabulary and verbal concept tasks). In contrast, older poor readers are closer to older normal readers on measures that rely heavily on sensitivity to and facility with the phonological components of language but are more disparate on those that rely heavily on semantic and syntactic development. However, these findings should not be taken to mean that poor and normal readers at younger age levels are equivalent in semantic coding ability or that poor and normal readers at older age levels are equivalent in phonological coding ability. Although either of these patterns may be observed in any individual case, group trends suggest that there are degrees of disparity between poor- and normal-reader groups in these information-processing capabilities, and those that are the primary source(s) of reader group differences in reading and other verbal coding tasks in early acquisition may not be the same as those that are the primary source(s) of group differences at later stages of acquisition.

Finally, we would like to add a qualification to the foregoing analysis. It is important to note that the data we have collected and our interpretations of these data, as reflected in the conceptualization of reading disability discussed throughout this chapter, have been derived from the study of the most severely impaired readers in normal classroom settings. These are children who have been selected for study in accord with accepted criteria for inclusion and exclusion and who are at the lowest end of the distribution of poor readers one might be inclined to study, which, in our research, is typically between the 4th and 10th percentile on an oral reading test (Gilmore & Gilmore, 1968). It is therefore possible that our findings would not generalize to a less severely impaired population. For example, we think that it is entirely possible, and even likely, that many children encounter reading problems primarily because of experiences that do not optimally attune them to all of the attributes contained in the printed word. The most obvious example is the child who has limited processing strategies because of exclusive exposure to either a meaning-based, whole-word approach or to a phonics approach to word identification. We surmise that, because of deficiencies in one of these subskills, such children will experience significant difficulties in learning to identify printed words, despite normal development in all of the cognitive and linguistic domains that are prerequisites to success in reading. However, they should not be as limited as the severely impaired readers we have been studying, and their difficulties should be less pervasive and more circumscribed. We have recently compared severely and moderately impaired poor readers, and our preliminary results suggest that this is indeed the case. Moreover, the results of the large training study discussed earlier make it clear that constrained and inflexible processing strategies can lead to deficiencies in word identification and that such strategies can be acquired by virtue of instructional biases and/or like experiences.

We have little doubt, however, that reading disability is a generic disorder that has multiple etiologies. Yet we firmly believe that, because of the nature of the reading process itself, and especially because reading is primarily a linguistic skill, these etiologies will implicate deficiencies in one or more aspects of language development and language functioning rather than deficiencies in other types of cognitive functioning.

### Notes

**1.** The term *phonetic* (decoding) is used here rather than *phonological* (decoding) because the identification of pseudowords draws on speech–motor representations that are less abstract than those implied in the use of the latter term. That is, phonetic codes are closer to the surface features of language than are phonological codes, and although the activation of phonetic codes depends on the availability of phonological codes, pseudoword decoding ultimately depends on one's ability to activate phonetic and articulatory representations.

**2.** Half of the stimulus sets could be categorized into three orthographic groupings, each with two members, or two semantic groupings, each with three members. The remaining half of the stimulus sets could be categorized into two orthographic groupings, each with three members, or three semantic groupings, each with two members.

**3.** Although the semantic distractors did not produce a significant increase in the false positive response rate in Condition A, it would seem possible that their mere presence may have encouraged a more semantically based approach to encoding.

**4.** Because there is some indication that the cognitive demands made by the Wug Test may lead to an underestimation of the mastery of inflectional morphemes in some individuals (Rosenberg, 1982), the results on this test were correlated with scores on the Verbal and Performance subscales on the WISC-R as well as with scores on the Peabody Picture Vocabulary Test (PPVT). Performance on the Wug Test did not correlate significantly with the WISC-R Performance IQ but did correlate positively and significantly with performance on the PPVT and WISC-R Verbal IQ. However, correlations between the Wug Test and the verbal measures (VIQ and PPVT) were much higher in the poor-reader groups, the only significant correlation among the normal-reader groups occurring between the Wug Test and the WISC-R Verbal IQ in second-grade normal readers. These results suggest that the Wug Test did not differentially tax the cognitive abilities of the poor and normal readers in our samples. Additional support for this possibility is provided by our observation that the second-grade normal readers performed better than the sixth-grade poor readers on this test. If younger, cognitively less mature subjects are able to perform better on a given task than older, more mature subjects, performance differences cannot be due to the cognitive demands of the task.

**5.** This test was constructed by Paula Menyuk, Boston University.

**6.** Because the number of subjects who received the PPVT ($N = 18$ to 29 per group) was not large enough to sustain the subdivisions of the poor- and normal-reader samples entailed in matching groups for WISC-R Verbal and Performance IQ, results on the PPVT are not reported for the IQ-matched groups.

**7.** Because the WISC-R Verbal- and Performance-IQ-matched subgroups discussed in this section represent nonrandom samplings from the "all subjects" groups and because data for some subjects are used in both the Verbal- and Performance-IQ-matched sets, the results are discussed in terms of general patterns rather than statistical trends since the latter would not be appropriate given the lack of independence among the groups.

**8.** In a pilot study, we equated for referential meaning the concrete and abstract word lists used in these studies by asking randomly selected subjects, at the same ages and grades as the research subjects evaluated in our studies, to define each separately. These lists were equated for connotative meaning by means of Osgood's semantic differential technique (Osgood, Suci, & Tannenbaum, 1957).

## References

Baddeley, A. D., & Hitch, G. (1974). Working memory. In G. H. Bower (Ed.), *The psychology of learning and motivation* (Vol. 8, pp. 47–90). New York: Academic Press.

Baron, J. (1979). Orthographic and word specific mechanisms in children's reading of words. *Child Development, 50,* 60-72.

Berko, J. (1958). The child's learning of English morphology. *Word, 14,* 150–77.

Biemiller, A. (1970). The development of the use of graphic and contextual information as children learn to read. *Reading Research Quarterly, 6,* 75–96.

Birch, H. G. (1962). Dyslexia and maturation of visual function. In J. Money (Ed.), *Reading disability: Progress and research needs in dyslexia* (pp. 161–9). Baltimore, MD: Johns Hopkins University Press.

Birch, H. G., & Belmont, L. (1964). Auditory–visual integration in normal and retarded readers. *American Journal of Orthopsychiatry, 34,* 852–61.

Blank, M., & Bridger, W. H. (1964). Cross-modal transfer in nursery school children. *Journal of Comparative and Physiological Psychology, 58,* 277–82.

Blank, M., & Bridger, W. H. (1966). Deficiencies in verbal labeling in retarded readers. *American Journal of Orthopsychiatry, 36,* 840–7.

Blank, M., Weider, S., & Bridger, W. (1968). Verbal deficiencies in abstract thinking in early reading retardation. *American Journal of Orthopsychiatry, 38,* 823–34.

Bradley, L., & Bryant, P. E. (1983). Categorizing sounds and learning to read: A causal connection. *Nature, 303,* 419–21.

Bryant, N. D. (1963). *Diagnostic Test of Phonic Skills.* Published by the author.

Byrne, B., & Shea P. (1979). Semantic and phonetic memory codes in beginning readers. *Memory and Cognition, 7,* 333–8.

Chomsky, N., & Halle, M. (1968). *The sound pattern of English.* New York: Harper & Row.

Denckla, M. B., & Rudel, R. (1976a). Naming of pictured objects by dyslexic and other learning disabled children. *Brain and Language, 39,* 1–15.

Denckla, M. B., & Rudel, R. (1976b). Rapid 'automatized' naming (R.A.N.): Dyslexia differentiated from other learning disabilities. *Neuropsychologia, 14,* 471–9.

Dunn, L. M. (1965). *Peabody Picture Vocabulary Test.* Circle Pines, MN: American Guidance Service.

Ehri, L. (1980). The role of orthographic images in learning printed words. In J. F. Kavanagh & R. L. Venezky (Eds.), *Orthography, reading and dyslexia* (pp. 155–70). Baltimore MD: University Park Press.

Felzen, E., Anisfeld, M. (1970). Semantic and phonetic relations in the false recognition of words by third and sixth grade children. *Developmental Psychology, 3,* 163–8.

Filbey, R. A., & Gazzaniga, M. S. (1969). Splitting the normal brain with reaction time. *Psychonomic Science, 17*(6), 335–6.

Firth, I. (1972). *Components of reading disability.* Unpublished docoral dissertation, University of New South Wales, Sydney, Australia.

Fox, B., & Routh, D. K. (1980). Phonemic analysis and severe reading disability in children. *Journal of Psycholinguistic Research, 9,* 115–19.

Gazzaniga, M. S., Bogen, J. E., & Sperry, R. W. (1965). Observations on visual perception after disconnection of the cerebral hemisphere in man. *Brain, 88,* 221–36.

Geschwind, N., & Fusillo, M. (1966). Color-naming defects in association with alexia. *AMA Archives of Neurology, 15,* 137–46.

Gibson, E. J. (1971). Perceptual learning and the theory of word perception. *Cognitive Psychology, 2,* 351–68.

Gilmore, J. V., & Gilmore, E. C. (1968). *Gilmore Oral Reading Test.* San Diego, CA: Harcourt Brace Jovanovich.

Goodman, K. S. (1973). Analysis of oral reading miscues: Applied psycholinguistics. In F. Smith (Ed.), *Psycholinguistics and reading* (pp. 158–76). New York: Holt, Rinehart & Winston.

Gough, P. B., Alford, J. A., & Holley-Wilcox, P. (1981). Words and contexts. In O. J. L. Tzeng & H. Singer (Eds.), *Perception of print: Reading research in experimental psychology* (pp. 85–102). Hillsdale, NJ: Erlbaum.

Harris, A. J., & Jacobson, M. D. (1982). *Basic reading vocabularies.* New York: Macmillan.

Hermann, K. (1959). *Reading disability.* Copenhagen: Munksgaard.

Jorm, A. F., & Share, D. (1983). An invited article: Phonological recoding and reading acquisition. *Applied Psycholinguistics, 4,* 103–47.

Keppel, G. (1973). *Design and analysis: A researcher's handbook.* Englewood Cliffs, NJ: Prentice-Hall.

Kleiman, G. M. (1975). Speech recoding in reading. *Journal of Verbal Learning and Verbal Behavior, 14,* 323–40.

Liberman, I. Y., & Shankweiler, D. (1979). Speech, the alphabet and teaching to read. In L. Resnick & P. Weaver (Eds.), *Theory and practice of early reading* (Vol. 2, pp. 109–32). Hillsdale, NJ: Erlbaum.

Liberman, I. Y., Shankweiler, D., Fischer, F. W., & Carter, B. (1974). Explicit syllable and phoneme segmentation in the young child. *Journal of Experimental Child Psychology, 18,* 201–12.

Morrison, F. J., & Manis, F. R. (1982). Cognitive processes and reading disability: A critique and proposal. In C. J. Brainerd & M. Pressley (Eds.), *Verbal processes in children* (pp. 59–93). New York: Springer-Verlag.

Orton, S. T. (1925). "Word-blindness" in school children. *Archives of Neurology and Psychiatry, 14,* 581–615.

Osgood, C. E., Suci, G. J., & Tannenbaum, P. A. (1957). *The measurement of meaning.* Urbana: University of Illinois Press.

Paivio, A. (1971). *Imagery and verbal processes.* New York: Holt, Rinehart & Winston.

Paivio, A., & Begg, I. (1971a). Imagery and comprehension latencies as a function of sentence concreteness and structure. *Perception and Psychophysics, 10,* 408–12.

Paivio, A., & Begg, I. (1971b). Imagery and associative overlap in short-term memory. *Journal of Experimental Psychology, 89,* 40–5.

Perfetti, C. A., & Hogaboam, T. W. (1975). The relationship between single word decoding and reading comprehension skill. *Journal of Educational Psychology, 67,* 461–9.

Perfetti, C. A., & Lesgold, A. M. (1979). Coding and comprehension in skilled reading and implications for reading instruction. In L. B. Resnick & P. A. Weaver (Eds.), *Theory and practice of early reading* (Vol. 1, pp. 59–84). Hillsdale, NJ: Erlbaum.

Perfetti, C. A., & McCutchen, D. (1982). Speech processes in reading. In N. Lass (Ed.), *Speech and language: Advances in basic research and practice* (Vol. 7, 237–69). New York: Academic Press.

Quigley, S. P., Steinkamp, M. W., Power, D. J., & Jones, B. W. (1978). *Test of Syntactic Abilities.* Beaverton OR: Dormac.

Rabinovitch, R. D. (1959). Reading and learning disabilities. In S. Arieti (Ed.), *American handbook of psychiatry* (pp. 857–69). New York: Basic Books.

Rosenberg, S. (1982). The language of the mentally retarded: Development, processes and intervention. In S. Rosenberg (Ed.), *Handbook of applied psycholinguistics: Major thrusts of research and theory* (pp. 329–92). Hillsdale, NJ: Erlbaum.

Smith F. (1973). Decoding: The great fallacy. In F. Smith (Ed.), *Psychlinguistics and reading* (pp. 70–93). New York: Holt, Rinehart & Winston.

Sperry, R. W. (1964). The great cerebral commisure. *Scientific American, 210,* 42–52.

Vellutino, F. R. (1979). *Dyslexia: Theory and research.* Cambridge, MA: MIT Press.

Vellutino, F. R., Bentley, W. L., and Phillips, F. (1978). Inter- versus intra-hemispheric learning in dyslexic and normal readers. *Developmental Medicine and Child Neurology, 20,* 71–80.

Vellutino, F. R., Harding, C. J., Phillips, F., & Steger, J. A. (1975). Differential transfer in poor and normal readers. *Journal of Genetic Psychology, 126,* 3–18.

Vellutino, F. R., Pruzek, R. M., Steger, J. A., & Meshoulam, U. (1973). Immediate visual recall in poor and normal readers as a function of orthographic–linguistic familiarity. *Cortex, 9,* 368–84.

Vellutino, F. R., & Scanlon, D. M. (1982). Verbal processing in poor and normal readers. In C. J. Brainerd & M. Pressley (Eds.), *Verbal processes in children* (pp. 189–264). New York: Springer-Verlag.

Vellutino, F. R., & Scanlon, D. M. (1985). Free recall of concrete and abstract words in poor and normal readers. *Journal of Experimental Child Psychology, 39,* 363–80.

Vellutino, F. R., & Scanlon, D. M. (1986). *Differential sensitivity to the meaning and structural attributes of printed words.* Manuscript submitted for publication.

Vellutino, F. R., & Scanlon, D. M. (in press). *Reading and coding ability: An experimental analysis.* Cambridge University Press.

Vellutino, F. R., Scanlon, D. M., & Bentley, W. L. (1983). Interhemispheric learning and speed of hemispheric transmission in dyslexic and normal readers: A replication of previous results and additional findings. *Journal of Applied Psycholinguistics, 4,* 209–28.

Vellutino, F. R., Scanlon, D. M., DeSetto, L., & Pruzek, R. M. (1981). Developmental trends in the salience of meaning versus structural attributes of written words. *Psychological Research, 43,* 131–53.

Vellutino, F. R., Smith, H., Steger, J. A., & Kaman, M. (1975). Reading disability: Age differences and the perceptual deficit hypothesis. *Child Development, 46,* 487–93.

Vellutino, F. R., Steger, J. A., DeSetto, L., & Phillips, F. (1975). Immediate and delayed recognition of visual stimuli in poor and normal readers. *Journal of Experimental Child Psychology, 19,* 223–32.

Vellutino, F. R., Steger, J. A., Harding, C. J., & Phillips, F. (1975). Verbal vs. non-verbal paired-associates learning in poor and normal readers. *Neuropsychologia, 13,* 75–82.

Vellutino, F. R., Steger, J. A., Kaman, M., & DeSetto, L. (1975). Visual form perception in deficient and normal readers as a function of age and orthographic linguistic familiarity. *Cortex, 11,* 22–30.

Vellutino, F. R., Steger, J. A., & Kandel, G. (1972). Reading disability: An investigation of the perceptual deficit hypothesis. *Cortex, 8,* 106–18.

Vellutino, F. R., Steger, J. A., & Pruzek, R. (1973). Inter- vs. intransensory deficit in paired associate learning in poor and normal readers. *Canadian Journal of Behavioral Science, 5,* 111–23.

Weber, R. M. (1970). First graders' use of grammatical context in reading. In H. Levin &

J. P. Williams (Eds.), *Basic studies in reading* (pp. 147–63). New York: Basic Books.

Wechsler, D. (1949). *Wechsler Intelligence Scale for Children*. New York: Psychological Corporation.

Wechsler, D. (1974). *Wechsler Intelligence Scale for Children-Revised*. New York: Psychological Corporation.

# 2 Research on the reading of mildly mentally retarded learners: a synthesis of the empirical literature

*Linda P. Blanton and Melvyn I. Semmel*
*with Sharyn S. Rhodes*

Although it is understood that problems in reading are not necessarily symptomatic of mental retardation, it is generally accepted that a diagnosis of mental retardation[1] is invariably indicative of significant developmental delay in the acquisition of reading skills. In fact, pupils characterized as mentally retarded frequently reveal a relatively broad variance of serious qualitative reading deficits in addition to slow acquisition of basic reading skills (Gillespie & Johnson, 1974). However, the ubiquity of reading deficiencies among mildly mentally retarded learners (MRLs) has not resulted in convincing empirically based explanations for these phenomena. Accordingly, the schools remain without particularly effective interventions to remediate the basic skills deficits of MRLs enrolled in special and/ or regular educational programs. Semmel, Gottlieb, and Robinson (1979) inferred from their extensive review of the literature that MRLs "never" reach a mean grade level of fourth-grade reading competency. These reviewers further conclude, "Instructional alternatives that have been offered to date have proven relatively ineffectual regardless of the environment in which these children are taught" (p. 237).

In searching the published literature on reading, we found a general failure to translate research into principles and methods for instructing MRLs. In fact, we discovered a general dearth of published empirically based reports related to reading and MRLs. A search of the contemporary literature failed to uncover a single comprehensive knowledge integration synthesis covering the research conducted in this substantive area since circa 1975. By contrast, numerous reviews that focused on reading and MRLs were published before that time (e.g., Blanton, Sitko, & Gillespie, 1976; Cawley, Goodstein, & Burrow, 1972; Cegelka & Cegelka, 1970; Gillespie & Johnson, 1974; Hurley, 1975; Kirk, 1964; Orlando, 1973; Reed, Rabe, & Mankinen, 1970; Spicker & Bartel, 1968).

The authors extend appreciation to Dr. William E. Blanton, Dr. Priscilla Drum, Dr. Carol Sue Englert, Dr. Susan Goldman, Dr. Steve Graham, Dr. Karen Harris, and Dr. Dorothy Semmel for valuable substantive and editorial contributions to this chapter. This work was supported, in part, by the Postdoctoral Training Program in Special Education, University of California, Santa Barbara, U.S. Department of Education.

70

The absence of a contemporary synthesis in the area of reading and MRLs is perplexing. It may well reflect a serious discrepancy in the emphasis on reading research with MRL groups before and after 1975. In considering this hypothesis, numerous questions arise about the reasons for this apparently diminished interest. Perhaps recently enacted federal and state mandates or policies (e.g., PL 94-142, *Larry P.* v. *Riles*) have directly or indirectly altered research. It is clear that legal and legislative mandates concerning the rights of the handicapped have resulted in differential categorical placements of children who formally would have been assigned to the MRL category. In California, for example, mildly mentally retarded pupils and learning-disabled children with normal intelligence are categorized as "learning handicapped." The California schools do not recognize the "educable retarded" or "mildly retarded" classification for state reporting and reimbursement purposes. These policy changes throughout the country may well have resulted in an inability on the part of researchers to select samples of specific clinically defined school-aged children, that is, MRLs (see Semmel et al., 1979). It appears equally plausible that policy-driven federal funding patterns have had an impact on research productivity, specifically in the area of the reading behavior and instruction of MRLs. Relatively few grants were awarded in this substantive research area between 1975 and 1985 by federal agencies, for example, the Bureau for the Education of the Handicapped or its successor, Special Education Programs, in the U.S. Department of Education (N. Safer, personal communication, June 18, 1985).

The present chapter reviews current research and attempts a synthesis of this information with earlier empirical work on MRLs in reading contexts. Initially, we summarize the research reported before 1975. Next, we review studies reported since that time with the intent of uncovering new trends, synthesizing consistent findings, and deducing implications for practice. We seek to provide the reader with a global understanding of where research on the reading of MRLs has been, where it is now, and where it might have to go.

We have searched the literature in special education, reading education, and cognitive psychology to locate the most accurate perspectives on research trends. The present chapter is limited to studies directly related to reading and is focused solely on the mildly mentally retarded population. No attempt was made to include the large body of research related to language variables and MRL populations.

## Reading research on mentally retarded learners before 1975

Two major trends are evident from a review of the research published before 1975. One strand of work concentrated on the identification of specific reading characteristics that differentiate MRLs from nonretarded pupils. This trend was accompanied by a search for correlates to the reading performance of MRLs. The second focused on comparative methods for teaching reading to MRLs, with the goal of identifying the most effective means of instruction. This section organizes early research on the reading of mildly retarded learners into the following categories: (1) comparisons of the reading characteristics of MRLs, (2) the efficacy of reading methods, and (3) the application of information-processing models to the comprehension of words and text.

## Comparisons of the reading characteristics of MRLs

**Between-group comparisons.** A persisting question in the field of mental retardation is, Do mentally retarded children differ from nonretarded children in the quantity and/or quality of their performance? When applied to reading skill acquisition, the question is translated to the issues of whether MRLs are inferior to nonretarded chronological age (CA) or mental age (MA) peers relative to all aspects of reading and whether MRLs acquire the same skills, at a slower rate, but in a similar developmental sequence.

Results of comparative studies generally confirm the expectation that nonretarded students are superior to retarded students on measures of reading ability. These findings were consistent with MA-matched groups for both silent and oral reading (Dunn, 1954). Nonhandicapped pupils' ability to use cues in print and other linguistic contexts was found to be superior to that of MRLs in a number of published investigations between 1954 and 1972 (e.g., Dunn, 1954; Goodstein, 1970; Hargis, 1972; Ramanauskas, 1972; Semmel, Barritt, & Bennett, 1970; Semmel, Barritt, Bennett, & Perfetti, 1968; Semmel & Bennett, 1970; Shotick, 1960). Dunn (1954) also reported superior comparative performance by nonretarded pupils on an analysis of patterns of reading errors and on visual efficiency and auditory acuity. Similar outcomes were reported for higher- and lower-order reading responses (Levitt, 1972), achievement in basal reading skills (Blake, Aaron, & Westbrook, 1967), and general reading levels (Cawley, Goodstein, & Burrow, 1968).

Although most studies comparing retarded and nonretarded pupils revealed differences in favor of nonretarded populations, some generated mixed results (e.g., Blake et al., 1967; Levitt, 1970). The Blake et al. (1967) study was probably the most comprehensive research project reported in this area. These researchers not only confirmed the overall findings of other comparative studies – that nonretarded pupils generally exceed retarded pupils in level of skill performance – but also found that MRLs do, in fact, learn the majority of reading skills that all students are expected to learn. More important, it was reported that MRLs acquire reading skills in the same scope and sequence presented by basal reading series used in the study. Although this finding does not furnish evidence that the sequence of skills taught is the best arrangement of skills for reading instruction, it does indicate that MRLs learn skills in the same sequence prescribed for nonretarded pupils. Of equal importance is the finding that MRL and nonretarded groups were more often similar in level of skill attainment at primary grade levels. At intermediate grade levels, however, differences favoring nonretarded groups became apparent.

Thus, a synthesis of early comparative studies suggests that MRLs acquire reading skills at a slower rate of development than their nonretarded peers. Perhaps of greater importance is the finding that MRLs apparently learn these skills in the same developmental sequence as do nonretarded students. Also, there is considerable evidence that an acceleration of the difference between groups in reading skill acquisition and performance occurs as the groups progress through school.

**Within-group comparisons.** Studies of within-group differences sought to identify specific variables that affect the reading performance of subgroups within the MRL population. Many early researchers concentrated on the identification of basic differences between different etiological groups of MRLs (e.g., endogenous and exogenous) or on the effectiveness of special methods of instruction for specific etiological classifications. This work was guided primarily by the earlier theoretical and pedagogical efforts of Alfred Strauss and his associates (Strauss & Kephart, 1955; Strauss & Lehtinen, 1947). Investigations of within-group differences among MRLs differentiated by etiology revealed no significant differences in academic achievement between brain-injured and non-brain-injured children (Capobianco, 1956; Capobianco & Miller, 1958; Cruickshank, Bentzen, Ratzeburg, & Tannhauser, 1961; Frey, 1960; Gallagher, 1960). In addition, the use of special methods or programs with brain-injured groups produced nonsignificant results (Cruickshank et al., 1961; Frey, 1960; Gallagher, 1960). Investigators apparently lost interest in the relation between etiology of mental retardation and reading variables since this line of inquiry contributed minimally to an understanding of the reading performance of MRLs. Though Strauss and his associates emphasized the importance of structured approaches to teaching reading, their theoretical and methodological foci had relatively little effect on the development of empirically validated methods of successfully teaching retarded children to read.

Interest in perceptual processes emerged from the failures to implicate neurological dysfunctions in the reading behaviors of MRLs. Perhaps emphasis on perceptual processes appeared somewhat less reductionistic at the time and represented a somewhat minimal concession to the growing influence of radical behaviorism. Alluding to perceptual processes eliminated the need to focus on central nervous system etiologies in accounting for reading behavior problems. Perceptual modality was the target of several studies employing aptitude-by-treatment interaction (ATI) designs to determine whether MRLs who were grouped and taught according to their modality preference would demonstrate significant reading achievement gains (Bracht, 1970; Sabatino & Dorfman, 1974; Sabatino,

Ysseldyke, & Woolston, 1973). Each of these efforts resulted in nonsignificant ATIs. Admittedly, methodological problems have characterized much ATI research (Berliner & Cahen, 1973; Carbo, 1983) and might have led to the rejection of teaching reading via modality strengths. Nonetheless, a review by Carbo (1983) indicated that numerous studies judged to be methodologically sound have produced reading achievement gains with nonretarded students who were instructed through their perceptual strengths.

With the absence of an adequate theory for guidance, researchers began to explore within-group approaches in an attempt to uncover significant correlates of the reading behavior of MRLs. Several investigators sought to determine the variables that differentiate relatively "good" from "poor" readers within the retarded population. Studies comparing adequate and inadequate readers were generally limited to descriptive comparisons of these two groups. Of the investigations reported, two (Merlin & Tseng, 1972; Sheperd, 1967) explored differences in reading ability and numerous associated factors, including psycholinguistic abilities, silent and oral reading, and patterns of reading errors. In both studies, good-reader groups demonstrated higher competence on specific psycholinguistic functions and on measures of reading skill, such as silent and oral reading, use of context clues, word recognition, listening comprehension, and sound blending. No significant differences were found between groups on certain psycholinguistic functions and on measures of handedness and lateral dominance. The results in general revealed that differences between groups favored the good-reader groups or were not significant.

Within-group studies such as those reviewed above have attempted to identify variables related to the reading performance of MRLs. Although a number of factors have been studied within the mildly retarded population, the evidence suggests that the reading performance of MRLs is not related to specifically identified variables such as the etiology of the condition or the perceptual characteristics of pupils within the MRL classification. It seems prudent to conclude that the within-group research paradigms before circa 1975 offered relatively little empirical evidence for solving service delivery problems presented by MRLs in the public schools.

### Efficacy of reading methods with MRLs

The effectiveness of specific approaches to teaching reading to MRLs has been the subject of numerous investigations reported in the literature. Most compared the efficacy of such approaches as language experience, basal reader, initial teaching alphabet (i t a), Words in Color, and programmed instruction, along with a wide array of published programs (Dunn & Mueller, 1966; Dunn, Neville, Bailey, Pochanart, & Pfost, 1967; Dunn, Pochanart, & Pfost, 1967; Vandever, Maggart, &

Nasser, 1976; Woodcock, 1967). The results of this line of research have generally failed to provide evidence for the superiority of one method over another.

Two studies (Neville & Vandever, 1973; Vandever & Neville, 1976) compared the effectiveness of synthetic and analytic approaches to beginning reading. In the synthetic approach, words are taught by initially emphasizing phoneme–grapheme relations. This method differs from the analytic approach, which initiates instruction with whole words. The results of both investigations suggested that synthetic instruction for MRLs is likely to promote the development of independent word attack skills.

Other areas of study included an investigation of letter versus configuration cues in word learning by retarded and nonretarded pupils (Vandever & Neville, 1974) and the examination of the effect of different questioning strategies on reading comprehension (Belch, 1974). Vandever and Neville's findings suggested that the mildly retarded group learned more words when letter cues were emphasized than when configuration cues were stressed. The results obtained by Belch (1974) indicated that high-order questioning strategies on the part of teachers of MRLs had a significant effect on subsequent reading comprehension.

A large number of investigations were conducted during the 1960s and 1970s on the effectiveness of programmed instruction techniques and teaching machine approaches (Blackman & Capobianco, 1965; Ellson, 1971; Haring, 1971; Hofmeister, 1971; Price, 1963). Greene's (1966) comprehensive review of the effectiveness of such approaches indicated that, in comparison with other approaches, neither programmed instruction nor teaching machines produced marked improvements in reading achievement. Her conclusion seems to hold true for subsequent studies of these interventions.

The research emphasis in special education during the 1960s and 1970s on contingency management techniques was particularly evident in studies of MRL academic performance. The effects of systematically imposed contingency management procedures – using incentives or reinforcers to obtain desired behaviors – produced significant reading performance gains in groups of MRL students (e.g., Busse & Henderson, 1972; Jenkins & Gorrafa, 1974). In addition to remarkable reading achievement gains, Busse and Henderson (1972) reported that approximately half of their sample, who were placed in regular classes at the completion of the study, were successful in the regular classroom when follow-up was conducted a year later.

In summary, studies that have compared different methods of and approaches to teaching reading to retarded learners do not provide substantial evidence for the superiority of any one method over another. However, the evidence must be interpreted in light of the fact that these relatively early investigations with retarded pupils most often placed emphasis on the word as the basic unit of study in contradistinction to comprehension of text.

*Application of information-processing models to the comprehension of words and text*

Beginning in the late 1960s, psycholinguists and cognitive scientists began to explore reading competence and performance. This interest emanated both from the "revolutionary" theoretical positions of transformational linguists (e.g., Chomsky, 1957) and from a growing influence of information theory (see Hildum, 1967). The focus during this period on the limited capacity of the human information-processing system led to an emphasis on organizational strategies used by learners to maximize the amount of relevant information that can be received, processed, and remembered. Since a detailed discussion of these important general trends is beyond the scope of this chapter, the reader is directed to relevant sources (Ausubel, 1968; Broadbent, 1958; Bruner, Goodnow, & Austin, 1956; Bruner, Olver, & Greenfield, 1966; Hunt, 1966; Mandler, 1967; Miller, 1956; Miller, Gallanter, & Pribram, 1960; Neisser, 1967; Olson, 1970; Tulving, 1962, 1966). These views conceptualized human memory as an active process of organization imposed on the stimulus input by the learner. Hence, the trend in research was significantly influenced by a prevailing view of the reader as a productive language processor of presented text.

Utilizing this theoretical framework, researchers began to investigate the ability to process and organize linguistic information in relation to the reading process and to reading difficulties of poor and/or retarded readers (Goodman, 1965, 1968, 1969, 1976; Kohlers, 1968; Lefevre, 1964; Neisser, 1967; Ryan & Semmel, 1969; Sitko & Semmel, 1973; Vellutino, Harding, Phillips, & Steger, 1975). In summarizing the various models for reading based on the active information-processing strategies of the reader, Ryan and Semmel (1969) contended that reading should be viewed as a "constructive active process in which the reader uses his cognitive and linguistic knowledge to reproduce a probable utterance from a careful sampling of cues and then matches that prediction for appropriateness" (p. 81). Furthermore, these authors suggested that the beginning reader should be encouraged to use appropriate higher-order language strategies – those already available from oral language usage. Reading behavior was seen as a psycholinguistic process whereby text provides cues for triggering cognitive and linguistic processing strategies.

The views of Semmel and his associates (e.g., Ryan & Semmel, 1969; Semmel, 1967) were incorporated into the rationale for a programmatic effort by Sitko, Semmel, Wilcove, and Semmel (1972) that sought to lay the groundwork for a psycholinguistically based reading program. An attempt was made to establish word-association norms for a group of mildly retarded children and to examine the effects of the group's word associations on reading performance. Although the results of the study produced no support for using high-association word pairs in sight vocabulary lessons for primary-aged children, the work was noteworthy in being one of the earliest attempts to explore linguistic organizational strategies that take advantage of the familiar structure of reading materials.

At the same time that studies began to provide evidence that short-term memory skills are related to reading achievement for retarded learners (Blackman, Bilsky, Burger, & Mar, 1976; Blackman & Burger, 1972; Samuels & Anderson, 1973), investigations were undertaken to explore the possibility that retarded learners have difficulty in reading comprehension because of a basic inability to organize verbal input for storage and retrieval during the act of reading. These investigations stemmed from the work of earlier researchers who studied organizational abilities of learners and provided the groundwork for future studies. One of the earliest reported studies with MRLs (Bilsky & Evans, 1970) found that organized, or blocked, presentation of words increased category clustering on subsequent random or nonorganized presentations. Following the same line of research, Evans (1970) reported that both clustering and recall performance were not significantly related to reading grade levels for MRLs. There were, however, methodological differences in the studies that help to explain the discrepant findings.

A study by Sitko and Semmel (1972) provided additional evidence that distinctive cuing of organizational or recoding strategies may result in the use of such strategies by retarded children and improve their processing of verbal stimuli. Expanding the work of Semmel and his associates, Blanton (1974) studied the relation of organizational abilities to the comprehension of written and oral connected discourse in MRLs and nonretarded children. She found that nonretarded learners scored significantly higher than MRLs on five measures of reading and listening comprehension; MRLs achieved significantly higher recall scores on distinctive-phrasal-cuing conditions, that is, pauses at phrase boundaries within the text of the passage, than on either no-cuing or distorted-phrasal-cuing conditions; nonretarded learners achieved significantly higher scores on a no-cuing condition than on a distorted-phrasal-cuing condition; and nonretarded learners scored higher on a distinctive-phrasal-cuing than on a distorted-phrasal-cuing condition. The differences obtained for Blanton's MRLs and nonretarded learners on a distinctive-phrasal-cuing paragraph compared with the differences obtained for MRLs and nonretarded learners on a no-cuing paragraph were significant for one recall measure but not for the other.

One of the major conclusions of the Blanton investigation was that the results supported Semmel's (1967) theoretical view that MRLs do possess the competence necessary for recoding certain types of information when they are given environmental cues that facilitate the use of higher-order organizational abilities. The contention that the difficulty experienced by MRLs in reading comprehension may be due to a basic inability to organize, recode, and retrieve verbal materials efficiently was also supported.

Considerable evidence, amassed from the studies cited above, has indicated that MRLs do possess the competence to recode linguistic units into hierarchical components when prompted. In addition, many of these researchers concluded that teaching retarded learners to impose organization on linguistic input may decrease their dependence on rote memory, and associative cues might be eliminated. Moreover, it might be that we can extend their memory capacity and, hence, comprehension of linguistic input.

In summary, a synthesis of the results of studies on the reading behavior of MRLs before 1975 reveals the following:

1. Mildly retarded learners are inferior to nonretarded learners in reading achievement and in the acquisition of specific reading skills.
2. Mildly retarded learners are capable of acquiring the same reading skills as their nonretarded peers but acquire them at a slower rate. Moreover, MRLs learn reading skills in the same sequence as nonretarded groups.
3. No particular reading method was found superior for groups of retarded learners, although some reading methods appeared to be effective for learners with specific characteristics and needs.
4. Studies of MRLs that explored etiology as a basis for reading difficulty lacked convincing results and essentially fell "out of favor" among behavioral researchers. A similar fate attended attempts to develop specialized pedagogical interventions with so-called minimally brain injured and perceptually handicapped MRL groups.
5. Linkages were clearly established between reading behaviors and organizational strategies for generating meaning from language.

The following section reviews reading research on MRLs from 1975 to 1985 and attempts to uncover changes in methodological and substantive trends from work reported before circa 1975.

## Reading research with mentally retarded learners since 1975

Recent research foci related to the reading of MRLs reflect the changing theoretical directions in the fields of cognitive psychology and reading education. These shifts include emphasis on the reader as an active rather than passive information processor and on the development of systems of discourse analysis (Kamil, 1984). Thus, research has been focused on aspects of the reader or features of text that can be manipulated to enhance the learner's understanding of what is read. Hence, recent research on reading with both nonretarded subjects and MRLs has been addressing issues related to the way learning occurs during reading.

The central goal of current applied "process" research is to determine *what* interventions can be predicted to improve the independent reading ability of all subjects and enhance their ability to derive meaning from words and text. Not all studies reviewed in this section reflect the foci described; however, the trend is evident in much of what is presented. Perhaps the most surprising outcome of our extensive literature search for the period from 1975 to 1985 was that so few studies related to the reading of MRLs have been published. For example, we found only four recent studies that directly investigated word identification skills.

To reflect the changing trends of reading research in the fields of special education, reading, and cognitive psychology, we have organized the research reviewed in this section under two headings: (1) reader-based needs of MRLs, specifically emphasizing learning strategies and instructional approaches for enhancing word identification and comprehension, and (2) text-based needs of MRLs, focusing on elements of text materials that may facilitate or debilitate learner comprehension and that can be manipulated to potentially improve reading performance.

### Reader-based needs of mentally retarded learners

Studies on reader-based needs of MRLs have explored a variety of interventions to enhance the learner's ability to identify words and comprehend text. These diverse investigations have targeted one or the other of these reading skills and generally made no attempt to enter the continuing debate in reading education over the relation between decoding and comprehension or word meaning and comprehension (Johnson & Baumann, 1984; Tierney & Cunningham, 1984).

As noted previously, early reading research with MRL populations began to establish links between reading behaviors of this group and cognitive strategies employed to generate meaning from language. This line of research has escalated in the past decade. In fact, there is now a body of empirically based evidence that cognitive skills frequently distinguish the performance of MRLs and nonretarded learners on intellectual tasks, and possibly on tasks such as reading skill acquisition. Both recent and past studies have documented that MRLs express cognitive deficits in comparison with nonretarded groups (Bilsky, Walker, Jones, Scheyer, & Black, 1982; Brooks & McCauley, 1984; Campione & Brown, 1979; Hagen & Stanovich, 1977). As yet, however, the bases or extent of cognitive deficits, particularly memory deficits, in MRL populations have not been clearly articulated. Moreover, many cognitive researchers emphasize "efficiency," or processing speed, as the critical feature on which MRL and nonretarded groups differ (Brewer & Smith, 1982; Brooks & McCauley, 1984; Davies, Sperber, & McCauley, 1981).

There is copious empirical literature supporting the contention that MRLs do possess cognitive processing competence that can be transformed into adaptive reading behaviors when direct instructional prompts or cues are provided (e.g., Bilsky, Whittemore, & Walker, 1982; Engle & Nagle, 1979; Glidden, 1977; Jarman, 1978). Research has also shown, however, that MRLs do not readily use cognitive strategies of their own volition (e.g., August, 1980; Brown, Campione, & Barclay, 1979; Campione & Brown, 1977). More important, MRLs have difficulty in generalizing learned strategies to new tasks (e.g., Brown, 1978; Glidden & Mar, 1978; Hamre-Nietupski, Nietupski, Vincent, & Wambold, 1982). This body of studies, along with past and recent studies demonstrating a relation between cognitive abilities and reading (e.g., Cummins & Das, 1980; Das & Cummins, 1978), has provided a framework for research that explores the effectiveness of strategy training in reading skill development. As already indicated, these "process" studies have been the trend since 1975 and are reflected in the research reviewed in the following sections on word identification and comprehension.

**Word identification research.** We found only four published investigations that directly investigated word identification skills of mildly retarded subjects (Blackman, Burger, Tan, & Weiner, 1982; Gickling, Hargis, & Alexander, 1981; Guthrie & Cunningham, 1982; Mason, 1978). This is surprising, because classroom instruction for MRLs generally emphasizes remediation and prevention of decoding problems (Brown, Palinscar, & Armbruster, 1984; Jenkins, Stein, & Osborn, 1981). The dearth of research on word recognition with MRLs is even more interesting when consideration is given to the current emphasis on the cognitive skills of this group. In particular, it might be expected that research on word recognition would be focused on the efficient use of cognitive strategies by MRLs with a goal of achieving automaticity. For example, when the learner must direct attention to decoding, the comprehension process is disrupted (Brooks & McCauley, 1984). Furthermore, the problem of attention may account for the cumulative deficits of MRLs on tasks such as reading comprehension.

Two of the four investigations identified explored cognitive processes in direct relation to word recognition skills. Mason (1978) sought to determine whether the mentally retarded use ineffective strategies for identifying and pronouncing printed words and for remembering the meanings of words. Subjects were required to pronounce words and to produce meaningful associates for words. The words used in the tasks were selected on the basis of frequency of use, concreteness, length, and vowel properties. On the pronunciation task, the results indicated that the subjects readily pronounced common words and usually mispronounced uncommon words. Further analysis revealed that the subjects depended on word frequency, which suggests that MRLs use a recognition strategy of memorizing whole words rather than cues such as letter patterns. On the meaning task, the retarded subjects depended on concrete referents to retrieve meanings of words.

Mason compared the results of the present study with her earlier research on nonretarded subjects and reported marked differences between the groups on identical pronunciation and meaning tasks. An examination of the distribution and kinds of errors made by both groups on the pronunciation task indicated that retarded subjects depended on whole-word retrieval, whereas nonretarded subjects used letter-sound information to pronounce words. An analysis of the meaning task revealed that nonretarded subjects gave responses to target words that reflected broad conceptual units. In contrast, the responses of retarded subjects revealed loosely organized concrete referents that were categorically distant from target words. These findings suggest the need to train retarded students in the use of cognitive strategies (e.g., categorical clustering), since the mentally retarded tend to use ineffective strategies on reading tasks when not prompted.

A study by Blackman et al. (1982) investigated the effect of training in specific cognitive and instructional strategies on the reading performance of MRLs with a mean CA of 11.78. Experimental and control groups were instructed in a reading program that emphasized decoding skills. In addition, the experimental group received a separate strategy training session during the intervention period. Strategy training consisted of a combination of cognitive and instructional strategies, to include chunking, rehearsal, sorting, and blending.

The results indicated no differences between experimental and control groups on criterion tests referenced to the reading program and on a standardized reading test. Several explanations were offered for the null results. One addressed the length of training and the possibility that the cognitive strategies were not fully developed by the training program. The other was that the experimental subjects were not successful in applying strategies to the different demands of the decoding tasks in the reading program. The first explanation was judged by the authors to be unlikely since subjects showed evidence of acquiring the trained strategies. The interpretation that the experimental group experienced difficulty in transferring learned strategies to a different task seems more plausible. Other reports have corroborated the finding that MRLs fail to generalize organizational abilities to new task demands (e.g., Engle, Nagle, & Dick, 1980).

Gickling et al. (1981) explored the effects of word imagery on the recall of the printed form of words among prereading retarded and nonretarded subjects. The subjects were taught 40 words they had not recognized during a pretesting session. Twenty words were classified as high-imagery nouns and 20 as low-imagery nouns. Small groups of learners were provided instruction in 10 training sessions. Instruction was limited to a verbal discussion of each word and was accompanied by a printed word card. Posttesting was carried out 2 days after training and once again 10 days after the first posttest. It was found that the imagery level of the words read facilitated sight word recognition for both retarded and nonretarded subjects. Furthermore, recall scores for both posttests were similar for the groups. The performance similarities of the two groups can be partially explained by the ages of the subjects. The CAs of the retarded subjects ranged from 9;4 to 16;5, whereas the CAs of the nonretarded subjects ranged from 5;2 to 6;0. These findings provide evidence that retarded learners rely on word recognition strategies similar to those used by younger, nonretarded learners at comparable MA levels.

The Gickling et al. (1981) and Mason (1978) findings provide evidence that MRLs most likely rely on ineffective strategies to identify words. Furthermore, the two studies suggest the need to train MRLs to use strategies that are predictive of success in reading skill development and/or that transfer to reading tasks.

Guthrie and Cunningham (1982) investigated the ability of 10- to 12-year-old mildly retarded students to compare and contrast unknown words with known words. The compare–contrast technique consisted of a series of steps designed to teach similarities and differences among words and the use of known words as a basis for decoding unknown words. Training was provided to the 15 students for 20 days at 30 min/day. The difference in pretest and posttest scores for the identification of unknown words was significant and led to the conclusion that teaching MRLs to use their known sight words to decode unknown words is an alternative available to teachers for teaching decoding. The results of the study must be interpreted with caution. The methodological limitations of the small sample size, the absence of a control group, and the use of rhyming words as the unknown words in the treatment all point to the need for additional research on this promising instructional strategy.

One obvious implication of the dearth of studies on the word identification abilities of MRLs is that there is a need for more research in this area. Moreover, it is surprising to find such limited emphasis on the word recognition skills of MRLs given that this has not been the case in reading research with nonretarded learners (Johnson & Baumann, 1984).

Although there has been a general shift in interest from word identification to comprehension for all learners, interest in word recognition research has continued with nonretarded learners, whereas it has decreased significantly since 1975 with MRLs. There are several possible explanations for the paucity of research on the word identification skills of MRLs. Special educators may be making the assumption that the early research emphasis on reading with MRLs provided a stronger knowledge base in word recognition than actually exists. Or investigators may have overreacted to the comprehension skill deficits of MRLs and are emphasizing comprehension to the point that word recognition research is being relegated to low-priority status. Whatever the explanation for the very limited research on the word identification skills of MRLs, sufficient evidence has not accrued to warrant diminishing further empirical study in this important area of inquiry.

**Comprehension research.** Recent research has elaborated the role of information-processing strategies in the reading comprehension of MRL groups. Several investigators have examined the role of metacognition in reading comprehension. A few have begun to explore how the MRL's prior knowledge affects his or her reading comprehension performance. There appears to be particular interest in cognitive processes that are likely to activate prior knowledge.

Relatively little is known about reading comprehension as a constructive process among MRLs since a limited number of studies were identified that examined reading comprehension processes in this group. Although there have been several investigations of the relation between specific information-processing strategies and reading skills, only a few studies have explored awareness of and/or self-regulation of strategies in reading comprehension. Even fewer studies have examined how prior knowledge affects MRLs' comprehension of text. Thus, there is no clear conceptualization of the linkages of various processing strategies to the reading comprehension of MRLs. To develop a greater understanding of possible relations between cognitive processes and the acquisition of reading comprehension by MRLs, it is critical that special education researchers analyze current conceptualizations guiding work in cognitive psychology and reading education toward understanding the reading comprehension of nonretarded learners.

We have organized the review of research on the reading comprehension of MRLs into two sections. The first reviews studies on the role of prior knowledge in reading comprehension and on the strategies employed by MRLs in utilizing prior knowledge to comprehend text. The other discusses investigations that have explored a variety of instructional strategies that are possibly helpful to MRLs in comprehending text.

*Learning strategies.* Two studies were found (Bilsky, Walker, & Sakales, 1983; Bos & Tierney, 1984) that examined the nature of constructive memory operations in the reading comprehension of MRLs and nonretarded children. Bilsky and her associates examined the ability of MRLs and nonretarded adolescent learners, matched on MA, to use categorical relations to read and interpret the meaning of sentences. A cued sentence recall task was employed using two types of sentences, one designed to encourage instantiation of a general noun (i.e., the process of selecting a specific meaning of a word from the family of meanings for the word) and the other designed such that interpretation of the same general noun was not constrained. Subjects were cued to recall sentences by presentation of the same general noun or with a specific noun from the same general category. It was hypothesized that this task would provide evidence for describing how prior knowledge of categorical relations is used to make inferences in constructing meaning from text.

Results revealed that the nonretarded group recalled more sentences than the MRL group. All the learners had better recall of sentences designed to encourage instantiation, and general cues produced better overall recall than particular cues. Further analysis, however, showed that, although general cues led to better recall for unconstrained sentences, there were no significant differences between groups for general or specific cues on sentences designed to encourage instantiation.

Bos and Tierney (1984) investigated the inferences generated by MRLs and nonretarded learners who were matched for reading comprehension level. Recall of third-grade-level expository and narrative passages was analyzed to determine the quality and quantity of inferences generated by the two groups of children. The results indicated that MRLs were similar to nonretarded children in the number of inferences generated during recall for both expository and narrative passages. The quality of inferences produced by MRLs for the expository passage, however, was inferior to that of the nonretarded group. These qualitative differences were indicated by the fact that MRLs generated fewer logical inferences based on their prior knowledge and the information explicitly stated in text. On the narrative passage, however, the groups did not differ significantly on qualitative measures of logical inferences, although the MRLs did generate more illogical inferences.

Both of the above studies suggest that MRLs, when matched with nonretarded peers for MA or reading comprehension level, do employ prior knowledge and inferential processes to construct and recall meaning obtained from text. Both studies, however, report inferior performance by MRLs: Bilsky et al.'s (1983) for overall sentence recall and Bos and Tierney's (1984) for the quality of inferences generated by retarded learners.

The prior knowledge that a learner brings to the instructional setting is considered a critical factor in determining the ability to comprehend what is read (Anderson & Pearson, 1984; Brown, Campione, & Day, 1981; Resnick, 1984). Prior knowledge provides relevant general, domain-specific, and rhetorical schemata that can be activated to construct meaning from text. Unless the learner possesses prior knowledge of situations and content presented in written material, he or she will not be able to understand or gain meaning from text (Resnick, 1984; Rumelhart, 1981). Mentally retarded students probably lack relevant schemata for much of the content encountered in reading instruction. The need to consider further the role of prior knowledge in the process by which MRLs gain meaning from text is underlined by the results reported by Bilsky et al. (1983) and by Bos and Tierney (1984).

In an investigation examining strategies used by learners to construct meaning from text, Bender and Levin (1978) reported the effects of subject-generated imagery and experimenter-generated pictures on the ability of MRLs to answer questions about a story. In addition to the two experimental conditions for imagery and pictures, two other conditions were included. One was a repetition-control condition in which pupils listened to sentences presented twice in succession and a control condition in which the group received no special instructions or aids.

Subjects were asked to answer two types of questions (i.e., verbatim and paraphrase) after hearing a story. The picture condition group performed significantly better for both verbatim and paraphrase questions than children in the other three conditions. In addition, no significant differences were found among the other three conditions for either type of question. Thus, this study provides evidence that the addition of pictures to reading instruction with intermediate- and secondary-level MRLs facilitates recall, regardless of the level of question asked. Furthermore, Bender and Levin's work (1978) suggests that prompting recall with repetition or imagery cues produces no significant effects on either older or younger MRLs.

Efficient use of contextual information has long been recognized to be particularly adaptive in comprehending text. Crossland (1981) compared MA-matched MRLs and nonretarded learners on the ability to use context in reading. A cloze procedure was used to design passages on which the pupils were individually tested. Cloze passages were matched to the instructional reading levels identified for the 15 subjects in the investigation. Group comparisons revealed that MRLs were inferior to nonretarded children in supplying exact words or in providing synonymous and grammatically correct words.

These findings suggest that mentally retarded readers have difficulty using context in reading. However, other studies of MRL context utilization reviewed by Streib (1976–7) produced inconclusive results. Streib indicated that the investigations reviewed relied almost exclusively on explorations of cloze procedures to study the use of context in obtaining meaning. Clearly, there is a need for extended study of the topic using additional paradigms that focus on analytic procedures such as error analysis.

The inability to utilize context to gain meaning from text is yet another area where MRL deficiencies can be explained from a variety of perspectives. These may include explanations of one or a combination of the following reader-based variables: a lack of prior knowledge, difficulty in spontaneously employing appropriate cognitive strategies to activate prior knowledge, or the inability to attend to relevant cues in the text needed for problem solving (Sternberg, Powell, & Kaye, 1983).

Although there have been numerous investigations of MRLs' memory processes, most studies have concentrated on specific strategies (e.g., rehearsal) and their acquisition rather than on MRLs' knowledge and use of strategies in thinking and learning. Considerable work has focused on the use of metacognitive skills by MRL children (Brown, 1978, 1980; Brown & Barclay, 1976; Brown, Campione, & Murphy, 1977; Brown & Lawton, 1977; Eyde & Altman, 1978; Kramer & Engle, 1981). Very few studies, however, have linked the use of metacognitive processes to the reading behavior of mentally retarded pupils (Brown et al., 1979). This dearth of research with MRL populations is surprising since research emanating from cognitive psychology and reading education has begun to demonstrate that metacognition may be a major factor in accomplished reading performance (Armbruster, Echols, & Brown, 1983).

In one of the earliest studies to explore metacognitive processes of MRLs, Brown and Barclay (1976) studied executive control in MRLs by training deliberate memorization strategies in a recall-readiness task. Sixty-six subjects were divided into groups based on age and were further assigned to treatment groups matched on the basis of pretest performance. Following pretesting, treatment groups were trained on three memorization strategies: label, anticipation, and rehearsal. The labeling strategy served as a control condition since it did not involve self-evaluation by the learner. At the completion of training, posttest sessions were conducted and students were prompted or unprompted to use the strategies they had been trained on earlier. Two of the three posttest sessions were held 2 days after training, and the third was held approximately 2 weeks later.

In general, the results revealed that older children (i.e., MA 8) performed significantly better than younger children with MAs of 6 for all training conditions. Anticipation and rehearsal conditions produced higher recall performance than did the label condition. Brown and Barclay reported that older children maintained unprompted high recall performance after 2 weeks for the rehearsal and anticipation conditions. However, although younger children improved in performance on an immediate prompted recall test, the effects were not maintained after 2 weeks for these conditions.

The effectiveness of both the anticipation and rehearsal conditions over the label condition was of particular interest since the effectiveness of these strategies can be attributed to self-testing features. The self-evaluation feature appears to lead to successful performance on a recall-readiness task because it requires maintenance of a mnemonic as well as judging its success in preparing for recall. It is important to note that the training of specific skills (i.e., anticipation and rehearsal) resulted in metamnemonic control in later recall even when the self-testing features of the strategies were not pointed out to the subjects. In addition, the age or cognitive maturity of the subject was shown to be related to the type of training necessary to induce memory monitoring.

In a follow-up and extension of the Brown and Barclay (1976) study, Brown et al. (1979) investigated the ability of MRLs to transfer learned strategies to a reading task. The same subjects were used to test long-term maintenance of strategies for comparable tasks, as well as generalization of strategies to a new task.

For the maintenance phase of the study, 58 of the original 66 MRLs were given unprompted and prompted posttests using stimulus material that differed from the comparable material used in the original study. As in the initial study, participants were divided into older and younger groups.

The results of the posttests for the younger group showed no evidence of maintenance, whereas the older group revealed clear evidence of maintenance. As in the original study, the anticipation and rehearsal groups outperformed the label group. The generalization phase of the investigation included only the older group. An additional 17 MRLs who were in classrooms with the 33 trained pupils were included, matched for CA, IQ, and MA with trained children, and served as a control group.

A transfer task was chosen for its representativeness to study activity required in typical classrooms. The task consisted of recall of idea units in simple stories. All pupils read between the second- and fourth-grade level. Stories were written so that each conformed to a readability score of approximately second-grade difficulty.

The results were analyzed for the importance level of idea units and for the study time taken by pupils. Again, the children were divided according to prior training in anticipation, rehearsal, and label strategies, with the inclusion of the untrained group. The results for recall of the importance level of idea units showed that the anticipation and rehearsal groups outperformed the label group and the naive controls. When study time was analyzed, the findings revealed that the anticipation and rehearsal trained groups studied longer than the older groups. The researchers interpreted the longer study time as indicative of more effective monitoring of recall readiness.

This study is of particular relevance since it demonstrated that long-term retention of mnemonics that embody self-testing routines can be achieved by MRLs. Furthermore, and perhaps more impressive, MRLs were shown to have the ability to transfer self-evaluation strategies to a prose-learning situation.

Hence, the role of metacognition in learning tasks is a promising area of study for MRL groups. This is especially true when one considers the poor performance of retarded pupils on cognitive tasks. And although research has demonstrated that MRLs can be taught to use a variety of strategies, they do not use them spontaneously. Since the use of such strategies is critical to the comprehension of text, research with retarded children must determine the reasons for poor performance on tasks requiring strategic intervention. It remains to be determined to what extent metacognitive factors other than those that have been studied to date in the area of mental retardation – for example, those having to do with phonological coding or grapheme–phoneme correspondence (Jorm & Share, 1983) – contribute to the difficulties experienced by MRLs in reading. Answers may be found in explorations of metacognitive functions of awareness, intention, monitoring, and evaluating strategies.

*Instructional strategies.* A number of studies have investigated the use of specific instructional strategies to aid MRLs in comprehending text (Belch, 1978; Bigler, 1984; Peleg & Moore, 1982; Rose, 1984). Teacher questioning, direct instruction techniques, previewing, and advance organizer effects have all been explored.

Belch (1978) studied the effects of high-order, low-order, and no-questioning strategies on reading comprehension scores of secondary-level MRLs who read at least at third-grade level. The treatment group tested with high-order questions was expected to be calling on higher cognitive processes such as evaluating and predicting outcomes. Subjects tested with low-order questions were expected to be recalling factual content. The third group was asked no questions about the high-interest, low-readability passage.

The subjects who were asked higher-order questions about the passages they read performed significantly better on a test of reading comprehension than did students asked low-order questions or students asked no questions. In addition, the low-order questioning groups and the no-questioning groups did not differ significantly on reading comprehension.

These findings suggest that MRLs are capable of processing higher-order information when questioned. In addition, when MRLs are challenged via high-order questioning, reading comprehension seems to improve. If, however, teachers rely on low-order questions, minimal gains can be expected from MRLs in reading comprehension.

Questioning effects were also considered by Bigler (1984), who explored the effectiveness of two direct instruction techniques on the performance of inference skills by MRLs reading at instructional levels of 2.0 to 3.0. Bigler compared a direct instruction strategy, "underlining key details," with a strategy that involved student practice in "thinking out loud" after hearing a teacher model specific steps in oral reasoning. The dependent variable in the study was an inferential comprehension measure of drawing conclusions and predicting outcomes. In addition, the investigation explored whether increased proficiency on one inferential comprehension skill would transfer to the other noninstructed skill under either instructional condition.

Story passages were used to instruct and evaluate student performance using a crossover experimental design. The results showed that (1) inference scores did not differ significantly for the two direct-instruction conditions, (2) student performance improved under both conditions, (3) more generalization of an instructed inference skill to a noninstructed inference skill seemed to occur under the modeling and thinking-out-loud condition, although the results were inconclusive, and (4) direct instruction of inference skills improved literal recall of passages. Bigler suggested that his results complemented those of Belch (1978) since high-order questioning appeared to be the explanation for increased performance scores on measures of predicting outcomes and drawing conclusions.

Bigler's work underlines the potential use of teacher explanation and modeling for skills instruction. In particular, these results call for further empirical exploration of different forms of explanation, modeling, and practice in frameworks designed to provide skills instruction for MRLs. Bigler's results also support the findings of Bilsky et al. (1983) and Bos & Tierney (1984) reviewed earlier in this section. That is, all provide evidence that MRLs are capable of using inferential processes to construct and recall meaning obtained from text.

The effects of an advance organizer (AO) on the reading comprehension scores of junior high school MRLs was investigated by Peleg and Moore (1982). The effects of the method were studied using two different presentation modes (written and oral) for three instructional conditions (introduction with AO, without AO, traditional), resulting in six experimental groups. Two types of learning outcomes (i.e., high-level and low-level questions) were tested across all experimental conditions.

For the oral presentation, the AO instructional condition was the least effective, whereas it was most effective when the mode of presentation was written. The subjects answered more low-level questions correctly than high-level questions, regardless of the instructional condition. However, more higher-level questions were answered correctly under the written mode of presentation.

Rose (1984) investigated the effects of previewing procedures, that is, methods that provide the opportunity for a learner to read or listen to a passage before instruction and/or testing, on the oral reading performance of MRLs. Both silent and listening previewing techniques were studied.

By means of an alternating treatments design, the five subjects were instructed in silent previewing and listening previewing. Both previewing conditions were more effective than no previewing. The previewing conditions led to improved oral reading rates, although gains for some subjects were minimal. In addition, listening previewing produced higher performance levels than silent previewing for most subjects.

Thus, research on the reading comprehension of MRLs has begun to parallel research currently being conducted with nonretarded groups. Investigations have begun to focus on the relations between cognitive processes and reading comprehension. There is also some exploration of the critical role of prior knowledge in reading comprehension, as well as some emphasis on strategic interventions to activate this knowledge. Similarly, studies of instructional strategies have emphasized the constructive nature of reading comprehension and the strategic use of skills by mentally retarded readers. Although work in this area must be considered to be in an embryonic stage, it is clear that the trends uncovered from work reported before circa 1975 in the areas of psycholinguistics and information processing have matured. It is equally clear that the contemporary emphasis on studying cognitive process variables in relation to the reading comprehension of MRLs is a most promising empirical tack for future research.

Most research that we identified on reader-based needs of MRLs focused on the comprehension skills of this group rather than on their word identification skills. And although the paucity of word identification research is particularly striking, the limited amount of comprehension research is equally disconcerting. Since so few studies were identified in these critical areas of reading, we expected to find extensive empirical investigations on other aspects of the reading behavior of MRLs. We searched the literature for research on such variables as effects of classroom organizations, influence of social structures, and the amount of reading instruction given to mentally retarded pupils. The search revealed only a few diverse studies of variables that influence the practical application of knowledge gleaned from the reader-based needs of MRLs. For example, we found an investigation on the effects of the "presence of others" and the "threat of evaluation" on the oral reading performance of MRLs (Gottlieb, 1982). The results revealed a significant main effect for evaluation but not for the mere presence of others. This study could have important instructional implications for teaching reading to MRLs.

Raber and Weisz (1981) investigated the effects of teacher feedback during reading instruction on learned helplessness in MRLs and nonretarded pupils of similar reading abilities. The findings indicated that MRLs received feedback more often than nonretarded students. Moreover, MRLs received negative feedback more often than their nonretarded peers. Interesting performance attributions directed to MRLs by their teachers were reported. Like the Gottlieb (1982) study, this investigation offers valuable information about psychosocial influences on the reading performance of MRLs. It is clear that investigations exploring the effect of psychosocial variables on MRLs, such as feedback and evaluative contexts, reveal instructional implications for consideration in both segregated and integrated administrative arrangements.

The amount of time spent teaching specific facets of reading to MRLs is expected to play a significant role in the acquisition of reading skills. We found only one published contemporary study that directly investigated time spent in reading instruction with mentally retarded pupils in resource room environments (Bromley & Carpenter, 1984). The descriptive data indicated that resource teachers spent the greatest proportion of instructional time on reading comprehension, the next highest percentage of time was spent on phonics and structure, and the least amount of time was spent on sight vocabulary. Hence, it would appear that the increasing interest in reading comprehension found in the research literature is reflected in the way specialists are prioritizing their instructional time in reading instruction for MRLs.

### Text-based needs of mentally retarded learners

In order to conceptualize more fully the parameters of reading behavior, the interactions between learner strategies and information presented to the learner in text must be better understood. Models of discourse analysis have been developed in recent years that provide greater understanding of text structure and processes used by learners to comprehend text. Furthermore, such models have provided the framework for investigations of the relation between text structure and reading comprehension (Meyer & Rice, 1984). Although research in this area has become active with nonretarded children, few investigations have included retarded learners.

Other text-based features have been investigated in an attempt to identify manipulatory aspects of text that might improve reading comprehension. Text adjuncts such as pictures, questions inserted in passages, and prefatory statements have been investigated extensively with nonretarded groups (Tierney & Cunningham, 1984). Once again, however, such research rarely includes MRL subjects.

Two recent studies were identified that explored MRLs' ability to rate and recall structurally important text units (Luftig & Greeson, 1983; Luftig & Johnson, 1982). Luftig and Johnson (1982) investigated the ability of MRLs to judge and use important information in reading material to aid recall. The design consisted of four experimental groups of retarded subjects who received treatment and two control groups, one consisting of retarded subjects and one of nonretarded subjects. All groups were matched for MA. Accuracy in judging the importance of units in a story and the number and type of prose units recalled were determined for all groups.

MRLs were capable of rating and recalling prose units that were high in structural importance. When receiving repeated prompts to use textual importance, MRLs demonstrated greater retention of a story. These findings suggest production deficits rather than mediational deficits in MRLs. That is, as stated previously, MRLs possess the specific strategies needed, in this case for determining important units in text, but may not use them unless trained to do so (Brown, 1978). This position stands in contrast to the view that MRLs suffer from mediational deficiencies that would lead to their inability to utilize specific strategies when cued to do so.

In a modification of an earlier study (Luftig & Johnson, 1982), Luftig and Greeson (1983) matched MRL and nonretarded groups on MA and CA to explore the effects of making ratings of both structural importance and idea saliency on story recall. For ratings of structural importance, the MRLs were less accurate in their judgments of high-, medium-, or low-importance story ideas than were nonretarded subjects. For recall of these idea units, MRLs who made ratings of importance recalled less of the total story than did nonretarded subjects. In contrast, the recall of stories was significantly higher for subjects (both MRLs and nonretarded groups) who made ratings of idea units before attempting recall. Furthermore, MRLs and nonretarded subjects who made prior judgments of idea importance recalled more high-importance and medium-importance idea units than low-importance ones. The findings were similar for idea saliency in that MRLs who made ratings of saliency performed poorly compared with CA-matched nonretarded subjects and more similar to MA-matched nonretarded subjects.

Like the findings with nonretarded subjects, the two studies reported by Luftig and his associates provide evidence that MRLs who make ratings of importance in text are aided in comprehension and recall of text. Furthermore, these investigations have provided some evidence that readers may not attend to the important ideas because they are distracted by their perception of what is more interesting in the text. Thus, training MRLs to make judgments of the importance of textual ideas may enhance comprehension skills. In addition, the provision of aids within text that cue the learner to important information may also aid in understanding.

Three studies reviewed earlier in this chapter provide support for the use of text adjuncts. Bender and Levin (1978) found that, when pictures were used as adjuncts to stories, performance on posttesting was greater than for other treatments. Rose (1984) reported positive findings when previewing was used as an aid to comprehension. In addition, the findings of Peleg and Moore (1982) favored the use of an advance organizer with written material.

The overall findings of research on text-based needs of MRLs reveal important implications for instruction in reading comprehension. There is evidence that cuing MRLs to relevant features of text and/or adding aids such as pictures, previews, and advance organizers enhance the reader's ability to comprehend written material. In addition to continued investigation with MRLs in areas where research has begun, there is a need to explore other text-based dimensions with this group. For example, we found no research on MRLs' interest in, or familiarity with, the content of text. Although there have been investigations with nonretarded learners on the ability to relate information presented in text to prior knowledge (Armbruster et al., 1983), research including MRLs is still needed.

## Conclusions and implications for instructional practice

Research on the reading of MRLs has changed its focus since 1975. Although these shifts seem to parallel the research of cognitive psychologists and reading educators on nonretarded subjects, investigations with samples of MRLs have been limited in scope as well as in number. Our search yielded approximately 25 data-based, published research studies with MRLs from 1975 to 1985. Clearly, on quantitative grounds alone, it can be argued that contributions to our empirical base of knowledge about the reading of MRL populations have been limited. In fact, one of the more salient outcomes of the present work is the irrevocable conclusion that this important area of inquiry has been seriously neglected.

### Policy influences on research productivity

The limited number and scope of research studies with MRLs in reading suggest several confluent policy forces that might explain why such a state of empirical neglect has existed since 1975. These issues focus on how public policy influences research agendas and ultimately influences the empirical knowledge in an area. In the present instance, we submit that our national mandates to protect the rights of handicapped children have, perhaps, inadvertently impinged on the productivity of reading research with MRLs.

The field of special education has undergone dramatic changes since the passage of PL 94-142 (Education for All Handicapped Children Act, 1975). Federal and state mandates and judicial edicts have required stringent protections in the assessment and identification of the handicapped in our nation's schools. As a result, many children who were formerly labeled mildly mentally retarded are no longer identified as such (MacMillan & Meyers, 1979). In fact, in some parts of the country (e.g., California) the educably mentally retarded category is no longer recognized by the schools.

The "mainstreaming" of MRLs from segregated special classes in the schools to "regular class" placements has increased dramatically since 1975 as a function of the least restrictive environment (LRE) provisions of the nation's legislative and judicial mandates (see Kaufman, Agard, & Semmel, 1985; Semmel, Gottlieb, &

Robinson, 1979). Furthermore, a relatively large number of MRLs have been receiving their education in regular class contexts.

We contend that these dramatic examples of the impact of policy on science may have made it difficult for researchers to secure samples reflecting the classically defined MRL population. It is also possible that access to MRL subjects has been severely curtailed as a function of their placements in regular class environments. The spirit engendered by LRE and integration efforts may have served to discourage researchers from attempting to identify MRLs in regular classes for the purpose of studying their reading behavior. However, it is interesting that, although the proportion of MRLs has increased in regular classes, there is little evidence that they have been included as subjects in studies reported by reading researchers working in the schools. It is equally interesting that with the diminished popularity of the homogeneous special class for the MRL population has come a decided decrease in reported studies of the reading behavior of members of this group by special education researchers interested in "mainstreaming."

PL 94-142 mandates that all MRLs receive individualized educational plans. This provision of the law may have led to the belief that, if the schools are held accountable for specific instructional goals, the operational instructional activities designed to meet these written objectives must be adequate. Should this be the case, we note that there is limited evidence in the literature related to the content or quality of regular class instruction for MRLs and that we have not found ample empirical data related to academic learning time variables studied in connection with this group.

The reading problems of MRLs may have also been overshadowed through the perception that special education services provided by the schools under PL 94-142 have been meeting the instructional needs of these students. Since individualized instruction is frequently provided for mainstreamed MRLs in settings such as resource rooms, parents and professional educators may assume that instructional needs in reading are being satisfied. Such complacency may well have reduced advocacy pressures to improve reading instruction for MRLs. Hence, they have probably indirectly reduced the motivation to prioritize research in this area.

Federal grant funding priorities may have also influenced the output of research conducted on the reading of MRLs. Considerable discretionary research funds were made available for the study of educational problems of MRLs following the passage of PL 94-142. However, relatively few of these dollars were allocated for contracts or grants to study the reading behavior of MRLs in the schools. The relatively low priority for funding in this area could be the by-product of a federal policy to shy away from involvement in educational issues related to curriculum in the local educational agencies within the states. Federal funding practices frequently stimulate research in a prioritized area. The cadre of researchers who have been traditionally interested in the MRL population is relatively small and dependent on extramural funds to support their empirical work. There is, then, little wonder that research focused on the reading performance of MRLs since 1975 has been relatively neglected.

Whatever the reasons for the limited amount and scope of research on the reading of MRLs, our current knowledge base is sorely lacking. There appears to be ample deductive evidence that, as a result of policy shifts regarding the rights of handicapped children in our nation's schools, there has been a confluence of forces mitigating against advancing knowledge and improving teaching techniques relative to the reading behavior of MRLs. Research on reading among MRLs has apparently "fallen between the cracks" in a research community that is generally disinterested in the variability of reading behavior injected into regular public school classes by federal and state mandates and a small cadre of special education researchers interested in the rights of the handicapped but apparently not particularly motivated to study their academic performance in the schools.

### Current state of knowledge

A result of this neglect since 1975 is that research on word identification of MRLs has progressed very little. The literature on reading comprehension has also been sparse, although more empirical activity was reported in this area than in word identification. Both areas have included investigations of strategic learning by MRLs and lend support to our conclusion that reading research with this group has begun to shift in directions similar to research with nonretarded learners.

Nevertheless, there seems to be no clear conceptualization of the linkages between various processing strategies and the reading behaviors of MRLs. For example, as noted earlier in this chapter, the role of prior knowledge in the reading of MRLs has just begun to be explored. Furthermore, only a few studies have investigated MRL awareness or self-regulation of strategies. We found no studies exploring the use of task-appropriate strategies by MRLs. It is clear that these promising areas of study need greater attention.

In addition to the recent focus on strategic behavior used by the learner, there have been investigations of the relation between text structure and reading comprehension. As discussed earlier in this chapter, only a few studies were found that explored this area with MRL groups.

### Consistent findings and implications for instruction

Although our literature search was disappointing in the extent of attention afforded the topic, we are nevertheless heartened by the fact that a number of results are consistent with the knowledge base that existed before circa 1975. These consistencies have direct implications for the instruction of MRLs in the schools.

The most robust finding in the literature on the reading characteristics of MRLs appears to be that these children develop their reading competencies more slowly but in the same general sequence as do nonhandicapped learners. It is equally well substantiated, however, that mildly retarded children rarely exceed a fourth-grade competency in reading on leaving school. Of particular importance is the copious evidence, dating back to the early 1960s, that mildly retarded learners have the *competence* to derive meaning from oral language or written text but do not naturally invoke the processes necessary for solving linguistic or reading problems (e.g., Semmel, 1967; Semmel & Bennett, 1970). Hence, MRLs may be considered to suffer from performance problems that suggest they lack a natural internal set for using highly adaptive cognitive or metacognitive skills for deriving meaning from oral or written language.

Semmel (1985) has defined MRLs as "children who must be taught in order to learn." We conclude from this review that MRLs in reading contexts are in need of powerful instructional interventions that are designed to cue their cognitive and metacognitive strategies. We are drawn to this view by the overwhelming number of demonstrations in the empirical literature of the facilitating effects of cuing adaptive strategies on the reading performance of MRLs.

## Needs for instructional practice

If we are to build a knowledge base for instructional practice, it is necessary that a variety of research foci be investigated. There is a pressing need for ecologically valid investigations of reading instruction with MRLs in different administrative and instructional school settings. The field is faced with a clear requirement that we determine the content and quality of, and the time devoted to, reading instruction with MRLs.

Instructional materials must be analyzed from the perspective of the characteristics of MRLs. Most instructional materials used in regular classrooms have not been developed with the performance deficiencies of MRLs considered. Since it appears that most regular class teachers use the same materials for all students and most follow teacher manuals that were not designed to meet the needs of MRLs, it is critical that these instructional materials and accompanying manuals be analyzed to determine how they should be modified by classroom teachers.

Lesson frameworks, to include models for direct instruction, should be explored with MRLs. Although these areas have begun to be investigated with this population, there is a need to explore frameworks and to evaluate their use for instruction in different strands of the reading curriculum.

Learner and text-based strategies require additional study. Although the results of studies in these areas are promising, we have not yet developed the necessary knowledge base with MRLs to feel confident of the shift to strategic instruction.

For the learner, the emphasis should be on word recognition and meaning, comprehension, lesson frameworks such as direct instruction, and self-regulated and strategic learning. Investigations addressing classroom variables should focus on determining what happens with MRLs in reading instruction and on ways to adapt and modify instructional materials to meet MRL needs (see Semmel & Englert, 1980).

Finally, we recognize the possibility that the period since 1975 reflects a significant change in the way our society views mildly handicapped populations in the schools. We have implied that the discontinuities in research from the period before 1975 to the present may be due, in part, to the melding of the MRL category into the nonhandicapped population. From a civil rights point of view this is obviously a positive social evolution. However, if this is the case, regular educators must address the problems that these children are bringing back to the regular classroom. We are aware that reading is a fundamental curriculum area that serves to predict most other aspects of a child's educational attainments. In reflecting on these policy-related issues we close this chapter by citing Semmel et al. (1979), who remind us of the dire need for programmatic research in stating:

Regardless of class placement, mentally retarded children read exceedingly poorly. [The] data suggest that the crucial need at present is to develop more appropriate instructional delivery systems for mentally retarded children. Instructional alternatives that have been offered to date have proven relatively ineffectual regardless of the environment in which these children are taught. (p. 237)

There is clearly a basic need for an accelerated program of empirical research to assist educators in coping with the challenges of teaching reading to mentally retarded children grouped heterogeneously in normalized and specialized instructional settings. As has been emphasized elsewhere (Semmel, Peck, & Lieber, 1986), we must identify, scale, and measure relevant variables within least restrictive instructional environments in order to develop an empirically validated pedagogy that fosters the realization of reading potential for all children.

### Note

1. A commonly accepted definition of mental retardation is the revised definition of the American Association on Mental Deficiency (AAMD), according to which "mental retardation refers to significantly subaverage general intellectual functioning resulting in or associated with concurrent impairments in adaptive behavior and manifested during the developmental period" (Grossman, 1983, p. 1). For mild mental retardation, significantly subaverage (general intellectual functioning) is defined as an IQ range between 50–55 and approximately 70 on standardized measures of intelligence. It should be noted that earlier AAMD definitions of mental retardation (Grossman, 1973) recommended slightly different upper-limit IQs. In the 1973 AAMD definition, the upper-limit IQ was set at less than 2 SD below the mean. The 1983 revised definition, however, does not specify exact standard deviation sizes.

### References

Anderson, R. C., & Pearson, P. D. (1984). A schema-theoretic view of basic processes in reading comprehension. In P. D. Pearson (Ed.), *Handbook of reading research* (pp. 255–91). New York: Longman.

Armbruster, B. B., Echols, C. H., & Brown, A. L. (1983). *The role of metacognition in reading to learn: A developmental perspective* (Tech. Rep. No. 40). Urbana–Champaign: University of Illinois, Center for the Study of Reading.

August, G. J. (1980). Input organization as a mediating factor in memory: A comparison of educable mentally retarded and nonretarded individuals. *Journal of Experimental Child Psychology, 30,* 125–43.

Ausubel, D. P. (1968). *Educational psychology: A cognitive view.* New York: Holt, Rinehart & Winston.

Belch, P. J. (1974). *An investigation on the effect of different questioning strategies on the reading comprehension scores of secondary level educable mentally retarded students.* Unpublished doctoral dissertation, West Virginia University, Morgantown.

Belch, P. J. (1978). Improving the reading comprehension scores of secondary level educable mentally handicapped students through selective teacher questioning. *Education and Training of the Mentally Retarded, 13,* 385–9.

Bender, B. G., & Levin, J. R. (1978). Pictures, imagery, and retarded children's prose learning. *Journal of Educational Psychology, 70,* 583–8.

Berliner, D. C., & Cahen, L. S. (1973). Trait–treatment interaction and learning. In F. N. Kerlinger (Ed.), *Review of research in education* (Vol. 1, pp. 58–94). Itasca, IL: Peacock.

Bigler, J. K. (1984). Increasing inferential comprehension scores of intermediate-age mildly retarded students using two direct teaching procedures. *Education and Training of the Mentally Retarded, 19,* 132–40.

Bilsky, L. H., & Evans, R. A. (1970). Use of associative clustering technique in the study of reading disability: Effects of list organization. *American Journal of Mental Deficiency, 74,* 771–6.

Bilsky, L. H., Walker, N., Jones, P., Scheyer, B., & Black, M. (1982). Use of categorical knowledge to aid recall. *Journal of Mental Deficiency Research, 26,* 11–20.

Bilsky, L. H., Walker, N., & Sakales, S. R. (1983). Comprehension and recall of sentences by mentally retarded and nonretarded individuals. *American Journal of Mental Deficiency, 87,* 558–65.

Bilsky, L. H., Whittemore, C. L., & Walker, N. (1982). Strategies in the recall of clusterable lists. *Intelligence, 6,* 23–35.

Blackman, L. S., Bilsky, L. H., Burger, A. L., & Mar, H. (1976). Cognitive processes and academic achievement in EMR adolescents. *American Journal of Mental Deficiency, 81,* 125–34.

Blackman, L. S., & Burger, A. L. (1972). Psychological factors related to early reading behavior of EMR and non-retarded children. *American Journal of Mental Deficiency, 77,* 212–29.

Blackman, L. S., Burger, A. L., Tan, N., & Weiner, S. (1982). Strategy training and the acquisition of decoding skills in EMR children. *Education and Training of the Mentally Retarded, 17,* 83–7.

Blackman, L. S., & Capobianco, R. J. (1965). An evaluation of programmed instruction with the mentally retarded utilizing teaching machines. *American Journal of Mental Deficiency, 70,* 262–9.

Blake, K. A., Aaron, I. E., & Westbrook, H. R. (1967). *Learning of basal reading skills by mentally handicapped and non-mentally handicapped pupils* (BEH Project No. 5-0391). Washington, DC: U.S. Office of Education.

Blanton, L. P. (1974). *The relationship of organizational abilities to the comprehension of connected discourse in educable mentally retarded and non-retarded children.* Unpublished doctoral dissertation, Indiana University, Bloomington.

Blanton, L. P., Sitko, M. C., & Gillespie, P. H. (1976). Reading and the mildly retarded: Review of research and implications. In L. Mann & D. A. Sabatino (Eds.), *The third review of special education* (pp. 143–62). New York: Grune & Stratton.

Bos, C. S., & Tierney, R. J. (1984). Inferential reading abilities of mildly mentally retarded and nonretarded students. *American Journal of Mental Deficiency, 89,* 75–82.

Bracht, G. H. (1970). Experimental factors related to aptitude–treatment interactions. *Review of Educational Research, 40,* 627–45.

Brewer, N., & Smith, G. A. (1982). Cognitive processes for monitoring and regulating speed and accuracy of responding in mental retardation: A methodology. *American Journal of Mental Deficiency, 87,* 211–22.

Broadbent, D. E. (1958). *Perception and communication.* London: Peragon.

Bromley, K., & Carpenter, R. L. (1984). Reading instruction in resource rooms. *Reading World, 23,* 209–17.

Brooks, P. H., & McCauley, C. (1984). Cognitive research in mental retardation. *American Journal of Mental Deficiency, 88,* 479–86.

Brown, A. L. (1978). Knowing when, where, and how to remember: A problem of metacognition. In R. Glaser (Ed.), *Advances in instructional psychology* (pp. 77–165). Hillsdale, NJ: Erlbaum.

Brown, A. L. (1980). Metacognitive development and reading. In R. J. Spiro, B. C. Bruce, & W. F. Brewer (Eds.), *Theoretical issues in reading comprehension* (pp. 453–81). Hillsdale, NJ: Erlbaum.

Brown, A. L., & Barclay, C. R. (1976). The effects of training specific mnemonics on the metamnemonic efficiency of retarded children. *Child Development, 47,* 71–80.

Brown, A. L., Campione, J. C., & Barclay, C. R. (1979). Training self-checking routines for estimating test readiness: Generalization from list learning to prose recall. *Child Development, 50,* 501–12.

Brown, A. L., Campione, J. C., & Day, J. D. (1981). Learning to learn: On training students to learn from texts. *Educational Researcher, 10,* 14–21.

Brown, A. L., Campione, J. C., & Murphy, M. D. (1977). Maintenance and generalization of trained metamnemonic awareness in educable retarded children. *Journal of Experimental Child Psychology, 24,* 191–211.

Brown, A. L., & Lawton, S. C. (1977). The feeling of knowing experience in educable retarded children. *Developmental Psychology, 13,* 364–70.

Brown, A. L., Palinscar, A. S., & Armbruster, B. B. (1984). Instructing comprehension-fostering activities in interactive learning situations. In H. Mandl, N. L. Stein, & T. Trabasso (Eds.), *Learning and comprehension of text* (pp. 255–86). Hillsdale, NJ: Erlbaum.

Bruner, J. S., Goodnow, J. J., & Austin, G. A. (1956). *A study of thinking.* New York: Wiley.

Bruner, J. S., Olver, R. R., & Greenfield, P. M. (1966). *Studies in cognitive growth.* New York: Wiley.

Busse, L. L., & Henderson, H. S. (1972). Effects of contingency management upon reading achievement of junior high educable mentally retarded students. *Education and Training of the Mentally Retarded, 7,* 67–73.

Campione, J. C., & Brown, A. L. (1977). Memory and metamemory development in educable retarded children. In R. V. Kail, Jr., & J. W. Hagen (Eds.), *Perspectives on the development of memory and cognition* (pp. 367–406). Hillsdale, NJ: Erlbaum.

Campione, J. C., & Brown, A. L. (1979). Toward a theory of intelligence: Contributions from research with retarded children. In R. J. Sternberg & D. K. Detterman (Eds.),

*Human intelligence: Perspectives on its theory and measurement* (pp. 139–64). Norwood, NJ: Ablex.

Capobianco, R. J. (1956). Studies of reading and arithmetic in mentally retarded boys: II. Quantitative and qualitative analysis of endogenous and exogenous boys on arithmetic achievement. *Monographs of the Society for Research in Child Development*, *19*(Whole No. 58).

Capobianco, R. J., & Miller, D. Y. (1958). *Quantitative and qualitative analyses of exogenous and endogenous children in some reading processes.* Syracuse, NY: Syracuse University Research Institute. (ERIC Document Reproduction Service No. ED 002 747).

Carbo, M. (1983). Research in reading and learning style: Implications for exceptional children. *Exceptional Children*, *49*, 486–94.

Cawley, J. F., Goodstein, H. A., & Burrow, W. H. (1968). *Reading and psychomotor disability among mentally retarded and average children.* Unpublished manuscript, University of Connecticut, School of Education, Storrs.

Cawley, J. F., Goodstein, H. A., & Burrow, W. H. (1972). *The slow learner and the reading problem.* Springfield, IL: Thomas.

Cegelka, P. A., & Cegelka, W. J. (1970). A review of research: Reading and the educable mentally handicapped. *Exceptional Children*, *37*, 187–200.

Chomsky, N. (1957). *Syntactic structures.* The Hague: Mouton.

Crossland, C. L. (1981). A comparison of retarded and non-retarded on the ability to use context in reading. *Journal for Special Educators*, *17*, 234–41.

Cruickshank, W. M., Bentzen, F. A., Ratzeburg, F. H., & Tannhauser, M. T. (1961). *A teaching method for brain-injured and hyperactive children.* Syracuse, NY: Syracuse University Press.

Cummins, J. P., & Das, J. P. (1980). Cognitive processing, academic achievement, and WISC-R performance in EMR children. *Journal of Consulting and Clinical Psychology*, *48*, 777–9.

Das, J. P., & Cummins, J. (1978). Academic performance and cognitive processes in EMR children. *American Journal of Mental Deficiency*, *83*, 197–9.

Davies, D., Sperber, R. D., & McCauley, C. (1981). Intelligence-related differences in semantic processing speed. *Journal of Experimental Child Psychology*, *31*, 387–402.

Dunn, L. M. (1954). A comparison of the reading processes of mentally retarded boys of the same mental age. In L. M. Dunn & R. J. Capobianco (Eds.), Studies of reading and arithmetic in mentally retarded boys. *Monographs of the Society for Research in Child Development*, *19* (1, serial no. 58), pp. 7–99.

Dunn, L. M., & Mueller, M. W. (1966). *The efficacy of the Initial Teaching Alphabet and the Peabody Language Development Kit with grade one disadvantaged children: After one year* (IMRID Papers and Reports, Vol. 3, No. 2). Nashville, TN: George Peabody College for Teachers, Institute on Mental Retardation and Intellectual Development.

Dunn, L. M., Neville, D., Bailey, C. F., Pochanart, P., & Pfost, P. (1967). *The effectiveness of three reading approaches and an oral language stimulation program with disadvantaged children in the primary grades: An interim report after one year of the cooperative reading project* (IMRID Behavioral Science Monograph No. 7). Nashville, TN: George Peabody College for Teachers, Institute on Mental Retardation and Intellectual Development.

Dunn, L. M., Pochanart, P., & Pfost, P. (1967). *The efficacy of the Initial Teaching Alphabet and the Peabody Language Development Kit with disadvantaged children in the primary grades: An interim report after two years* (IMRID Papers and Reports, Vol.

4, No. 7). Nashville, TN: George Peabody College for Teachers, Institute on Mental Retardation and Intellectual Development.

Ellson, D. G. (1971). *The effect of programmed tutoring in reading on assignment to special education classes: A follow-up of four years of tutoring in the first grade.* Unpublished manuscript, Indiana University, Bloomington.

Engle, R. W., & Nagle, R. J. (1979). Strategy training and semantic encoding in mildly retarded children. *Intelligence, 3,* 17–30.

Engle, R. W., Nagle, R. J., & Dick, M. (1980). Maintenance and generalization of a semantic rehearsal strategy in educable mentally retarded children. *Journal of Experimental Child Psychology, 30,* 438–54.

Evans, R. A. (1970). Use of associative clustering technique in the study of reading disability: Effects of presentation mode. *American Journal of Mental Deficiency, 74,* 765–70.

Eyde, D. R., & Altman, R. (1978). *An empirical study of the development of memory and metamemory in mild and moderately retarded children* (Rep. No. 443AH60046). Paper presented at the World Congress on Future Special Education, Stirling, Scotland. (ERIC Document Reproduction Service No. ED 157 286).

Frey, R. M. (1960). *Reading behavior of brain-injured and non-brain-injured children of average and retarded mental development.* Unpublished doctoral dissertation, University of Illinois, Champaign–Urbana.

Gallagher, J. (1960). *The tutoring of brain-injured mentally retarded children.* Springfield, IL: Thomas.

Gickling, E. E., Hargis, C. H., & Alexander, D. R. (1981). The function of imagery in sight word recognition among retarded and nonretarded children. *Education and Training of the Mentally Retarded, 16,* 259–62.

Gillespie, P. H., & Johnson, L. (1974). *Teaching reading to the mildly retarded child.* Columbus, OH: Merrill.

Glidden, L. M. (1977). Stimulus relations, blocking, and sorting in the free recall and organization of EMR adolescents. *American Journal of Mental Deficiency, 82,* 250–8.

Glidden, L. M., & Mar, H. H. (1978). Availability and accessibility of information in the semantic memory of retarded and nonretarded adolescents. *Journal of Experimental Child Psychology, 25,* 33–40.

Goodman, K. S. (1965). A linguistic study of cues and miscues in reading. *Elementary English Review, 42,* 639–43.

Goodman, K. S. (Ed.). (1968). *The psycholinguistic nature of the reading process.* Detroit, MI: Wayne State University.

Goodman, K. S. (1969). Words and morphemes in reading. In K. S. Goodman & J. T. Fleming (Eds.), *Psycholinguistics and the teaching of reading* (pp. 25–33). Newark, DE: International Reading Association.

Goodman, K. S. (1976). Reading: A psycholinguistic guessing game. In H. Singer & R. B. Ruddell (Eds.), *Theoretical models and processes of reading* (pp. 497–508). Newark, DE: International Reading Association.

Goodstein, H. A. (1970). Performance of mentally handicapped and average-IQ children on two modified cloze tasks for oral language. *American Journal of Mental Deficiency, 75,* 290–7.

Gottlieb, B. W. (1982). Social facilitation influences on the oral reading performance of academically handicapped children. *American Journal of Mental Deficiency, 87,* 153–8.

Greene, F. M. (1966). Programmed instruction techniques for the mentally retarded. In

N. R. Ellis (Ed.), *International review of research in mental retardation* (pp. 209–39). New York: Academic Press.

Grossman, H. J. (Ed.). (1973). *Manual on terminology and classification in mental retardation*. Washington, DC: American Association on Mental Deficiency.

Grossman, H. J. (Ed.). (1983). *Classification in mental retardation*. Washington, DC: American Association on Mental Deficiency.

Guthrie, F. M., & Cunningham, P. M. (1982). Teaching decoding skills to educable mentally handicapped children. *The Reading Teacher*, *35*, 554–9.

Hagen, J. W., & Stanovich, K. E. (1977). Memory: Strategies of acquisition. In R. V. Kail & J. W. Hagen (Eds.), *Perspectives on the development of memory and cognition* (pp. 89–111). New York: Wiley.

Hamre-Nietupski, S., Nietupski, J., Vincent, L. J., & Wambold, C. (1982). Effects of strategy training on the free-recall performance of mildly and moderately mentally retarded adolescents. *American Journal of Mental Deficiency*, *86*, 421–4.

Hargis, C. H. (1972). A comparison of retarded and non-retarded children on the ability to use context in reading. *American Journal of Mental Deficiency*, *76*, 726–34.

Haring, N. G. (1971). *Investigation of systematic instructional procedures to facilitate academic achievement in mentally retarded disadvantaged children* (Final Report). Seattle: University of Washington, Child Development and Health Retardation Center.

Hildum, D. C. (Ed.) (1967). *Language and thought*. New York: Van Nostrand.

Hofmeister, A. (1971). Programmed instruction: Revisited implications for educating the retarded. *Education and Training of the Mentally Retarded*, *6*, 172–6.

Hunt, E. B. (1966). *Concept learning: An information processing problem*. New York: Wiley.

Hurley, O. L. (1975). Reading comprehension skills *vis-à-vis* the mentally retarded. *Education and Training of the Mentally Retarded*, *10*, 10–14.

Jarman, R. F. (1978). Patterns of cognitive ability in retarded children: A reexamination. *American Journal of Mental Deficiency*, *82*, 344–8.

Jenkins, J. R., & Gorrafa, S. (1974). Academic performance of mentally handicapped children as a function of token economies and contingency contracts. *Education and Training of the Mentally Retarded*, *9*, 183–6.

Jenkins, J. R., Stein, M. L., & Osborn, J. R. (1981). What next after decoding? Instruction and research in reading comprehension. *Exceptional Education Quarterly*, *2*, 27–39.

Johnson, D. D., & Baumann, J. F. (1984). Word identification. In P. D. Pearson (Ed.), *Handbook of reading research* (pp. 583–608). New York: Longman.

Jorm, A. F., & Share, D. L. (1983). An invited article: Phonological recoding and reading acquisition. *Applied Psycholinguistics*, *4*, 103–47.

Kamil, M. L. (1984). Current traditions of reading research. In P. D. Pearson (Ed.), *Handbook of reading research* (pp. 39–62). New York: Longman.

Kaufman, M., Agard, J. A., & Semmel, M. I. (1985). *Mainstreaming: Learners and their environment*. Cambridge, MA: Brookline Books.

Kirk, S. (1964). Research in education. In H. A. Stevens & R. Heber (Eds.), *Mental retardation* (pp. 57–99). University of Chicago Press.

Kohlers, P. A. (1968). Reading is only incidentally visual. In K. S. Goodman & J. T. Fleming (Eds.), *Psycholinguistics and the teaching of reading* (pp. 8–16). Newark, DE: International Reading Association.

Kramer, J. J., & Engle, R. W. (1981). Teaching awareness of strategic behavior in combination with strategy training: Effects on children's memory performance. *Journal of Experimental Child Psychology*, *32*, 513–30.

Lefevre, C. A. (1964). *Linguistics and the teaching of reading.* New York: McGraw-Hill.

Levitt, E. (1970). The effect of context on the reading of mentally retarded and normal children at the first grade level. *Journal of Special Education, 4*, 425–9.

Levitt, E. (1972). Higher-order and lower-order reading responses of mentally retarded and non-retarded children at the first-grade level. *American Journal of Mental Deficiency, 77*, 13–20.

Luftig, R. L., & Greeson, L. E. (1983). Effects of structural importance and idea saliency on discourse recall of mentally retarded and nonretarded pupils. *American Journal of Mental Deficiency, 87*, 414–21.

Luftig, R. L., & Johnson, R. E. (1982). Identification and recall of structurally important units in prose by mentally retarded learners. *American Journal of Mental Deficiency, 86*, 495–502.

MacMillan, D., & Meyers, C. E. (1979). Educational labeling of handicapped learners. In D. C. Berliner (Ed.), *Review of research in education* (Vol. 7, pp. 151–94). Itasca, IL: Peacock.

Mandler, G. (1967). Organization and memory. In K. W. Spence & J. T. Spence (Eds.), *The psychology of learning and motivation* (pp. 328–72). New York: Academic Press.

Mason, J. M. (1978). Role of strategy in reading by mentally retarded persons. *American Journal of Mental Deficiency, 82*, 467–73.

Merlin, S. B., & Tseng, M. S. (1972, April). *Psycholinguistic and reading abilities of educable mentally retarded readers.* Paper presented at the annual meeting of the American Educational Research Association, Chicago.

Meyer, B. J. F., & Rice, G. E. (1984). The structure of text. In P. D. Pearson (Ed.), *Handbook of reading research* (pp. 319–51). New York: Longman.

Miller, G. A. (1956). The magical number seven, plus or minus two: Some limits on our capacity for processing information. *Psychological Review, 63*, 81–97.

Miller, G. A., Gallanter, E., & Pribram, K. H. (1960). *Plans and the structure of behavior.* New York: Holt, Rinehart & Winston.

Neisser, U. (1967). *Cognitive psychology.* New York: Appleton-Century-Crofts.

Neville, D., & Vandever, T. R. (1973). Decoding as a result of synthetic and analytic presentation for retarded and non-retarded children. *American Journal of Mental Deficiency, 77*, 533–7.

Olson, D. R. (1970). Language acquisition and cognitive development. In H. C. Haywood (Ed.), *Social–cultural aspects of mental retardation* (pp. 113–202). New York: Appleton-Century-Crofts.

Orlando, C. P. (1973). Review of the reading research in special education. In L. Mann & D. Sabatino (Eds.), *The first review of special education* (pp. 261–83). Philadelphia: Journal of Special Education Press.

Peleg, Z. R., & Moore, R. F. (1982). Effects of the advance organizer with oral and written presentation on recall and inference of EMR adolescents. *American Journal of Mental Deficiency, 86*, 621–6.

Price, J. E. (1963). Automated teaching programs with mentally retarded students. *American Journal of Mental Deficiency, 68*, 69–72.

Raber, S. M., & Weisz, J. R. (1981). Teacher feedback to mentally retarded and nonretarded children. *American Journal of Mental Deficiency, 86*, 148–56.

Ramanauskas, S. (1972). Contextual constraints beyond a sentence on cloze responses of mentally retarded children. *American Journal of Mental Deficiency, 77*, 338–45.

Reed, J. C., Rabe, E. F., & Mankinen, M. (1970). Teaching reading to brain damaged children: A review. *Reading Research Quarterly, 5*, 379–401.

Resnick, L. B. (1984). Comprehending and learning: Implications for a cognitive theory of instruction. In H. Mandl, N. L. Stein, & T. Trabasso (Eds.), *Learning and comprehension of text* (pp. 431–43). Hillsdale, NJ: Erlbaum.

Rose, T. L. (1984). The effects of previewing on retarded learners' oral reading. *Education and Training of the Mentally Retarded, 19,* 49–53.

Rumelhart, D. E. (1981). Schemata: The building blocks of cognition. In J. T. Guthrie (Ed.), *Comprehension and teaching: Research reviews* (pp. 3–26). Newark, DE: International Reading Association.

Ryan, E. B., & Semmel, M. I. (1969). Reading as a constructive language process. *Reading Research Quarterly, 5,* 59–83.

Sabatino, D. A., & Dorfman, N. (1974). Matching learner aptitude to two commercial reading programs. *Exceptional Children, 41,* 85–90.

Sabatino, D. A., Ysseldyke, J. E., & Woolston, J. (1973). Diagnostic–prescriptive teaching utilizing perceptual strengths of mentally retarded children. *American Journal of Mental Deficiency, 78,* 7–14.

Samuels, S. J., & Anderson, R. H. (1973). Visual recognition memory, paired-associate learning, and reading achievement. *Journal of Educational Psychology, 65,* 160–7.

Semmel, M. I. (1967). Language behavior of mentally retarded and culturally disadvantaged children. In J. F. Magary & R. B. McIntyre (Eds.), *Fifth Annual Distinguished Lecture Series in Special Education* (pp. 31–47). Los Angeles: University of Southern California Press.

Semmel, M. I. (1985). *Identification and classification of handicapped children in the schools.* Unpublished manuscript, University of California, Santa Barbara.

Semmel, M. I., Barritt, L. S., & Bennett, S. W. (1970). Performance of EMR and non-retarded children on a modified cloze task. *American Journal of Mental Deficiency, 74,* 681–8.

Semmel, M. I., Barritt, L. S., Bennett, S. W., & Perfetti, C. A. (1968). A grammatical analysis of word associations of educable mentally retarded and normal children. *American Journal of Mental Deficiency, 72,* 567–76.

Semmel, M. I., & Bennett, S. W. (1970). Effects of linguistic structure and delay on memory span of EMR children. *American Journal of Mental Deficiency, 74,* 674–80.

Semmel, M. I., & Englert, C. S. (1980). *A reading media simulation: Teaching reading to special needs children.* Bloomington: Indiana University, Center for Innovation in Teaching the Handicapped.

Semmel, M. I., Gottlieb, J., & Robinson, N. M. (1979). Mainstreaming: Perspectives on educating handicapped children in the public school. In D. C. Berliner (Ed.), *Review of research in education* (Vol. 7, pp. 223–79). Itasca, IL: Peacock.

Semmel, M. I., Peck, C., & Lieber, J. (1986). Effects of special education environments: Beyond mainstreaming. In C. J. Meisel (Ed.), *Mainstreaming handicapped children: Outcomes, controversies, and new directions* (pp. 165–92). Hillsdale, NJ: Erlbaum.

Sheperd, G. (1967). Selected factors in the reading ability of educable mentally retarded boys. *American Journal of Mental Deficiency, 71,* 563–70.

Shotick, A. (1960). *A comparative investigation of the performance of mentally retarded and normal boys on selected reading comprehension and performance tasks.* Unpublished doctoral dissertation, Syracuse University, Syracuse, NY.

Sitko, M. C., & Semmel, M. I. (1972). The effect of phrasal cueing on free recall of EMR and non-retarded children. *American Educational Research Journal, 9,* 217–29.

Sitko, M. C., & Semmel, M. I. (1973). Language and language behavior of the mentally retarded. In L. Mann & D. A. Sabatino (Eds.), *The first review of special education* (pp. 203–60). Philadelphia: Journal of Special Education Press.

Sitko, M. C., Semmel, D. S., Wilcove, G., & Semmel, M. I. (1972). *The relationship of word- and sentence-associations of EMR children to reading performance* (Tech. Rep. No. 6.33). Bloomington: Indiana University, Center for Innovation in Teaching the Handicapped.

Spicker, H. H., & Bartel, N. R. (1968). The mentally retarded. In G. O. Johnson & H. D. Blank (Eds.), *Exceptional children research review* (pp. 38–109). Washington, DC: The Council for Exceptional Children.

Sternberg, R. J., Powell, J. S., & Kaye, D. B. (1983). Teaching vocabulary-building skills: A contextual approach. In A. C. Wilkinson (Ed.), *Classroom computers and cognitive science* (pp. 121–43). New York: Academic Press.

Strauss, A. A., & Kephart, N. C. (1955). *Psychopathology and education of the brain injured child: Vol. 2. Progress in theory and clinic.* New York: Grune & Stratton.

Strauss, A. A., & Lehtinen, L. E. (1947). *Psychopathology and education of the brain injured child* (Vol. 1). New York: Grune & Stratton.

Streib, R. (1976/1977). Context utilization in reading by educable mentally retarded children. *Reading Research Quarterly, 120,* 32–54.

Tierney, R. J., & Cunningham, J. W. (1984). Research on teaching reading comprehension. In P. D. Pearson (Ed.), *Handbook of reading research* (pp. 609–55). New York: Longman.

Tulving, E. (1962). Subjective organization in free recall of unrelated words. *Psychological Review, 69,* 344–54.

Tulving, E. (1966). Subjective organization and effects of repetition in multitrial free-recall learning. *Journal of Verbal Learning and Verbal Behavior, 5,* 193–7.

Vandever, T. R., Maggart, W. T., & Nasser, S. (1976). Three approaches to beginning reading. *Mental Retardation, 14,* 29–32.

Vandever, T. R., & Neville, D. D. (1974). Letter cues vs. configuration cues as aids to word recognition in retarded and non-retarded children. *American Journal of Mental Deficiency, 79,* 210–13.

Vandever, T. R., & Neville, D. D. (1976). Transfer as a result of synthetic and analytic reading instruction. *American Journal of Mental Deficiency, 80,* 498–503.

Vellutino, F. R., Harding, C. J., Phillips, F., & Steger, J. A. (1975). Differential transfer in poor and normal readers. *Journal of Genetic Psychology, 126,* 3–18.

Woodcock, R. W. (1967). *The Peabody–Chicago–Detroit reading project: A report of the second-year results* (IMRID Papers and Reports, Vol. 4, No. 15). Nashville, TN: George Peabody College for Teachers, Institute on Mental Retardation and Intellectual Development.

# 3 Schooled language competence: linguistic abilities in reading and writing

*Charles A. Perfetti and Deborah McCutchen*

In this chapter, we pose a general question and develop an argument concerning the kind of answer that is required. The question is whether there are some general principles of language competence that can be applied to the development of both reading and writing skills. The short answer to the question we pose is yes – there are some general principles of language competence that serve both reading and writing. At the same time, there are some distinctive features of writing not shared by reading, and we shall try to specify some of these. The general form of our argument is that schooled language competence is a restricted set of abilities; that is, it cannot be identified with the full range of cognitive skills. The essential activity of both reading and writing is linguistic symbol manipulation.

In what follows, we first define schooled language competence. Then we critically discuss other approaches to language competence, arguing that nonlinguistic approaches are inadequate. We then demonstrate, first for reading and then writing, that language competencies play a central role.

## Schooled language competence

By *schooled language competence*, we intend to suggest a set of language abilities that build on basic linguistic competence and are heavily modified by learning. By assumption, schooled language competence underlies performance on every language task. For the performance side, we restrict our discussion to the ordinary text reading and mundane writing activities of elementary school children, although we intend that the underlying competence serves other language performances as well.

One problematic component of the concept of schooled language competence is its relation to basic language competence. We can make the relatively weak assumption that a child entering school at age 6 has basic language competence in the sense of knowing the grammar of his or her language. Furthermore, the child

Some of the research described in this chapter was funded by the National Institute of Education through a grant to the Learning Research and Development Center, University of Pittsburgh.

has a high degree of pragmatic competence, implicitly understanding conditions on communication, turn taking, and so on. Effects of schooling on language competence appear, at least by informal observation, to lie in two areas: (1) an increase in vocabulary size and, concomitantly, an increase in semantic precision of words and (2) an increase in syntactic options. It is the syntactic growth that is clearly connected to initial language competence, although vocabulary growth is also, to the extent that word morphology is used generatively, for example, adding *unable* to the vocabulary based on an appreciation of the negative prefix. In general, increased competence in syntax is the part of schooled competence that builds on *basic* language competence.

What is problematic is how to understand this "building on" relationship. One possibility is that new structures are learned. Another possibility is that the number of syntactic options merely increases from basic knowledge of syntactic forms. The difference between these two alternatives is whether, for example, the increased use with schooling of subordinate clauses (Loban, 1976) reflects the acquisition of subordination structures (or rules) or merely the productive control of structures that have been part of basic competence for some time. There has been a profound neglect of the mechanisms by which language growth occurs beyond early childhood, and, accordingly, there is little reason to choose one syntactic growth hypothesis over the other. A weak assumption seems appropriate and sufficient: The growth of language competence with schooling reflects a basic language competence developed at an early age that, with appropriate experience and linguistic dispositions, drives subsequent grammatical development. Extended grammatical competence is especially important in writing, as we shall argue.

Schooled language competence develops in the context of the acquisition of literacy. There are two parts to this general claim. One is that the development of schooled language competence serves the acquisition of both reading and writing. The second is that the development of schooled language competence occurs primarily through the influence of literacy. The relationship between writing and reading, on the one hand, and schooled language competence, on the other, is reciprocal. Although both claims have interesting entailments, we focus here on the first one, that reading and writing are served by schooled language competence. That such competence arises through reading and writing rather than through spoken language is an interesting hypothesis, but largely beyond our purpose here (see, however, Perfetti 1985, in press).

## Knowledge and problem solving are insufficient

In contrast to the approach we develop here, there are some approaches to skilled performance that include virtually no roles for a generalized language competence. We shall discuss two briefly to show that they are inadequate.

*Knowledge*

The first approach emphasizes the critical role of knowledge in skilled performance. The basic thrust is that cognitive task performance in general, including reading comprehension, is driven by conceptual knowledge of the task domain. The methodology behind this approach has been the comparison of experts with nonexperts in a domain, for example, physics (Chi, Glaser, & Rees, 1982; Larkin, McDermott, Simon, & Simon, 1980), chess (Chase & Simon, 1973), social science (Voss, Greene, Post, & Penner, 1983), and baseball (Spilich, Vesonder, Chiesi, & Voss, 1979). The conclusion that seems to cut across the different domains is that performance on a task depends qualitatively on the individual's expertise in the domain. When an individual is knowledgeable in a domain, his or her problem solving is qualitatively different from that of a nonexpert in its reliance on the conceptual structures of the domain. Performance, in short, is driven more by the deep conceptual structure of the domain than by more general principles of skilled performance.

In the case of reading and writing, such an approach can be characterized as schematic or, more generally, semantic. It suggests that understanding a text and producing one are activities largely driven by the application of knowledge structures or schemata that are specifically appropriate for the text domain. To a considerable extent, this knowledge approach seems to be on target. It not only allies with common sense; it is supported by empirical demonstrations that domain knowledge is important in text comprehension. To cite only a few examples, there is Bransford and Johnson's (1973) classic demonstration that comprehension of a vaguely worded passage is virtually impossible in the absence of a topically relevant title given in advance of the text. Dooling and Lachman (1971) provide a similar demonstration. There is also the demonstration of Anderson, Reynolds, Schallert, and Goetz (1976) that the interpretation of ambiguously worded passages can depend on the background knowledge of the reader. Anderson et al. found that physical education students interpreted an ambiguous text in terms of a wrestling match and other students interpreted the same text in terms of a prison break. Finally, there is the demonstration of Spilich et al. (1979) that individual differences in topic knowledge produce corresponding differences in comprehension of texts about the topic.

Despite the demonstrated importance of topic knowledge in text comprehension, the strong knowledge approach to comprehension is limited. Indeed, it is impossible to hold simultaneously both to a strong knowledge approach to reading comprehension and to a concept of reading ability. At minimum, reading ability is what remains after specific knowledge effects are accounted for. Now, it may turn out that reading ability is an illusion that masks innumerable topic-specific comprehension procedures. If so, tests of reading comprehension skill would essentially be tests of knowledge differences in which students vary in the extent of their knowledge of the mundane topics covered by such tests. To see that such a view is not completely far-fetched, one might think of the long-standing controversy over the knowledge-dependent nature of IQ tests. If it is possible to believe that IQ tests reflect specific knowledge, it is possible to believe the same of reading comprehension tests.

Although it is possible that this view could be mainly correct in the long run, there is no reason to accept it in the absence of strong supporting evidence. The strong knowledge position indeed contains a knowledge paradox. If comprehension is strongly dependent on knowledge, how is new knowledge acquired through comprehension? The strong semantic approach would have to claim that, given some metric of knowledge-relatedness, learning new material is possible only within some knowledge distance of the learner's present knowledge.

The concept of general language ability provides part of the answer to the knowledge paradox. New knowledge can be acquired through language because of general mechanisms that are part of language competence. Syntactic abilities, coupled with broader-scope discourse abilities, allow comprehension to proceed by linking together word concepts in such a way as to establish a text base, that is, a representation of what the text "says," even if this is short of a deep representation of the referent world described by the text. This distinction between the text base (the propositions of the text) and the situational base (the relations in the referent world described by the text) has proved to be a useful one (van Dijk & Kintsch, 1983). It is possible for a reader to understand a text, to a limited but useful extent (e.g., to be able to summarize its contents) without being able to learn from it. For example, students who lack LISP programming knowledge can read and summarize a LISP programming text even when they are not learning much about programming from the text (Kintsch, 1986). Certainly, such superficial comprehension is short of deep understanding, and learning ultimately seems to depend on deep understanding. Building (permanent) new knowledge structures depends on a base of related knowledge for the foundation. However, these learning processes themselves depend on a logically prior, more elementary sort of comprehension that does not build permanent knowledge structures but rather builds temporary representations of texts. Of course, the sooner these text representations can be integrated with knowledge-building processes, the better for the learner. Temporary representations without integrating knowledge structures are at risk.

This learning–comprehending distinction may help mark out the boundaries of knowledge effects in text performance, and it allows a role for language ability in comprehension, on which learning depends. However, it does not seem to explain the results of Bransford and Johnson (1973), Dooling and Lachman (1971), or Anderson et al. (1976). The effects in these experiments were on comprehension, but they were on the situational model rather than the text model. Once subjects were informed that the vague text of Bransford and Johnson (1973) was about "washing clothes," they knew the situation referred to by the text. Once Dooling and Lachman's subjects were told that a certain story was titled "Christopher Columbus," they could interpret such phrases as "an egg not a table correctly typifies this unexplored planet" in terms of a situation. Thus, when most of the words and phrases are referentially vague (Bransford & Johnson, 1973; Dooling & Lachman, 1971) or referentially ambiguous (Anderson et al., 1976), knowledge of the situation is important for selecting a situational model for comprehension. This demonstrates the limits of comprehension based only on an impoverished text model. However, when mundane texts are involved, the referential value of many words and phrases will be clear and the reader or listener will be able to construct a text model and a situational model simultaneously. The key to the construction of a situational model is that the reader have an *interpreted* representation of the text, that is, one that is referentially and inferentially rich. This process depends both on knowledge and on a basic meaning representation, a point we return to later.

### Strategies

A second nonlinguistic approach to skilled performance emphasizes strategies. The thrust of this approach is that the individual applies either general or task-specific strategies in the course of cognitive task performance. In the case of reading, such strategies as self-questioning and summarizing are applicable to text learning (Palinscar & Brown, 1984). In the case of writing, planning and goal setting are especially prominent (Hayes & Flower, 1980), although these strategies apply to reading as well. There are complicating features in concepts of strategy use. Normally, strategies may be conscious or unconscious; they may support learning or memorizing; they may have, in principle, wide applicability or they may be task specific. However, since only relatively weak claims have been made for strategies, we will not be concerned with the many useful distinctions that can be made. That is, whereas it is in principle possible to imagine a knowledge approach to comprehension that ignores all but the most basic general language ability, it is not possible to imagine a stand-alone strategy approach to comprehension. Nor are we aware of any claims that reduce comprehension to strategy application. Thus, it is sufficient to note simply that reading and writing cannot be understood as the acquisition and use of general cognitive strategies.

Nevertheless, it is clear that there are strategies for reading and learning from text. They begin, perhaps, with the reader setting some purpose for his or her reading. Once set, this purpose can control the percentage of words fixated and the fixation duration per word. This speed control then influences the degree of detailed comprehension achieved. In addition, there are direct comprehension strategies that may be applied. Readers who ask themselves the main point of each paragraph are applying such a strategy. Self-testing and summarization are other examples of explicit comprehension monitoring strategies.

In our view the interesting thing about all strategies – except for general purpose setting, which affects comprehension because it controls the density and duration of lexical processes – is that skilled reading can get by without them. The skilled reader may be doing the *functional equivalent* of summarizing or self-questioning when he or she derives a higher-order representation of text sentences, but there does not seem to be any meaningful sense in which such processing amounts to a strategy. It does indeed depend on the timely activation of relevant knowledge and the concomitant rapid construction of necessary inferences. (Texts are never fully explicit.) However, such knowledge activation and inference making may be more appropriately thought of as tied to basic text processes than as detachable strategies. They are, in ordinary circumstances, triggered by comprehended text elements.

It is only the appearance of reading failure that allows notice of the potential for strategies. It is possible, although not yet established, as far as we know, that text-based processes that apply readily to spoken language apply, for some readers, only unreliably to print. For such persons, instruction in strategy application sometimes may be worthwhile, and such instruction has been strongly advocated (Ryan, 1982). As one example of the strategy approach, Palinscar and Brown (1984) showed that teaching comprehension monitoring strategies was successful but only if the strategies were learned through a socially interactive reciprocal teaching procedure. The strategies themselves may be less important than whatever learning potentials are allowed by reciprocal teaching. Even if this is not the case generally, the importance of strategies would be limited. They are procedures to apply to texts for individuals who have trouble reading. Their difficulty with reading, it is worth noting, is not necessarily caused by their lack of monitoring skills. Indeed, many, perhaps most, individuals who have comprehension problems, we predict, will turn out to lack monitoring skills only as a secondary derivative problem. They will also lack more fundamental language competence skills that serve reading.

In the case of writing, the strategies approach emphasizes planning, especially establishing goals and subgoals in connection with audience, tone, and writing purpose. It is clear that skilled writers attend to such goal setting and that children and writers of low skill often do not (Scardamalia & Bereiter, 1982). The school setting, in fact, often makes such goal setting difficult, and the appearance of arbitrary writing goals has been one of the noted shortcomings of writing instruction (Applebee, 1982). Learning to write with a purpose and audience in mind is certainly part of the process of learning how to write. Similarly, learning to plan beginnings and endings and in-between expositions is part of the acquisition of writing.

On the other hand, the contribution of such planning and goal setting to writing competence should not be overemphasized (see McCutchen, 1984, for a related discussion of the limitations of planning models as complete accounts of writing).

Just as strategy deficiencies are seldom the only problem faced by a *reader* of low skill, planning deficiencies are seldom the only problem faced by a *writer* of low skill. Writing competence is the productive control over the grammatical devices of language in the service of some communicative intent. It is our impression that the communicative intent, in a general way, comes easier to writers than the productive control. Nevertheless, we do not wish to argue against planning and strategy applications. We do, however, want to assert that writing is primarily a process of productive control of linguistic symbols. We think that acquiring this control in the context of communicative intentions that are often arbitrary or underspecified is what makes writing acquisition nontrivial. However, it is linguistic manipulation that lies at the heart of writing and thus makes it a cognitive skill that must be understood as one based on schooled language competence.

In summary, we have argued for a concept of schooled language competence that serves both reading and writing as well as other language performances. We have further argued that alternative approaches to cognitive skills that, respectively, emphasize knowledge and strategies provide insufficient accounts of reading and writing skills despite their value in explaining some aspects of cognitive performance. In what follows, we illustrate the schooled language competence analysis of reading and writing.

## Linguistic and nonlinguistic sources of reading skill

There is a substantial body of reading research that informs us about word identification and comprehension and, to a lesser extent, learning how to read. We can extract general principles of language-based competence from this research and also from a rational analysis of reading. We argue that certain basic linguistic abilities drive skilled reading and that these abilities are both highly generalized (i.e., independent of domain) and restricted (i.e., especially suitable for language processing). The argument extends to both word identification and comprehension.

### Reading and knowledge

We have already argued that reading ability cannot be identified with knowledge. Here we try to specify why this is the case. Two general principles are critical to our argument. First, we claim a distinction between meaning and interpretation. Second, we note the possibility that certain language processes are relatively impenetrable. The consequence of accepting these two principles is that important parts of reading cannot be influenced by knowledge.

First, there is a matter of definition. It is natural to suppose that the validity of theoretical claims about reading hinge critically on the definition of reading. One can define reading in such a way that it is similar to thinking, or at least so that it includes a wide range of inference, interpretation, and construction. Or reading can be defined more narrowly as the translation of written elements into language. The latter is essentially the decoding definition of reading, and there are some reasons to prefer it, although it is probably the nonpreferred definition among reading researchers (see also Perfetti, 1984). However, we take the position that the definition of reading does not matter much for our argument, provided that an extremely broad thinking definition is rejected. We argue that *reading* is a generalized language ability; however, there is no reason to make this argument about thinking. Indeed, we want to make a distinction between unconstrained higher-level mental processes that take full advantage of all information sources and relatively constrained lower-level processes that cannot take full advantage of all information sources. We will accept a definition of reading that includes comprehension or one that stops at print-language translation, but not one that suggests that reading is thinking guided by print. To put it another way, if one insists on the broadest definition, our argument will apply to only part of reading. In any case, we do intend it to apply to reading comprehension.

### Meaning and interpretation

Reading comprehension, like comprehension generally, is the construction of veridical mental representations of situations described in written text. The text itself can be said to have a range of possible representations, because texts are ambiguous. To the extent that there is overlap between one of these potential text representations and a mental representation constructed by a reader, we can speak of the reader achieving a reading of the text, or comprehending the text. Ordinarily, we speak of comprehending the text as if there were one idealized text representation rather than a range of possible interpretations. No harm comes from this fiction. The important point is that comprehension is the overlap between the reader's obtained (or constructed) representation and a text representation. This is a reasonable understanding of comprehension, perhaps without contention, except for such tricky details as assessing what the possible readings of a text are (let alone what *the* reading is).

However, we know there is both more (and less) to comprehension than this concept of overlap between representations. Consider a perhaps classic sentence from an experiment described by Bransford and Johnson (1973):

(1) *The haystack was important because the cloth ripped.*

In the experiment, such a sentence was relatively difficult to recall in a cued recall situation with the subject noun (*haystack*) as a cue. However, when the sentence was accompanied by a context cue, the word *parachute*, its recall was dramatically improved. The usual interpretation of this result is that *parachute* provides a context that enables one to comprehend the sentence and that things, including sentences, that are comprehended are better remembered than things that are not comprehended. Comprehension, by this conclusion, is a matter of relating a sentence to knowledge of the world. In this case, relevant knowledge about parachutes and parachuting is activated and linked to the sentence.

The parachute example represents a well-known approach to comprehension in general. It assumes that language comprehension strongly depends on knowledge. We agree with this assumption, but only if we appreciate some distinction between interpretation and meaning. "Comprehension" is an equivocation between two possibilities: achieving a meaning for a text and achieving an interpretation of a text. Identifying comprehension only with interpretation leads to the claim that comprehension depends on knowledge. Identifying comprehension with meaning leads to a different perspective: Comprehension depends on meaning, a symbol-based process, whereas interpretation depends on meaning plus knowledge.

To return to the parachute example, it is not that the sentence *The haystack was important because the cloth ripped* is not comprehensible. Indeed, its meaning is fully represented by a set of elementary propositions. In effect, the propositions of this sentence presuppose the existence of two objects, assert a predication for each concept (*important*) and (*ripping*), and, centrally, assert a predication (*because*) linking these two predications. The meaning of a sentence is embodied in the combination of its propositions and its symbol values or word meanings. Propositional analysis, although not without problems (e.g. there is no algorithm for it), is a widely accepted text research tool thanks to the research of Kintsch and van Dijk (1978; Kintsch, 1974).

However, word meanings present a deep problem of long standing. The tradition represented by Wittgenstein (1892/1953) holds that there are no necessary and sufficient conditions on word meaning and that meaning is a matter of language use. The tradition represented by Katz and Fodor (1963; Katz, 1966), among others, holds that there are systematic components that comprise word meaning. It is beyond our purpose to join the historical controversy in the philosophy of language concerning meaning. However, it is useful to examine some of the implications for comprehension of what we call the *symbol* approach compared with *context* approach.

The context approach is represented by the work of Bransford already cited and by a number of other important psychological studies of comprehension. For the issue of word meaning, a study of Anderson and Ortony (1975) is a good representative of the contextualist approach. Anderson and Ortony report a cued recall experiment for sentences such as the following:

    (2) *The accountant pounded the stake.*
    (3) *The accountant pounded the desk.*

There were two different recall cues for these sentences: *hammer* and *fist*. The idea was that *hammer* would be a better recall cue for (2) and *fist* would be a better cue for (3). The reasoning was that sentences are comprehended and remembered as contextually particularized mental representations. If so, a cue's effectiveness will depend on whether it is consistent with the particularized representation. The results of the experiment confirmed this expectation: *Hammer* was a better recall cue for (2), and *fist* was a better recall cue for (3).

The question is what to make of such a result. We agree with Anderson and Ortony (and Bransford & Johnson, 1973) that "sentence comprehension and memory involve constructing particularized and elaborated mental representations" (Anderson & Ortony, 1975, p. 167). Thus, a reader, or a listener for that matter, is apt to understand "pounded the stake" as a particular action that is different from "pounded the desk." The mental representations that result may not be identical in the two cases, although experiments on recall do not demonstrate anything about the representation formed during comprehension. Indeed, the question of when different kinds of inferences and elaborations are made remains an open one.

What we reject is the stronger position that the words only loosely constrain the mental representation. Indeed, the words strongly constrain the representation to elaborations consistent with the basic semantics of the word. Thus, how *pounding* will be understood will be consistent with the semantic constraints of *pound*: *pound* (agent, object, instrument). The difference between sentences (2) and (3) lies in the way the reader is apt to fill in the instrument case, which is not explicit in either sentence. Presumably the reader would have no trouble understanding (4):

(4) *The accountant pounded the stake with his fist.*

The explicit mention of an instrument fills in the variables allowed by the verb frame and, no matter how pragmatically unconventional, forces an interpretation of (4) that is, at the action level, more similar to (3) than (2).

What is not possible, in general, is to use *The accountant pounded the stake* to mean that the accountant pounded the desk. Nor can it mean that the accountant pulled up the stake or that the bartender pounded the desk. The fact is that mental representations (i.e., *interpretations*) are constrained by *meanings*. One cannot use any sentence to carry any interpretation. There is a range of likely interpretations and there even seems to be a default interpretation when meanings are underspecified, but there are constraints imposed by both symbol meaning and syntax.

At this point, the counterargument may be that anything can "mean" anything in the right context. On the contrary, it seems correct only to say that words can be used to "refer to" anything, and any sentence can be given such and such "interpretation." There is nothing gained by this claim. Interpretation is indeed a matter of context, and reference can be assigned by convention or whim. However, the distinction between meaning and interpretation makes context stretching an idle exercise. Comprehension is the link between meaning and interpretation, and there is no reason to identify it only with interpretation.

Finally, it is important to note that nothing in our argument requires a "fixed-meaning" view of language. It is perfectly possible to accept the Wittgenstein analysis of meaning as family resemblance and simultaneously hold a distinction between meaning and interpretation. We can understand concepts, particularly natural categories, as organized around prototypical instances (Rosch, 1973), rather than as sets of necessary and sufficient features. Indeed, we need make no strong assumptions about the mental representation of word meaning. The only assumption needed is that word meanings *are represented* rather than merely constructed de novo on each token occurrence. The represented word meaning, which may have probabilistic family-resemblance characteristics, places significant constraints on comprehension.

If the meaning–interpretation distinction is maintained, we take interpretation to be determined by meaning plus context. The role of knowledge is clarified by this distinction. In general, knowledge has a limited effect on comprehension; it has a profound effect on interpretation. The many studies that have shown knowledge effects on text processing, by this view, have demonstrated such effects on the way the reader interprets a passage. In some cases the passage is so vague that interpretation is very poorly constrained. This is the case with the Bransford and Johnson (1973) washing machine and balloon experiments. When subjects were given pictorial cues, they were able to make a uniform interpretation of the text. In the case of Anderson et al. (1976), who presented subjects with an ambiguous text, the subjects' interpretation of the text was influenced by their specific background. An ambiguous passage that refers to "Rocky" getting up from a mat was more likely to be interpreted as one about a wrestler by students from a weight-lifting class than by education students, who were more likely to construct a prison-escape interpretation. It is probably significant that such experiments have used very odd texts. Even a cursory examination of the Bransford and Johnson texts and the Anderson et al. texts shows their vagueness of reference. The words seem to float in the air above the referential ground. Presumably, readers either fail to construct an interpretation or construct one based on their individual experiences. It is far from clear that ordinary texts, written to communicate rather than obfuscate, would show such a strong effect of knowledge. However, this is a minor point, for knowledge surely affects interpretation. In ordinary texts, interpretation and meaning (comprehension) are usually highly overlapping. In these experimental texts, they are not.

A final point must be addressed. It may be possible to defend a strong distinction between linguistic knowledge and "real-world" knowledge, but it is unnecessary except for special purposes beyond our own. Moreover, it is difficult to argue this distinction in the case of semantics. Indeed, this difficulty was the most critical criticism of the semantic theory of Katz and Fodor (1963), which attempted to hold a sharp distinction between a finite set of systematic meaning features that defined concepts and an indefinitely large set of nonsystematic features that individuated concepts. Bolinger (1965) argued, successfully we believe, that such a distinction was ultimately unprincipled.

The question is, Are we not in the same position as Katz and Fodor in claiming that some kinds of knowledge (world knowledge) affect interpretations, whereas other kinds of knowledge (linguistic knowledge) affect meaning comprehension? No. The critical difference is that we are not assuming a sharp distinction between linguistic knowledge and world knowledge for concepts in general. Whereas a distinction between meaning and interpretation is critical, the epistemological source of the meaning features is not.

The words *hammer*, *accountant*, *stake*, and *desk* all refer to concepts that are organized through real-world experience. However, their common attributes constitute their typical meanings, and it is these meanings that constrain comprehension. Thus, whether some object is called a *desk* or a *table* can be a matter of doubt, but its preferred designation will reflect the typical usage pattern of a broad language community. In short, the more an object resembles a typical desk, the more likely it is to be referred to by the word *desk*. On the comprehension side, the reader's "default" particularization (interpretation) of *desk* is presumably based on the prototype. There is no issue here of linguistic versus nonlinguistic, except for the syntactic category, *noun* in this case, which plays a specific role in comprehension not necessarily dependent on conceptual structure.

Verbs present a slightly different situation, because their semantic values comprise a real semantic structure rather than a loosely structured feature list. *Pound*, for example, is a verb that semantically takes three arguments – a pounder, a thing pounded, and a pounding instrument. This is the basic schema of the action of pounding and constitutes its core meaning. Assigning values to the variables – who pounded what in what manner – is the process of particularization or, more generally, interpretation. There are syntactic consequences of the argument structure, with the arguments mapping into syntactic functions such as subject, direct object, and object of a preposition. Nevertheless, even in the case of verbs, it is not necessary to assume a sharp boundary between linguistic and nonlinguistic knowledge in the representation of the verb meaning. (The syntactic constraints on the verb are another matter.) Instead, we assume that the argument structure constitutes part of the core meaning of the verb. Obviously, learning the core meaning of a verb like *pound* is a matter of extracting the core properties from pounding instances observed in the world. Thus, for both nouns and verbs as names of concepts there are two kinds of knowledge, although the distinction is not linguistic versus nonlinguistic. The relevant distinction is between the knowledge that comprises the core meaning of the concept and knowledge that comprises the particularization of the concept in context. This distinction appears to be roughly parallel to that originally made by Frege (1892/1952) between sense and reference. With such a distinction, it is important to make clear where the effects of knowledge are. We think that comprehension of core meaning is not typically subject to the effects of knowledge. Demonstrations of knowledge effects have typically shown effects on interpretation, not on meaning comprehension.

### *The impenetrability of some comprehension processes*

The second part of the argument is that some processes of comprehension are not easily penetrated by "outside" sources of information. Any such impenetrable process is not, therefore, influenced by knowledge. Thus, we assume that comprehension occurs within a processing system that has some constraints on the interaction of its components. A strong form of this argument is that a language processor consists of noninteracting autonomous components (Forster, 1979).

Such an argument has taken on new life as the modularity thesis (Fodor, 1983). We find the modularity thesis congenial, but there are aspects of it that are quite beyond our present purpose. For example, the assumption that modular cognitive systems are innate is reasonable but probably unnecessarily strong for our more modest purpose, which is to argue that knowledge does not affect comprehension at all levels. For this, we need argue only that processes of comprehension, in some sense of comprehension, do not have much access to knowledge, expectations, beliefs, or any other source of imported information. Such a comprehension process would be "informationally encapsulated" (Fodor, 1983) in that it has access only to certain kinds of information and not others. Such a process is a rapidly executing computational process that is driven by data structures for which it is specialized.

**Acquired modularity.** What we want to add to the modularity concept is the idea that modularity can be acquired. More specifically, the characteristic of impenetrability or information encapsulation can be acquired as a result of extended practice. The mechanism for modularity acquisition is the gradual specialization of data structures that are sufficient to trigger the computation. Whether a process that acquires its modularity has just the characteristics of modules that are assumed to be based on innate mental structures is an open question. However, the property they would share under any analysis is impenetrability, so we should perhaps refer to acquired impenetrability rather than acquired modularity. At least two comprehension processes are impenetrable by knowledge, beliefs, and expectations. One has acquired impenetrability, whereas the impenetrability of the second one may reflect some innate components. The first is a word identification and the second is sentence parsing.

### Word identification

In the case of word encoding, the process of lexical access, understood as some minimal identification of a word, appears to be relatively impenetrable. In skilled reading, the identification of a printed letter string is under the control of the input string through its connections with a mental representation of the word. The information in the letter string is sufficient to activate the word representation, and this activation process executes so rapidly that there is little possibility for knowledge to penetrate the process.

This observation was developed by Perfetti and Roth (1981) to account for individual differences in reading skill. A result in the literature on children's reading is that high-skill readers' word identification is facilitated by context to a lesser extent than is low-skill readers' (Perfetti, Goldman, & Hogaboam, 1979; Perfetti & Roth, 1981; Stanovich & West, 1981; West & Stanovich, 1978). The studies showing this result have used latencies to name printed words and lexical decision tasks, with sentence and discourse contexts arranged to facilitate or inhibit the recognition of a word. It is particularly interesting for our argument that Perfetti and Roth (1981) showed that degree of context facilitation for word identification is a function of the word's identification time in isolation. In their analysis the time to identify a word in isolation was variable either because of the perceptual quality of the word – it varied in its degree of visual degrading – or because of the speed of a particular reader in identifying the word in context. It did not matter which of these two was the source of the word's "basic" identification speed. Whether measured by individual subjects or individual words, the word's basic identification rate determined the degree of context facilitation. A word that was identified slowly in context showed greater context facilitation than a word identified rapidly. This is exactly the result one would expect according to the impenetrability argument. The penetration of the word identification process by knowledge, belief, or expectations is possible only to the extent that the identification process is slowly executing. In skilled reading with a high-quality perceptual input, word identification is too rapid for penetration. With a reader of low skill or a perceptual input of low quality, word identification is not too rapid for penetration, and context effects become more likely.

This raises the question of whether a rapidly executing impenetrable process differs fundamentally from a more slowly executing penetrable process or whether it is merely faster. The answer we prefer is that there may be some qualitative differences, but this preference is not critical for our argument. According to this view the impenetrable process is triggered when a stimulus pattern, a letter string, activates the word representation that contains that pattern. The slower penetrable process seems to take whatever incomplete output it obtains from this initial process and adds information to it in the form of expectations and so on. Word identification may have some of the characteristics of problem solving in such a case. This is the work of an executive central processor rather than a word recognition module. There may be little reason, however, to prefer this qualitative description of the difference to one that says that time to execute is the only difference. This alternative description is simply that expectations and knowledge potentially affect every process, but they usually lose the race when a skilled reader processes a familiar word. Either description will serve the present argument.

This account appears to overlook the fact that there are facilitative effects in word recognition that do not depend on slowly executing recognition processes. Priming effects have been observed in lexical decision tasks in which the interval between a priming word and a target word is less than 250 msec (DeGroot, 1983; Neely, 1977), a time probably too short to allow any facilitating expectation processes to execute. Furthermore, priming effects have been observed under conditions in which the prime itself was not perceived because of a brief-exposure-plus-masking procedure (Fowler, Wolford, Slade, & Tassinary, 1981). Such cases suggest a very fast acting context effect and are consistent with a two-process theory of context effects, one operating quickly and automatically and the other operating slowly and only with attention shifts (Neely, 1977; Posner & Snyder, 1975; Stanovich & West, 1981).

A rapidly executing contextual priming process is consistent with the impenetrability hypothesis, especially if this process is restricted to superficial lexical links. That is, activation may spread locally through a memory network from one word to a related neighbor. If the neighboring word is then quickly presented visually, it will be "recognized" more quickly than otherwise. (The usual way of thinking about this quicker recognition is to assume that recognition is a decision process relative to some threshold value. The threshold is reached more quickly after priming because a word's representation already has some activation from the priming connection [Morton, 1969].) This is consistent with the impenetrability hypothesis, because the effect does not involve imported knowledge or expectations. It involves only a very local lexically based effect that occurs, in modularity terms, within the lexical module.

It is interesting in this regard that the spread of activation may be even more local than is usually implied by the concept of "spreading activation." DeGroot (1983) has shown that within 240 msec (SOA), priming of a lexical decision occurs across one associative link but not across two links. Thus, the word *bull* can prime *cow* and *cow* can prime *milk*, but *bull* does not seem to prime *milk*. On the basis of DeGroot's results, we are inclined to say that the spread of activation is very restricted, perhaps to immediate lexical neighbors.

Providing stronger support for the impenetrability hypothesis are the results of the experiments of Swinney (1979) and Onifer and Swinney (1981). Swinney (1979) used a cross-modal priming paradigm in which subjects heard an ambiguous prime word as part of a sentence. The priming word triggered a visual presentation of a word for lexical decision. For example, the auditory prime *bug* was presented in a biasing sentence, *The man was not surprised when he found several spiders, roaches, and other* bugs. The lexical decision followed immediately for *ant* or *spy*, each related to one sense of *bug*, or a control word. The result was a priming effect for both related words, compared with the control, even though context should have biased only one word, *ant* in this case. Thus, we have a case in which a contextually based expectation cannot penetrate lexical processing. There is the basic lexical priming effect but no effect based on what the word means in context. After a longer interval, however, the priming is selective, only *ant* and not *spy* showing an effect. Such a result suggests a two-process account of semantic encoding, a preliminary short-lived stage in which all the multiple meanings represented by a word are activated and a second slower stage in which the contextually appropriate meaning is selected. The first stage is impenetrable; the second is penetrable.

There is an important additional result from Swinney's paradigm for impenetrability. Kintsch and Mross (1985) replicated the Swinney experiment but in addition included a condition of "thematic" priming. Thematic primes derive from the model of the text presumably being constructed by the reader. For example, in a text about a man who is in danger of missing a very important plane, the word *gate* would be presented for lexical decision (at the asterisks) as the subject heard this sentence: . . . *so he hurried down to his plane* ***. The result was no priming effect, presumably because there were no local associations between *plane* and *gate*. By contrast, a lexical decision on *fly* was facilitated because of its strong association with plane. This result supports the hypothesis that thematic knowledge from a text does not penetrate word recognition, specifically meaning activation.

### Sentence parsing

The second component of comprehension that may show relative impenetrability is sentence parsing. Although we think that sentence parsing is properly understood as a process that operates on a specialized linguistic vocabulary and thus lends itself to strong claims about syntactic modules, we again think that a weaker assumption is sufficient for our argument. We assume that an early stage of comprehension involves a preliminary attachment of words and phrases to other words and phrases. The process by which these attachments are made is parsing. The output of parsing is the basis for a semantic analysis of the sentence, and, in particular, it is preliminary to the propositional representation of sentences.

When a reader or listener encounters *The beer is in the refrigerator next to the milk*, the parsing process readily attaches the phrase *next to the milk* to *beer* rather than to *refrigerator*. However, an attachment to *refrigerator* is possible, and in a context in which there are two refrigerators this attachment is readily made. However, it appears that attaching the final prepositional phrase to the immediately preceding noun phrase is not the preferred strategy. It requires an intermediate noun phrase node to be constructed "above" the noun phrase node that represents *by the refrigerator*, in violation of what Frazier (1979; Frazier & Rayner, 1982) calls the minimal attachment strategy. Attaching *next to the milk* to *the beer* is a minimal attachment with no higher syntactic node being required.

Of course, what is interesting about minimal attachment, or any other syntactically defined parsing principle, is exactly its lack of reference to nonsyntactic information. In the refrigerator example, however, semantics and pragmatics add their weight to the minimal attachment reading. In a sentence such as *The beer is in the refrigerator next to the wall*, the influence of semantics is in the opposite direction. Minimal attachment prefers the same attachment as before, *next to the wall* with *beer*, but clearly this interpretation is not working as well here as the alternative attachment – *next to the wall* with *refrigerator*. However, there is evidence that the preference for the minimal attachment is strong enough that readers take longer to read a sentence that requires the nonminimal attachment (Frazier & Rayner, 1982). Furthermore, even when story contexts encourage the nonminimal reading, the preferred reading may still be the minimal attachment reading, at least for some sentence types (Ferreira & Clifton, in press).

The basis for syntactic preferences is a matter not easily resolved. They may reflect constraints on syntactic tree building that in turn reflect psychological processing principles (e.g., minimal attachment), or they may reflect knowledge about environments associated with lexical items, especially verbs (Ford, Bresnan, & Kaplan, 1982). For our argument, the ultimate source of parsing principles is not critical, except that it cannot lie primarily in a general knowledge component. Parsing principles reflect linguistic knowledge that is *essentially* (as opposed to "under all conditions") independent of general knowledge. Most important is the possibility, now demonstrated for at least some sentence construction, that these principles are not overridden by knowledge, context, and expectations (Ferreira & Clifton, in press; Frazier & Rayner, 1982). That is, they are impenetrable.

## Summary

In this section, we have argued that reading is a restricted-general ability. Two related arguments make the case for this claim. One is that meaning comprehension and interpretation are not the same. Meaning comprehension is driven by the text in accord with constrained principles of symbol meaning and syntax. Interpretation is unconstrained and *inference rich*. The effects of knowledge are largely on interpretation through such processes as particularization and inference building. Meaning comprehension is relatively free of knowledge influences.

The second argument is that some comprehension processes, at least some that comprise meaning comprehension, can acquire impenetrability. Such processes can be thought of as modular, but their significant feature is their resistance to knowledge penetration. They are rapidly executing and computationally autonomous. Both lexical access and sentence parsing are candidates for impenetrable modular processes. Word identification becomes impenetrable with increasing reading skill, and parsing seems to follow structural principles. The implication of this argument is that skilled reading is a general ability free of specific knowledge influences in the processes of (1) word identification and (2) syntactic parsing.

These are early-occurring processes on which depends the assembly of propositions from sentences. Thus, there are grounds for identifying general reading ability with the linguistic processes that make possible the encoding of propositions.

### *Implications for research on reading ability*

The argument that reading is in large part a restricted-general linguistic process has implications for theories and research in reading ability. Most important is that ability in reading depends on linguistically based processes that support word identification, parsing, and proposition encoding. It depends less on abilities to apply special knowledge, draw inferences, make elaborations, and apply interpretative schemata to the outcome of meaning comprehension. The latter processes are important for the reader's construction of an interpreted representation, that is, a situational model or, more generally, a mental model (Johnson-Laird, 1984). However, they are peripheral abilities in two ways, according to our argument. First, those inferential processes that are necessary to maintain coherence are often triggered automatically for skilled readers by local text features in mundane texts. Second, for difficult texts, such processes are qualitatively peripheral, in that conscious problem-solving procedures must be applied. Again, we see no reason yet to identify reading with problem solving or thinking.

This is not an entirely definitional matter. Suppose that in an idealized experiment free of all measurement and sampling error, we can identify a group of low-ability comprehenders as defined by poor performance in answering inference questions based on their reading. To explain this inference-making "deficit" there appear to be these four theoretically interesting possibilities: (1) specific knowledge deficits, (2) no specific knowledge deficits but a systematic failure to apply knowledge to text reading, (3) an unspecified inability to make inferences in texts, and (4) a reduced ability to encode propositions.

The strong form of the knowledge hypothesis predicts (1). It might also predict that further testing of subjects changes their ability classification as different knowledge requirements are encountered. However, it is not falsified by the finding that repeated measures over variable knowledge domains does not change classification. Individuals obviously can differ in total knowledge across many domains. A weak form of the knowledge hypothesis would predict (2), that knowledge use, not knowledge itself, is decisive. A general strategy hypothesis would predict (3), but in fact, (2) and (3) would be very difficult to distinguish. Both depend on demonstrating the availability of knowledge and its nonuse during reading. Alternative (4) is consistent with the restricted-general model of reading ability, but this outcome is not predicted by it without an additional assumption concerning processing efficiency. With the addition of such an assumption, alternative (4) predicts that *observed* difficulties in inferential comprehension arise in unobserved difficulties in meaning comprehension (i.e., proposition encoding).

Naturally, a real experiment is likely to produce complicating results. Many readers of low ability can be expected to show deficits in knowledge, inference making, and meaning comprehension. Such interskill correlations are so common that determining causal directions in abilities has been very difficult. In fact, no hypothesis has to claim that it accounts for all higher-level comprehension variance, but to be taken as central, rather than peripheral, in the theory of reading ability it must account for a large share. That is, in principle, the inference-deficit model of ability must predict many cases of poor inference performance in the absence of basic meaning comprehension deficits. The restricted-general model must make just the opposite prediction.

In fact, little actual research can provide adequate tests of these alternatives, despite the considerable amount of informative research on reading. Studies that have shown low-ability readers to have inference problems have not adequately assessed their basic meaning comprehension abilities, including word identification. Similarly, studies that have shown links between basic processes and reading ability have not assessed knowledge-related and inference factors. Of course, it is difficult to functionally separate meaning and inferences sufficiently for testing, even though we have argued for a clear conceptual separation. (It is not impossible, however, to achieve functional separation.)

Although decisive studies are lacking, there are some suggestive ones. For example, Oakhill (1982) identified groups of 7- and 8-year-old children who were equivalent on word identification accuracy but unequal on a test of comprehension.[1] In a subsequent test they were presented spoken three-sentence "stories" and were then given a recognition memory test. The key data were false recognition responses to inferences based on a plausible interpretation of the "story." Although both groups made more false recognitions to plausible inferences than to implausible ones, this difference was greater for skilled comprehenders. However, skilled comprehenders also showed a nonsignificant advantage over less skilled comprehenders in recognition of actually occurring sentences. Thus, although it is tempting to interpret these results as singling out inference making as the key problem for low-skill comprehension, they do not strongly rule out the hypothesis that skilled readers establish a more accurate meaning representation from which to make inferences. It is our conclusion that other studies of inference and elaboration have also largely failed to separate these factors.

Of course, research on children's reading ability has shown a pervasive association between comprehension and lower-level linguistic processing (Perfetti, 1985). Of the many factors that have distinguished high- and low-comprehension groups, the most pervasive in our research (summarized in Perfetti, 1985) have been the following. Compared with less skilled readers, skilled readers show (1) word identification processes that are more accurate and more rapid, less affected by stimulus variables (e.g., word frequency and lexicality), and less affected by discourse context; (2) a greater working memory capacity, as assessed in linguistic memory tasks in both spoken and written forms; and (3) shorter times to understand simple one-proposition sentences.

Thus, in this picture, the skilled reader is characterized by rapidly executing context-free word identification processes and an effective linguistic memory that enables sentence comprehension. It is possible that a richer characterization is needed, specifically one that adds an ability to use knowledge or inference making to turn a meaning representation into an interpreted representation. However, although such factors are clearly important for a theory of interpretation, their centrality in a theory of reading ability is less certain at the moment.

Finally, on the specific question of the role of knowledge in reading ability, we refer to some results of an ongoing study of fourth- through seventh-grade children. Although tentative, they strongly suggest an important but limited role of knowledge in children's reading of knowledge-demanding texts. Subjects are assessed for domain-specific knowledge in football and for general reading comprehension ability, producing four groups defined by the four combinations of high and low knowledge and high and low reading ability. (Low-knowledge subjects can be characterized as having very little knowledge of the goal structure and rules of football.) The subjects read football and nonfootball texts and are given a test of speeded word identification.

According to the restricted-general model of reading ability, we expect to find that a skilled reader can attain some comprehension of a knowledge-demanding text even when he or she lacks much knowledge. Of course, to the extent that specific knowledge is required for text interpretation, we should find, as other studies have, that high-knowledge subjects comprehend more of the text than low-knowledge subjects. The results so far are fully consistent with these predictions. High-knowledge subjects show better comprehension but only for a football text. High-ability readers outperform low-ability readers for both texts at both levels of knowledge.

These, of course, are very superficial results. We need to know much more about *what* low-knowledge, high-skill readers are comprehending in a knowledge-demanding text and how this differs from what both high-knowledge subjects and low-skill subjects are comprehending. Can we see more evidence of a meaning representation in the high-skill, low-knowledge subjects and more evidence of an interpreted representation in high-knowledge subjects? There are related questions concerning control of processing times. For example, does a knowledge-demanding text change the reading rate of subjects lacking knowledge? If research similar to the study described here can provide some answers to these questions, the claim that there are restricted but generalized reading abilities can be given a serious test.

### Linguistic and nonlinguistic sources of writing skill

We think that the same issues of language competence present in reading are also present in writing. The processes of reading and writing are different in important ways, and writing is not simply the inverse of reading. However, to the extent that general language competence is in fact *general* and to the extent that it involves the processes we suggest here, we should observe those processes in writing.

### Meaning and interpretation

The distinction between intention and meaning is again important, although because of the nature of writing, important in different ways. We stated that comprehension requires both meaning and interpretation, and the reader's goal is one of constructing an interpretation from meaning. The writer's goal, however, is to guide the reader to some particular interpretation through the meaning of specific text. As we have argued, there are factors beyond the text that affect readers' interpretations, an important one being the reader's prior knowledge. The knowledge that a given reader brings to bear on a text, however, is largely beyond the control of the writer of that text. The writer has direct control only of the text meaning; he or she has only a probabilistic indirect influence on interpretation.

Nevertheless, the skilled writer uses meaning to influence interpretation as much as possible. From this perspective, the writing of texts such as those in the Bransford and the Anderson experiments, because of ambiguities or underspecified reference, did not use meaning to constrain (or even establish) their interpretations. This situation is not entirely unfamiliar to teachers of writing who, during conferences with students, frequently hear detailed explanations of "What I meant there," explanations that often have little to do with what actually appears in the students' compositions. Writing well entails controlling meaning and, only through that, interpretation.

In order to control meaning, however, the writer must first deal with his or her own "semantic intention," the writer's counterpart to the reader's interpretation. That is, the writer's intention derives from the writer's idiosyncratic experiences, knowledge, point of view, and so on, and it is the writer's task to forge that often unwieldy mix of purpose and message into a text – a text with a meaning that is both relatively unambiguous (if not precise) and independent of personal context (if not universally comprehensible). Thus, the writer must be concerned with two levels of interpretation, his or her own intention and the reader's interpretation, as well as with the text's meaning, which mediates the two.

This mediation is far from perfect, however, because of the idiosyncratic nature of intention and interpretation. Rather than the pristine "transformer" metaphor popular in communication theory, which involves sender, message, and receiver, we have something more like the following:

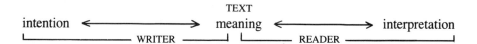

The writer's personal knowledge and purpose interact with a text during its creation, affecting the text's developing meaning and, in turn, being affected by it. The situation is similar for the reader, as the Anderson and Bransford experiments demonstrate. For there to be much correspondence at all between the writer's intention and the reader's interpretation, the text's meaning must be clear and well articulated.

### Turning intention into meaning

Research on the development of writing skill indicates that less skilled writers often fail to make the distinction between intention and meaning. Rather than focusing on their text's meaning, some writers remain locked within their own intention. Flower (1979) describes such writing as "writer-based" in contrast to "reader-based." In reader-based prose, meaning is clearly specified: concepts are well articulated, referents are unambiguous, and relations among concepts are presented within some logical organization. The result is an autonomous text (Olson, 1977) that adequately imparts its meaning to the reader without relying on unstated knowledge or external context. In contrast, writer-based prose is full of idiosyncratic phrases that are loaded with semantic content for the writer – meaning that is not, however, articulated for the reader. Textual referents are often ambiguous or even completely lacking, as the writer works from a position of privileged knowledge not shared with the reader. Furthermore, the overall text organization is often idiosyncratic, reflecting the writer's associative path of discovery rather than an organization that aids the reader's interpretation. Flower (1979) points out that writer-based prose is often produced by accomplished writers in early drafts. Skilled writers, however, rework those early drafts, expanding compressed meaning and supplying an organization that will be clear to the reader.

Flower's (1979) descriptions pertain to less skilled college-age writers, but similar descriptions also apply to children's early writing. Bartlett (1982) found that younger children are often incapable of resolving pronominal ambiguity in their own writing, although they are somewhat better at doing it in the writing of others. Again the explanation seems to involve the writer's privileged knowledge, that is, the writer's intentions that never get expanded into meaning in the text. When forced to become an external reader who is no longer immersed in underlying intention, a child can better see the limitations of a text's meaning.

That the problem is one of *linguistic specification* rather than one of *cognitive recognition* of potential ambiguity was made clear by a study of children's use of referential devices in narratives (Bartlett & Scribner, 1981). In narrative contexts in which there were multiple characters of the same sex and same age (i.e., contexts in which references to *the man* or *the girl* would lead to ambiguities), children tended to use a wider variety of referring expressions. They may not have been successful in consistently avoiding referential ambiguity, but they did seem aware of potential difficulties. Thus, it is not the case that children's representations (i.e., interpretations) are somehow faulty or underspecified. Rather, children fail to turn their *private* interpretations into adequate *public* meaning.

Young children's texts also typically reflect the child's own discovery process, with little reorganization to make the ideas coherent for the reader. Scardamalia and Bereiter (1982) describe how this "knowledge-telling" strategy reduces the cognitive load of text production. Children interpret the writing task as a request to indicate what they know about the topic, and they comply with that request by giving their private intention, not by creating a text with its own public meaning. Children's texts typically contain information in exactly the form and order it was retrieved from memory. Even with explicit tutoring in prewriting planning behaviors, children younger than 12 often generate actual sentences while "planning" and then simply recopy them verbatim while "writing" (Burtis, Bereiter, Scardamalia, & Tetroe, 1983).

Thus, for many young children writing is a "first come, first served" serial process of information retrieval. Little editing is done to change the form of the final text from the form of the retrieved information. The National Assessment of Educational Progress (1977) showed that 40% of the 9-year-olds tested, 22% of the 13-year-olds, and 32% of the 17-year-olds made no revisions after their first drafts were completed. As Nold (1981) points out, the NAEP did not assess whether any editing had taken place during the generation of the first draft, but this criticism seems relevant only for the older writers. Among the children we have observed up to the age of 14, relatively little on-line editing occurs routinely.

For example, we (McCutchen & Perfetti, 1982) found that the writing of children in second and fourth grade directly reflected memory search processes rather than text-constrained processes. The writing of these children was simulated by a model that had direct memory readout as the main process in writing. Increasing text constraints began to emerge in the model of older children's writing (but even there to only a limited extent).

This description of writing as controlling the interpretation of the reader through the meaning of the text is, of course, derived from an adult perspective of literacy. Just as skilled writers may produce "writer-based" first drafts with no intention of passing them on to readers, young children may also write with no expectation of a reader. In both cases – the first draft of a skilled writer and the idiosyncratic writings of a young child – the main objective may be to explore one's private interpretations. The skilled writer, having completed this self-discovery process, then goes on to reformat the text for presentation to the public. The young child, however, may have no such goal. Especially for children just learning to write (ages 5 to 7, or even younger), writing may not be the communicative act we describe here. Rather, writing for the young child may simply be another form of symbolic play, much like drawing and make-believe, the purpose of which lies more in the *process* than in the *product* (Gundlach, 1981; Read, 1981; Vygotsky, 1978). Evaluative statements by children around age 7 typically concern their own affective responses to texts' topics (i.e., their own *interpretation* of the texts), and only later do children's comments come to reflect such aspects of the texts as coherence and creativity (Hilgers, 1984).

Perhaps, then, children's earliest writing should not be evaluated in the way we describe here. However, just as invented spellings of precocious children gradually come to conform to standard English spellings (Bissex, 1980; Read, 1981), children's written texts (especially those produced in school) are eventually required to be more than private symbolic play. Writing is eventually required to be a communicative act between writer and reader, and children generally come to realize that fact, as early writing behaviors such as drawing and talking aloud are replaced by more adult-like writing behaviors such as rereading and silent transcription (Cioffi, 1984). It is this aspect of writing – writing as schooled language competence – that we are addressing here. However, this early function of writing as symbolic play might help to explain why some writers find it so difficult to move from private interpretation to public meaning.

### *Restricted-general linguistic processes in writing*

We have argued that the writer's goal is to create meaning from his or her own intention. In the same way that the reader's knowledge can affect the reader's interpretation of a text (Anderson, Spiro, & Anderson, 1978; Bransford & Johnson, 1973; Spilich et al., 1979), the writer's knowledge affects the writer's intention and thus the text itself. However, just as there are general reading processes that seem impenetrable to knowledge and expectations, such as word recognition processes and syntactic parsing processes, there also seem to be generalizable writing skills that are independent of domain-specific knowledge.

McCutchen (1986) showed that developmental differences observed in children's writing skill were not solely attributable to differences in domain-specific knowledge. Groups of children high and low in knowledge of football were studied, with subject pairs matched on reading ability and equally distributed across grades 4, 6, and 8. (Football was chosen as a knowledge topic since it is a recreational interest that, as such, seems not to be correlated with school performance.) Although there was an effect of knowledge of topic in that study such that children generated more coherent texts when they were knowledgeable in the topic, this effect did not eliminate developmental differences. Even with knowledge controlled, older children generated more coherent texts than did younger children, thus demonstrating a role for general language competence independent of domain-specific knowledge. Furthermore, older children's ability to write more coherently reflected those areas of language competence we assume are most affected by schooling: (1) vocabulary size and semantic precision and (2) syntactic repertory. Older children more often linked their sentences into a coherent discourse using linguistic devices such as semantically related lexical items and subordinate clauses, and they did their best to articulate their arguments, even when their lack of detailed knowledge forced them to argue in generalities, citing, for example, famous players or team spirit as reasons a given team would win the championship. Younger children who had a large amount of relevant knowledge often offered more penetrating analyses of a team's strengths and weaknesses (e.g., a quarterback's passing ability, an offense's running game), but their texts still reflected a "knowledge-telling" approach to writing, with simple lists of reasons and no substantiation of their arguments.

There are two points to be made about these observations. First, and most obvious, is that domain knowledge is not sufficient for coherent writing. Second, domain knowledge, beyond some minimum, may not be necessary. Of course, it presumably is necessary for informed, interesting, and well-argued writing. However, the ability to use language competence to bootstrap discourse processes, even in the absence of a high level of domain knowledge, is the essence of schooled language competence.

Certainly, linguistic knowledge and procedures require semantic content on which to operate, and the richness of the underlying knowledge base has important implications for the quality of the resulting text. What is expressed in the text comes ultimately from the knowledge base of the writer. Let us assume, for convenience, that the knowledge representation can be described by a semantic network. When the network contains a large number of differentiated concept nodes and a richly elaborated network of relational ties among them, the writer has an excellent source of semantic "raw material" to turn into a discourse. A writer who lacks knowledge of a given topic must work from an impoverished knowledge base containing few concept nodes and a sparse network of relational links among them. Thus, the writer low in relevant topic knowledge must work harder to create a coherent discourse, making inferences and indirect memory searches through a sparse and disjoint knowledge base. By contrast, the writer high in topic knowledge can, to a large extent, simply *retrieve* coherent information structures from memory.

Even for the high-knowledge writer, however, coherent information retrieved from memory does not necessarily guarantee a coherently related discourse. The transformation of semantic information into language is a nontrivial cognitive task. Sets of propositions do not comprise a text. Those propositions must be specified *in language*, that is, specified by particular words within particular syntactic arrangements, and empirical evidence demonstrates that considerable planning time is required during speech production which corresponds to manipulating propositions and turning them into syntactic units (Ford & Holmes, 1978). Thus, even after semantic information is retrieved from memory, the speaker or writer is still faced with the task of coordinating semantic propositions within appropriate syntactic sentence frames and then, within an extended discourse, coordinating those sentences within appropriate discourse frames.

### Components of generalized writing competence

Earlier we defined writing competence as productive control over the grammatical devices of language in the service of some communicative intent. What sorts of knowledge comprise writing competence under this definition? Likely candidates seem to be (1) discourse schema knowledge, (2) lexical knowledge, and (3) syntactic knowledge and procedures, all of which interact. The first seems most relevant to clarifying the writer's communicative intent, whereas the remaining two constitute productive control over the symbol systems of language.

Discourse schema knowledge, which has been the focus of considerable research (Meyer, 1975; Stein & Glenn, 1979; Stein & Trabasso, 1981), is the knowledge of discourse forms. Although it is possible to think of some discourse schemata, story grammars, for example, as derivative from nontextual, event-world knowledge, our assumption is that they must include linguistic and textual information. They include knowledge of the general structure and ordering of information within a given discourse, the typical qualitative nature of that information, and the kinds of linguistic ties that link that information into a coherent discourse. Knowledge of a general narrative schema, for example, specifies that events revolving around one or more main characters be temporally and causally linked, typically with linguistic connections such as *then* and *so*, although inferences based on real-world event knowledge often permit the omission of explicit links (McCutchen, 1985). There are substantial data suggesting that even relatively young children have at least rudimentary narrative schemata (Brown, 1976; Brown & Smiley, 1977; Stein & Glenn, 1979). Expository texts, however, have a very different structure built on the presentation of a main point followed by explanation, description, or argumentation in support of that main point. Rather than temporal-causal relations among events, expository texts require logical-causal relations among arguments, which often take such linguistic forms as *but*, *also*, *because*, or *since* (McCutchen, 1985). Though not typically appearing as early as narratives, expository (and other nonnarrative) schemata do seem to develop eventually (Bereiter & Scardamalia, 1981; Freedle & Hale, 1979; Meyer, 1975; Waters, 1980).

A second source of linguistic knowledge important in the writing process is lexical – the knowledge of words, including their meanings, their form class, and their orthographic, phonemic, and morphemic structure. Some of this knowledge, such as orthographic knowledge (i.e., spelling), may be rather explicit, whereas knowledge of form class or morphological derivation may be more implicit – less available for articulation but available for use at a functional level in sentence generation. A writer may, for example, nominalize a verb from an earlier sentence in order to maintain textual coherence. Or, as in the case of a young person we studied, a writer could move from a discussion of being the "hero" of the football game to his next point with the phrase *Besides glory*. The semantic relatedness of *hero* and *glory* permitted the writer to make this rather sophisticated transition, freeing him from more mundane coherence devices such as verbatim repetition.

Also available as part of general linguistic knowledge, often implicitly, is knowledge of syntactic constructions and procedures for coordinating those constructions during sentence generation. This syntactic knowledge is more than the knowledge of grammar that underlies basic language competence, more, that is, than the tacit knowledge of all possible permissible linguistic strings. It is knowledge of the strings that are locally appropriate within the developing discourse. By *locally appropriate* we mean a fairly restricted region of text development that influences the syntactic form of a given sentence. Locally appropriate syntactic knowledge and flexibility enable a writer to construct sentences that, for example, honor the given–new constraint (see Clark & Haviland, 1977). Furthermore, together with adequate lexical knowledge, syntactic flexibility permits the coordination of multiple concepts within a single sentence, for example, highlighting some concepts in main clauses as others are relegated to subsidiary or explanatory roles within subordinate clauses. Such coordination of multiple concepts is especially crucial in discourse production, where the main thread of the developing discourse may be carried along in main clauses whereas subordinate clauses often serve to maintain coherence – clarifying or affirming presuppositions, specifying relations, and the like.

The relation among these three types of linguistic knowledge is not specifiable in detail, but they probably contribute to actual writing performance through fairly complex interactions. Discourse schema knowledge specifies the general nature of the discourse and the types of relations typically required to maintain discourse coherence. Lexical and syntactic knowledge enable one to manipulate words and phrases to honor the discourse requirements of the schema. The interplay among these knowledge sources – recognizing discourse requirements and having the linguistic competence to fulfill those requirements – is a large component of the schooled language competence underlying writing skill.

### Impenetrability revisited

In our discussion of reading we suggested that reading skill entails the acquisition of rapidly executing linguistic processes, specifically word identification and syntactic parsing, processes that are largely impenetrable to external (i.e., nonlinguistic) knowledge, expectations, or beliefs. Skilled reading thus involves linguistic processes that operate independently of an executive processor, although executive control may be required during high-level text processing, such as repair of text, comprehension failures, and monitoring of reading rate.

Such an executive processor, however, has a much larger role in writing. The fact that sentence production is both slower and less automatic than sentence parsing is a clear indication of this. Moreover, studies of on-line writing behaviors (Flower & Hayes, 1980, 1981, 1984; Hayes & Flower, 1980; McCutchen, 1984) reveal the multiple sources of information that skilled writers continually consult: information in the writing assignment itself, information about the topic from long-term memory, information about the perceived audience, information about the writer's goals and how to achieve them (e.g., being clear, being interesting, being humorous), and information from the text as it develops (e.g., what points have and have not been made, what words or syntactic constructions have been used so far).

The main point to be made about this work is that the writing process is cyclic and interactive. Skilled writing is not the serial operation of autonomous sentence generation procedures, but a process of sentence generation continually interrupted by editing and planning procedures, which in turn are interrupted by generation procedures. Skilled writing necessitates breaking out of serial "knowledge-telling" processing (Scardamalia & Bereiter, 1982) and replacing it with more flexible processing that moves from the writer's knowledge base, to the developing text, to the potential reader's interpretation of the text, and back again. Moreover, the syntactic processes that may be relatively impenetrable in comprehension are very penetrable in the much slower process of producing a sentence under multiple discourse constraints. An executive processor, in a sense, has to have access to the information that is otherwise concealed in the syntactic module.

Thus, a critical difference between reading and writing is the importance of executive control during writing and, in particular, the growing control of executive processes over general language skills. During both reading and writing, however, these language skills have to be up to the demands placed on them. Both reading and writing require efficient manipulation of the symbol structures that comprise language, at the word level as well as at the syntactic level. During reading, word meanings must be rapidly retrieved in response to orthographic strings and their contextually appropriate meanings encoded. Sentences must be parsed and semantic roles assigned. During writing, semantic intentions must prompt retrieval of appropriate syntax and lexical items, often several since text constraints can make some wordings more appropriate than others.[2] The difference between reading and writing, however, is that to a large extent the text dictates the reader's options, and thus control strategies play a lesser role. The writer is not so constrained, and control processes gain importance. Extending these descriptions, we might characterize developmental and individual differences in writing skill in terms of the adequacy of general linguistic skills and their amenability to executive control.

Using a serial, knowledge-telling strategy, young children make few executive decisions about how ideas are arranged in their texts or how sentences are syntactically constructed. Information is retrieved from memory and apparently clothed in the first linguistic expression that comes to mind. As we described earlier, young children are often satisfied with writing down their own idiosyncratic intention. They do not attempt to create explicit meaning in their texts apart from that privileged knowledge, and they make few demands on language competence. They write relatively simple sentences and, as a result, often produce relatively incoherent texts (McCutchen, in press; McCutchen & Perfetti, 1982). It does not seem that language competence itself is lacking, since young children often use more complex syntactic constructions in their speech than they do in their writing (Loban, 1976; O'Donnell, Griffin, & Norris, 1967). Rather, children seem not to shape their written sentences in response to the multiple discourse demands heeded by skilled writers (e.g., audience, tone, clarity, textual constraints). Thus, the language skills of many children have not come under the executive control that writing requires. For such writers, linguistic procedures remain relatively impenetrable.

In the normal development of writing skill this situation seems to change. With age, and especially with schooling, most children become better able to shape their language to the discourse requirements of their texts, and they write more coherent texts as a result. In fact, older children come to use more complex syntax in their writing than in their speech (Loban, 1976; O'Donnell et al., 1967).

However, attention to the discourse demands of written texts is not all there is to writing skill. As the writer allows such factors as clarity, audience, tone, and coherence to affect his or her linguistic choices, the language required to address simultaneously all those factors can become increasingly complex. For example, the writer might want to interject a comment that will amuse but not sidetrack the reader from the main point. This might require some sort of subordination, a parenthetical phrase, or some other complex syntactic construction. Once the need for syntactic complexity is recognized, an extended linguistic competence must be there to meet that need. This extended linguistic competence, as opposed to basic linguistic competence, is far from universally acquired.

There are many adolescents and young adults who have not mastered the syntax they need to coordinate the complexity they wish to express. They can be found across the country in remedial writing classes, and they have syntactic problems unlike those of younger children. Rather than ignore the complex discourse demands in written language, these writers "mismanage" that complexity (Shaughnessy, 1977). That these writers are different from *young* immature writers is a point worth emphasizing. Younger writers may occasionally omit a word, but they rarely garble syntax. Young writers seem not to tax their syntactic competence because, we suggest, their sense of discourse never demands it of them. It is not until writers reach a certain level of maturity that they even attempt to express many ideas (e.g., more than five distinct propositions) within a single sentence. It is that complexity, and the sophisticated syntax that it requires, that proves so problematic for many older writers.

One eighth-grade writer we have studied shows some recognition of the complex discourse demands in written language, and it is his attempt to address that complexity, without adequate control over the requisite syntax, that seems the source of his problem. Consider one of his sentences:

> *It was late in the fourth quarter with 50 seconds left on the clock with the steelers quarterback Terry, who throw a long pass in which John had cot and scored a touchdown and game went into overtime with the score 7 to 7.*

The writer has at least eight propositions he is trying to coordinate: (1) It was late in the game; (2) 50 seconds remained; (3) Terry threw a pass; (4) Terry was the Steeler quarterback; (5) John caught the pass; (6) John scored a touchdown; (7) the score was tied at 7; and (8) the game went into overtime. With some work, all eight propositions can be combined into a single sentence: *It was late in the game, with only 50 seconds remaining, when Steeler quarterback Terry threw a pass, which John caught and took in for a touchdown, tying the score at 7 and sending the game into overtime.* There are, of course, other possible phrasings, but all require rather sophisticated clausal subordination. Such sophistication is beyond this writer, but his attempt is revealing. He does not write several short sentences, as a much younger writer would. He seems to have an impressionistic sense of what formal written English is like, but he does not have mastery of the linguistic structures that give written language its peculiar form. This writer attempts to respond to the discourse demands of written language, but he does not have productive control over the grammatical devices that would express his intent.

### *Reading, writing, and language competence*

We have argued here that general language competence underlies both reading and writing skills, and we have tried to distinguish this schooled language competence from more basic communicative language skills. We have suggested that schooled language competence builds on more basic language competence and, like basic competence, depends at its core on linguistic symbol manipulation. Schooling, however, extends both the linguistic options open to children (increasing their vocabulary and syntactic repertoire) and the linguistic demands placed on them. With each year in school, children are increasingly required to acquire information through reading and demonstrate their learning through writing (although the second perhaps too infrequently). These forms of linguistic interactions, stripped of much of the contextual information inherent in conversational interactions, require different competence from the child – competence based more on language and less on real world knowledge.

Furthermore, we suggest that reading and writing do not have only shared features, and for this reason, we might expect some disassociation between reading skill and writing skill. Whereas skilled reading entails increasing encapsulation and automaticity of linguistic subskills (Perfetti, 1985), skilled writing requires that language processes become increasingly open to external discourse demands, for example, purpose and audience in a given text. Reading requires that linguistic procedures fire smoothly and rapidly, accessing a particular meaning when confronted with a given grapheme string or computing a particular syntactic parse when confronted with a given clause arrangement. Alternative words or phrasings are irrelevant, since reading requires recovering a meaning and an interpretation from the specific words and phrases present in the text being read. Consideration of such alternatives, however, is part of writing skill, since some choices are more appropriate than others within a given discourse.

A person could be skilled at reading and *not* at writing for several reasons. First, one might not subject discourse production procedures to executive control – an executive that is largely unnecessary for skilled comprehension, we have argued. Although active strategy use has been successfully applied as a remedial technique to improve *poor* comprehension skills, *skilled* reading is a more passive cognitive activity than writing, since a by-product of skill in reading is increased automaticity of many processes. Second, one might be able to derive meaning from lexical and syntactic forms without having enough control over those forms to generate them. Such asymmetries between comprehension and production are not uncommon in language learning.

What seems somewhat surprising is the apparent rarity of severe disassociation between reading and writing skill. In a correlational analysis of McCutchen's (1986) data, the overall correlation between reading ability and writing skill was .50 for all grades combined (as measured by the Spearman rank-order correlation coefficient), and as might be expected, the correlations were higher when each grade was analyzed separately: .65 for fourth graders, .62 for sixth graders, and .78 for eighth graders. The measure of reading ability was percentile rank on the reading subsection of the California Achievement Test, and the measure of writing ability was an index of coherence in the children's texts (see McCutchen, in press, or McCutchen & Perfetti, 1982, for a description of the coherence analysis). Although our coherence analysis taps local features of discourse, it is probably correlated with more global evaluations of writing quality, if we may extrapolate the results of a study of college students' essays by Witte and Faigley (1981) using a similar coherence analysis. In their study, texts that were subjectively rated high contained more cohesive ties than did texts rated poor. Thus, if coherence, as an analytic index of writing skill, is associated with reading comprehension skill, it is likely that other less analytic indexes are also. Furthermore, other analytic measures also show reading and writing to be associated (Loban, 1976).

Such correlations lend support to our claims about general language competence underlying both reading and writing skills. It is especially interesting that the correlation in the McCutchen (1986) data was highest for the older children. By grade 8, children may have recognized the general discourse demands of text production, abandoning early knowledge-telling strategies in favor of more sophisticated executive strategies. If so, what remains to determine writing ability is the child's productive control of lexical and grammatical devices. We have argued that such linguistic processes also underlie reading ability. Thus, an increased correlation for older children could reflect the central role in both reading and writing of linguistic symbol manipulation that becomes more visible as basic strategies for writing are partly acquired. There are other possible explanations, however. We imagine that many would argue that the increased knowledge and inference demands of writing, on the one hand, and of comprehension tests, on the other, account for any increased correlations that might be observed.

It is obvious that there is much more to be learned about the relation between reading and writing. The view that inference-rich knowledge-driven processes form their most compelling link may be correct in some sense. Our purpose has been to provide a different perspective, one that allows the commonalities of reading and writing to be seen in the basic linguistic skills that they share and their differences to be seen in their vastly unequal reliance on other things.

### Conclusion

We have argued that a set of restricted-generalized abilities underlie both reading and writing. A major entailment of this argument is the rejection of knowledge-based and strategy-based approaches to language competence. The central features of schooled language competence arise from linguistic skill: a schooled extension of basic linguistic abilities. Prominent among these are skilled extensions of basic syntactic abilities and lexical knowledge.

Important to our argument is a principled distinction between meaning and interpretation. Comprehension implies achieving text representations that are richly interpreted. However, it equally implies a process of relatively uninterpreted representations on route to more richly interpreted texts. These meaning representations are achieved in part by comprehension processes (e.g., word identification and syntactic parsing) that have low penetrability. They are not readily influenced by knowledge and expectations when carried out skillfully and routinely. Reading ability is centrally the reflection of these processes and only peripherally the reflection of knowledge-dependent inferential processes.

Writing shares these features with reading. However, whereas the "passive" language processes are central in reading, writing calls much more on the active control of these processes. Although knowledge remains only peripheral in writing, language abilities must be considerably extended. Language processes come to be visible to an executive control process, losing much of their impenetrable flavor. They operate under more complex demands imposed by discourse requirements and multiple writing goals. Linguistic abilities retain their central importance; indeed, they must be better to meet these demands.

There are specific empirical consequences of our analysis, although for both reading and writing, existing research results are not decisive. We conclude, however, that recent research demonstrates a role for knowledge-free general abilities in both reading and writing.

### Notes

**1.** Such groups have been identified in other research, always, as far as we know, equating accuracy of word identification and not speed of identification. It is much better to assess the speed as an index of processing facility.

**2.** Note that the same processes occur in *speech* production (see Fromkin, 1973, 1980). Writing differs from speaking primarily in its higher standards for well-formedness and its expanded opportunities for planning and editing.

### References

Anderson, R. C., & Ortony, A. (1975). On putting apples into bottles: A problem of polysemy. *Cognitive Psychology, 7*, 167–80.

Anderson, R. C., Reynolds, R. E., Schallert, D. L., & Goetz, E. T. (1976). *Frameworks for comprehending discourse* (Tech. Rep. No. 12). Urbana: University of Illinois Laboratory for Cognitive Studies in Education.

Anderson, R. C., Spiro, R. J., & Anderson, M. C. (1978). Schemata as scaffolding for the representation of information in connected discourse. *American Educational Research Journal, 15*, 433–40.

Applebee, A. N. (1982). Writing and learning in school settings. In M. Nystrand (Ed.), *What writers know: The language, process, and structure of written discourse* (pp. 365–81). New York: Academic Press.

Bartlett, E. J. (1982). Learning to revise: Some component processes. In M. Nystrand (Ed.), *What writers know: The language, process, and structure of written discourse* (pp. 345–63). New York: Academic Press.

Bartlett, E. J., & Scribner, S. (1981). Text and context: An investigation of referential organization in children's written narratives. In C. H. Frederiksen & J. F. Dominic (Eds.), *Writing: The nature, development, and teaching of written language* (Vol. 2, pp. 153–68). Hillsdale, NJ: Erlbaum.

Bereiter, C., & Scardamalia, M. (1981). From conversation to composition: The role of instruction in a developmental process. In R. Glaser (Ed.), *Advances in instructional psychology* (Vol. 2, pp. 1–64). Hillsdale, NJ: Erlbaum.

Bissex, G. L. (1980). *Gyns at wrk: A child learns to read and write*. Cambridge, MA: Harvard University Press.

Bolinger, D. (1965). The atomization of meaning. *Language, 41* (Oct.–Dec.), 555–73.

Bransford, J. D., & Johnson, M. K. (1973). Considerations of some problems of comprehension. In W. G. Chase (Ed.), *Visual information processing* (pp. 383–438). New York: Academic Press.

Brown, A. L. (1976). The construction of temporal succession by preoperational children. In A. D. Pick (Ed.), *Minnesota Symposium on Child Psychology* (Vol. 10). Minneapolis: University of Minnesota.

Brown, A. L., & Smiley, S. S. (1977). Rating the importance of structural units of prose passages: A problem of metacognitive development. *Child Development*, *48*, 1–8.

Burtis, P. J., Bereiter, C., Scardamalia, M., & Tetroe, J. (1983). The development of planning in writing. In B. M. Kroll & G. Wells (Eds.), *Explorations in the development of writing* (pp. 153–74). New York: Wiley.

Chase, W. G., & Simon, H. A. (1973). The mind's eye in chess. In William G. Chase (Ed.), *Visual information processing* (pp. 215–81). New York: Academic Press.

Chi, M. T. H., Glaser, R., & Rees, E. (1982). Expertise in problem solving. In R. J. Sternberg (Ed.), *Advances in the psychology of human intelligence* (Vol. 1, pp. 7–76). Hillsdale, NJ: Erlbaum.

Cioffi, G. (1984). Observing composing behaviors of primary-age children: The interaction of oral and written language. In R. Beach & L. S. Bridwell (Eds.), *New directions in composition research* (pp. 171–90). New York: Guilford.

Clark, H. H., & Haviland, S. E. (1977). Comprehension and the given-new contract. In R. O. Freedle (Ed.), *Discourse production and comprehension* (pp. 1–40). Norwood, NJ: Ablex.

DeGroot, A. M. B. (1983). The range of automatic spreading activation in word priming. *Journal of Verbal Learning and Verbal Behavior*, *22*, 417–36.

Dooling, D. J., & Lachman, R. (1971). Effects of comprehension on retention of prose. *Journal of Experimental Psychology*, *88*, 216–22.

Ferreira, F., & Clifton, C., Jr. (in press). *The role of context in resolving syntactic ambiguity*. Amherst: University of Massachusetts.

Flower, L. (1979). Writer-based prose: A cognitive basis for problems in writing. *College English*, *41*, 19–37.

Flower, L. S., & Hayes, J. R. (1980). The dynamics of composing: Making plans and juggling constraints. In L. W. Gregg & E. R. Steinberg (Eds.), *Cognitive processes in writing* (pp. 31–50). Hillsdale, NJ: Erlbaum.

Flower, L., & Hayes, J. R. (1981). Plans that guide the composing process. In C. H. Frederiksen & J. F. Dominic (Eds.), *Writing: The nature, development, and teaching of written language* (Vol. 2, pp. 39–58). Hillsdale, NJ: Erlbaum.

Flower, L., & Hayes, J. R. (1984). Images, plans, and prose: The representation of meaning in writing. *Written Communication*, *1*, 120–60.

Fodor, J. D. (1983). *Parsing, constraints and the freedom of expression*. Montgomery, VT: Bradford Press.

Ford, M., Bresnan, J. W., & Kaplan, R. M. (1982). A competence-based theory of syntactic closure. In J. W. Bresnan (Ed.), *The mental representation of grammatical relations* (pp. 727–95). Cambridge, Mass.: MIT Press.

Ford, M., & Holmes, V. M. (1978). Planning units and syntax in sentence production. *Cognition*, *6*, 35–53.

Forster, K. I. (1979). Levels of processing and the structure of the language processor. In W. E. Cooper & E. C. T. Walker (Eds.), *Sentence processing: Psycholinguistic studies presented to Merrill Garrett* (pp. 27–85). Hillsdale, NJ: Erlbaum.

Fowler, C. A., Wolford, G., Slade, R., & Tassinary, L. (1981). Lexical access with and without awareness. *Journal of Experimental Psychology: General*, *110*, 341–62.

Frazier, L. (1979). *On comprehending sentences: Syntactic parsing strategies*. Unpublished doctoral dissertation. Bloomington: Indiana University.

Frazier, L., & Rayner, K. (1982). Making and correcting errors during sentence comprehension: Eye movements in the analysis of structurally ambiguous sentences. *Cognitive Psychology*, *14*, 178–210.

Freedle, R. O., & Hale, G. (1979). Acquisition of new comprehension schemata for expository prose by transfer of a narrative schema. In R. O. Freedle (Ed.), *New directions in discourse processing* (pp. 121–35). Norwood, NJ: Ablex.

Frege, G. (1952). Ueber Sinn und Bedeutung. *Zeitschrift fur Philosophie und philosophische Kritik*, vol. 100, pp. 25–50. Translated in P. T. Geach & M. Black (Eds.), *Philosophical writings of Gottlob Frege*. Oxford: Blackwell. (Original work published 1892.)

Fromkin, V. A. (Ed.) (1973). *Speech errors as linguistic evidence*. The Hague: Mouton.

Fromkin, V. A. (Ed.) (1980). *Errors in linguistic performance*. New York: Academic Press.

Gundlach, R. A. (1981). On the nature and development of children's writing. In C. H. Frederiksen & J. F. Dominic (Eds.), *Writing: The nature, development, and teaching of written language* (Vol. 2, pp. 133–52). Hillsdale, NJ: Erlbaum.

Hayes, J. R., & Flower, L. S. (1980). Identifying the organization of the writing process. In L. W. Gregg & E. R. Steinberg (Eds.), *Cognitive processes in writing* (pp. 3–30). Hillsdale, NJ: Erlbaum.

Hilgers, T. L. (1984). Toward a taxonomy of beginning writers' evaluative statements in written composition. *Written Communication*, *1*, 365–84.

Johnson-Laird, P. N. (1984). *Mental models*. Cambridge, MA: Harvard University Press.

Katz, J. J. (1966). *The philosophy of language*. New York: Harper & Row.

Katz, J. J., & Fodor, J. A. (1963). The structure of a semantic theory. *Language*, *39*, 170–210.

Kintsch, W. (1974). *The representation of meaning in memory*. Hillsdale, NJ: Erlbaum.

Kintsch, W. (1986, April). *General strategies for comprehension*. Talk presented at the American Educational Research Association Annual Meeting, San Francisco.

Kintsch, W., & Mross, F. (1985). Context effects in word identification. *Journal of Memory and Language*, *24*, 3.

Kintsch, W., & van Dijk, T. A. (1978). Toward a model of text comprehension and production. *Psychological Review*, *85*, 363–94.

Larkin, J. H., McDermott, J., Simon, D. P., & Simon, H. A. (1980). Expert and novice performance in solving physics problems. *Science*, *80*, 1335–42.

Loban, W. D. (1976). *Language development: Kindergarten through grade twelve* (Research Rep. No. 18). Urbana, IL: National Council of Teachers of English.

McCutchen, D. (1984). Writing as a linguistic problem. *Educational Psychologist*, *19*, 226–38.

McCutchen, D. (1985). *Children's discourse skill: Form and modality requirements of schooled writing*. Unpublished manuscript.

McCutchen, D. (1986). Domain knowledge and linguistic knowledge in the development of writing ability. *Journal of Memory and Language*, *25*, 431–44.

McCutchen, D., & Perfetti, C. A. (1982). Coherence and connectedness in the development of discourse production. *Text*, *2*, 113–39.

Meyer, B. (1975). *The organization of prose and its effect on memory*. Amsterdam: North Holland.

Morton, J. (1969). Interaction of information in word recognition. *Psychological Review*, *76*, 165–78.

National Assessment of Educational Progress (1981). *Three national assessments of reading: Changes in performance, 1970–80*. Denver, CO: NAEP.

Neely, J. H. (1977). Semantic priming and retrieval from lexical memory: The roles of inhibitionless spreading activation and limited-capacity attention. *Journal of Experimental Psychology: General*, *106*, 1–66.

Nold, E. W. (1981). Revising. In C. H. Frederiksen & J. F. Dominic (Eds.), *Writing: The nature, development, and teaching of written language* (Vol. 2, pp. 67–79). Hillsdale, NJ: Erlbaum.

Oakhill, J. (1982). Constructive processes in skilled and less skilled comprehenders' memory for sentences. *British Journal of Psychology*, *73*, 13–20.

O'Donnell, R., Griffin, W., & Norris, R. (1967). *Syntax of kindergarten and elementary school children: A transformational analysis* (Research Rep. No. 8). Champaign, IL: National Council of Teachers of English.

Olson, D. (1977). From utterance to text: The bias of language in speech and writing. *Harvard Educational Review*, *47*, 257–81.

Onifer, W., & Swinney, D. A. (1981). Accessing lexical ambiguities during sentence comprehension: Effects of frequency of meaning and contextual bias. *Memory & Cognition*, *9*(3), 225–36.

Palinscar, A. S., & Brown, A. L. (1984). Reciprocal teaching of comprehension-fostering and comprehension-monitoring activities. *Cognition and Instruction*, *1*(2), 117–75.

Perfetti, C. A. (1984). Reading acquisition and beyond: Decoding includes cognition. *American Journal of Education*, *93*, 40–60.

Perfetti, C. A. (1985). *Reading ability*. New York: Oxford University Press.

Perfetti, C. A. (in press). Language, speech, and print: Some asymmetries in the acquisition of literacy. In R. Horowitz & S. J. Samuels (Eds.), *Comprehending oral and written language*. New York: Academic Press.

Perfetti, C. A., Goldman, S. R., & Hogaboam, T. W. (1979). Reading skill and the identification of words in discourse context. *Memory and Cognition*, *7*, 273–82.

Perfetti, C. A., & Roth, S. F. (1981). Some of the interactive processes in reading and their role in reading skill. In A. M. Lesgold & C. A. Perfetti (Eds.), *Interactive processes in reading* (pp. 269–97). Hillsdale, NJ: Erlbaum.

Posner, M. I., & Snyder, C. R. (1975). Attention and cognitive control. In R. L. Solso (Ed.), *Information Processing and Cognition: The Loyola Symposium* (pp. 55–85). Hillsdale, NJ: Erlbaum.

Read, C. (1981). Writing is not the inverse of reading for young children. In C. H. Frederiksen & J. F. Dominic (Eds.), *Writing: The nature, development, and teaching of written language* (Vol. 2, pp. 105–18). Hillsdale, NJ: Erlbaum.

Rosch, E. (1973). On the internal structure of perceptual and semantic categories. In T. E. Moore (Ed.), *Cognitive development and the acquisition of language* (pp. 111–44). New York: Academic Press.

Ryan, E. B. (1982). Identifying and remediating failures in reading comprehension: Toward an instructional approach for poor comprehenders. In G. E. MacKinnon & T. G. Waller (Eds.), *Advances in reading research* (Vol. 3, pp. 223–61). New York: Academic Press.

Scardamalia, M., & Bereiter, C. (1982). Assimilative processes in composition planning. *Educational Psychologist*, *17*, 165–71.

Shaughnessy, M. (1977). *Errors and expectations: A guide for the teacher of basic writing*. New York: Oxford University Press.

Spilich, G. J., Vesonder, G. T., Chiesi, H. L., & Voss, J. F. (1979). Text-processing of domain-related information for individuals with high and low domain knowledge. *Journal of Verbal Learning and Verbal Behavior*, *18*, 275–90.

Stanovich, K. E., & West, R. F. (1981). The effect of sentence context on on-going word recognition: Tests of a two-process theory. *Journal of Experimental Psychology: Human Perception and Performance*, *7*, 658–72.

Stein, N. L., & Glenn, C. G. (1979). An analysis of story comprehension in elementary school children. In R. Freedle (Ed.), *Advances in discourse processing 2: New directions in discourse processing* (pp. 53–120). Norwood, NJ: Ablex.

Stein, N. L., & Trabasso, T. (1981). What's in a story: An approach to comprehension and instruction. In R. Glaser (Ed.), *Advances in instructional psychology* (Vol. 2, pp. 213–67). Hillsdale, NJ: Erlbaum.

Swinney, D. A. (1979). Lexical access during sentence comprehension: Reconsideration of context effects. *Journal of Verbal Learning and Verbal Behavior, 18*, 645–59.

van Dijk, T. A., & Kintsch, W. (1983). *Strategies of discourse comprehension.* New York: Academic Press.

Voss, J. F., Greene, T. R., Post, T. A., & Penner, B. C. (1983). Problem solving skill in the social sciences. In G. H. Bower (Ed.), *The psychology of learning and motivation: Advances in research theory* (Vol. 17, pp. 165–213). New York: Academic Press.

Vygotsky, L. S. (1978). *Mind in society: The development of higher psychological processes* (M. Cole, V. John-Steiner, & E. Soubermen Eds. and Trans.). Cambridge, MA: Harvard University Press.

Waters, H. S. (1980). "Class News": A single-subject longitudinal study of prose production and schema formation during childhood. *Journal of Verbal Learning and Verbal Behavior, 19*, 152–67.

West, R. F., & Stanovich, K. E. (1978). Automatic contextual facilitation in readers of three ages. *Child Development, 49*, 717–27.

Witte, S. P., & Faigley, L. (1981). Coherence, cohesion, and writing quality. *College Composition and Communication, 32*, 189–204.

Wittgenstein, L. (1953). *Philosophical investigations* (G. E. M. Anscombe, Trans.). New York: Macmillan. (Original work published 1892.)

# 4 Knowledge telling and knowledge transforming in written composition

*Marlene Scardamalia and Carl Bereiter*

At a certain level of description everyone's language processes are the same. At another level of description everyone's language processes are different. A major task for applied cognitive scientists is to find levels of description that capture educationally significant differences. In the emerging field of research on composing processes, the search for appropriate descriptions has been carried out largely through the comparison of expert and novice writers (Burtis, Bereiter, Scardamalia, & Tetroe, 1983; Flower & Hayes, 1980; Scardamalia & Paris, 1985). Models of the composing process, however, have been aimed at universality, that is, at providing a description applicable to writers at all levels of skill (de Beaugrande, 1984; Hayes & Flower, 1980a). This has created a gap between theory and data. Empirical research has produced a wealth of data on differences between what experts and novices do when they write, but the available models have been too general to be very helpful in bringing order out of this mass of observations.

In this chapter we set forth two models of composing processes, one intended to capture essential features of immature composing and the other features that distinguish mature writers. We use the terms *mature* and *immature*, rather than *expert* and *novice*, because the reference groups for these models are advanced undergraduates and graduate students, on one hand, and elementary school students, on the other. Thus, the "mature" reference group includes many who are by no means experts in the use of the written word, and the "immature" group includes some who are very skillful in the kinds of writing they do. But, as we shall try to show, the difference in the overall way of writing that typifies these two groups is a difference of profound educational significance.

The contrasting models are called *knowledge telling* and *knowledge transform-*

The work reported in this chapter was supported by the Ontario Ministry of Education through a block grant to the Ontario Institute for Studies in Education and by grants from the Alfred P. Sloan Foundation and the Social Sciences and Humanities Research Council of Canada. We gratefully acknowledge the research assistance of Clare Brett, Jud Burtis, Pamela Paris, Rosanne Steinbach, and Jacqueline Tetroe. The authors also thank John Bransford for his discussion of an oral presentation of this material at the American Educational Research Association, 1984, and Jane Zbrodoff for comments on an earlier draft.

*ing*. These labels reflect the idea that the principal difference between mature and immature composing is in how knowledge is brought into the writing process and in what happens to knowledge in that process. Discussions by expert writers are replete with testimonials to the effect that their understanding of what they are trying to say grows and changes in the course of writing (Lowenthal, 1980; Murray, 1978; Odell, 1980). A major implication of the contrasting models is that this knowledge-transforming effect is not a universal property of writing but is the result of certain complex problem-solving procedures that form part of one way of writing and are absent from the other.

Perhaps the most convincing way to present these models would be to itemize the many expert–novice and developmental differences that have been observed and then show at the end how the two models account for these differences. The matter is not that simple, however. There are few unequivocal differences. Thinking-aloud protocols show, for instance, that children do little or none of the goal-directed planning evidenced in the protocols of mature writers (Burtis, 1983; Burtis et al., 1983). But without a theory that suggests how it might be possible to produce coherent texts without such planning, one is likely to reject the finding – to argue, for instance, that it is merely an artifact of children's more limited vocabularies for reporting mental events. So we have chosen the opposite manner of presentation – to explain the models in some detail first and then itemize observable differences that we believe make more sense when they are interpreted in terms of the two models.

The final section of the chapter deals with instructional intervention. As noted in the opening paragraph, the applied cognitive scientist's task is not merely to describe cognitive processes but to describe them in ways that capture educationally significant differences. The instructional efforts to be described are based on the premise that helping students move from a knowledge-telling to a knowledge-transforming approach to writing is an important and realistic educational objective. It will be argued that the importance of this objective extends beyond writing instruction, having broad implications for the way students develop their knowledge.

### Knowledge telling

Knowledge telling is a way to generate text content, given a topic to write about and a familiar genre (factual exposition, personal opinion, instructions, etc.). The knowledge-telling model (Figure 1) shows how text generation can take place under these circumstances without the need for an overall plan or goal, for an elaboration of problem constraints (Flower & Hayes, 1980), or for the problem-solving procedures characteristic of mature composing processes (Hayes & Flower, 1980b).

The knowledge-telling process works as follows. The writer constructs some

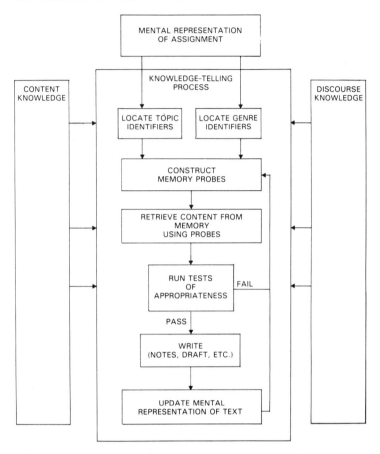

Figure 1. Structure of the knowledge-telling model. This model is an adaptation of a model first presented in Bereiter and Scardamalia (1985).

representation of the assignment. Then topic and genre identifiers are located. If the assignment is "Should boys and girls play on the same sports team?" topic identifiers might be *sports teams*, *equality*, and *female liberation*. These topic identifiers serve as cues for memory search, and these cues automatically prime associated concepts. Thus, information in memory becomes available for use in composition through a process of spreading activation (Anderson, 1983; Caccamise, in press; Collins & Loftus, 1975), initiated by cues drawn from the writing assignment. Although this process does not ensure that all the information activated will be relevant, there is a built-in tendency toward relevance. As Anderson explains, "Spreading activation identifies and favors the processing of information most related to the immediate context (or sources of activation)" (Anderson, 1983, p. 86). Therefore, text generated by the knowledge-telling process tends to stay on topic automatically, by the nature of spreading activation, without need of the writer to monitor or plan for coherence.

In addition to identifying topics, the writing assignment typically also prescribes or implies the genre. In the sports team assignment used for the present illustration, the question format identifies the intended genre as an opinion essay calling, minimally, for the presentation of an opinion and a reason. In the knowledge-telling model, genre identifiers function in much the same way as topic identifiers. They result in memory probes like *statement of belief* and *reason*, which operate in combination with the topical memory probes to increase the likelihood that spreading activation will bring forth content appropriate to the writing assignment. For example, the topic probe *equality*, combined with the genre probe *statement of belief*, might activate content for an opening sentence that would appear in the text as "I think that boys and girls should play on the same sports teams."

Once a unit of text has been produced (mentally, as a note, or as part of a text draft), it serves as an additional source of topic and genre identifiers. These additional identifiers not only aid the retrieval of additional content but also increase the tendency toward coherence, for the next item to be retrieved will be influenced by the items previously retrieved. In our example, after the opening statement of belief was produced, the young writer's knowledge of the opinion essay genre would likely generate the memory probe, *reason*. This probe, together with probes associated with *girls*, *boys*, *sports*, and *equality*, might result in an addition to the text such as "Girls are as good in sports as boys are." This think–say process continues until the page is complete or the store of ideas that comes to mind is depleted.

Note that in the knowledge-telling model coherence and well-formedness do not depend on deliberate or conscious application of world knowledge or knowledge of literary genres. The writer's attention may be wholly occupied by the activity of finding a next thing to say, and yet coherence, well-formedness, and a valid expression of the writers' beliefs and knowledge may all result from automatic processes set in motion by that activity.

### Knowledge transforming

A model of mature writing, the knowledge-transforming model, is presented in Figure 2. Note that this model is not a mere elaboration of the knowledge-telling model presented previously, but neither is it a complete departure. Rather, the new model retains the former model as a subprocess, embedding it within a complex problem-solving process.

This problem-solving process involves two different kinds of problem spaces (Scardamalia, Bereiter, & Steinbach, 1984). Following Newell (1980), we conceive of a problem space as an abstract entity consisting of a number of knowledge states and operations, the operations having the effect of producing movement

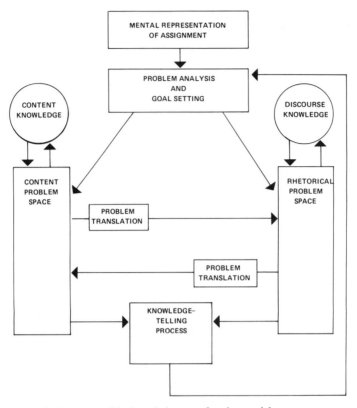

Figure 2.  Structure of the knowledge-transforming model.

through the problem space – that is, from one knowledge state to another. In the content space, the knowledge states can be roughly characterized as beliefs, and the operations are the inferring, the hypothesizing, and so on that lead from one state of belief to another. In the rhetorical space, the knowledge states are various representations of the rhetorical situation, which includes the text and the goals it subserves. The operations, accordingly, are ones that alter the text, goals, or relations between them.

Such a distinction between problem spaces is implicit in standard conceptions of rhetoric. Rhetoric, as Bryant (1965, p. 18) explains, is "distinct from the learnings which it uses." It is not concerned with the ideational content of discourse per se but rather with the "relationships of ideas to the thoughts, feelings, motives, and behavior of men." In the knowledge-transforming model these "learnings" (i.e., the ideational content of discourse) are operated on in the content space. The rhetorical space, in contrast, is concerned with achieving goals of the discourse and therefore with the relation between ideational content and the possible reactions of a reader.

The transformation of knowledge (which is what the model is intended to account for) takes place within the content space, but in order for the writing process to play a role in knowledge transforming, there must be interaction between the content space and the rhetorical space. The key requirement is for problems encountered in the rhetorical space to be translated into subgoals to be achieved in the content space and vice versa. For instance, difficulties that are encountered in the rhetorical space, in making a statement clear or convincing, may be translated into subgoals of generating examples of a concept, reasons for a belief, intermediate steps in a chain of reasoning, arguments against a competing belief, and so on. Operations carried out within the content space to achieve such subgoals may in turn lead to changes in the writer's belief, elaborations, new connections, or goals for future study and thought. In this way, the dialectical interaction between the two problem spaces can produce changes in the content and organization of the writer's knowledge.

The rhetorical side of this dialectical process is illustrated in a thinking-aloud protocol drawn from research by Flower and Hayes (1980). The protocol segment of interest begins with the writer rejecting a previously generated idea on purely rhetorical grounds (" . . . it ain't a bad idea but it's *too abstract*)." But rather than simply go back and retrieve another idea from memory, as a writer following a knowledge-telling strategy would do, he first specifies rhetorical subgoals that a new candidate idea must meet: "Okay, how do I put this in a *particular situation without letting the paragraph take over the whole paper* . . . also, *without seeming to stereotype English teachers*." The protocol continues with the writer retrieving a new idea that meets these rhetorical specifications.

A question to which the knowledge-transforming model attempts to provide an answer is, How does such generation of an idea (which usually appears in protocols as a spontaneous event) take place? The model implies that there is a transformation of the rhetorical requirements into content-related subgoals. We presume that one cannot search memory for ideas labeled "will not take over the whole paper" or "does not seem to stereotype English teachers." Criteria such as these must be translated into subgoals related to ways that information is actually coded in memory. Thus, the subgoal might be "Find an instance of idea X that is concrete, not complex, and not highly associated with English teachers." Such a subgoal could then provide memory probes likely to elicit content meeting the original specifications.

The actual retrieval of information from memory, we presume, is like that involved in the knowledge-telling process – a matter of spreading activation from nodes activated by the memory probes, but there are many more memory probes reflecting rhetorical subgoals. The consequence is that the information retrieved should not merely fit topical and genre requirements but should have a good likelihood of fitting the specific constraints set out by the writer's analysis of the rhetorical problem (cf. Flower & Hayes, 1980). Furthermore, by meeting these distinctive constraints, the newly retrieved information is likely to bring to attention some previously unrecognized relation between ideas – in the present case, for instance, some previously unrecognized generalization about English teachers. This new item of knowledge may in turn be translated into some new subgoal for the composition – for instance, the goal of modifying the plan for the text to incorporate a discussion of the new insight. Pursuit of this subgoal may lead to new rhetorical problems, which are translated back into new subgoals to be achieved in the content space, and so on – hence, the continual revision and rethinking that mature writers go through in a serious piece of writing (Murray, 1978). This does not happen in the knowledge-telling process, however, because in effect there is no rhetorical problem solving. Content retrieved from memory either is passed directly into the composition or else is rejected and other content is retrieved, but in either event there is no dialectical process that leads to the elaboration of subgoals for the composition or that leads memory search into new areas of memory.

### Psychological plausibility of the two models

The knowledge-telling and knowledge-transforming models have been presented as alternative ways of producing compositions, making use of known processes and capabilities of the human cognitive system. It has been implied that these models represent what actually goes on in the minds of typical immature and mature writers. It is time now to deal more explicitly with that issue.

Chomsky (1980) has emphasized that a cognitive theory can be valid in the sense of accounting for a body of facts and yet not bear any resemblance to what actually goes on in the mind. For cognitive models to offer promise as guides to instruction, however, it would seem that they must meet the latter condition as well. That is, in order to map on to any reasonable conception of educational growth, cognitive models must have psychological reality.

Psychological reality is a very strong claim, however, one that cannot be made for any cognitive model in its early stages of verification. A more immediately addressable claim is that of psychological plausibility – the claim that a model might reasonably be thought to describe what actually goes on in the mind. With respect to the knowledge-telling and knowledge-transforming models, two questions of psychological plausibility can be addressed: Are the models compatible with people's subjective experience of writing? And is there any plausible account of how the cognitive structures described by the models might come to be acquired?

*Subjective accounts of the composing process*

Such reports as we have been able to draw from children about their composing processes have tended to conform to the knowledge-telling model. Here, for instance, is the composing strategy reported by a grade 6 student:

> I have a whole bunch of ideas and write down till my supply of ideas is exhausted. Then I might try to think of more ideas up to the point when you can't get any more ideas that are worth putting down on paper and then I would end it.

A very similar report comes from another grade 6 student:

> I have a whole bunch of good ideas and I start writing the major ones first because they are the ones that are in the front of my mind. Then the smaller ones start coming three quarters of the way in the page and maybe a whole bunch of those . . . a swarm of those . . . so I might write as many of them as I can . . . . It doesn't take that long.

At first glance this student seems to have a sense of relative importance among ideas, which might imply more sophisticated rhetorical judgments than are provided for in the knowledge-telling model. In fact, however, the belief that the major ideas are those that come first to mind is fully congruent with a spreading-activation process that starts with information most closely related to contextual cues.

In contrast to the straightforward generating process described by these novice writers is the more recursive and problem-fraught process described by some expert writers. Here, for instance, is Aldous Huxley describing the process of constructing a piece of prose:

Generally, I write everything many times over. All my thoughts are second thoughts. And I correct each page a great deal, or rewrite it several times as I go along . . . . Things come to me in driblets, and when the driblets come I have to work hard to make them into something coherent. (Cited in *Writers at Work*, 2nd series, 1963, p. 197)

Not all mature writers labor over their writing the way Huxley reports, of course. Some skilled academic writers tell us they generate first drafts in much the same way that our grade 6 students report, but then revise extensively. Others appear to work out their ideas through lectures and discussion, so that when they finally come to putting their ideas into writing, a straightforward process of knowledge telling is sufficient. These would appear to be variations of knowledge transforming rather than indications of a radically different process.

As noted previously, expert writers frequently attest to the role of writing in developing their thoughts and knowledge. C. Day Lewis (cited in Murray, 1978, p. 102) goes so far as to claim that "we do not write in order to be understood; we write in order to understand." Writers sometimes refer to writing as a process of discovery, or they express a sense that the piece of writing acquires autonomy to such an extent that it influences the writer's thinking, rather than the influence being entirely in the other direction. Peter Elbow (1973, p. 15) states that writing helps "*free* yourself from what you presently think, feel and perceive." Within the knowledge-transforming model such impressions could all be attributed to the effect that problems generated in the rhetorical space have on search through the content space.

Our youthful informants report no such liberating or discovery-producing effect of writing. One grade 6 student, indeed, reports just the opposite, in commenting on the quotation from Elbow:

> It's the other way around actually; when I'm writing, usually it gets more and more contained. When it's in my mind it's freer than ever, and when it's on the paper it seems more trapped . . . . The idea can't come out in its full form.

Young writers tend rather to describe writing as a knowledge-telling process in which the only problems are problems of expressing what is already formed in their own minds. Here is one grade 6 student's view:

> My main idea . . . is to make my ideas as clear to someone else, but only to someone else and not to me . . . . It's automatically going to be clear to me, especially if I put myself in someone else's shoes . . . because I wrote it.

Most young writers are not as lucid or explicit as the ones cited in this section. These young writers were in fact selected for interview because they were especially talented writers. Therefore, it is all the more remarkable that in describing the writing process as a whole they should refer to it in terms that are much more compatible with the knowledge-telling than with the knowledge-transforming model.

### *How do the models get into the mind?*

Human beings, including children, are noteworthy for their goal-seeking and problem-solving propensities. We should make it clear that the knowledge-telling model does not imply that young people have no goals or concerns when they write. It implies only that their executive system lacks the means of bringing these goals and concerns actively into the composing process and applying strategies to them. Nevertheless, it may seem implausible that children should develop such an approach to writing. The notion of their doing so becomes more plausible if we recognize that *knowledge telling as a whole constitutes an elegant solution to a large problem faced by beginning writers.*

The large problem faced by beginning writers is that of converting a language production system developed for conversation, a system dependent at every level on inputs from the social environment, to a system that is capable of functioning autonomously. As we detail at length in another publication (Bereiter & Scardamalia, 1982), this conversion involves finding ways to sustain discourse beyond the turn-taking pattern of conversation, ways to activate and search memory stores in the absence of prompts from other people's contributions to the discourse, and the development of schemas to ensure appropriateness, coherence, and completeness in the absence of a responsive audience.

In tackling this problem during the early years of school, children are of course handicapped by their limited knowledge and by the fact that their written language skills, such as handwriting and spelling, are not yet automatic and therefore draw mental effort away from higher-level aspects of text production. Consequently, any solution to the problem of generating written discourse must be one that makes few knowledge demands and that economizes on mental effort. Economizing on mental effort generally means reducing the number of task features that need attending to, reducing procedures to routines, avoiding recursive loops in favor of linear procedures that allow items to be processed once and then ignored, and avoiding means–end analysis. On all of these counts the knowledge-telling model represents a winning strategy. All it requires is a set of schemas that specify appropriate structural elements for texts and some nodes in memory capable of being activated by cues from an assigned topic. Its demands on processing capacity are minimal. The result is a highly efficient procedure, capable of initiating writing within seconds after a topic has been assigned and sustaining discourse within topical and structural bounds.

We would argue therefore that the knowledge-telling model is at least a plausible outcome of the situation children typically face in the early years of literacy. What is harder to account for plausibly is the emergence of a cognitive structure resembling the knowledge-transforming model. It should be evident from a comparison of Figures 1 and 2 that the knowledge-transforming model is not an outgrowth of the more primitive model. Rather, it is a novel structure that subsumes the more primitive one as a component.

One possibility is that people who eventually develop a full-fledged knowledge-transforming approach to writing are different from the beginning, that instead of passing through a stage of knowledge telling they take a more goal-directed approach to writing even in their earliest efforts. Case studies of somewhat precocious writers provide grounds for such a speculation (Britton, 1982; Calkins, 1979, 1983), as do retrospective reports of able adult writers (Scardamalia & Bereiter, 1982). In later sections of this chapter we describe instructional efforts to move students from a knowledge-telling to a knowledge-transforming way of writing. Although the results of these efforts offer support to the belief that knowledge-transforming strategies can be learned, they leave open the question of how far instruction can go in changing knowledge tellers into knowledge transformers and what proportion of students can be expected to undergo such a change. Therein lies what we judge to be the main challenge facing applied cognitive research on writing.

### Characteristics of immature and mature writing interpreted in light of the contrasting models

One virtue to be sought in theoretical models is that they bring a unified set of explanatory principles to bear on phenomena that had previously been treated separately. In this section we deal with some commonly observed failings of immature writers, such as lack of adaptation to audience, lack of planning, and paucity of revision. Also, however, we note some of the typical positive characteristics of immature writing, for these require explanation as much as the negative characteristics. We try to show how these various characteristics fit together into a coherent picture that is compatible with knowledge telling and knowledge transforming as models, respectively, of immature and mature composing processes.

### Text characteristics

Although the knowledge-telling model deals with how texts are generated and not with what those texts will be like, the model does suggest certain text characteristics that would tend to be affected by knowledge telling.

**1. Topical coherence.** Texts generated by knowledge telling should tend to stick to their simple topics. McCutchen and Perfetti (1982) found that, in texts written by fourth graders, sentences were coherent with the simple topic but other linkages among ideas were lacking – a result consistent with the premise that content is retrieved from memory primarily by topical and structural cues. The typical result of such limited coherence is that a text on the topic of whether television is a good or bad influence on children will deal with television watching and children, but will not necessarily deal with the influence of the former on the latter, which would constitute a more complex linking of ideas.

**2. Well-formedness.** The knowledge-telling model predicts that texts will tend to conform to the structural requirements of literary types, although not necessarily achieving the goals of those literary types. In persuasive writing, therefore, knowledge telling ought at a minimum to produce a statement of belief accompanied by a list of reasons, but not a developed line of argument. Texts fitting this description are reported to be the modal type for both 13-year-olds and 17-year-olds in the National Assessment of Educational Progress (1980a, 1980b) evaluations of persuasive writing.

**3. Writer-based prose.** Typical novice writing was diagnosed by Flower (1979) as "writer-based prose" – prose that reflects the writer's train of thought rather than being adapted to the train of thought of the intended reader. Such writing, Flower noted, is appropriate for a first draft, but with novice writers it tends to persist in the final draft. Such a result is predictable from the knowledge-telling model, because the knowledge-telling process provides no means whereby the writer can deliberately apply knowledge about the reader. Thus, efforts by knowledge tellers to adapt their writing to reader characteristics would have to depend on controls over surface structure (e.g., control of register, carried over from oral language skills) but would not include the ability to reorganize information according to reader needs.

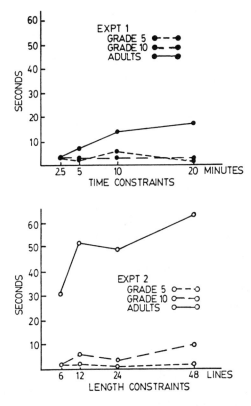

Figure 3. Time taken to start writing simple script-based stories on assigned topics (e.g., "Rick goes to a restaurant"). In Experiment 1 stories were written under different time constraints. In Experiment 2 they were written under constraints specifying the number of lines to be written (with unlimited time). (From Zbrodoff, 1984. Reprinted by permission.)

### Start-up times

As we have noted previously, the knowledge-telling process should permit a rapid start on writing, given a familiar topic and genre. Since no overall goal setting or planning are involved, the time to get started should be the time it takes to retrieve a first item of content fitting the requirements of the topic and genre. A corollary is that start-up time should not vary with other requirements.

Figure 3 (from Zbrodoff, 1984) shows the time people spent before starting to write when given a simple story-writing assignment and a certain length of time or a certain number of lines in which to complete the story. Grade 5 children behaved exactly as would be expected from the knowledge-telling model. The start-up times were very brief, just a few seconds, and they did not vary with either the amount of time allowed or with the size of text to be produced.

In contrast, adults showed adaptations consistent with a more well planned approach to writing. The more time they were allowed, the more time they spent before beginning to write, and when no time constraints were imposed they spent much more time than under even the most liberal time limits. Their start-up times also increased depending on the length of the story they were required to produce.

### Notemaking

In a study reported in Burtis et al. (1983), students were asked to plan and take notes before writing an assignment. Since the knowledge-telling model is geared to text generation, it would be expected that immature students' notes would closely resemble text. Students following a knowledge-transforming model, however, would be expected to represent a variety of ideas in notes that were not simply ideas for inclusion in a text. Figure 4 shows notes typical of 10-year-olds in the study. They are essentially texts written in list form. In contrast, the notes of graduate students are more like worksheets. Writers enter ideas at several different levels of abstraction, evaluate, and build structures out of them.

### Planning protocols

The knowledge-telling model would suggest that what goes on mentally in the young writer while composing should bear a close resemblance to what appears on the page. The knowledge-transforming model, however, would suggest that among more mature writers there should be a great deal of activity revealed in thinking-aloud protocols that is not directly represented in the text. Figure 5 gives a gross quantitative indication of adult–child differences. The darkened bars show the mean number of words in thinking-aloud protocols produced during the planning of compositions. Plain bars show the mean number of words in corresponding essays. At all ages writers say more than they write, but the difference for adults is proportionately much larger. (The study from which these data are drawn is reported in Burtis, 1983.)

Figure 6 presents a portion of an adult protocol. Material printed in boldface duplicates or paraphrases material that actually ended up in the writer's story. The remainder, by far the bulk of the protocol, consists of provisional ideas, goal statements, comments, and problem-solving attempts, in relation to which the boldface statements are like tips of icebergs.

In contrast, Figure 7 presents the complete thinking-aloud protocol of a 10-year-old in the same study, coded in the same way. Except for a couple of procedural comments, the student's planning consists entirely of content subsequently put into the story.

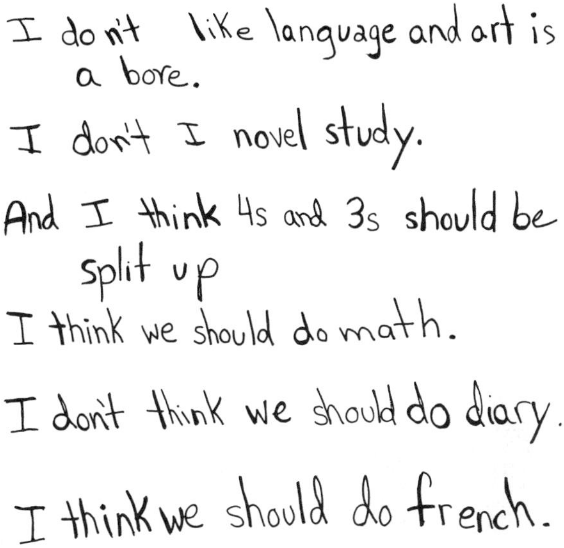

I don't like language and art is a bore.

I don't I novel study.

And I think 4s and 3s should be split up

I think we should do math.

I don't think we should do diary.

I think we should do french.

Figure 4. Example of notes taken by a grade 4 student while planning an essay on the topic "Should children be allowed to choose the subjects they study in school?"

*Revising*

Another manifestation of the mental processes of composing is the changes writers make in their texts. A typical elementary school manuscript may show no revisions at all (National Assessment of Educational Progress, 1977), and there is a tendency at all school levels for revisions to be merely "cosmetic" (Nold, 1981). With certain kinds of support or instruction, however, elementary school children do begin to make revisions of some consequence (Bereiter & Scardamalia, in press, chap. 11; Calkins, 1983; Graves, 1979). In 6 weeks of group instruction (Bereiter & Scardamalia, in press) it was possible to increase the number of ideational changes that students made in their texts; these were reflected in significant improvements for all but two students between pre- and posttest writings. Changes were of the order of adding an introductory sentence, adding a conclusion, providing additional descriptive information, and inserting missing information.

Figure 8 shows the original text plus the revisions made by a grade 6 student in the 6-week instructional experiment. Besides a number of stylistic improvements, the student made a major structural improvement through the addition of a topic sentence that tied together the rest of the text. With respect to the distinction between knowledge telling and knowledge transforming, however, what we must note is that even changes of this comparatively high level represent alternative ways of saying the same thing or additions to rather than transformations of information. Thus, the revisions do not indicate any actual transcending of the knowl-

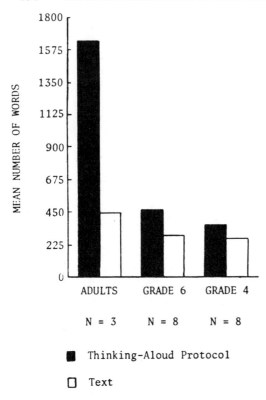

Figure 5. Mean number of words in thinking-aloud protocols of subjects planning compositions compared with mean number of words in the resulting texts.

edge-telling model. The kind of reprocessing that does not appear to go on in immature writers is that involving goals and main ideas (Perl, 1979; Sommers, 1980).

The issue of revision illustrates the value of having a coherent model of immature composing. Teachers of writing have tended to regard revision as an important but distinct part of the writing process, which students for some reason avoid. However, direct efforts to get students to revise have tended to be ineffectual (Faigley & Witte, 1981). Significant revision presupposes a system of goals and goal-seeking procedures. Students who lack such a system, whose text production system corresponds to the knowledge-telling model, need more than encouragement to revise and guidelines for improving their texts. They need help in developing a system within which revision can be a goal-directed process. Planning and audience adaptation, beyond a superficial level, also depend on such a system. But for students who lack such a system, lessons in outlining and notemaking or exercises in writing to different audiences are not likely to touch the heart of the difficulty.

Topic: A Kid Who Lost Things

... Right now, he's isolated - and how I would... If I have a connection made there - how I want to do that: Do I want an adult to intervene? Or do I want this to be that realistic? Or fairy tale-ish? Or...because I can make it any way I want. Okay, maybe I ... weird!! Ah, let me see ... I know. **He makes this model of a ship, and on this ship he makes a little model of himself, and he loses it!** And this little model of himself happens to end up in his back pocket. Oh, why not? I can do anything I want with this story! Okay, so he just doesn't have any friends, and he's still losing things, and he doesn't know where he's put his ship and this little model he made of himself. But - magic!! The little model starts to talk to him, and helps him to find things! Let me see now ... I want to get some other kids involved, here. There's always one kid that shines through. **Okay, one kid likes his work, his art work, and, and, helps him. So, this kid who loses things and ends up giving - instead of losing things, he gives things away!** What a mixed-up story! Imagine, giving things away!! Okay, it's not too clear right now because there's kind of ... I have different directions - whether to go with the notion of this other child helping him out, or staying with the idea of some magic happening for him. Maybe I'll have both. You wanted a story? Once upon a time ... Okay. Not quite, not quite! I am just writing the title again, just to get a feel for it. " The kid who lost things". I think what I'm going to do here is have development of sharing that he gives, not everything away, but gives things away to this other kid. **This other kid, in return, without knowing it, helps him out in locating his losses...**

Figure 6. Portion of adult thinking-aloud protocol. Segments printed in boldface closely resemble material appearing in the final text.

When interpreted within the framework of the knowledge-telling and knowledge-transforming models, the oft-lamented weaknesses of students' writing may be seen to follow naturally from the overall structure of their composing processes rather than being a collection of separate and exasperating deficiencies.

## Mental representations in knowledge-transforming and knowledge-telling processes

In the preceding sections there has been the suggestion that mature writers work at a number of levels in composing a text, whereas children stay within a narrower range of levels, comprising mainly specific items of content and linguistic concerns related to expressing those items. This implies that with immature writers

Topic: A Kid Who Lost Things

I could put him going to school and he probably loses a shoe. And then he's trying to find it and someone else finds it. And he goes home and tells his mother and his mother... and then the person that finds it gives it back and the next day, and then the next day, the person that found it, so the boy says thank you to the person that found it. Then the next day he goes to school, he loses something else. And the teacher asks him what he lost and he says his short pants. He said his short pants. And they were in the washroom. And he goes home and brings them back. And then it's Saturday and school is over. And that's all. He goes back to school on Monday, he goes and plays, comes back in, he does his work, and he loses his gold ring and his mother says, "you lose everything." And he says it's true. And then he goes back to school and he never loses anything else. And his mother was happy because she doesn't want to buy him any more stuff. And they were happy from that day on. That's finished.

Figure 7. Child thinking-aloud protocol obtained under same conditions as the adult protocol shown in Figure 6. Again, segments printed in boldface closely resemble material appearing in the final text.

the text on the page should fairly completely reflect the text as it is represented in the mind, whereas for mature writers the text on the page would correspond to only a part of the mental representation. Other parts of the mental representation would include more abstract encodings of text content, of structures, goals, strategy decisions, and the like.

The issue of what kinds of mental representations writers have available and what they are able to do with them is vital to understanding writing competence psychologically (Flower & Hayes, 1984). Models like those presented in Figures 1 and 2 provide a framework for investigating this issue, but they do not provide answers. A theoretical framework is necessary, however, because mental representations cannot, of course, be observed. They must be inferred from indirect evidence. In this section we discuss two kinds of indirect evidence that can be interpreted within the framework of knowledge-telling and knowledge-transforming models.

## Representations used in recall of text

One indirect means of testing hypotheses about mental representations of text is the use of recall protocols (a detailed account of procedures is available in Scar-

DO YOU THINK THAT CHILDREN SHOULD BE ABLE TO WATCH
AS MUCH TELEVISION AS THEY WOULD LIKE?

❶ →

I THINK THE PARENTS SHOULD REMIND THEIR CHILDREN NOT TO
WATCH TO MUTCH T.V. BUT I THINK THE CHILD SHOULD HAVE SOME
RESPONSIBILITY TO KNOW THAT THEY HAVE WATCHED ENOUGH.
HE OR SHE SHOULD BE ENVOLVED WITH OTHER ACTIVITIES TOO
SUCH AS SPORTS READING A GOOD BOOK OR JUST PLAYING A GAME. THEY
SHOULD ALSO MAKE TIME IN THEIR DAY TO DO THEIR HOME-
WORK OR PRACTICE THEIR MUSICAL INSTRUMENTS IF THEY
HAVE ONE, AND TELEVISION SHOULDN'T INTERFERE. WITH IT

❷ NO I DON'T THINK THAT KIDS SHOULD
BE ALLOWED TO WATCH AS MUTCH T.V. AS
THEY WANT BECAUSE EVERY KID WANTS
TO WATCH T.V. DAY IN AND DAY OUT.

Figure 8. Original text and revisions by a grade 6 student who had been through a 6-week program of instruction in diagnosis and revision of texts. Original text is in printed characters; revisions are in hand-drawn characters placed as they actually were by the student.

damalia & Paris, 1985). The assumption is that, in trying to recall things about their texts, writers make use of whatever stored knowledge is connected with what they are trying to recall. We therefore expect that mature writers use complex routes to retrieving text information, passing through representations of a variety of kinds, whereas immature writers should make use of a smaller variety of representations and depend more on direct recall of whatever is asked.

**Problem solving and content recall.** Twelve writers at each of three ages were asked to think aloud as they tried to recall the exact words of a text they had previously written. A rough idea of the amount of information used from outside the text can be obtained by comparing the number of words in the thinking-aloud protocols with the number of words in the texts. Such data are presented in Figure 9 for adults, grade 10 students, and grade 6 students. ($n = 6$ per group. The other half of the participants received an experimental treatment that might have biased their output. For details of the full study see Scardamalia & Paris, 1985.) Only the adults took, on average, more words to recover what was written in the text than it took to write the text.

Sources of differences in adult and student performance can be identified if we consider the kinds of activity going on in the recall protocols. Figure 10 shows a portion of an adult protocol. Boldface material duplicates or paraphrases material that actually ends up in the essay. The remainder indicates problem solving: Goals

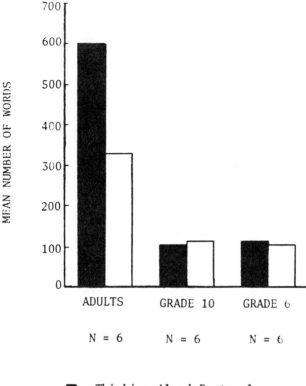

Figure 9. Mean number of words in thinking-aloud protocols of subjects attempting verbatim recall of previously written texts compared with number of words in the actual texts.

and gists are reconstructed and used to aid recovery of what was said in the text. The following excerpt illustrates the use of goals, gists, and structural representations to aid recall is: "From there I think I went on to a *third paragraph*, where *I was trying to draw those things together, to say something like . . .* " (a statement of the gist of the next section follows).

For contrast, Figure 11 shows the complete recall protocol of a 12-year-old in the same study, coded in the same way. This protocol represents the only case in grade 6 where the number of words in the thinking-aloud protocol exceeded those in the text by more than 10 words. None of the additional activity is of the sort found in the adult protocol. Everything is a paraphrase of the contents of the text

Topic: Should Children be Allowed to
Choose What Subjects They Study in School?

... I can't remember what the next sentence was, but the general idea was **as a result of all of this the school could no longer perform the function that it was performing in the past, and therefore was left in a semi-chaotic situation.** I did not in fact include that idea. What I just said now was not in there, it has not been brought out, come to think of it. So then I said something like **a lot of these changes are reflected in the demise of a core curriculum, and a reluctance to use, and** that wasn't the word, **but somehow standardized testing to determine achievement was no longer existent.** And I don't quite remember what I said. From there I think I went on to a third paragraph where I was trying to draw those things together to say something like **although it can be argued that a child's desires, and something or other, should** something to the effect **that although it can be argued that the child should be able to choose his own subjects because this satisfies his needs and desires, it can also be argued that by doing so** .. I can't remember what I said, I can't remember the argument of the other side. I was struggling with it, and it wasn't all that clear. Then the rest of it is all a jumble. That's where I was running into further problems, the point that I was trying to make, **was ...**

Figure 10. Portion of adult recall protocol. Segments printed in boldface closely resemble actual text the subject was trying to recall.

except for the unmarked sections. In the unmarked sections the student is telling about personal experiences related to the topic of her essay: " . . . like we couldn't understand the packaging and it started, like, no more English on some things, and all French, and then started mostly French television."

It is impressive that the youngest students remembered as much of their texts as adults. Seemingly, young writers do not stray far from an easily accessible network of ideas in the production of their texts, and thus they do not have far to return when it comes to recalling the text. In comparison, adults work considerably harder, retracing a complex maze of ideas, and do not recall more of their content for all of that effort.

It might be noted that, since the younger writers wrote shorter compositions, they had less to recall. It could therefore be argued that they might have had the more abstract text representations available but had no need to use them. If our overall analysis is correct, however, the lesser use of abstract representations by immature writers applies during text production as well and therefore is involved

Topic: Should Children Have to Learn
to Speak a Second Language?

I think it depends on what country they live in. I moved to Montreal when I was five, and we had a lot of French every day, and my dad had to learn french at his office, and he brought home books home every night to study the French language, and I could see that he was having trouble, and I haven't had French before until I moved to Montreal, and when Rene Levesque went into the provincial election the whole province started turning bilingual, and on all the packaging there were two languages, and on the road signs there were both English and French, and about two years ago the English language started disappearing and like it started being more and more French, and we were finding it more and more difficult to cope with it, like we couldn't understand the packaging and it started like no more English on some things, and all French, and then started mostly French television, and we were finding it hard to learn the french language, like my dad is old, and he was finding it hard to learn it and I was finding it hard, so we decided to move back here again, and I think that if you have no other opportunity to like, move, and you can't go to a school that's English, then you can't do anything else but learn the French language, or any other language that's not your own, then you just have to, you have no other choice.

Figure 11. Grade 6 thinking-aloud protocol obtained under the same conditions as the adult protocol shown in Figure 10. Segments printed in boldface closely resemble actual text the subject was trying to recall.

in their production of shorter and less complex texts. Accordingly, rather than trying to "unconfound" text differences and process differences by experimental manipulations, it seems preferable to keep testing further implications of the knowledge-telling and knowledge-transforming models to see whether the results continue to support them (as is done, for instance, in the research on mental representation of main point reported in a later section).

**Variety of representations used.** In the adult protocol shown in Figure 10, the writer makes reference to intentions (e.g., "I was trying to draw those things together"), to gists (signaled, e.g., by "to say something like . . . "), and also to structural features of the text (e.g., "third paragraph"). The protocol from the grade 6 student, however, shows only verbatim recall or paraphrases of material in the text – what we will here refer to as representations of content. Recall protocols of all 36 students in the study were scored for the extent to which recall was mediated through each of the aforementioned kinds of representation: intention, gist, structure, and content. The largest number of different types of representations ever used (maximum, 4) was determined. The four-way pattern representing complete interconnectedness between different forms of representation was found, with one exception, only among adults. Children's protocols showed little reference to gist and intention and an absence of the rich mediational networking of ideas found with adults. For the most part, students in the two younger age groups showed direct access to the content of their texts.

Presumably, transformations on ideas are made possible by representing text in abstract and gisted forms. Such representations free the author from needing to hold in active memory a representation of the literal contents of the text. If this is true, it follows that young students must use short-term memory capacity simply to hold onto their ideas, leaving little, if any, surplus capacity to weigh ideas against one another and to consider alternatives.

By constructing higher-level representations of their texts, mature writers also provide themselves with a source of memory retrieval cues not provided by the text itself. Flower and Hayes (1981) found expert writers generating most content ideas in response to their own elaborations of the rhetorical problem, whereas novice writers generated 70% of their ideas in response either to the topic assignment or to the last content item considered. These findings suggest that the knowledge teller not only is limited to a much smaller set of memory probes but also is limited to probes that are less likely to be related to high-level goals or points of the composition.

### Representations of main points of texts

One kind of mental representation that de Beaugrande (1984) hypothesizes to play a significant role in text production is what he calls ideas, but what might more commonly be referred to as main points – central propositions that the text is fashioned around and that other propositions are intended to support. From the standpoint of the composing process, what matters is not how main points are presented in the text but how they function in the mind of the writer. In a skilled writer main points would be expected to function as goals, exerting a directive influence over the composing process. With immature writers, however, it is not certain whether main points are represented in their minds at all (regardless of whether they are recoverable from the texts such writers produce). The knowledge-telling model would predict that main points would not play a role in the composing processes of immature writers, simple topics and structural schemas taking over the job of holding the text together.

Writers' mental representations of main points were also investigated indirectly through recall tasks (Bereiter, Burtis, Scardamalia, & Brett, 1983). The students wrote an essay and subsequently wrote a statement of their main point. The experimenters then prepared three different statements of main point for each essay. One labeled "upgraded version" was an attempt to elicit from the essay writer a comment such as, "Ah, that's precisely what I was trying to say. This makes the main point clearer than I did." The downgraded version was meant to elicit something like "That wasn't my main point – I may have mentioned that lifeguards get good tans but I just kinda' added that. It's not important." The third version was a paraphrase of the author's own statement of main point, to which we expected a response of the order of "Yeah, that's what I was trying to say."

The underlying assumption of the study was that if students constructed and used representations of their main points in writing, they should be accurate in recognizing distortions of their point and should base their judgments on their remembered intentions. Students who did not construct or use such representations, however, should be more willing to accept any main point statement that was compatible with text content and should not refer to their remembered intentions in judging a main point statement. The study was run with students in grades 5 and 11. The majority of grade 11 students behaved in the manner expected of people who had active mental representations of their main points. They reliably preferred upgraded or paraphrased versions of their main point statements to downgraded versions and could point out that certain propositions, although included in their texts, were not ones they intended as main points. Grade 5 students, however, tended to respond equally positively to upgraded, downgraded, and paraphrased versions of their main point statements and seldom appealed to their own intentions in judging a statement. Thus, it was as if they were in the position of readers rather than creators of their own texts.

From these studies and other, more complex data reported in Scardamalia and Paris (1985), a picture of mental representations emerges that is consistent with but that adds psychological depth to the pictures sketched by the knowledge-telling and knowledge-transforming models. Consistent with the idea that knowledge telling is a process focused at the level of item-by-item text generation, young writers' mental representations of their own texts are confined mainly to specific items of content or language. The only other kind of representation to appear with any frequency in text recall is representation of structural elements (reason, example, etc.). This is consistent with the memory-cuing role assigned to such information in the knowledge-telling model. Mature writers show the full range of mental representations suggested in general descriptions of the composing process (de Beaugrande, 1984). Moreover, their recall protocols show that the different kinds of representation are connected: Adults, for instance, appeal to intentions or gist in an effort to reconstruct text verbatim. This interconnectedness of representations, we presume, enables them to work on different levels of text problems, such as problems of meaning, expression, or organization, in a coordinated fashion, without losing hold of the process as a whole.

It might be tempting, in light of these findings, to conclude that writing instruction should focus on helping students construct higher-level representations of their texts – especially representations of intentions or goals and of gists or main points. But, of course, it is not merely having such representations that makes a mature writer; it is being able to operate on them. If students are locked into a knowledge-telling process, there is no function for higher-level representations. In such a case it is not clear how students could learn to create such representations. We return, therefore, to the conclusion that it is the composing process as a whole that has to develop, not some aspect or component of it. Rather than pointing to a particular focus for writing instruction, research on mental representations contributes to understanding what it means for the composing process as a whole to develop to higher levels.

### Instructional strategies

How does a student change his or her approach to writing from one of knowledge telling to one of knowledge transforming? If it is correct that these approaches derive from qualitatively distinct cognitive structures and that the more advanced structure is not a direct outgrowth of the other, rich and varied writing experience and motivation to improve may not be sufficient. Or even if they are sufficient for some students, there are likely to be many other students who could profit from more direct assistance.

Two general approaches have been used in our instructional research, which is summarized in detail in Bereiter and Scardamalia (in press). One is to introduce what can be called reflective loops into children's composing routines. The clearest example comes from a study in which students had to stop after every sentence and select an evaluative statement from a set of possibilities (Scardamalia & Bereiter, 1983b). They were then led through a loop of diagnosis, choice of action, and possible revision before proceeding to the next sentence. (A less intrusive and more generalizable procedure will be described presently.) The idea is to modify the straight-ahead course of knowledge telling by getting the student to rethink decisions, to consider alternatives, and to shift attention to aspects of the writing task other than generation of the next item of text content. Such reflective activities, it is hoped, will cause the student to create small problem spaces for dealing with the issues that reflection brings to light, and this will be the beginning of the rhetorical and content problem spaces that are the main structural features of the knowledge-transforming model.

The other approach to structural change depends on giving students insight into their own composing processes (Scardamalia & Bereiter, 1983a) and exposing them to a view of what the more mature composing process is like. We can hardly expect children, except perhaps those fortunate enough to be in close contact with professional writers, to have much sense of the complexities that underlie expert performance. Our primary objective in designing instruction has been to open up this world to them. What follows is a brief sketch of how we applied these ideas of introducing reflective loops and demonstrating mature composing processes with a grade 6 class. (For a more complete presentation of research procedures and results see Scardamalia et al., 1984.)

### Opportunity to view adult composing processes

Students suggested topics for essays – for example, "Rock stars are more talented today than ever." Then they watched an adult think aloud while struggling to write an essay on that topic. The adult would say things like the following:

> I don't know a thing about modern rock stars. I can't think of the name of even one rock star. How about David Bowie or Mick Jagger . . . *But many readers won't agree that* . . . they are modern rock stars. I think they're both as old as I am. Let's see, *my own feelings about this are* . . . that I doubt if today's rock stars are more talented than ever. Anyhow, how would I know. I can't argue this . . . *I need a new idea* . . . *An important point I haven't considered yet is* . . . ah . . . well . . . what do we mean by talent? Am I talking about musical talent or ability to entertain – to do acrobatics? Hey, I may have a way into this topic. *I could develop this idea by* . . .

The actual modeling was much more convoluted. This brief segment took, in real time, about 10 min.

### Scaffolding for the mature process

To help students sustain planning and to go beyond "what next?" content generation, they were provided with cards containing cues that they could incorporate into their thinking. The underlined phrases in the preceding example of an instructor's planning monologue are some of the planning cues used. The monologue illustrates how they were used – as if they were natural parts of protocol statements. A sampling of cues used in opinion essay planning is shown in Figure 12. A sample from a parallel set used for factual exposition is presented in Figure 13. Each student had on index cards a more extensive set of phrases pertaining to the particular genre being worked with. All modeling – including that done by adults – was carried out with the cards. These planning supports aided students as they took turns, on a voluntary basis, thinking aloud in front of the class. The activity became a favorite, and students put in bids for their turn at what came to be known as soloing.

**Monitoring kinds of mental activities that need attention.** At first students selected cards at random. When they became more proficient at planning with the help of the cards, they were encouraged to monitor their own thinking to determine whether they needed a new idea, needed to elaborate or improve an idea, needed to assess their goals, or needed to try to put together what they had so far. Cards

NEW IDEA

> AN EVEN BETTER IDEA IS ...
> AN IMPORTANT POINT I HAVEN'T CONSIDERED YET IS ...
> A WHOLE NEW WAY TO THINK OF THIS TOPIC IS ...
> NO ONE WILL HAVE THOUGHT OF ...

ELABORATE

> AN EXAMPLE OF THIS ...
> MY OWN FEELINGS ABOUT THIS ARE ...
> ANOTHER REASON THAT'S GOOD ...
> I COULD DEVELOP THIS IDEA BY ADDING ...
> A GOOD POINT ON THE OTHER SIDE OF THE ARGUMENT IS ...

IMPROVE

> I COULD MAKE MY MAIN POINT CLEARER BY ...
> I REALLY THINK THIS ISN'T NECESSARY BECAUSE ...
> I'M GETTING OFF TOPIC SO ...
> BUT MANY READERS WON'T AGREE THAT ...
> TO LIVEN THIS UP I'LL ...

GOALS

> A GOAL I THINK I COULD WRITE TO ...
> MY PURPOSE ...

PUTTING IT TOGETHER

> IF I WANT TO START OFF WITH MY STRONGEST IDEA I'LL ...
> I CAN TIE THIS TOGETHER BY ...
> MY MAIN POINT IS ...

Figure 12. Examples of planning cues provided to help students plan opinion essays. Each cue was printed on a separate card and could be drawn on at will to help formulate a thought while planning. Cues were not intended to be used in the resulting texts.

were subdivided into the categories indicated in Figures 12 and 13 to aid this process. The students learned to select cards in accordance with the kind of thinking they needed to do.

**Dialectic between rhetorical and content concerns.** A combination of rhetorical concerns, including obligations that arise out of expectations of the genre, reader concerns, and concerns for personal feelings, were incorporated into planning cues. Phrases such as "No one will have thought of" and "An important distinction is" often led students to retrieve information that surprised and delighted them. It appeared, therefore, that such cues were achieving the intent of setting

| NEW IDEA | An important distinction is ... |
| | A consequence of (this is) ... |
| | The history of this is ... |
| | Something that is similar is ... |
| | A cause of (this is) ... |

| ELABORATE | I'm impressed by ... |
| | An explanation would be ... |
| | An example of (this is) ... |
| | This results in ... |
| | My own experience with this is ... |

| IMPROVE | I could describe this in more detail by adding ... |
| | This isn't exactly how it is because ... |
| | I could give the reader a clear picture by ... |
| | This isn't true of all ... |
| | To put it more simply ... |

| GOALS | A goal I think I could write to ... |
| | My purpose ... |

| PUTTING IT TOGETHER | If I want to start off with my strongest idea I'll ... |
| | I can tie this together by ... |
| | My main point is ... |

Figure 13. Examples of planning cues provided to help students plan factual expository essays. Method of use was the same as for cues displayed in Figure 12.

into motion the knowledge-transforming processes resulting from interaction of rhetorical and content concerns. That is, the rhetorical concerns stimulated by the cue cards were being translated into content probes that brought out previously unrecognized connections between items of knowledge.

The instructor tried, by modeling and explanation, to encourage repeated cycles of thinking and rethinking of the kind shown in protocols of expert writers. The students were also encouraged to function as independently as possible. Planning cues were seen as a transitional device for this purpose. They provided a means of support that enabled students to plan their compositions without guidance from the teacher. As expected, the students gradually became less dependent on the cue cards, planning for extended periods of time on their own, referring to the cards only when stuck.

This experiment yielded evidence of statistically significant effects on reflectivity both in thinking-aloud composing protocols and in the essays students wrote. The experimental group showed itself to strongest advantage when given unlimited time to plan, moving from the instant starts characteristic of knowledge telling to the point where they spontaneously spent up to four class periods planning before starting to draft a major paper. Even under time-limited test conditions their factual exposition essays showed significantly greater reflectivity than those of controls, although their opinion essays did not. On the whole, weaknesses in the essays of experimental students could be traced to difficulties in maintaining coherence. This we attribute to their retrieving more and more varied information than they were accustomed to handling.

A year after this intervention we had an opportunity to collect writing samples and notes from six experimental and six control students. We shall illustrate the kinds of advances we traced with the work of one student. It should be noted that this student is not representative. She was the most successful of the small group whose writing development was followed up. Rather, her work illustrates what might reasonably be aimed for in instructional efforts to produce global change in children's composing processes.

**Notemaking.** Figure 14 illustrates the notes produced by this student. They reflect types of mental representations and concerns identified with the knowledge-transforming model. First she surveys the kinds of information that might be included in her essay. Only then does she begin to expand individual ideas, some of which were not included in her original list. She makes decisions based on rhetorical qualities – for instance, she rejects content because it is unoriginal. She works out ideas in point form – giving the gist of what she might say rather than writing full sentences. A comparison between these notes and her text shows that the order of presentation in the text bears little relation to the order in which the ideas are presented in her notes.

**Planning.** This young writer worked on her essay for four class periods. Although she used encyclopedias as a resource, she did not spend a great deal of time copying material from them, nor did she use them as her primary source of ideas. She worked out her own thoughts on the topic and used reference books to fill in gaps in her thinking. This amount of planning was typical of children in the experimental program and sharply distinguished them from students in the control group.

**Revising.** The text that this student deletes (see Figure 15) is well-formed text. If we look closely we can see that this young writer has already done a considerable

- MANNERS AT MEALS
- AT SCHOOL
- ON THE BUS
- TO YOUR ELDERS
- AROUND THE WORLD
- WITH STRANGERS
- BEING A HOST/HOSTESS

PHRASES
- PLEASE
- THANK - YOU
- PASS THE BUTTER PLEASE        *maybe (unorginal)*
- MAY I ...(INSTEAD OF CAN I)

ACTIONS
- HOLDING DOOR OPEN
- HOLDING CHAIR
- DON'T GET UP UNTIL HOST OR HOSTESS DOES - ALSO DON'T START
  EATING BEFORE HOST/HOSTESS.
- TIP YOUR HAT
- SHAKE HANDS (RIGHT)           *maybe*
- SETTING OF TABLE
- HELP CLEAR & WASH

ETIQUETTE - MEANS GOOD MANNERS   *For sure*

AROUND THE WORLD

JAPAN - TAKE OFF SHOES BEFORE ENTERING HOUSE   *NO*

WEALTHY PEOPLE - COMPLICATED & RIGID RULES   *NO*

SMALL TOWN - EVERYONE KNOWS EACH OTHER AND VISIT NEW
                NEIGHBOURS TO WELCOME THEM        *NAH*

LARGE TOWNS - DON'T KNOW NEIGHBOURS AND WAIT TO BE INVITED

PROTOCOL
AT SOCIAL FUNCTIONS ATTENDED BY GOVERNMENT OFFICIALS, MILITARY
OFFICERS, AND FOREIGN DIPLOMATS.
MEN AND WOMEN RECEIVE THE RESPECT DUE THEIR OFFICE.   *NO*
DINNER - IN ORDER OF RANK                              *WAY*
PROPER TITLES - NOT HEY YOU BUT GENERAL ETC.

ORIGINS
HANDSHAKE: DEVELOPED WHEN TWO MEN SHOOK HANDS TO SHOW THEY  *Maybe*
WEREN'T CARRYING WEAPONS

CHIVALRY: DURING MIDDLE AGES IN EUROPE BOYS BECOMING KNIGHTS
LEARNED IT

      KNIGHT DEVOTED TO THE CHRISTIAN CHURCH AND HIS COUNTRY
      AND WOMEN WERE TREATED WITH GREAT RESPECT

TODAY'S FORMAL ETIQUETTE ORIGINATED IN THE FRENCH ROYAL COURT   *FOR SURE*
DURING THE 1600'S AND 1700'S

ETIQUETTE - CAME FROM OLD FRENCH WORD TICKET.  ✓

Figure 14. Notes made in planning an essay by a grade 6 student after about 10 weeks
of instruction in reflective planning. Hand-lettered notes are ones added by the student
after the initial drafting of notes.

amount of local revising before giving up on this segment. The major revision indicated in this figure suggests that the writer undertook at least one major re-framing of her discourse.

**Knowledge retrieval.** It is clear from this student's notes that she managed to uncover more content than she used, and her comments suggest that at least some of this content was uncovered by self-constructed memory probes related to goals for the composition.

It might be noted that none of these observations is directly related to the quality of the student's compositions. Although enabling students to produce more fully elaborated, more effective, or better organized writing is a worthy goal, it can be achieved by simply helping students to become better knowledge tellers. It is a different kind of challenge to help students become knowledge transformers. It means more than teaching them certain procedures or motives. It requires helping them develop a cognitive structure within which the process of composing pro-duces reconstruction of knowledge. We think that is an educational objective wor-thy of the best efforts of instructional researchers.

### Conclusion

Novice writers depend on having knowledge already assembled (either in memory or through teacher-directed writing activities) in forms ready for written presen-tation. Experts can make use of complex knowledge-processing procedures to transform knowledge that is not so assembled into coherent and effective form. Accordingly, what we see in the performance of expert writers is the execution of powerful procedures that enable them to draw on, elaborate, and refine available knowledge. For novices, however, writing serves more to reproduce than to refine knowledge.

Two profoundly different approaches to knowledge can be detected among writ-ers. One approach, knowledge telling, leaves the structure of knowledge essen-tially unaltered. The other, knowledge transforming, develops new understanding through the interaction of rhetorical and substantive concerns. In this chapter we have presented models of these distinctive approaches and reviewed data on ob-servable features of notemaking, planning, and revising that support this two-model view. We also discussed evidence for markedly different mental representa-tions of text underlying these models. Finally, we presented results from instruc-tional research that has aimed to promote a knowledge-transforming approach.

This research suggests that an additional order of educational objective is re-quired if we are to help students acquire a knowledge-transforming structure for composing. They need explicit models of mature competence and means of cop-ing with procedures that extend the competence they bring naturally to the task. Instructional efforts suggest that it is possible to convey the complex problem-

ETIQUETTE IS REALLY BEING POLITE AND USING MANNERS.

IT COMES FROM THE OLD FRENCH WORD TICKET.

ETIQUETTE ~~WAS FIRST~~ ORIGINATED AGES AGO WHEN PEOPLE

REALIZED THEY WOULD HAVE . HAVE EVEN SIMPLE MANNERS ~~LIKE~~

~~A HANDSHAKE~~ TO LIVE NICELY.

~~HANDSHAKES DEVELOPED~~

THE HANDSHAKE WAS TO SHOW THAT NEITHER PERSON WAS

CARRYING A WEAPON. IT SERVED AS A DISPLAY OF FRIENDSHIP

~~AND~~ though EVEN TODAY IT IS STILL COURTESIOUS TO used to be SHAKE YOUR RIGHT HAND

IN A CLASP OF FRIENDSHIP.

~~ETIQUETTE~~

MUCH OF TODAY'S FORMAL ETIQUETTE ~~CAME~~

### ETIQUETTE (EHTUHKEHT)

ETIQUETTE IS ANOTHER WORD FOR MANNERS. IT COMES UP
IN ALL DIFFERENT PLACES FROM INVITING PEOPLE TO PARTIES TO
DRIVING A CAR. ETIQUETTE TODAY IS LESS STRICT THAN ~~IN THE~~
~~1600'S TO THE BEGINNING OF THE~~ IT WAS AWHILE AGO. BEFORE
THE 1900'S MEN WOULD BE TERRIBLY COURTEOUS TO WOMEN. THEY
WOULD HOLD DOORS, PUSH IN CHAIRS, AND ON DATES WOULD CHOOSE
THE ACTIVITY AND PAY THE EXPENSES. SIR WALTER RALEIGH PUT
HIS CLOAK DOWN OVER A PUDDLE FOR QUEEN ELIZABETH I TO WALK
ON. NOW THAT IS WHAT I CALL POLITENESS. THESE DAYS, ETI-
QUETTE IS LESS STRICT. FOR EXAMPLE, ON DATES THE BOY AND
GIRL SHARE THE COST AND BOTH DECIDE WHERE TO GO.
IT IS STILL THE THAT
AT THE TABLE ~~IT IS~~ MAN ~~STILL~~ HOLDS THE CHAIR FOR THE
LADY BUT SOME MANNERS APPLY TO EVERYONE.

AT THE START OF A FORMAL MEAL NO ONE SHOULD BEGIN EATING
UNTIL THE HOST OR HOSTESS ~~BEGINS~~ PICKS UP HIS OR HER FORK AND
~~STARTS EATING.~~ PEOPLE SHOULD NOT ~~EA~~ TALK WITH THEIR MOUTHS
FULL AS IT IS UNPLEASANT FOR OTHERS TO WATCH. EVERYONE MUST
BE FINISHED EATING BEFORE THE NEXT COURSE OR BEFORE THE TABLE
IS CLEARED. EVERYONE STAYS AT THE TABLE UNTIL EXCUSED BY THE
HOST OR HOSTESS.

THESE MANNERS MAKE EVERYTHING EASIER FOR DAILY LIVING AND
A LOT MORE ATTRACTIVE TO LOOK AT.

WEALTHY PEOPLE AND ARISTOCRATS HAVE MORE RIGID RULES OF
ETIQUETTE THAN MIDDLECLASS AND POOR PEOPLE--PROBABLY BECAUSE
THEY GET TO EAT IN PALACES AND MUST LEARN THE KING'S OR QUEEN'S
MANNERS.

I THINK MANNERS MAKE THE WORLD AN EASIER PLACE TO LIVE IN
AND IF EVERYONE LEARNED THE RULES OF ETIQUETTE THERE WOULD BE
LESS ARGUMENTS AND FIGHTS.

Figure 15. Facsimile of text, showing revisions, by the same student whose notes for
the composition are shown in Figure 14.

solving procedures that underlie expertise, and that in so doing the abilities that students bring to writing are extendable. Instructional studies also suggest, however, that moving from a knowledge-telling to a knowledge-transforming way of writing is not an incremental process but rather the rebuilding of a cognitive structure.

### References

Anderson, J. R. (1983). *The architecture of cognition.* Cambridge, MA: Harvard University Press.

Bereiter, C., Burtis, P. J., Scardamalia, M., & Brett, C. (1983, April). *Developmental differences in mental representation of main point in composition.* Paper presented at the meeting of the American Educational Research Association, Montreal.

Bereiter, C., & Scardamalia, M. (1982). From conversation to composition: The role of instruction in a developmental process. In R. Glaser (Ed.), *Advances in instructional psychology* (Vol. 2, pp. 1–64). Hillsdale, NJ: Erlbaum.

Bereiter, C., & Scardamalia, M. (1985). Cognitive coping strategies and the problem of "inert knowledge." In S. F. Chipman, J. W. Segal, & R. Glaser (Eds.), *Thinking and learning skills: Research and open questions* (Vol. 2, pp. 65–80). Hillsdale, NJ: Erlbaum.

Bereiter, C., & Scardamalia, M. (in press). *The psychology of written composition.* Hillsdale, NJ: Erlbaum.

Britton, J. (1982). Spectator role and the beginnings of writing. In M. Nystrand (Ed.), *What writers know: The language, process, and structure of written discourse* (pp. 149–69). New York: Academic Press.

Bryant, D. C. (1965). Rhetoric: Its function and scope. In J. Schwartz & J. A. Rycenga (Eds.), *The province of rhetoric* (pp. 3–36). New York: Ronald Press.

Burtis, P. J. (1983, April). *Planning in narrative and argument writing.* Paper presented at the meeting of the American Educational Research Association, Montreal.

Burtis, P. J., Bereiter, C., Scardamalia, M., & Tetroe, J. (1983). The development of planning in writing. In G. Wells & B. M. Kroll (Eds.), *Explorations in the development of writing* (pp. 153–74). New York: Wiley.

Caccamise, D. J. (in press). Idea generation in writing. In A. Matsuhashi (Ed.), *Writing in real time: Modelling production processes.* New York: Longman.

Calkins, L. M. (1979). Andrea learns to make writing hard. *Language Arts, 56,* 569–76.

Calkins, L. M. (1983). *Lessons from a child: On the teaching and learning of writing.* Exeter, NH: Heinemann.

Chomsky, N. (1980). *Rules and representations.* New York: Columbia University Press.

Collins, A. N., & Loftus, E. F. (1975). A spreading activation theory of semantic processing. *Psychological Review, 82,* 407–28.

de Beaugrande, R. (1984). *Text production: Toward a science of composition.* Norwood, NJ: Ablex.

Elbow, P. (1973). *Writing without teachers.* New York: Oxford University Press.

Faigley, L., & Witte, S. (1981). Analyzing revision. *College Composition and Communication, 32,* 400–14.

Flower, L. S. (1979). Writer-based prose: A cognitive basis for problems in writing. *College English, 41,* 19–37.

Flower, L. S., & Hayes, J. R. (1980). The cognition of discovery: Defining a rhetorical problem. *College Composition and Communication, 31,* 21–32.

Flower, L. S., & Hayes, J. R. (1981). The pregnant pause: An inquiry into the nature of planning. *Research in the Teaching of English, 15*, 229–44.

Flower, L. S., & Hayes, J. R. (1984). Images, plans and prose: The representation of meaning in writing. *Written Communication, 1*, 120–60.

Graves, D. H. (1979). What children show us about revision. *Language Arts, 56*, 312–19.

Hayes, J. R., & Flower, L. S. (1980a). Identifying the organization of writing processes. In L. W. Gregg & E. R. Steinberg (Eds.), *Cognitive processes in writing* (pp. 3–30). Hillsdale, NJ: Erlbaum.

Hayes, J. R., & Flower, L. S. (1980b). Writing as problem solving. *Visible Language, 14*, 388–99.

Lowenthal, D. (1980). Mixing levels of revision. *Visible Language, 14*, 383–7.

McCutchen, D., & Perfetti, C. A. (1982). Coherence and connectedness in the development of discourse production. *Text, 2*, 113–39.

Murray, D. M. (1978). Internal revision: A process of discovery. In C. R. Cooper & L. Odell (Eds.), *Research on composing* (pp. 85–103). Urbana, IL: National Council of Teachers of English.

National Assessment of Educational Progress (1977). *Write/rewrite: An assessment of revision skills; selected results from the second national assessment of writing.* (Tech. Rep.). Washington, DC: U.S. Government Printing Office. (ERIC Document Reproduction Service No. ED 141 826)

National Assessment of Educational Progress (1980a). *Writing achievement, 1969–79: Results from the third national writing assessment: Vol. 1. 17-year-olds* (Tech. Rep.). Denver, CO: National Assessment of Educational Progress. (ERIC Document Reproduction Service No. ED 196 042)

National Assessment of Educational Progress (1980b). *Writing achievement, 1969–79: Results from the third national writing assessment: Vol. 2. 13-year-olds* (Tech. Rep.). Denver, CO: National Assessment of Educational Progress. (ERIC Document Reproduction Service No. ED 196 043)

Newell, A. (1980). Reasoning, problem solving, and decision processes: The problem space as a fundamental category. In R. S. Nickerson (Ed.), *Attention and performance VIII* (pp. 693–718). Hillsdale, NJ: Erlbaum.

Nold, E. W. (1981). Revising. In C. H. Frederiksen & J. F. Dominic (Eds.), *Writing: The nature, development and teaching of written communication* (pp. 67–79). Hillsdale, NJ: Erlbaum.

Odell, L. (1980). Business writing: Observations and implications for teaching composition. *Theory into Practice, 19*, 225–32.

Perl, S. (1979). The composing processes of unskilled college writers. *Research in the Teaching of English, 13*, 317–36.

Scardamalia, M., & Bereiter, C. (1982). Assimilative processes in composition planning. *Educational Psychologist, 17*, 165–71.

Scardamalia, M., & Bereiter, C. (1983a). Child as co-investigator: Helping children gain insight into their own mental processes. In S. Paris, G. Olson, & H. Stevenson (Eds.), *Learning and motivation in the classroom* (pp. 61–82). Hillsdale, NJ: Erlbaum.

Scardamalia, M., & Bereiter, C. (1983b). The development of evaluative, diagnostic, and remedial capabilities in children's composing. In M. Martlew (Ed.), *The psychology of written language: Developmental and educational perspectives* (pp. 67–95). New York: Wiley.

Scardamalia, M., Bereiter, C., & Steinbach, R. (1984). Teachability of reflective processes in written composition. *Cognitive Science, 8*, 173–90.

Scardamalia, M., & Paris, P. (1985). The function of explicit discourse knowledge in the development of text representations and composing strategies. *Cognition and Instruction, 2*, 1–39.

Sommers, N. (1980). Revision strategies of student writers and experienced adult writers. *College Composition and Communications, 31*, 378–88.

*Writers at work: The* Paris Review *interviews* (2nd series). (1963). New York: Viking.

Zbrodoff, N. J. (1984). *Writing stories under time and length constraints.* Unpublished doctoral dissertation, University of Toronto.

# 5    Cognitive processes in revision

*John R. Hayes, Linda Flower, Karen A. Schriver,*
*James F. Stratman, and Linda Carey*

The primary purpose of this chapter is to present a new model of the revision process in written composition – a model based on the results of thinking-aloud protocol studies. We proceed by first discussing earlier observations and theories of
revision. We then describe the model and, finally, discuss in detail the protocol
data on which the model is based.

### Earlier observations

Although there have been relatively few empirical studies on revision, those that
are available provide valuable guideposts for the development of theory. The literature reviewed below establishes four points:

1. There are large differences in the amount of revising writers do. Experts make
   more revisions than do novices.
2. Expert revisers attend to more global revising problems than do novices.
3. Writers have more difficulty detecting faulty referring expressions when revising
   their own text than when revising the texts of other writers.
4. The ability to detect text problems appears to be separate from the ability to fix
   these problems.

*Writers differ greatly in the amount of revising they do*

Reviewing the testimony of eminent writers, Murray (1978) concludes that for
them "writing is rewriting." Here, Murray is describing the propensity of skilled
writers to spend far more time in revision than in the production of the original
draft. Bracewell, Scardamalia, and Bereiter (1978) found, however, that fourth
graders hardly revise at all, that eighth graders' revisions hurt more than they help,
and that for twelfth graders, helpful revisions narrowly outnumber harmful ones.

This work was supported in part by Grant BSN-8210492 from the National Science Foundation,
1982.

Bridwell's (1980) results were slightly more positive about twelfth graders' revisions than were those of Bracewell et al. (1978). She found that twelfth graders' second drafts were considerably better in "general merit" and mechanics than their first drafts. Pianko (1977) reported that first-year college students devote less than 9% of their composing time to rereading and revising. Clearly, writers differ widely in the amount they revise. In general, it appears that the more expert the writer, the greater is the proportion of writing time the writer will spend in revision.

## *Experts attend more to global problems than do novices*

The literature suggests that experts and novices define revising in very different ways. Broadly, revision can be defined as the writer's attempt to improve a plan or text. Within this definition, experts appear to attend *more* systematically to different aspects of the text than do novices.

Stallard (1974) found that only 2.5% of twelfth graders' revisions were focused above the word and sentence level. Bridwell (1980), who also studied twelfth graders, found about 11% of revisions above the sentence level. Bridwell's figure of 11% may be higher than Stallard's because Bridwell counted each sentence in a multisentence revision as a separate occurrence of a multisentence revision. If Bridwell had counted each multisentence revision just once for each group of revised sentences as Stallard did, the percentage of such revisions could not exceed 5.9% (if each multisentence revision consisted of just two sentences) and would be lower if some revisions involved three or more sentences.

Beach (1976), studying college juniors and seniors, found that students who revised extensively "tended to conceive of the paper in holistic terms" and to infer "general patterns of development." Students who did not revise extensively "evaluated only separate bits" of their papers.

Sommers (1980) found that first-year college students "understand the revision process as a rewording activity. . . . They concentrate on particular words apart from their role in the text" (p. 381). In contrast, experienced writers (e.g., journalists, editors, and academics) "describe their primary objectives when revising as finding the form or shape of their argument" (p. 384). Furthermore, Sommers (1980) found that "experienced writers have a second objective; a concern for their readership" (p. 384). Moreover, Sommers says, "At the heart of revision is the process by which writers recognize and resolve the dissonance they sense in their writing" (p. 385).

Faigley and Witte (1981), who studied changes in meaning resulting from revision, found that experts were more likely to change meaning through revision than were novices. They observed that the revisions of inexperienced college writers resulted in changed meaning in 12% of cases; the revisions of experienced college writers, in 25% of cases; and the revisions of expert adult writers, in 34% of cases.

These results suggest that experts define the task of revision as being more global and more focused on meaning and audience than do novices.

### Writers have difficulty detecting faults in their own text

Bartlett (1981) compared the revision processes of fifth-grade students who were revising both their own and other writers' texts. In one study, she found that when the children were revising their own texts, they were able to find 56% of missing subjects or predicates but only 10% of faulty referring expressions. In contrast, when they were revising the text of other writers, they detected about half of each type of problem. Knowledge of their own intention as writers apparently made it difficult for them to detect faulty references in their own texts.

### Finding and fixing problems appear to be separate skills

In a second study, Bartlett asked sixth and seventh graders to revise paragraphs that embodied one of two types of reference problem. The first type of problem involved sentences of the form "A boy named Joe. . . . Another boy named Bill. . . . He. . . ." The second involved sentences of the form "A boy. . . . Another boy. . . . He. . . ."

Confronted with the first problem type, the children were able to detect 62% of the problems and then corrected 95% of those they detected. With the second problem type, they detected 52% of the problems (about the same as before) but were able to correct only 58% of those they detected. The children's ability to solve the second type of problem, then, appeared to be limited in two ways. First, the students were able to detect only half of the problems and, of course, they did not solve those problems they did not detect. Thus, they were limited by their ability to *detect* problems. Second, the children were able to solve only about half of the problems they did detect. Thus, they were also limited by their ability to solve identified problems. The children's capacity to solve the first type of problem appeared to be limited only by the ability to detect problems since the students solved almost all of the problems they detected. However, we have no evidence that the children could have solved the problems they failed to detect if they had been pointed out to them. Thus, the children's ability to solve the first problem type was certainly limited by their ability to detect problems but might also have been limited by their ability to solve them.

Scardamalia and Bereiter (1983) have suggested that sixth to eighth graders' ability to revise is limited much more by their ability to fix problems than by their ability to detect them. On the basis of current data, our best guess is that both the ability to detect problems and the ability to fix them once they are detected act independently to limit students' ability to revise.

### Earlier theory: cues initiating revision

Several researchers have suggested that the cue or initiating condition for revision is a dissonance or incongruity between intention and execution. For example, Bridwell (1980) suggests that, when rereading the text, "the writer may either verify what is on the page or perceive some dissonance" (p. 220). Perception of dissonance is a cue that may lead to a decision to change the text. According to Sommers (1980), "The anticipation of a reader's judgment causes a feeling of dissonance when the writer recognizes incongruities between intention and execution" (p. 385). It is this recognition, Sommers asserts, that leads the writer to make revisions.

The most complete model of revision to date is Scardamalia and Bereiter's (1983) C.D.O. (compare, diagnose, and operate) model. According to Scardamalia and Bereiter, "During the course of composition, two kinds of mental representations are built up and stored in long-term memory. These are a representation of the text as written up to the time, and a representation of the text as intended. The C.D.O. process is initiated by a perceived mismatch between these two representations" (p. 4).

Although the idea that revision is initiated by the discovery of dissonance between intention and execution is attractive, we believe that it is not adequate to account for all of the phenomena we observe in revision. To make it clear why we think so, we shall first define some concepts. When we speak of intention, we refer to the author's writing plan to produce a text that will accomplish a purpose such as conveying facts or convincing an audience. This writing plan or network of working goals was itself constructed out of the writer's knowledge of goals, plans, constraints, and criteria for discourse and for problem solving in general. By text, we mean the external written product the writer produces (with greater or lesser skill) in an attempt to carry out the writing plan. If the text is reasonably well written, a reader can usually infer the major aspects of the writing plan from the text alone. The writing plan, then, although most available to the writer, is also available in various degrees to others.

With these definitions in mind, we see that the reviser may engage in evaluations of several kinds:

1. The reviser may evaluate the text against general criteria for texts such as standards of spelling, grammar, and clarity. Such evaluations can be carried out even if the reviser is not aware of the writer's plans for the text. Certainly, a text will fail to meet these general criteria if it is so badly garbled that the reader is unable to decipher the writer's intention.
2. The reviser may evaluate the text against the writer's intention. When writers revise their own texts, they frequently find that the text does not fully express their intended meaning. They may find that the words and examples they have chosen, though close to the intended meaning, are not fully accurate and have to be revised. When the reviser is not the writer, he or she must infer the writer's plan

from the text. The inferred plan can then be compared with the text. For example, the reviser may say, "I see what he is trying to do, but he needs a better example."
3. The reviser may evaluate the plan against criteria he or she believes plans should meet. For example, a writer might plan to present a list of examples supporting a point and then, reflecting on the plan, decide that the listing approach would not be convincing because it is boring. An interesting case is one in which the writer plans an argument and then executes it in writing. On reading the text, he or she finds that it accurately represents the plan but that the plan is built on contradictory assumptions. Thus, the text matches the plan (a positive type 2 evaluation) but the plan itself is rejected.

Of these three types of evaluation, the second involves the comparison of text and intention but the first and third do not. Of the three, we believe that the third is the most important in producing high-quality revisions. In fact, we propose that the superiority of an expert's revisions is based not on a better comparison of text and intention, but on a better evaluation of plans with respect to the writer's general goals.

## The model

In this section we introduce a theoretical model of the revision processes we observed. However, before we explicate the features of this model, we believe it is important to address several questions about the value and place of such models in research and instruction. In particular, we shall explain how models induced from protocol data help us to create more testable theories of writing task performance. Recently, model building based on protocol data has been attacked as a poor method of understanding underlying cognitive skills in writing (e.g., Cooper & Holzman, 1983, 1985). Indeed, because a recent essay by Cooper and Holzman (1985) contains most of the serious (and recurrent) criticisms leveled at protocol methodology, we shall briefly address the objections it raises.

### Goals and criticisms of protocol-derived models

Three criticisms of the use of protocols to study writing have been advanced by Cooper and Holzman (1985):

1. Cooper and Holzman claim that valid empirical research can begin only with a "well-defined" object of research. Cognitive processes in writing are ill-defined; therefore, protocols cannot be used to study these processes until the precise nature of the processes is clearly and unambiguously explicated.
2. They claim that writing theories induced from protocol data cannot be tested in principle, because writing processes are too complex to capture in protocols and because the protocol verbalizations themselves do not provide any information about these writing processes.
3. They imply that experts and novices differ in their capacity to give reports of their activities while writing; therefore, comparisons of experts and novices are likely

to reflect differences in this capacity, not necessarily differences in particular skills or processes.

Let us take up each of these criticisms in turn.

**1.** Cooper and Holzman have contended that we have not sufficiently defined our "object of research." They point out that such a definition is necessary before any theory of cognitive processes can be "tested." Unfortunately, in making these points, they mistakenly assume that the purpose of protocol methodology in our studies is to *test* – or validate – a theory of cognitive processes in writing. For instance, Cooper and Holzman argue that, before using the methodology, we should be able to define the difference between the cognitive processes underlying writing and those underlying speech generation in an oratorical context. However, two unfortunate (and, we believe, mistaken) assumptions lie at the base of their criticisms.

First, so far in our research we have used protocol methodology primarily to *construct* and *enrich* theories of writing task performance, not to *test* our theories or models. The problem with current research on writing as we perceive it is that, where underlying cognitive processes are concerned, there has been no strong or "well-defined" theory to test – certainly none before Emig (1971). To that extent, we agree with Cooper and Holzman in their concern for creating testable theories, but because we have noted the absence of empirically based process theories, we began building theories using the untried observational method of protocols. The goal of such theory building, in contrast to theory testing (or hypothesis testing), is to locate processes that might be more carefully studied, that is, to locate and explore phenomena not previously observed that might have theoretical significance. The methodological research indicates that protocols are ideal for this theory-building purpose (Ericsson & Simon, 1984, chap. 1).

However, observers like Cooper and Holzman (1985) appear to demand that phenomena be perfectly understood before they can be *either* observed or tested. They state, "As a theory is useful to science only when applied to a well-defined object of research, so a methodology is useful only to the extent that it can be used to test a carefully articulated theory" (p. 98). We reject both assertions. They are based on a conception of the relation between methodology and theory that is unnecessarily narrow – one that would severely limit the way many scientists do productive research. In the first instance, many a theory has been useful to science when the object of that theory was only partially defined – Freud's theory of dreams is just one powerful case in point. (Whatever else his current detractors might say, we doubt they would say his theory is "useless.") In the second instance, many an important theory has been *built* (or discovered) using a different methodology than the one used subsequently to test or validate its hypotheses. To make the kind of sweeping claim that Cooper and Holzman do (above) is blithely to ignore the fact that there may be separate methods for building, testing, and interrelating theories.

Indeed, our situation with protocol methodology is somewhat analogous to the scientific situation that emerged with the invention of microscopes. Early microscopes were initially important as means of *generating* new theories of disease etiology – theories that no one quite knew how to test or validate at the time but that stimulated an entirely new direction of hypothesis testing. In a similar way, we are using protocols to make novel but (as far as possible) systematic observations about the information-processing activities of writers. Our search for interpretations of what we observe necessarily proceeds in parallel with the search for a better (i.e., more testable) model or theory (see Ericsson & Simon, 1984, pp. 5–10).

**2.** Cooper and Holzman (1985) also claim that the writing theories induced from protocol data are not testable *in principle* (Cooper & Holzman, 1985, p. 98). For instance, citing Ericsson and Simon (1984) in their support, Cooper and Holzman state that "laboratory protocol methodologies cannot deal with complicated cognitive processes" and that "common experience shows that cognitive processes in non-laboratory conditions are also unreachable in this fashion" (p. 99). Both statements are wholly unfounded (Cooper and Holzman offer not a single study in support) and reflect a superficial reading (at best) of the research on protocol methodology reported by Ericsson and Simon. Indeed, Cooper and Holzman's statements disregard the thrust of Ericsson and Simon's entire book, for although Ericsson and Simon go to great lengths to describe the limitations of protocol methodology for specific purposes and under specific conditions, they never state prima facie that it cannot deal with complicated cognitive processes. On the contrary, they conclude, after a massive review of empirical studies, that such a criticism is unfounded (see especially Chapters 4 and 5). Protocol data are shown to be a powerful means of both testing and building theories – not merely theories about simple processes, but theories about higher-level processes as well. As they plainly state, " . . . higher-level activities like reading and writing are made up of numerous sub-processes that use short-term memory for inputs and outputs. [Protocol] subjects' awareness of these inputs and outputs enables them to report the occurrence and duration of higher-level activities" (p. 243).

As for tracing cognitive processes outside the laboratory, numerous successful protocol studies of subjects executing "real" complex tasks have been conducted (see the bibliography in Ericsson & Simon, 1984). The evidence produced by these studies indicates that many supposedly "unreachable" or "unreportable" cognitive processes can be either reported or inferred from transcripts. Many "ecologically valid" studies are also discussed by Ericsson and Simon.

Another criticism, often closely following the preceding one, is that the verbal data produced by protocols have nothing to do with the cognitive processes in question (i.e., with cognitive processes in writing). In other words, the protocol data are merely "epiphenomenal." For example, Cooper and Holzman (1985) contend that protocol methodology merely "produces interesting narratives, data for a theory about what certain writers will say about the writing process, but not data about *the* writing process, nor even, given its limitations, particularly useful data about the cognitive processes of writers in this particular situation" (p. 99). But this charge that verbal reports of writers are epiphenomenal has little or no empirical basis. Again, Cooper and Holzman offer not one study to support their claims. Indeed, this criticism is also carefully addressed by Ericsson and Simon, and it would appear that Cooper and Holzman ignored their discussion or failed to comprehend it. As Simon and Ericsson note, "Whenever verbalizations correspond to plausible intermediate states in a processing model for the problem solving activity, we can plausibly infer that this information is *actually used* in generating the problem solution" (p. 171, our emphasis). In addition, Ericsson and Simon describe three criteria for assessing the relevance of verbalizations to a given task:

> The verbalizations should be relevant to the given task.
> The verbalizations, to be pertinent, should be logically consistent with the verbalizations that just precede them.
> A subset of the information heeded during task performance will be remembered.

We take our protocols to satisfy all three of these criteria (pp. 171–2) and suggest that Cooper and Holzman apply the strong form of the epiphenomenality "test" detailed by Ericsson and Simon to our (or indeed any) protocols (p. 172).

Moreover, with particular reference to the studies and model of revision presented in this chapter, we must also reject both of the above criticisms. We do not take our data here as "irrefutable proof" of the accuracy or completeness of our revision model, but we do think the model, together with the data, sets forth interesting, useful, and testable hypotheses about the kinds of skills experts and novices are likely to exhibit differentially, particularly on controlled revision tasks of the type we have used. We reiterate that we are more interested in *building* a theory of revision processes and showing its plausibility than in testing the predictions that might be implied by this theory. We nevertheless invite research that tests our model against new data obtained in a similar context. And with Ericsson and Simon (1984), we believe that protocol methodology, if carefully used, would be one valid means of testing some of the hypotheses connected with our model.

**3.** A final criticism, which is implied by Cooper and Holzman (1985), concerns the educational value of expert–novice comparisons (such as the one we are about to report), especially in relation to teaching. In short, they seem to be asking, "Why make models of expert–novice differences? What good are these models for improving students' work?" To answer these questions, we must place the present model in the context of our earlier work with experts and novices.

Our previous studies have strongly suggested that writing involves a number of subprocesses whose presence, organization, and degree of automaticity (i.e., accessibility to focal attention) vary with expertise as well as other factors, such as type of writing task and experimental instruction. We assume that expertise affects not only what *information* a subject may heed in short-term memory, but also to some extent the subject's *ability to report* what he or she heeds. Thus, it may be that experts, because they have "overlearned" or "automated" a certain process, cannot verbalize this process, whereas novices can. For example, an expert might use parallelism in sentences unconsciously and therefore not report information indicating the deliberate decision to use this technique. A novice, however, having just learned what parallelism is, may vocalize information indicating a conscious choice. Conversely, both experts and novices might consciously use the same sub-process, but only experts – as a result of having better "verbal skills" – might be able to report that they were doing so. Both of these effects of "expertise" are inherent in expert–novice studies of the type we report here and can probably never be wholly eliminated. In particular, we realize that what may appear to be a difference between experts and novices in underlying writing or revising processes may sometimes partly be an artifact produced by the interaction between the degree of expertise a subject possesses and the constraint of giving a protocol. Despite these possible confounds in comparing experts and novices, however, there is nevertheless much benefit in reporting the differences we find, and for two reasons.

First, we assume that some high-level processes (e.g., selection of relevant content in writing or revising) can never be "automated," no matter how expert the expert, and that traces of the information used or produced in the process will be available for reporting in short-term memory. How these higher-level processes are handled seems likely to reflect genuine expert–novice differences, and not merely developmental effects of learning (automaticity) or ancillary effects of verbal "reporting skill." Second, we examine not only verbal reports but also textual data (in the revisions that subjects actually produce) to support the inferences we are making about likely expert–novice "process" differences. These textual data allow us to check our assumptions about what processes experts and novices appear to employ. In nearly all cases, the process data are paralleled by differences in written output.

As for the usefulness of the model itself, we believe it helps us more than any other model produced to date to see more precisely where in the complex process of revision students may experience problems. As Bereiter and Scardamalia (1981) put it, "In order to make advances in teaching a subject like composition, it isn't enough to know what needs to be learned. One has to get to the heart of the difficulties people have in learning it" (p. 3). In particular, the model divides the revision process into several major subprocesses, each of which we describe in detail. We wish to show that any number of subprocesses can be the source of trouble for novices and that each of these subprocesses may constitute a skill worthy of separate instructional effort. In other words, to improve students' performance in revision, one may have to improve their *ability to perform* on a number

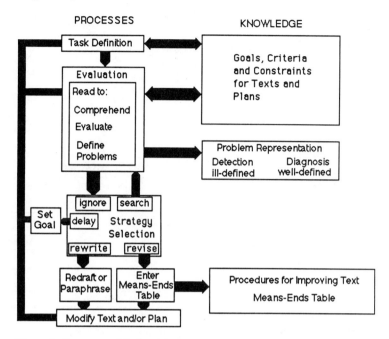

Figure 1. Process model of revision.

of discrete subtasks – as well as increase *what they know* about texts, writing, and revision.

In summary, we continue to be impressed by the value of expert–novice protocol studies for theory-building purposes. If better, more "well-defined" theories were available, more theory testing, using classical psychological performance measures, might be possible. But it is precisely the lack of theory about cognitive processes in writing that motivates our research. With Patrick Suppes (1974), we "want to see a new generation of trained theorists and an equally competent band of experimentalists to surround them, and [we] look for the day when they will show that the theories [we] now cherish were merely humble way stations on the road to the theoretical palaces they have constructed" (p. 3).

*Parts of the model*

We present the model first, largely as a means of organizing our observations. Each subprocess is treated in a separate section. The revision model (Figure 1) is an elaboration of the review process described in our previous research on writing (Figure 2). The model is divided into two major sections. Processes in which the reviser engages are on the left, and categories of knowledge that influence these processes or result from their action are on the right. Before describing the results

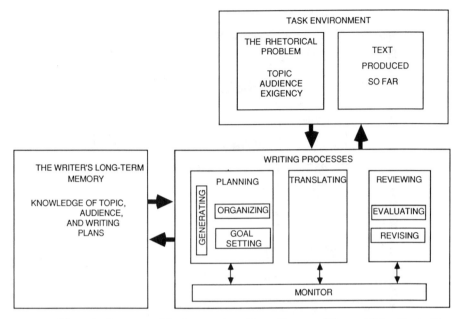

Figure 2. Process model of composing. (From Flower and Hayes, 1981a. Used with permission.)

of our protocol analyses, we shall first present an overview of the subprocesses represented in the model.

To perform a task, a person must have a definition of the task to be performed. The task definition for revision specifies, among other things,

> The goals of the reviser, for example, revision for clarity or elegance.
>
> The features of the text that should be examined, for example, global features, local features, or both.
>
> How the revision process should be carried out. For example, should the text be examined in one pass or in several? Should the "gist" of the text be extracted before revision begins?

We shall make two important points about task definition. First, revisers may modify their task definitions during the course of revision. Second, the definition of revision varies from person to person. In particular, experts appear to differ systematically from novices in their goals for revision and in the features of the text they believe should be examined.

The goals, criteria, and constraints that define acceptable texts and plans may be ones the reviser brings to the revising task, or they may be ones that are suggested in the course of the revision process. For example, if the reviser notices several wordiness problems in a text, he or she may set the goal to be aware of such problems. Goals, criteria, and constraints, then, may be dynamically modified during revision.

The evaluation process applies the goals and criteria relevant to the reviser's task definition to texts and plans. We believe that evaluation is best viewed as an extension of the familiar process of reading for comprehension. The primary output of evaluation is an initial problem representation and sometimes important discoveries that influence the revision process. The evaluation process, operating under the goal to modify the text, may thus generate useful alternatives to text features and text goals.

Problem representations vary in specificity or well-definedness. At the ill-defined end of the spectrum are simple detections – the reviser recognizes that some sort of problem exists, but the exact nature of the problem is not clear (e.g., "It just doesn't sound quite right here"). At the well-defined end of the scale are highly specific problem diagnoses (e.g., "That word is misspelled"). Between these two extremes are representations that contain some information about the nature of the problem but are not yet specific enough for the reviser to take appropriate action without further effort. Problem representation, then, varies on a continuum from simple detection through relatively vague diagnoses to very specific diagnoses.

The reviser's strategy selection depends on the initial problem representation. Two sorts of strategy are available:

1. Those that modify or control the revision process itself: ignoring the problem, delaying action, searching for more information to clarify the problem representation
2. Those that modify the text: revising the text or rewriting the text

Ignoring a problem occurs, for instance, when the reviser determines that the problem, however it is defined, is not worth fussing over or, for instance, when the definition or nature of the problem itself is not clear to the reviser. Delaying action often occurs when the reviewer decides to deal with the text in two passes – one pass for high-level problems and one pass for surface problems. On the first pass, the reviewer may notice that the text has spelling problems but decide to wait until the second pass to fix them. Searching for more information may occur when the reviewer's diagnosis is not specific enough to suggest a clear choice of action. The search for more specific information has the purpose of moving the representation from the ill-defined toward the well-defined end of the continuum.

When revisers decide to modify the text, they have two major options: rewriting and revising. By *rewriting*, we refer to the strategy by which the writer abandons the surface structure of the text, attempts to extract the gist, and rewrites that gist in his or her own words. Rewriting may be done at a relatively local level when the reviser paraphrases individual sentences or at a global level when the reviser redrafts a large section of the text. Rewriting may be chosen either when the reviser does not have an adequate strategy for fixing the text problem (as is frequently the case for novices) or when the reviser judges that the text has too many problems to make revision worthwhile (as is often the case with experts).

Because of common usage, we have used *revising* to refer to the whole process by which the reviser attempts to improve a text. At this point, however, we want to use the term in a more restricted sense, as the strategy by which the writer attempts to fix the text problem while preserving as much of the original text as possible. We assume that successful revising requires that the writer diagnose the text's problems and fix them without completely rewriting the text.

Indeed, although this distinction between revising and rewriting is somewhat difficult to establish, we shall present empirical evidence indicating its foundations in the reviser's processes. Specifically, rewriting and revision can be viewed as points on a continuum whose positions depend on the extent to which the writer attempts to save the original surface of the text. We assume that writers' devotion to preserving the original text varies continuously over a range of values from high, when one is editing one's boss's memo, to low, when one is repairing the work of a less than competent assistant. We shall attempt to show that, in comparison with rewriting, revision operates as a focused "repair" procedure based on rich diagnostic information about the problem.

In carrying out the revision process, writers may vary in the goals and criteria they bring to the task, in the kinds of problems they are able to identify in text, and in the sophistication of the methods they employ. Each reviser can be thought of as having a "means–ends table" in which the problem to be fixed (the ends) is associated with appropriate rules, maxims, and problem-solving procedures (the means). As we shall see, expert revisers have more detailed and complex means–ends tables than do novice revisers.

To summarize, our purpose in presenting this preview of the parts of the model has been to show that revision is indeed a complex process, containing a number of critical subprocesses for investigation. However, before we proceed to a discussion of our findings concerning these subprocesses, we shall describe the basic components of our experimental task and method. The remainder of the chapter is structured as follows:

> Method
> Task definition
> Evaluation
> Problem representation: detecting text problems
> Problem representation: diagnosing text problems
> Strategy selection

## Method

### The task

Our goal was to create a realistic task that called for a full range of rhetorical and stylistic revisions. In order to acquaint themselves with the protocol method, the subjects completed a practice task (see Appendix B). They were given a letter written to the Carnegie-Mellon University athletic coach by another coach, discussing why women are unnecessarily reluctant to participate in college sports. The subjects were asked to revise this letter into a handout for first-year women (see Appendices A and C). We designed this to be a naturalistic task demanding both high- and low-level revisions. That is, although the information in the letter was appropriate, the task implicitly called for changes in voice, genre, rhetorical stance, perceived audience, and style. In addition, we planted a set of stylistic and rule-governed errors in the text, including problems with spelling, punctuation, grammar, wordiness, and diction (see Appendix C). The subjects were paid and told that the Writing Center would select the best revision.

### Subjects

The 14 subjects in the study included seven undergraduate students (two of whom were identified by grades and teachers as very capable writers, the others as inexperienced); three professional writer-editors who frequently did revision but typically did not have to diagnose or explain problems in texts; and four experienced writing instructors who had also had experience as editors.

### Method and analysis

The study involved three stages during which the subjects were asked to think aloud as they worked. In Stage 1 they revised the faulty text. Stage 2, immediately afterward, was a cued recall session in which the subjects were asked to explain the changes they had made. In Stage 3, one week or more later, the subjects were given sentences from the original containing the 26 "planted problems" in random order and asked to describe any problems they saw. These three measures enabled us to collect converging evidence on what problems people actually saw and to separate what people might "know" on the less demanding single-sentence task from what they actually used during revision.

The protocols from the three sessions were first parsed to identify instances of *reading*, *proposed changes*, and *comments*. The comments were further parsed into numbered clauses as the basic unit of analysis. The texts were analyzed for revisions. All changes made on the text were also traced to the protocol, a procedure that enabled us to compare comments in the protocol with actions taken. All comments were then typed on individual 3 × 5 cards, which allowed a variety of blind sortings that are described in the following studies.

## Defining the task of revision

The first study attempted to define the process of "task definition" as it occurs in our model of revision. The study presented data suggesting important differences in task definition processes between experts and novices and discussed the implications of these differences for our overall understanding of revision skill.

### Task definition versus problem representation

The first process illustrated by our revision model is task definition. In a sense, this process is the foundation of all other revision skills, for it reflects writers' underlying conceptions of what it means to revise or improve a text. That is, the task definition process reflects writers' conceptions of what activities are involved in revision as well as their conception of how these processes are to be managed. Experimental research on problem solving tells us that the ability to report or describe our task definitions while we are at work on a problem is limited (Ericsson & Simon, 1984). Unless specifically directed to talk about their concept of a particular type of problem solving, experimental subjects are not likely to do so to any great extent. Nonetheless, the pervasive effect of apparently "tacit" task definitions on task performance is noted again and again in research. People appear to create and draw on knowledge when they anticipate complex tasks.

For this reason, we place the task definition process at the top of our model, not because the definition itself is necessarily fixed or unchanging during revision, but rather because of its underlying importance. Its products are the goals, constraints, and criteria that will guide the overall revision process. Moreover, we distinguish the task definition process from the problem representation process, also shown in our model. We can characterize the difference as follows. Whereas task definition processes reflect writers' conception of relevant revision criteria, revision activities, and ways of managing these activities over time (e.g., when to read "for comprehension" and when to evaluate), problem representation processes reflect writers' understanding of what is wrong with the text or what it needs and how to respond to these errors or needs. We shall further clarify the differences between these two major processes here, because we believe that each contributes independently to revisers' difficulties and successes, and therefore each may be the locus of important (and perhaps teachable) skills.

1. The kind of knowledge that makes up *task definitions* is generally regarded as "metacognitive" knowledge, since a task definition implies control over the use of other kinds of knowledge (Bracewell, 1983; Flavell, 1977). In other words, metacognitive knowledge consists of the things one has to know in order to make use of other kinds of knowledge one has. With Bracewell (1983), we assume that metacognitive processes are conscious processes (i.e., ones deliberately chosen) because knowledge of them can be verbalized. A task definition for revision contains a person's knowledge of what general processes might be used in the revision of a text and in what possible orders these processes might be invoked. Let us look at a concrete example.

If I am given a text to revise by an experimenter, I may know that I can either read the whole text first before making changes or read one small section at a time and make my changes as I proceed. Hence, I am making a decision about what general processes to use and in what order to apply them. As another example, I may read completely through the text, then decide to evaluate the text (on a second pass) for only certain within-sentence problems, such as faulty pronouns. A reviser's task definition controls such decisions about overall goals for the text, the constraints that may limit achieving these goals, and the evaluative criteria to be applied. At any given point I may be more or less conscious of the fact that I am making such choices, but certainly the fact that I may switch from one goal, process, or criteria to another indicates that to some extent I can manipulate my definition of the task.

In our description of revision, then, the task definition process creates and stores metacognitive, or regulatory, knowledge. Moreover, we do not wish to give the impression that task definitions are static, or fixed, by the reviser at the beginning of a task and never altered later. Rather, we hypothesize that task definitions are periodically "updated" during the course of revision. As dynamic constructs, they depend partly on stored conceptions (in long-term memory) of what it means to revise and partly on what information is provided (continually) by the task environment. By *task environment* we include all those sources of information outside a reviser, including the writer's text with the changes made in it so far (Flower & Hayes, 1981a). Whenever a reviser accesses new information from the task environment, the reviser's priorities for executing various subprocesses associated with the task may be altered; thus, the reviser's (current) task definition may change.

2. Problem representation differs from task definition in the following way. Although problem representations, like task definitions, involve regulatory knowledge, problem representation is a process that focuses on some particular difficulty or need in the text. As shown in the model (Figure 1), problem representation refers to the information processing prompted by some specific unit of text, whether this unit is small or large.

We can clarify this difference between task definition and problem representation with an extended illustration. First, here is what we mean by the "regulatory control" effected by the task definition process. Suppose I am reading a letter my boss has asked me to improve. When I read the letter for the first time, I am likely to be reading primarily to comprehend it, that is, to build a representation of its meaning – the more so if I have no idea of what it is about. However, even such a naive reading is still directed by the higher-level goal of improving the text – so I am not reading purely to comprehend, as the recipient might be. Such a shift in goals, between reading purely to comprehend (i.e., for some purpose other than revision) and reading to revise (or improve) the text, is controlled by a person's task definition. And task definition controls decisions about other kinds of processes as well.

For instance, in the course of reading with the goal to improve the text, my effort to comprehend per se may become sidetracked. That is, I may encounter many difficulties or needs in the letter and begin to try to *evaluate* them. In attempting an evaluation (e.g., "Should the text be this way or some other way?"), in effect I cease to read for comprehension. I shift processes further, and this shift is controlled by my task definition. Of course, task definitions may also limit in an a priori way some of the evaluative procedures I will use. I may, for example, choose to read the first and last line of each paragraph, or skim the text rapidly several times in succession. I may decide to read the entire text in several discrete passes, searching in each pass for only a few kinds of related problems, or I may decide to read the entire text in a single pass, evaluating each sentence after I read it for a large range of criteria. A person's task definition will delimit, and monitor, these options.

Finally, task definitions set boundaries to the evaluative criteria that may be applied. For instance, for a certain type of writing, the reviser may opt to ignore spelling errors or, conversely, to search chiefly for such errors. Or the reviser may look chiefly to see if certain questions are answered (e.g., the journalist's who, what, where, when, and why), if repetition is justifiably used, if sentences exceed a certain length, or if sentences are written in a certain pattern (e.g., active vs. passive voice). Thus, the task definition process sets up certain criteria in addition to setting underlying goals and constraints.

The problem representation process is quite different, as we can see by returning to the letter scenario just described. For example, suppose as I read my boss's letter I come upon a sentence that brings me to a complete stop – a sentence I have difficulty understanding and that seems unacceptable. I may represent the sentence's problem to myself as one caused by its three embedded dependent clauses, or I may simply say to myself, "It has too many words." One of these two representations may be more specific than the other. We refer to the processing called for in making such diagnostic choices as the *problem-representation process*. The important point to be made about this process is that the problem representation I have determines the value, or power, of the procedures I will use to correct the problem.

An analogy with manufacturing may provide another way of understanding the difference in our model between task definition, problem representation, and strategy selection. In revision, task definition acts much like a quality control *manager* in a complex assembly process. The quality control manager sets the goals, criteria, and constraints by which assembly and evaluation of the product proceed. In particular, the quality control manager schedules different inspection processes, determining what inspections are absolutely required for product quality. The manager constructs a list of the general evaluative processes that are essential and feasible. On the basis of this list he may also decide which evaluation routines *must* come before others, which routines *may* (but do not necessarily have to) come before others, and which routines may *interrupt* others. In a similar way, task definition in revision determines (1) the reviser's choice of major revision goals, (2) the availability of evaluative subprocesses needed to meet those goals, and (3) the general "schedule" by which these subprocesses might be carried out.

Problem representation is analogous to a quality control *inspector*, who actually makes performance evaluations and assesses (or defines) specific problems with the product. Moreover, just as important interaction occurs between the quality control manager and the inspectors in a manufacturing environment, so we hypothesize that considerable interaction occurs between revisers' task definition process and their problem representation process. For example, depending on the results of diagnostic processes brought to him by the inspector, the quality control manager may change his goals and priorities and thus call a halt to – or temporarily interrupt – other evaluative processes just getting underway. Similarly, task definition during revision may set goals that are periodically modified by information generated later during the problem representation process. We shall describe in greater detail how we think this interaction occurs (in the discussion section of this first study and again in the "Strategy Selection" section).

Finally, in our model, strategy selection might be usefully compared to the *line manager*, who works just below the level of the quality control inspector. The line manager decides how to tackle the problems assessed by the inspector and carries out the adjustments indicated. In strategy selection, as we later discuss, the reviser determines what to do in response to particular text problems. Just as we hypothesize that the problem representation process may change the reviser's task definition, so we also hypothesize that strategy selection may change the goals, criteria, and constraints that make up this definition.

## Differences between experts' and novices' task definitions

Having defined the basic differences between task definition and the other major processes in our model, we shall describe the specific objectives and method of analysis used in the present study. Our basic question was this: What overall conceptions of revision, or what kinds of task definitions, would the early portions of the protocols reveal? This question actually has several parts, as follows.

First, we wanted to see whether experts and novices give themselves the same or different tasks to perform – that is, do they define their tasks differently, and if so, how?

Second, we wanted to find out if experts pay more deliberate attention to the construction of their task definitions than do novices. For instance, do experts create revision plans and agendas or other kinds of process or problem "inventories" that shape their subsequent efforts to improve the text?

Third, we wanted to find out if experts tailor their task definition to the occasion more so than novices. For instance, other revision researchers have suggested that most revisers are likely to invoke stored, relatively fixed criteria and procedures for guiding the process rather than adapting their task definition to the underlying purpose of the text and the difficulties inherent in that purpose. The implication of text-based studies of revision, in particular, seems to be that few revisers – regardless of whether they are experts or novices – deliberately or consciously attend to the task definition process. For example, Nold (1982) concludes that revisers do not set goals and make "plans" for guiding the revision process unless specifically prompted to do so by teachers or experimenters; instead, they simply invoke static, well-learned subroutines, much like the college student who, instead of performing the task of comparison and analysis set by essay directions to "analyze the function of the black veil in Hawthorne's 'The Minister's Black Veil,'" defines his task as a narrative one, in which he merely recounts the events of the story (Nold, p. 11). Similarly, Nold theorizes that most revisers operate largely out of tacit, stored conceptions of revision; in her view, they do not consciously build a representation of the task's demands, nor do they forecast the goals, criteria, and constraints they might use before setting to work.

However, this theory is based on scant direct evidence. Few (if any) revision studies have attempted to produce evidence of revisers' deliberate attention to the task definition process and to the tailoring of revision goals that might be part of this process. In other words, no revision studies have tried to capture and describe how revisers produce task definitions under experimental conditions. The study reported here is the first to take a close look at how expert and novice revisers initially construct task definitions and to observe some of the variables apparently involved in this process.

### Method

As noted above, studies of a wide variety of problem-solving tasks indicate that task definitions usually are not verbalized by subjects in detail (Ericsson & Simon, 1984). Indeed, it appears to be difficult for many people to verbalize task definition information concurrently with problem solving, unless such information can be heeded in short-term memory. To deal with this problem, we designed our directions so that revisers could more directly heed the information associated with task definition. Specifically, although our directions implied a distinction between *revising* and *rewriting*, the directions themselves did not offer an explicit explanation of this distinction. We deliberately created a sense of dissonance. We wanted subjects to work with the existing text to whatever degree they considered appropriate, so we left it to them to make their own interpretations of the revise–rewrite distinction, with only one constraint imposed: We instructed them not to rewrite the text completely. That is, we did not allow subjects simply to read the target text, set it aside, and then create a new, altogether original text on a separate sheet of paper. We directed subjects to make all their changes on the target text and to use extra paper only when they wished to make additions or do extensive restructuring. Otherwise, they were free to do as they wished, adding whole new sections if they desired.

Thinking-aloud protocols of seven experts and seven novices were examined. To determine any differences between the task definitions of experts and novices, we examined all transcripted comments made by both subject groups, beginning with the moment they began reading the task directions and ending when the subjects made their first text change. In particular, we thought that comments in the early stages of the revision task might provide useful evidence of the different features of experts' and novices' task definition process.

To clarify our method, we shall briefly explain how the initial phase of the protocols was segmented.

1. *Direction-reading phase.* We transcribed the subjects' comments during the direction-reading phase of the task because we hoped to observe the effects, if any, these directions had on the reviewers' initial attempt to build task definitions. The direction-reading phase included all comments made during the time the subjects read the task directions up to the point where they began reading the target text (i.e., the letter).
2. *Initial text-reading phase.* This phase included all comments the subjects made between the time they first began reading the target text and the time they made their first text change (i.e., actually added or deleted a word, phrase, etc.). Our major assumption in examining the subjects' comments during this phase was that the amount and kind of information processing done here might have powerful implications for the task definitions they subsequently used to guide task performance.

The comments made by revisers during both the direction-reading and text-reading stages were carefully analyzed. The comments appeared to fall into one of seven "activity" categories (Table 1). These categories were established by an inductive process; that is, all comments made by subjects within the segments described above were sorted into piles, according to the kind of activity the comments seemed to imply. The categories were not generated before the data had been inspected. Though the first category, "Reads letter completely," is probably self-explanatory, the others may not be and will be briefly explicated here. Category 2 refers to comments in which the subject introduces either a plan or goal for the task that was not explicitly provided by the task directions and that was not a mere paraphrase of these directions. For example, a subject might have said, "My objective here is to really pump up the enthusiasm of freshman women for sports." Category 3 refers to comments in which the subject summarizes the contents of the letter or its purpose, as in "Basically this handout just compares advantages of intramurals with something else you might do in your leisure time at school." Category 4 refers to comments in which the subject focuses on the audience's possible needs, as in "I think this kind of document ought to be simple, because freshman students have very short attention spans!" Category 5 refers to comments in which

Table 1. *Differences in experts' and novices' task definitions*

| Task definition activity | Experts | Novices |
|---|---|---|
| 1. Reads letter completely before attempting to revise | 6/7 | 5/7 |
| 2. Establishes process plans or goals that are more specific than directions before revising | 4 | 1 |
| 3. Offers "gist" of letter content or purpose | 2 | 0 |
| 4. Establishes audience needs before attacking first sentence | 2 | 1 |
| 5. Offers inventory of problems detected in first read | 2 | 0 |
| 5. Detects global problems (other than audience problem) during or just after first read | 5 | 2 |
| 7. Makes critical comments (other than global or audience) during or just after first read | 5 | 2 |
| Total number of instances | 20 | 6 |
| Percentage of total possible | 47.6 | 14.4 |

the subject builds a list or schedule of things he or she thinks will have to be done. For example, "The first thing I'll do is remove all the spelling errors, then the vague pronouns. Then I'll try to get the larger organizational matters taken care of." Category 6 refers to comments in which the subject mentions some negative impression created by the text as a whole or some negative trait that cannot be localized. The subject might comment, for instance, "Somehow the voice is wrong" or "It's really boring." Finally, Category 7 refers to comments in which the subject identifies a particular fault that must be corrected, though the subject does not immediately proceed with correction, as in "Those exclamation points have to go," or "That's a vague pronoun if ever I saw one."

The reliability of these categories was checked by four independent coders, each of whom coded 26 comments in an actual protocol. The average intercoder agreement was 81% and was found to be statistically significant.

### Results

Two of the novices and one of the experts (a professional writer) did not read the target text completely before beginning to make changes. Instead, they read the first few sentences of the text and then immediately began adding and/or deleting portions. Obviously, revisers who do not read a text completely at least once do not draw on the same amount of information in constructing their task definitions as those who do. Accordingly, one might assume their task definitions will be less appropriate than those of subjects who do read completely through. Not reading the text completely might be taken as an indication of poor revision skill, that is, a failure to attend to all the necessary information. A possible explanation as to why some subjects did not read the text completely is simply that they might have found the task so familiar or routine that reading all the way through did not seem important to them. Thus, on the face of it, such behavior should not necessarily be construed as a sign of poor revision skill, or even as a handicap on performance, without other data being taken into consideration. This behavior does indicate, however, that incomplete readers are likely to form a rather different task definition than are complete readers.

The first two columns of Table 1 show the number of subjects from each group making one or more comments in a specific category. As the table indicates, experts scored more than the novices when the various comment categories are aggregated. Note that the summary data in the table are for Categories 2 through 7. Experts scored in 20 of the 42 cells, compared with the novices' score of 6 of 42 cells, or 47.6% (experts) versus 14.4% (novices). These results were statistically significant.

### Discussion

We do not assert that comments in these categories constitute unequivocal evidence that specific processes were occurring during task definition. However, the categories do point to metacognitive skills that we believe are worthy of further investigation. By the time expert revisers make their first text change, our data suggest that they have created richer, more complex task definitions than novices. Experts are much more attentive to the rhetorical context of the document and to the "global" problems associated with this context. Indeed, not only have experts processed different information about the task, establishing markedly different revision goals and plans, but also they apparently have more regulatory processes available for storing and retrieving information during subsequent efforts to improve the text. In particular, the evidence supports the following observations:

1. *Experts have more knowledge about how to make process plans to guide task performance (Category 2).* For example, during his initial reading of the target text, one expert (HD) commented that "one of the things that I do normally day to day is, when I first look at a piece I very quickly see the spelling errors, and I tend to make the changes in that *in my first run through* because sometimes as you read through it later you may miss them." The comments of another expert (JP), upon reading the text through once, indicate his awareness that revision is a complex task whose subtasks must be regulated; he asks rhetorically, "Do I describe *each revising pass* as I do it?" Only one of the novices made any comments suggesting knowledge of process plans.
2. *Experts deliberately create an "inventory" of problems in anticipation of subse-*

*quent work (Category 5)*. For example, an expert (JP) revealed that he tries initially to organize the "problems" he will focus on in a kind of list – a list that may also serve as a means of managing the flow of his attention: "The first thing I will do at least as I read the sentences [again], . . . it seems to me the person does have a sense of organization, does write what I call topic sentences, and . . . there's just plain errors, and there's wordiness in the prose. . . . I have two basic biases in revising, or three. One, of course, is mechanics . . . one is cutting out as many adjectives as don't seem necessary, and the [other] is saying things like "assume" instead of "possess the assumption that" . . . I know I'm going to come back – want to come back and do something with what seems to be a bad voice." Another expert (HD) also constructs an initial inventory of problems as a way of managing his attention. He remarks, "The thing that jumps out at me here . . . is . . . the exclamation points. . . . Maybe it's my personality, but I'm not into that kind of thing. I think where I find exclamation points I'll quickly dump them. . . . I don't like overstatement, and there's some of that in here." Although it is true that only two of seven experts made comments suggesting that they built inventories, we nevertheless find it striking that none of the novices made such comments. Moreover, the behavior of novices later in the course of revision suggested that they were not operating under the direction of such inventories. The experts, including those who made no initial comments suggesting they use inventories, nevertheless seemed to be using them as they revised (see "Strategy Selection" below).

3. *Experts' task definitions include "global" goals for revision that take into account the purpose of the text in the communication situation (Category 6)*. One expert subject (BA), for example, remarked in the course of her first reading, "It seems to me that if the goal of this article is to get women involved, it ought to be clear whether they want them to be involved in intramural or varsity sports, or both . . . right at the beginning." By contrast, only two of the novices made any comments that suggested awareness of "global" problems with the text before making text changes.

Although the data for each category of results (1 through 7), taken separately, are insufficient for determining statistical significance, the overall pattern of results between the two groups suggests that experts build strikingly different task definitions than novices and also bring greater "managerial" skill to performance. (This managerial skill is further evidenced by choices in revision strategy selection, a process we discuss in detail later.)

First, when the data for Categories 2, 5, 6, and 7 are taken together, it becomes strikingly clear that from the outset experts are building completely different task definitions than novices. Experts make an effort to tailor their conception of revision to the task at hand. Ultimately, experts are performing a different task, focusing much more globally on the purpose of the text. In contrast, novices appear to conceive of revision in a radically different way, by searching for problems in the text without giving much attention to the text's purpose or to global aspects of the communication situation. The evidence further suggests that they are not attending to their task definitions and therefore not actively constructing or tailoring them before they revise. Indeed, the evidence from the initial segments of the protocols leads us to infer that they do not set goals or make plans for approaching the task in a comprehensive way. Rather they seem much more directly dependent on the order in which problems appear in the target text. They do not revise on the basis of problem "inventories" or similar ad hoc "schedules" for regulating subprocesses. Thus, whereas many experts in the initial stages of their protocols did appear to tailor their task definitions as they read, most novices seemed to apply a fixed, stored routine.

Second, the results suggest that experts may see revision as a collection of more or less distinguishable processes that must be approached iteratively, in successive passes. Indeed, protocol comments suggest that experts are more aware than novices of the complex demands revision places on attentional capacity and, as a result, consciously try to break down revision processes into more discrete subprocesses. This inference, at least, is supported by the results for Categories 2 and 5, where experts "forecast" the kind of criteria they may employ over the course of discrete subsequent passes. Some experts explicitly set about evaluating a text for certain kinds of problems before others, thus recognizing a principle of economy of effort, or what we call "precedence guidelines." The experts seem aware that revising involves applying many different kinds of procedures over time and that determining in advance a rough order for these procedures is likely to make them more efficient.

To summarize, key differences in revision behavior appear in the way experts represent their goals for the task from the outset, in the way they represent the structure of the process to themselves (i.e., single pass with no priorities vs. many passes with some priorities), and also in the way experts manage the processes associated with the task. Given these findings, there are several skills associated with task definition that might be assessed independently: Novices must learn not only (1) what information to attend to in the text they revise, but perhaps more importantly (2) how to set goals and make plans for revising, and (3) how to support (or "monitor") their attentional capacities while work is under way. Such expert control methods as informal inventories or plans that assign different subtasks to different passes might reduce information overload and thus make revision more efficient. In particular, to build these inventories and set priorities (or hierarchies) within them means that the novice reviser must also learn (4) to attend to the underlying purpose of the communication and the problems inherent in this purpose. Without such attention, it would seem difficult (if not impossible) for a reviser to construct meaningful revision plans or to monitor progress in carrying them out. Where such attention to purpose is lacking, the reviser is likely to pick out problems more haphazardly.

On the basis of this first study, then, we believe several issues deserve more investigation. First, we need to investigate the reasonable assumption that revisers' task definitions, and in particular revisers' goals for revision, vary in response to a host of factors. Although the experts as a group clearly created different initial task definitions and goals than the novices, there was nevertheless a wide range of initial definitions and goals among the experts themselves. These differences are indicated by the fact that individual experts did not have the same pattern of comments in the categories (Table 1). The factors affecting initial task definition and goals include (at least) the following:

1. Attention to the purpose, length, and genre of text to be revised
2. Attention to the explicit verbal demands or directions presented to the reviser by an instructor, experimenter, or other instigator
3. Attention to the implicit demands represented by the intended audience and by the context this audience shares with the reviser
4. Attention to stored conceptions of the revision process and to textual knowledge in the reviser's long-term memory
5. Attention to changes introduced to the text as the reviser works at the task
6. Attention to the number, density, and complexity of problems and errors in the target text

The two initial segments of the protocols we examined in this study showed that attention to all of these factors influenced task definitions. Because this list of factors is probably incomplete, we feel safe in concluding that there is no such thing as an "optimal" task definition for any particular revising task. Depending on how many and which of these factors are attended to, a number of different, but equally appropriate task definitions might result. However, by experimentally manipulating the amount of attention the reviser may place on one or more of these factors, we might be able to discover more about how each affects the task definition process and the goals the reviser initially establishes. For instance, here is how we might examine the effect of (1) error number, (2) error complexity, and (3) error "density" in texts (item 6 in the list above) on task definition: Texts varying along these three dimensions could be submitted to revisers to determine whether there is a "saturation point" at which both novices and experts alike will opt to rewrite a text completely instead of revising it in piecemeal fashion. Indeed, some of our experts commented that they wanted to simply rewrite the text because of the large number and complexity of problems they found. One subject (DS) commented, "I wouldn't even write it this way. I'm just so . . . This thing is so ridiculous. . . . I want to rewrite it."

Another study might focus on the effects of "problem inventories" on attentional capacity and "managerial" control of the revision process. For instance, novices might be trained to read completely through stimulus texts to make prioritized inventories of the problems they find as they proceed. Their control over the revision process, along with the effectiveness of their final revisions, could then be compared with that of a group of (matched) novices who attempt the task without such training in inventory making. To establish the precise contribution of the inventory method, both groups could be carefully instructed in methods for solving the types of problems presented (e.g., faulty pronoun reference, faulty parallelism).

As noted earlier, we hypothesize that task definitions are not static but rather dynamic entities. Task definitions appear to change as work on the revision task progresses, and we believe our results here justify the study of how and why they change. Specifically, our protocols suggested that experts' task definitions and problem representations will interact more than those of novices over the course of the whole revision process. We can explain what we mean by "interact" by referring again to our model and our earlier hypothetical example. Suppose that I have chosen to read my boss's letter and revise it as I proceed. That is, I do not read all the way through the text before beginning to make changes. Now, as I am reading and checking, suppose that I encounter (detect) an unacceptable sentence and I pause to represent its problem as being triple dependent clauses. I decide to remove immediately two of these clauses to solve the problem. However, in so doing, I reconsider whether I ought to go ahead and simply read through the rest of the text without stopping, merely flagging other sentences with this or a similar problem. After pondering a moment, I do decide to finish reading the text and to postpone further correction, merely flagging other instances of the same type of problem.

Notice what has happened in this scenario. My detection and problem representation have altered my initial task definition and thus changed my process plan for the task. In particular, I have updated my initial (or working) task definition, which directed me simply to revise as I read. At this point my task definition changes because I have now decided to read all the way through, paying special attention to dependent clauses as I go.

We feel this interaction, or "feedback loop," between the problem representation and the task definition is very significant, for it may be that experts are more capable than novices of adjusting their task definition in response to specific problems detected in the course of revising. In other words, the experts will continue to adjust their task definition and process plans in response to new information, whereas novices may continue inappropriately to force an initial, low-level task definition to do the job, not making later adjustments in their revision process plans. Though our evidence in this first study does not specifically address this point, our findings here (and in the other studies in this group) lead us to hypothesize such a difference between expert and novice performance. In other words, we predict that the task definitions of experts will be both more tailored in the initial phases of the task and more flexible over the course of performance.

Our data also indicate that the reverse process is a significant one for distinguishing experts from novices. For instance, the data in this study strongly imply that the information in the initial task definition (i.e., goals and criteria) subsequently influences both the detection and representation of problems in the text. To express this phenomenon in a metaphor, the task definition acts as a pair of colored glasses: If I have a task definition that considers revision to be primarily the deletion of excess words, I may not detect other sorts of problems in the text (e.g., lack of specificity in examples). I simply will not see certain kinds of difficulties. What is equally interesting, the task definition may influence the strength or definedness of diagnoses that revisers make of specific problems they do detect.

Indeed, later studies in this series provide evidence that inappropriately narrow task definitions may be the culprits that prevent novices from making detections, independently of a lack of specific knowledge about the problems themselves. That is, unless a more global task definition is tailored for the occasion by the reviser, even problems for which the novice has the requisite diagnostic knowledge may go unsolved. In the model, we show this influence of task definition on problem representation with an arrow from the reviser's goals and criteria for text to the evaluate function (Figure 1).

## Evaluation

In this section, we present a more detailed model of the evaluation subprocess and suggest its relation to the process of reading. We believe that evaluation is best viewed as an extension of the familiar process of reading for comprehension. We first discuss reading for comprehension and then describe how this process is modified to evaluate and define problems in text.

### Reading for comprehension

Reading for comprehension is a process by which the reader attempts to construct a satisfactory internal representation of the meaning of the text. Consistent with Thibadeau, Just, and Carpenter's (1982) model of reading, we assume that the process by which a reader constructs an internal representation of the text involves the interaction of subprocesses on many levels. Our proposal for such a multilevel representation process is shown in Figure 3. The processes we include in the model differ from those in the Thibadeau, Just, and Carpenter model, particularly on the more complex levels. Our choice of processes is based on our analysis of thinking-aloud protocols of subjects reading and attempting to understand fairly difficult technical prose (see Schriver, 1984). The levels of processing include at least the following:

1. Decoding words, that is, identifying individual words and retrieving their meanings from memory.
2. Identifying the grammatical structure of sentences.
3. Applying elementary semantic knowledge, for example, interpreting sentences such as "The pen is in the coat" and "The coat is in the pen."
4. Making factual inferences.
5. Applying schemas and world knowledge.

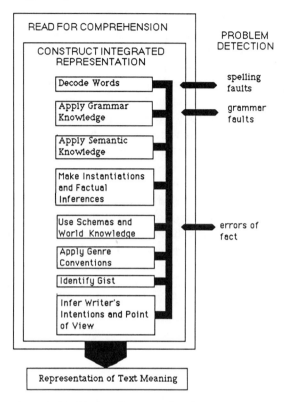

Figure 3. Model of reading comprehension process.

6. Making use of genre conventions, for example, "I guess he is summing up here."
7. Identifying gist.
8. Inferring the text's function or the writer's intentions and point of view.

We are not asserting that these subprocesses act in sequence. Rather, we assume that they may occur in any order and that they cooperate with one another in the effort to produce a satisfactory text representation. For example, finding the grammatical structure of ambiguous sentences such as "They are sinking ships" may depend on identifying the gist of the text. Furthermore, we assume that all of these subprocesses may make use of all of the information about the text that is available at the time – that is, that readers integrate their interpretations of the new text with the interpretation they have made of the text so far. Thus, all decisions about the meanings of words, grammatical structure, and the writer's plans and goals in the newly read text are made so as to produce an integrated representation of the text and of the author's intentions.

Reading for comprehension, by itself, can lead to the detection of some problems under the following circumstances. When everything goes smoothly, as it usually does in reading well-constructed text, the reader's attention is focused primarily on the representation being produced and very little on the comprehension process that is producing it. With poorly constructed texts, however, the reader may, by following any of the subprocesses, encounter comprehension difficulties that bring text problems to his or her attention. Predictably, when people are reading for comprehension, they appear not to be nearly as sensitive to text problems as they are when they are revising. However, reading protocols indicate that, even while reading for comprehension, readers do retain sensitivity to some kinds of text problems. For example, if the reader sees *revise* in the text, decoding this string as the word *receive* may require some conscious problem solving. As a by-product of this effort, the reader will likely be aware that there is a misspelling. Similarly, the reader may become aware of other text faults such as grammatical problems and errors of fact. For some problems, the editor never sleeps. The right-hand side of Figure 3 shows some problem categories to which readers appear to retain sensitivity. The arrows in the diagram indicate that the detection and diagnosis of different text problems are associated with different levels of the comprehension process. That is, the detection and diagnosis of spelling faults are typically the result of the word-decoding process, and the detection of incoherence is usually the result of the process of identifying gist.

### Reading to evaluate and/or to define problems

People may read a text with a variety of purposes. They may read to comprehend. They may read simply to evaluate – for example, "Is this essay sufficiently well written to be included in my anthology?" Or they may evaluate in order to revise. When writers read a text to revise it, they still read to comprehend it, but they adopt several goals in addition. First, they read with the goal of detecting and characterizing text problems. This goal makes them more responsive to a much wider variety of text problems than people reading simply for comprehension (compare the right-hand sides of Figures 3 and 4). Second, they adopt the goal of fixing the text problems that they find. This goal leads them to take a more active attitude toward the text, searching for ways to improve it at all levels from wording to overall text structure. Searching for possible improvements may lead to discoveries associated with various levels of the comprehension process, as shown in the left-hand column of Figure 4. For example, searching for an alternative word in order to avoid repetition may trigger an association to another part of the text and reveal a surprising relation within the text. Or searching for an example to illustrate a principle may lead to the discovery of a way to make contact with the special interests of the audience. Third, if revisers are skilled, they adopt the goal of shaping the text to the needs of the intended audience. This goal has a profound effect on performance at all levels. For example, it leads skilled revisers to consider not only

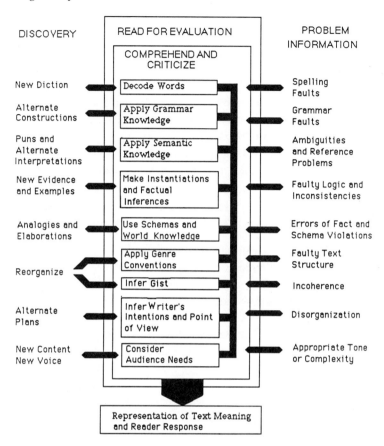

Figure 4. Model of reading to evaluate.

whether the words of the text are intelligible to themselves but also whether they are intelligible and acceptable to the intended audience.

These additional goals make the behavior of the reviser quite different from that of the person reading for comprehension. The reviser is more concerned with detecting and diagnosing text problems, is more actively searching for alternative text features, and is therefore more likely to make useful discoveries about the text than is a person reading for comprehension.

The three activities included in the evaluation process in Figure 1 – reading to comprehend, reading to evaluate, and defining the problem – can be distinguished by a number of measures: (1) They produce different results (ranging from automatic detections to evaluative judgments to elaborated problem diagnoses). (2) They often take different amounts of time (e.g., defining the problem often requires considerable problem-solving effort beyond that entailed in reading to evaluate or simply to understand). (3) Finally, they are associated with expert–novice differences. Here again, defining the problem is normally a demanding process that novices rarely display.

We see that the sequence in the evaluation process in Figure 1 reflects an escalation of goals and constraints from reading for comprehension as the least constrained to reading to define problems as the most constrained.

Although revision may involve all of the levels we have specified in Figure 4, novices appear to entertain fewer constraints, and they typically make less use of the three most complex levels than do experts. Novices are less likely than experts to (1) infer gist, (2) infer the writer's intentions, and (3) consider the reader's needs.

### Special revising situations

To discuss the reviser's performance in more detail, we must distinguish among three rather different evaluation situations: (1) revisers evaluating another writer's text, (2) revisers evaluating their own text, and (3) revisers evaluating plans, whether their own or those of another writer.

**Revisers evaluating another writer's text.** When revisers are evaluating text written by another writer, they have only indirect access through the text itself to the writer's underlying plans. In many cases, the evidence in the text is clear enough that the reviser can be confident of the writer's original intent. In some cases, however, the evidence is not clear. For example, one of our revisers said of the text, "I hope that's what she did say."

**Revisers evaluating their own text.** Revisers who are revising another writer's text can reconstruct the writer's intentions only from the text itself. Revisers who are revising their own text have privileged access to the intentions that gave rise to the text. This difference in access to writers' intentions can be both a help and a hindrance. It can be a help because in many cases only the writers know if a given word or phrase accurately matches their intention. It can be a hindrance when, as Bartlett (1981) has shown, writers' knowledge of their own intentions may blind them to certain faults in their texts.

**Writers revising plans.** According to the model shown in Figure 1, when revisers evaluate a text, they may also evaluate the text plan. We distinguish the evaluation of plans from the evaluation of text at this point for three reasons. First, plans are sometimes evaluated separately from text. A writer may construct a plan for writing a text and then evaluate and revise that plan before writing any text. Second, the process of evaluating a plan is somewhat different from the process of evaluating a text. Evaluating a plan typically does not involve consideration of the surface structure of the text that the plan would produce. Indeed, writers frequently find that plans that seemed quite adequate simply do not work when they attempt to write them down, because there is no acceptable surface structure to embody the plan. A common example is attempting to express too many ideas in one sentence. We simply do not recognize the weakness of the plan until we try to execute it. Finally, we want to emphasize the importance of the evaluation of plans in the revision process whether or not the writer is dealing with a text. Although, as we will show, experts are superior to novices in detecting and diagnosing surface-level faults in a text, the weight of evidence suggests that the real advantage of experts lies in the greater attention they devote to the evaluation and revision of text plans.

### Problem representation: detecting problems in text

Anyone who has tried to advise a friend (or oneself) on a poorly written draft is likely to say that reading even a difficult text is far easier than trying to diagnose or revise it. Perhaps it is this intuition that has led most revision theorists to treat evaluation as an isolated act of comparison and testing. In contrast, one of the chief suggestions made in the previous section was that evaluation is best understood as an extension of the reading process. The subprocesses we identified within evaluation represent distinct locations on a continuum marked by an increasing number of goals and constraints imposed on one's representation of the text. As reader-revisers move along this continuum, they metaphorically turn up the power or work load of the process – subjecting their growing representations of the text to more stringent demands and attempting to define its failures more fully.

The output of the evaluation process – at whatever level it is conducted – is a problem representation (see Figure 1). Problem representations also vary along a continuum for which the metric is not power or effort but the amount of information the evaluation process has produced. In discussing evaluation, then, we focused on the conduct of a process. Now we turn to its output – the writer's problem representation – as it is reflected in our data from expert and novice revisers.

The process of revision simply cannot proceed until the reviser perceives that the text, or a plan for producing a text, has problems. Problem detection, then, is a necessary precondition for revision. In this section, we describe two differences between college students and experts in detecting text problems: First, college students persistently fail to detect some problems that experts detect easily. Second, experts are much more likely to detect global problems than are college students.

As noted above, our experimental procedures involved the collection of thinking-aloud protocols from subjects as they revised a text with 26 planted errors and a number of global problems. The plants included misspellings, faulty parallelism, and the like. Most of these plants were problems at the sentence level or below. The global problems included such things as inappropriate focus on the audience and improperly sequenced topics. The protocols allowed us to determine when the revisers were reading each text problem and exactly what their responses to the problem were as they examined the text.

The novice revisers typically read each problem more than once. In some cases, they read particular problems as many as eight times. Their responses included detection of the problem, failure to detect the problem without comment, and failure to detect the problem accompanied by comments indicating approval of the text containing the problem. For example, the novice reviser GB persistently failed to detect text problems in the following sentence while reading it on four separate occasions: "In sports like fencing for a long time many of our varsity team members had no previous experience anyway." After his first reading GB said, "OK." After the second, he made no direct comment. After the third reading he said, "OK, that sounds good right there." And after the fourth, "OK." Another novice reviser commenting on this sentence said, "Freshmen would like that."

The novices' insensitivity to text problems appears in some cases to be relative rather than absolute. For example, GB repeatedly read the sentence that began "Many naive women students possess the assumption that . . . " On the first reading, he deleted "naive" but made no other changes. On the second reading, he said "OK, that's good . . . " Finally, on the third reading, he said, "No, no, no . . . shorten it up" and changed "possess the assumption" to "think." Although some of the difference in sensitivity is relative, some is, in the practical sense, absolute. That is, some text errors the novices never caught despite repeated rereadings of the text. Thus, another novice read this sentence seven times and never found fault with it.

In total, the novice subjects read text segments that contained planted errors on 327 occasions. On 26% of these occasions, they detected the error. On 6% of the occasions they actively expressed approval of the error, and on 68% of occasions they read the error without comment. Thus, in 74% of the occasions, our novices failed to detect the problems in the text segments they read.

We cannot provide a comparable summary for the experts because, as will be discussed below, many of the experts were playing a different game than the novices. That is, their strategy of revising did not require them to comb the text systematically in order to detect problems. Rather, some decided that the text had too many errors to make repairing each one individually worthwhile. They decided, therefore, simply to extract the gist of the text, rewrite it in their own words, and ignore the individual errors. As a point of comparison, the expert whose revision strategy most closely resembled that of the novices had a failure rate of 36% in comparison with 74% for the novices.

It is conceivable that, despite the lower efficiency of their detection processes, novices might, through persistence, have found as many of the errors as the ex-

Table 2. *Comparison of experts' and novices' ability to detect, diagnose, and fix text problems*

| Subjects | Protocol or cued recall | | Single-sentence task | | Fix or eliminate |
|---|---|---|---|---|---|
| | Detection | Diagnosis | Detection | Diagnosis | |
| *Teachers* | | | | | |
| JP | 18 | 14 | 21 | 20 | 26 |
| SE | 9 | 9 | 18 | 13 | 25 |
| BA | 20 | 20 | 17 | 16 | 23 |
| DS | 18 | 11 | 20 | 10 | 24 |
| *Professionals* | | | | | |
| DE | 9 | 2 | 15 | 12 | 25 |
| HL | 14 | 8 | 9 | 7 | 23 |
| HD | 18 | 14 | 21 | 19 | 20 |
| Total experts | 106 | 78 | 121 | 97 | 166 |
| % of possible responses | 58 | 43 | 66 | 53 | 91 |
| *Experienced students* | | | | | |
| CC | 8 | 5 | 11 | 5 | 26 |
| JJ | 12 | 4 | 15 | 12 | 14 |
| *Novice students* | | | | | |
| NG | 13 | 6 | 10 | 5 | 13 |
| GB | 3 | 1 | 9 | 2 | 12 |
| MM | 6 | 2 | 8 | 4 | 21 |
| ML | 12 | 6 | 13 | 8 | 16 |
| KC | 12 | 3 | 11 | 6 | 15 |
| Total students | 66 | 27 | 77 | 42 | 117 |
| % of possible responses | 36 | 15 | 42 | 23 | 64 |

perts did. However, as Table 2 shows, they did not. Evidence from the protocols indicated that, by the end of the revision sessions, the experts had detected 58% of the planted problems whereas the students had detected only 36%.

When we examine the percentage of problems eliminated[1] in the revisions, we notice an anomaly. The experts eliminated 91% of the errors and the novices eliminated 64%. In each case, these figures are about 30% higher than the percentage of problems detected. There are, it seems to us, two possible reasons for this anomaly:

1. Some problem detections were missed in the protocols. Thus, some apparently undetected problems that were fixed were in fact detected by the revisers but not mentioned in the protocols.
2. Problems were eliminated that, in fact, were not detected. This might have hap-

pened in two ways: (a) Revisers who adopted a rewriting strategy extracted the gist of the text without attending to its errors. They then generated new text on the basis of their own production grammars, which were relatively error free. (b) Revisers accidentally eliminated a problem they had not detected while attempting to fix other problems they had detected.

Our protocol evidence indicates clearly that the second hypothesis is correct. The evidence for this is best seen in novice revisers. One novice, for example, deleted the sentence "Intramural sports are not quite the same as varsity sports, in which the rules are better, equipment is better, and with the techniques of the players being more developed" because she believed it would not be persuasive. She gave no evidence that she noticed the parallelism problem in the sentence but eliminated it nonetheless. Deciding whether the first hypothesis is also correct will require further experimental work.

Examining the protocols makes it clear that there was a difference not only in the number of errors the experts detected but also in the kinds of errors they detected. The experts detected not only more sentence-level problems – the kind of problem to which novices devote almost all of their attention – but more global problems as well – the kind of problem novices rarely detect.

With one exception, the planted problems were strictly sentence-level problems. The global problems the experts detected (e.g., the recognition that a sentence was placed in the wrong paragraph) were, in most cases, additional to those counted in Table 2. Thus, the data in Table 2 underestimate the difference in problem detection between expert and novice because they focus primarily on sentence-level problems. The protocols strongly suggest that the experts were more concerned than the students with global problems.

To provide quantitative confirmation of this hypothesis, we selected two expert and two novice protocols at random and analyzed them in the following way. First, the protocols were divided into problem-solving episodes. (Judges can identify such episodes quite reliably.) Typically, the episodes corresponded to a single problem-solving event, for example, "OK, what am I going to do about this monster? I'm going to delete it, that's what."

After the protocols were divided into episodes, each episode was evaluated to determine whether it was concerned with a problem above the sentence level or with a problem at or below the sentence level. Table 3 shows the proportion of episodes in each category for both experts and students. For the novices, only 15% of the episodes involved problems above the sentence level in contrast to 42%, or nearly three times as many, for the experts.

## Problem representation: diagnosing problems in text

We have noted that people detect many problems simply because their own reading process is derailed by the text, but when people are reading to evaluate, their sensitivity to text problems is heightened and directed in specific ways. We have also

Table 3. *Comparison of experts' and novices' episodes showing detection of local and global text problems*

|  | Local | Global | Other | Total |
|---|---|---|---|---|
| *Experts* | | | | |
| Number | 54 | 42 | 5 | 101 |
| Percentage | 54 | 42 | 5 | — |
| *Novices* | | | | |
| Number | 71 | 13 | 3 | 87 |
| Percentage | 82 | 15 | 3 | — |

noted that evaluation per se is a constructive process: Just as reading builds a representation of a text, evaluation builds a representation of problems. In this section, we look more closely at the nature and content of these representations. First, we describe our model of the continuum along which revisers' problem representations exist; we also explain what we believe are the conceptual advantages of using this continuum to characterize problem representations. Second, we explain the significance of a critical segment (or "range") of the continuum – a segment composed of what we call "diagnoses." Third, we discuss a variety of findings in our protocols that helped us to generate our continuum model of problem representations.

### The continuum of problem representations

To begin with, the problem representations people actually create appear to exist along a continuum. Representations range from spare representations that contain little information about the problem to richly elaborated diagnoses that offer both conceptual and procedural information about the problem. Problem representations found at the low end of this continuum might be expressed by a protocol comment such as "I don't like this." Or when asked why a change was made, the writer might simply assert, "I don't know, it just didn't sound right." In Figure 5 we have labeled such representations "detect." They contain little information beyond the recognition that a problem exists. Such representations are simple, efficient, and often sufficient for the task, but they also indicate that the writer is working with limited information and an unelaborated representation of the problem. He or she has an ill-defined problem to solve.

The continuum in Figure 5, then, is based on the amount and specificity of information contained in a reviser's representation. (Note that this continuum is not a quality scale based on an assumption that some representations are inherently better than others.) At the far right we find those representations that contain a good deal of highly specified information about the problem and, as a conse-

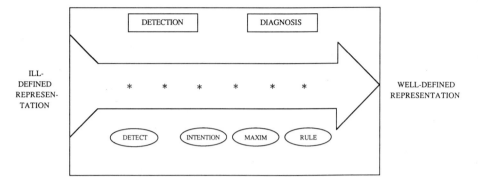

Figure 5. Model of problem representation continuum.

quence, give the writer a well-defined problem with which to work. Such well-defined problems are most frequently associated with violations of a spelling or grammatical rule as in the sentence "Athletics is an important aspect of college." When the reviser represents the problem as "a disagreement between the subject and verb," he has pinpointed the location of the problem he perceives (to the two words "athletics" and "is"), has identified the cause (disagreement in number), and in the process has specified a clear solution procedure (change the verb). The subject whose "detect" represents the problem as "this sentence just doesn't sound right" has identified a substantially different problem.

Unfortunately for writers, most of the significant problems in adult text cannot be turned into completely well defined problems and are located by necessity somewhere short of the far right of this continuum. For example, matters of diction and style (e.g., whether to use a technical term or when to use "I") are governed not by rules but by judgment, taste, and a sense of appropriateness. More global problems such as voice, persuasiveness, or organization are by nature even less well defined. They are harder to attach to a specific word, their effect is more diffuse, and there are fewer explicit procedures for dealing with them. Revision, unlike simple proofreading, is the process of solving a series of interlinked problems, some of which are relatively ill defined.

Two variables appear to affect where a given representation fits on this continuum. One is the nature of the problem itself, as discussed above. The other is how fully the writer chooses (or is able) to represent the problem. For example, a perception of incoherence in a paragraph could be represented with a detect ("Wait, this is confusing"), with additional information about location ("These two sentences don't work"), with a general rhetorical concept such as "flow," or with a more technical concept such as "topic shift," which contains procedures for tracing and testing the topic development and heuristics for repairing shifts.

As our model emphasizes, problem representations range along a continuum from ill- to well-definedness. However, striking substantive differences in some of these representations led us to identify a special class of high-information representations, for which we have reserved the term *diagnosis*. A bona fide diagnosis, unlike other forms of representation, depends on concept recognition. When diagnosing, the reviser recognizes that the current problem belongs to a class or category of text problems the reviser already knows. For instance, people often detect that they feel peaked and have a fair amount of information about their condition, but still do not know what the problem is. That is when a doctor's representation is called for. By analogy, a diagnosis is a problem representation one would be willing to pay for. When revisers say such things as "That's terribly wordy" or "This never comes to a point" or "I don't see the logical connection between *x* and *y*," they place the problem in a conceptual framework that contains information about typical problem features, tests for refining the definition, and likely procedures for fixing the problem.

Diagnosis depends on concepts and categories, but note that it does not depend on names. A reviser does not have to know a technical term or even a name at all in order to diagnose a current problem as yet another "whatchamacallit." The critical feature of a diagnostic concept is not its name, of course, but the useful prior knowledge about texts and discourse that it brings with it.

### *Conceptual advantages of a continuum model*

Defining problem representation as an ill- to well-defined continuum with the special category of diagnosis at the upper end has certain advantages for building a theory of revision processes. Such a continuum allows us, for instance, to account for some of the limitations of novice performance. Scardamalia and Bereiter (1983) found that sixth- and eighth-grade students could identify certain problems such as "People may not believe this" or "I think this could be said more clearly" with some reliability (they agreed with an adult). And yet when asked to explain or support why they had chosen one of these evaluative statements from a set of cards, they could go no further – they made uninterpretable comments or simply reiterated the statement on the evaluative card. Why? One explanation is that these students, with the aid of their evaluative cards, are working rather effectively at the level of midrange detection. Their problem representations can indeed go beyond the level of detect: They include information about the reviser's reading experience, the general location of a problem, and social knowledge about how readers respond to topics. However, they are not able to diagnose the problem more fully or move up to a categorical representation, much less one that involves specific rhetorical knowledge about discourse patterns and text. A second conceptual advantage of this continuum is that it helps us to account for the behavior of expert writers who frequently go through a series of problem representations. Although experts may begin like anyone else, with a detection, they often exercise the search option (see Figure 1) to loop back into problem representation. By reconsidering the problem, they typically move their representation farther and farther to the right, turning a detection into a more fully defined and more manageable problem.

### The range of diagnoses

In the previous section we pinpointed the key difference between detecting a problem and diagnosing a problem: In order to diagnose, the writer develops a relatively well defined representation of a text problem that is based on a categorization of the problem type. However, *diagnoses themselves* vary in their level of specificity and in the kinds of problem they define. At one extreme (at the left of our continuum in Figure 5) we find relatively vague and ill-defined diagnoses. One form these diagnoses take is an attempt to simulate a reader's response, as in the following examples:

> I think I'd just read that first sentence and say, "Why bother?"
> No one would believe that.

In these verbalizations the category of problem is implicit; it may not have a name. However, the reviser has clearly recognized a problem type. Some problems seem to demand these ill-defined diagnoses and cannot be "reduced" to more well defined ones. Other problems, however, admit very specific, well-defined diagnoses, such as diagnoses of mechanical errors that exhibit an explicit and recognizable category (e.g., ambiguous relative pronoun reference).

In analyzing the diagnostic comments of our expert and novice revisers we distinguished three overall types of diagnosis:

1. The least well defined diagnoses we classified as *intentional* diagnoses. Here revisers attempt, with whatever rhetorical knowledge they have at their disposal, to compare their representation of the text's purpose and/or the author's intentions with what is actually written and then to decide how to change the text (or a text plan) to satisfy these apparent intentions. An example of such an intentional diagnosis might be: "The purpose of this thing is to get women into a large active group to lobby for funding. And the way to do this is to recruit for teams." From this statement, the reviser proceeded to plan possible ways of changing the text to meet its apparent intended purpose.
2. The most well defined diagnoses we classified as *rule-based*. Here revisers have a ready-made problem representation based on their knowledge of violations of standard rules of grammar, punctuation, and spelling. They also have a built-in action: If a spelling is wrong, fix it.
3. A number of statements, which fell between these two extremes, we classified as *maxim-based*. Here revisers have some established guidelines, but not any clear-cut rules on which to base their diagnoses. Such maxims incorporate those found in standard handbooks, such as "Avoid wordy prose" or "Use parallel structure." They may also be personal to the writer – either general rhetorical guidelines the writer always employs (such as avoiding negative constructions) or more genre-specific guidelines the writer has developed, through experience, for example, in writing public-relations handouts.

## *Results of protocol analysis: differences between experts and novices*

The results listed in Table 2 show that experts and novices differed not only in their detection rate but in the number of problems they diagnosed and eliminated. If we consider the 26 planted problems (which ranged from spelling to diction to sentence style to organization) the experts diagnosed 43% of these problems to the novices' 15%. On the single-sentence task, which called for problem representation alone, the pattern is the same. The experts diagnosed 53% to the novices' 23%.

The difference in the amount of expert and novice diagnosis on the 26 planted problems is significant even though these include many small and/or local errors we might expect experts, in particular, to handle relatively automatically without explicit diagnosis. When we look at the amount of diagnosis of whole-text problems, the contrast between experts and novices becomes dramatic. In this analysis we looked for a diagnostic statement that showed the writer's concern with a problem that (1) extended over more than one sentence and/or (2) reflected a generalized problem with the text, such as "This is a sexist letter" or "In a recruiting letter you don't want to focus on what is wrong with the team." Our original text was in fact a hot bed of such whole-text problems since we had given subjects a text with one purpose, audience, genre, and style (a rather stuffy, disorganized letter to a colleague) and asked them to revise it for a different purpose, audience, genre, and style (a persuasive handout for students). It seemed reasonable to believe students could deal with this topic, audience, and genre, even if they could not make successful revisions. Although the novices did draw on their world knowledge and sense of audience and purpose, they appeared to manage the revision process itself by limiting their attempts at diagnosis to the boundaries of a single sentence. The novices diagnosed a mean of 3.0 whole-text problems compared with the experts' mean of 10.4. Even more striking was the amount of processing devoted to these problems once they were noted. That is, once the experts detected one of these whole-text problems, they followed up with attempts at further diagnosis, the creation of subgoals and text plans, and the use of a variety of other problem-solving strategies. We will illustrate what we mean by a greater "amount of processing" from specific protocols later in this section.

Whole-text problems such as "There's really a contradiction in here" are typically complex, ill-defined problems that may demand both extra attention and some rhetorical knowledge. This study suggests that experts meet the demands of whole-text diagnoses by devoting a good deal of attention to the problem; novices manage by avoiding the difficulty altogether.

There are other differences in the way experts and novices represent text problems. Let us examine some of the general differences between the ways in which our two subject groups represented problems to themselves. In other words, what separates expert and novice diagnosis?

Table 4. *Comparison of experts' and novices' diagnoses*

| Subjects | Total diagnoses | Type of diagnosis | | | Multisentence intentional |
|---|---|---|---|---|---|
| | | Rule | Maxim | Intentional | |
| *Experts* | | | | | |
| Instructors | 324 | 14 | 80 | 230 | 82 |
| % of total | | 4.3 | 24.7 | 71 | 35.6 |
| (*n* = 4) | | | | | |
| Professional | 107 | 18 | 19 | 70 | 13 |
| writers | | 16.8 | 17.7 | 65.4 | 18.6 |
| % of total | | | | | |
| (*n* = 3) | | | | | |
| Total experts | 431 | 32 | 99 | 300 | 95 |
| % of total | 61.6 | 7.4 | 23 | 69.6 | 31.6[a] |
| average | | | | | |
| Total novices | 214 | 15 | 64 | 135 | 14 |
| % of total | 30.5 | 7 | 29.9 | 63.1 | 10.3[a] |
| average | | | | | |
| (*n* = 7) | | | | | |

*Note:* Expert–novice difference in total diagnoses significant at $p < .05$.
[a] Percentage of intentional diagnoses.

As Figure 5 shows, diagnosis can take at least three significantly different forms depending on whether it is based on a rule, a maxim, or a sense of the text's intentions. Intentional diagnoses seem to be the most difficult to perform, because they are based on a comparison of the text and an image of the purpose, audience, or point of the text. Unlike rules or maxims, which are part of the reviser's *prior* knowledge, these intentions are often *created* afresh for each text; they may require the writer to make inferences about the audience and to construct a sense of gist or logic of the text. The procedures for solving such problems are also more complex, depending on heuristics rather than rules. In the case of many such problems, there is not even a standard heuristic procedure and the reviser must return to planning (see Figure 2) and generate new text.

We expected our experts to use a greater proportion of these intentional diagnoses, assuming they would recognize the difficult problems of audience, purpose, paragraph, and interparagraph coherence, and that they would have appropriate rhetorical knowledge to solve these ill-defined problems. Previous research (Beach, 1976; Nold, 1982; Sommers, 1980), which showed that students' revisions were typically limited to sentence-level corrections with no changes in meaning, would lead one to expect a parallel limitation in the revising *process* of novices and a failure to consider the more global issues of audience and purpose.

Our results, however, did not support this hypothesis (see Table 4). Both experts and novices used intentional diagnoses with roughly the same relative frequency. (Given the difference in the overall number of diagnoses, there was no significant difference in relative frequency: experts, 69.6%; novices, 63.1%.) This finding raised an important question: Were the novices actually attending to *global problems* just as the experts were?

A more detailed analysis of the novices' diagnoses showed that, although their efforts were indeed global in their concern for *intentionality*, they were not global in terms of *scope*. Novices regularly demonstrated these inferential responses to the text, to its purpose and audience, but these intentional diagnoses were applied to problems only within the scope of a simple sentence, often to single words or phrases. For example, a novice reading the phrase "Very fine friendships are often a further dividend [of sports]" responds, "Wait! This sounds really bad. 'A further dividend' . . . That sounds like some sort of banking instruction or something. . . . This 'very' I don't like . . . . This sounds pretty pushy." This novice is clearly attuned to the way readers respond to diction and to ill-concealed intentions. However, the chances of making significant changes in the text are probably low if one's unit of analysis is limited to individual words, phrases, or sentences.

The ability to deal with global features of the text, it appears then, has two dimensions. One is a concern for *intentionality* – which these novices had in abundance – and the other is the ability to apply that concern to problems of some *scope*. Our initial findings showed that novices largely failed to see problems at the whole-text level; novices diagnosed a mean of 3.0 whole-text problems compared with the experts' mean of 10.4. In addition, we found that the overall percentage of multisentence intentional diagnoses was 31.6% for the experts versus 10.3% for the novices (see Table 4).

This interesting surprise in the data suggests that assumptions about the writer's thinking process based on the evidence of the written product may lead to poor inferences about the skills a novice possesses and about the processes the task actually requires. Given this single-sentence strategy, urging inexperienced writers to attend to global issues of purpose and audience, for instance, might do little to affect the part of the process that is really limiting performance. An increased concern with intentionality could be incorporated quite easily into the novice reviser's current, limited-scope strategy with little effect on performance.

The results of the detection study show that novices simply give themselves far fewer problems to deal with from the start. As we now demonstrate, when we look at how the remaining problems are represented (i.e., when we look at bona fide diagnoses on both planted and whole-text problems) we see an even further decrease in the amount and quality of information attached to the novice's problem representation. Whereas novices create a spare image of a few problems, experts richly elaborate representations of many. Therefore, given that diagnosis is a prominent part of the expert's process, the next question to ask is, What role does it play?

*What role does diagnosis play in expert revision?*

Insofar as literary critics, rhetorical analysts, and writing instructors can serve as role models, one would expect diagnosis to be standard operating procedure for effective revisers. However, the reality appears to be more complex, for at least three reasons.

**1. Diagnosis is clearly not an obligatory step in revision.** Although the experts successfully fixed 91% of the planted problems, they chose to diagnose actively only 43% of them. Furthermore, on the diagnostic single-sentence task itself, they explicitly diagnosed only 53% of these common problems (see Table 2). Why? The answer is that even experts miss things other experts would see. Moreover, most subjects brought a narrower set of criteria to the single-sentence task, ignoring many of the more global problems of tone and style they had attended to during their revision. Finally, and perhaps most importantly, some problems appear to be solved more easily by the detect and rewrite strategy than by the more demanding path of diagnose and revise.

**2. Rewriting is often more efficient than trying to diagnose and revise.** As Figure 1 shows, the simplest path through revision is simply to detect and rewrite without calling on the special knowledge or extra attention diagnosis requires. Experts, like novices, often choose a paraphrase procedure that involves reading a faulty sentence or paragraph, extracting the gist, and then rewriting it in the way they normally produce prose. The rewrite strategy depends on the writer's normal language production skills. In the case of the expert these may be considerable. In the case of a novice these skills may be limited but still considerably in advance of his or her diagnostic skills. Evidence of the rewrite strategy in our study came in many forms: in the speed of revision, the absence of diagnosis, the fluent production of whole new sentences or chunks of text, and explicit comments by subjects, for example, "I'm rewriting, not revising this now" or "What I'm doing is trying to say it in my own words." In the cued recall, subjects regularly justified changes with the comment "I don't know why, this just sounds better." The frequency of the "sounds right" metaphor gave the impression that revisers often work as some musicians play – by ear. This finding is not surprising since this generate and test process draws on the writer's vast knowledge of language patterns and a body of relatively automated production skills.

Diagnosis, then, as we have defined it, appears to be an optional, strategic choice made against the backdrop of the simpler, more dominant procedure of rewriting. These strategic choices will be discussed in detail in the next section.

**3. Diagnosis is the expert's option.** Diagnosis is neither obligatory nor as pervasive as the simpler detect–rewrite strategy. However, it appears to be a strategy of considerable power that experts have a greater option of using.

To begin with, the experts are able, *when asked*, to diagnose more problems. (Compare 53% of the planted problems on the single-sentence task with the novice's 23% in Table 2.) More importantly, experts do significantly more diagnosis, *by choice*. Table 4 shows the total number of diagnostic comments made on both the protocols and cued recall. This number includes responses not only to the 26 planted problems, but to any problem the subject perceived. The experts averaged 62% diagnoses over the task to the novices' 31%, significant at the .05 level. Perhaps an even more meaningful figure emerges when we look at the subjects whose overall strategy predicts that they would use diagnosis if they could. That is, early in the study (and independent of this analysis) we identified four subjects whose explicit definition of the task effectively precluded a diagnostic strategy. As we discuss later, three subjects (a teacher, professional, and student) worked as rewriters and a fourth (a professional) worked as a deleter. Both of these strategies can increase efficiency by eliminating the *need* for diagnosis. When we look at the remaining bulk of the subjects, for whom diagnosis is a meaningful option, we find the experts averaging a striking 89% diagnoses over the task to the novices' 33%.

One final analysis supports this notion that diagnosis is an option experts can choose. If we look at those problems the writers actively detected – ones we can be *sure* they noticed – we find that the experts (including the rewriters and deleter) chose to diagnose 72% of these, whereas the students diagnosed only 39%.

To summarize, our analysis suggests that, although diagnosis is an optional strategy, it is the expert's option – and that option is actively exercised. In more general terms, it points to the fact that revision itself is a strategic process – not a simpler task of detecting and repairing errors. Most of the significant problems in adult texts are ill-defined problems writers must represent to themselves. In such revision, problem representation is no easy task; it calls on both knowledge and judgment. A diagnosis, as we have defined it, is a high-information representation, which places the problem in a category and may call up a repertory of procedures and tests. Diagnosis, it seems, is the expert's option for use on demanding problems. Although it requires more time, attention, and knowledge, it is a powerful problem-solving strategy, which, as we might expect, experts choose to use on significant problems.

### What constitutes an "expert" diagnosis?

Experts not only choose to make more diagnoses, they appear to create qualitatively different problem representations when they do so. The following excerpts from the protocols of an expert and two novices will illustrate some of the differences. Notice the dimensions of the problem noted in the expert's extended representation, compared with novice 1's simpler conceptualization and novice 2's reliance on a rewrite strategy. Notice also that the expert sees problems in relation

to the purpose of the whole text, whereas neither novice looks beyond the immediate context of the individual local problems.

The expert's text, which is a discussion of varsity sports, starts a new paragraph
with:

> I don't want to infer that the only chance women get for participating in sports is
> on varsity teams. Intramural sports are not quite the same as varsity sports in
> which the rules are better, equipment is better, with the techniques of the players
> being more developed.

The expert's response is spread over two passes at the text (P = protocol line):

P8    Aside from the fact that the sentence isn't parallel –

P9    Again I don't see the connection between the two sentences. [She had seen a con-
      nection problem in previous sentences.]

P10   It seems to me that if the goal of this article is to get women involved . . . a . . .

P11   It ought to be clear whether they want them to be involved in intramural or in var-
      sity sports or both . . . .

P12   Right at the beginning.

P13   I'll just go on.

*

*

      [*Reads* "intramural sports" . . . intramural sports."]

P42   I have to go back and look at the purpose of this thing once more.

P43   It does not say everything that probably needs to be said about student pressure.

P44   The purpose of this thing is to get women into a large active group to lobby for
      more funding,

P45   and the way to do that is to recruit more women for teams.

P46   In that case, if we want to recruit more women for the varsity teams, why for intra-
      mural sports?

P48   I don't know.

P49   I don't know because I don't understand enough about the subject

P50   to know if women in intramural sports would be part of what she's calling the
      teams

P51   and would therefore be part of a group to lobby for more funding

P52a  I suppose that they –

P53   if they were interested in sports, even if it were only intramural,

P52b  they could conceivably still be interested in lobbying for funding.

P54   On the other hand, if the focus here is on varsity teams,

P55   then this paragraph on intramural has absolutely no purpose in the thing.

P56   I think I'm going to take the paragraph out

P57   because it really doesn't say anything very helpful about intramural sports anyway.

P58 It just says they can be fun and take less time.

P59 It doesn't say anything very positive or convincing for intramural sports.

P60 So I'm just going to cross the whole paragraph out.

P61 That takes care of that one.

P62 Now I'll come back to the opening paragraph

P63 and see if I can make it make a little more sense.

*Novice 1*

[*Reads* "I don't want . . . "]

P41 This is all negative stuff.

[*Reads* "in which the rules are better, equipment is better, etc."]

P42 It can all be cut out.

P43 [*Writes* "Intramural sports are not the same as varsity sports."]

[*Speaks*] Period.

P44 They [are] a little casual, I guess. [She later adds this idea to her rewrite of the sentence.]

*Novice 2*

P103 OK, so – a – that's bad.

P104 Looks like a total rewrite.

[*Reads* "I don't want to infer. . . ."]

P111 That's bad.

Novice 2 chose to avoid diagnosis and take a direct path from detect to rewrite. Novice 1 chose to diagnose the problem she detected in the first sentence and to revise both the sentence and the information it contained. The expert chose to exercise her option to diagnose, building a quite complex representation of the problems with this paragraph.

We believe that further research will show other qualitative differences in expert diagnoses, not merely differences in frequency. As the expert protocol excerpt shows, experienced writers use diagnosis to explore ill-defined problems – problems for which they, like the novices, have no ready-made procedures or heuristics. This expert created an elaborate problem representation that included information about parallelism, logic, topic focus, and coherence, as well as her inferences about the alternative purposes of the text and her plans for meeting those purposes. Her diagnosis, however, is not a mere list of faults, but a hierarchically structured representation of the problem. For instance, she interprets the local problem of a topic shift between sentences 1 and 2 (P42) as a failure to maintain the purpose and focus of the entire handout. Her diagnosis of local incoherence between sentences is subordinated to the problem of global coherence. Likewise her solution is based on converging evidence – the text is incoherent *and* it is low in information. Note, too, how her abstract diagnoses concerning purpose are clearly connected to specific features of the text. This ability to build elaborated representations that integrate diagnoses into networks of related problems at various levels of the text appears to be an important feature of expert performance (Flower, Carey, & Hayes, 1984). Diagnosis in the hands of an expert leads to the creation of a problem that is substantially different from that the novice sees.

Diagnosis appears to be the expert's option for good reason. It is an exceptionally powerful means of managing complex problems. However, that power often comes at a price. On the one hand, diagnosis allows writers to grapple with larger, more global problems; it consolidates problematic features of a text into a conceptual whole, and it points to ways of dealing with the whole text. On the other hand, as writers begin to detect and represent these more global problems to themselves, they move from local, well-defined problems with explicit procedures to more complex, ill-defined problems for which there are no clearly defined ways to proceed. Diagnosis is a double-edged sword. Representing a complex and global problem is often tantamount to giving oneself an ill-defined and unmanageable problem. In further studies of diagnosis, we hope to see how writers handle this dilemma and use diagnosis to create manageable problems.

### Strategy selection

Revising prose requires the skill to construct solutions to problems – solutions that are unique to any given task. Because many text problems are ill-defined, writers usually have a range of means for solving them. Writers vary widely, however, in the problems they choose to solve, the strategies they use to solve them, and the quality of solutions they create.

Novices, as one might expect, have an impoverished set of problem-solving strategies, tending to use a few rule-governed procedures to solve most problems they detect. Aside from invoking rigid rules (Rose, 1980), novices deal with many text problems by using a default strategy of simply "eliminating the obstacle by deleting it" (Bridwell, 1980; Sommers, 1980). In contrast, experts use a range of procedures that enable them to satisfy a more complex set of goals and constraints than novices.

Research into the revision processes of both experienced and inexperienced writers indicates that revision requires making strategic decisions about how to modify text. Beach (1976) found that revisers could predict changes necessary for subsequent drafts. Having described a writing problem, "they would predict ways of solving that problem on their next draft" (p. 162). Nonextensive revisers were less likely to predict solution strategies or to make many changes on later drafts. Beach's findings implied that, if students can be taught to revise more extensively, their drafts will improve. However, Bridwell's (1980) findings contradict Beach's assertion that more extensive revisers are better writers. Her study reveals that *more* revision does not necessarily mean *better* revision: The most extensively revised papers received a range of quality ratings from the top to the bottom of the scale. In fact, her results show that novice revision can often make a text worse. Similarly, Bracewell (1983) found that novices often lack the ability to exercise deliberate control over the syntactic productions they make – that there is often a disassociation between goals and actual performance. Success in revision, then, appears to lie not in the amount of revision but in how effectively the revision solves the text problem.

We find that the best revisions are produced by writers whose strategies are adapted to the text's purpose and goals. But what does it mean to make this adaptation? In this section, we shall discuss a range of strategies that help give writers control over their revision process, as well as strategies for modifying text. We shall also see how strategy selection reflects changes in the writer's task definition, as we discussed earlier.

*Strategy selection* encompasses the critical decisions writers must make about what action to take after they have defined the task, evaluated the text or plan, and represented its problems. This decision process is represented by the *select strategy* component of the model (see Figure 1). Of course, decisions are made throughout the revision process. Our focus here is on the writers' active strategies for monitoring the writing process and for modifying text. When writers define their task, evaluate the text, and represent problems in the light of goals and plans, they have at least five actions from which to choose:

1. Ignore (the problem)
2. Delay (the effort to solve the problem)
3. Search (for more information to solve the problem)
4. Rewrite (the text by redrafting or paraphrasing)
5. Revise (the text by relying on diagnostic information)

The first three actions often assist the writer in managing the process, in clarifying the problem representation, and in determining the scope of particular text problems. The second two describe means of modifying the text. Our results suggest that expert and novice revisers are quite distinct in their ability to exercise these strategies.

### *Managing the revising process: to ignore, to delay, to search*

**Ignore.** The first action on the left side of the *select strategy* area in Figure 1, ignore, describes what writers do when they detect text problems they believe do not merit serious attention. Typically, experienced writers ignore detections associated with optional grammatical or stylistic rules such as "never end a sentence with a preposition." Maxine Hairston's (1981) study on style points out that often grammatical and stylistic rules are applied arbitrarily and are frequently influenced by personal taste.

Our results support Hairston's findings; not only is there a wide difference in the range of text problems experts and novices pay attention to and ignore, but experts differ from experts and novices from novices. For example, one expert in our study noticed a split infinitive and said: "I see we have a split infinitive here, but they never bother me so I think we'll leave it." Another expert who spotted the same split infinitive remarked, "I always feel compelled to fix split infinitives. I just hate the way they sound." A novice who noticed a problem with word choice said, "I know it's not quite the right word, but I won't change it; they'll never notice it anyway, so why bother. I'll just go on to the next sentence." Another novice who detected a problem with an undefined abbreviation read it and commented, "I wonder what the term *AIAW* means? I can't figure it out, but it must be important, so I'll leave it there."

Moreover, we found that expert and novice writers often distinguish the text problems they ignore using one of two criteria: (1) The problem will not create confusion for the reader, or (2) finding a solution is too difficult or not worth the effort. Sometimes both criteria are used simultaneously. Making effective decisions about what to ignore depends on skill in knowing when to apply these criteria – skill that often requires exercising subtle discrimination. The ability to exercise this discrimination is one factor that separates novices from experts. We find that *ignoring* can be a sophisticated strategy for controlling the revision process but that too often it acts as a default strategy in the hands of inexperienced writers.

**Delay.** To delay action describes the writer's conscious decision to divide the revision process into parts. Delaying action allows the writer to focus attention selectively on one part of the task while *setting a goal* to deal with another part later. This strategy is used when:

1. The writer chooses to prioritize revision activity – dealing with a class of problems such as those associated with the text's meaning first, with grammatical and stylistic problems second, and with polishing last. Experts, as we pointed out in our task definition study, often read a text for gist before repairing surface structure features.
2. The writer may need to reread the text to evaluate whether the problem is major or minor in relation to other modifications that have to be made. We saw that expert writers frequently re-evaluate the problems detected during a first reading to determine the order in which problems will be addressed.
3. The writer may not have a ready procedure for remedying the text problem and may choose to "write around" the difficulty until the solution becomes apparent. One of the better novices in our study noticed that the original text did not say much about sports being fun and could not decide how to convey that idea. She made a note to herself to "include why sports are fun" – "as soon as I figure out where to put it and how to say it."
4. The writer realizes that invention is called for but needs to evaluate the text more critically in order to discover the best way to proceed. For example, several of the experts in our study decided that a revised handout "on sports for freshman

women" should list the sports the college offers. They put off generating the list, however, until they had decided on the argument's main points.

5. The writer has to revise a particular section of text before knowing how to solve problems in other parts of the text (see Figure 2). For example, the writer may need to revise sections in the body of a text before revising introductions. One expert in our study remarked, "If this is a handout, we need to get the facts straight first; then I'll know what to do with this deadly introduction."

As we can see from these examples, delaying action often sends writers back to planning, reevaluating, and reformulating goals for the text. Both expert and novice writers tend to create verbal cues for themselves, such as "develop this point as soon as I see how it relates to the next section," as well as visual cues, such as checking or starring sections of text as reminders of changes they need time to consider.

To delay action effectively requires the writer to attend to text features that need further work. We found that, although revisers often intend to come back to places in the text that require more attention, they frequently fail to do so. For example, one of the novices in our study noticed that the original text set up a negative contrast between intramural and varsity sports, implying the superiority of varsity sports. She remarked, "If this handout is to recruit people for both kinds of teams, maybe it shouldn't say that varsity sports have better players, rules and equipment. That's like saying, you know, your equipment is going to be worse, and the rules are going to be worse, and you may get hurt." She then said, "Well, I'll come back to that and change it later. I think it should make both kinds of teams sound good." Her final revision, however, kept the pejorative contrast.

Although the reason revisers sometimes fail to act on problems they flag is not entirely clear, we offer several hypotheses:

They may lack the strategies and procedures for acting on their goals.

They may lack the managerial skill to coordinate a number of revisions.

They may lack the perspective to judge the appropriateness of a proposed solution.

They may experience memory overload and forget the problems they detect.

They may ignore their early detections, feeling satisfied with revisions already made.

They may feel that the effort needed to make the revision is too great in relation to the impact it will have on the text.

**Search.** Search is a strategy used to refine and elaborate the problem representation. Writers typically search in response to a feeling that their representation is incomplete or inadequate. Search is a process of representation in which writers try to define the problem more explicitly. The output of problem representation, as we have suggested previously, is a continuum from ill- to well-defined problems. In using a search strategy, writers try to push their representation from ill- to well-defined. This process provides them with a sharpened representation, which in turn gives them a better idea of how to solve a problem.

To re-represent a problem involves many processes; prominent among these are memory search and text search. By *memory search*, we are referring to the process of retrieving experience and knowledge relevant to the problem. Memory search often occurs rapidly. Writers may detect a problem and characterize it generally but then generate several successive re-representations of its nature. Consider the following example of a novice who searches memory to sharpen his problem representation, finds relevant and useful information, yet fails to accomplish his revision goal.

The novice has just read a sentence describing a lack of competition in varsity sports: "Therefore, many of the teams are less competitive than many students expect." He responds, "Wait a minute, there's something wrong there. I don't know if I want to say that sports are less competitive. Is this true anyway? Well, when I played varsity sports, I noticed that students were *more* competitive than I'd ever seen before. So that's wrong. Maybe it should say less strenuous . . . no . . . maybe less rigorous. You know, some women may be a little intimidated to come out. How about 'Teams are not less competitive.' No, that sounds bad. I don't know how to get across the fact that they're less than major college sports but they're just as competitive. OK, I'll just cut that whole thing out."

In this case, the subject found that the information was imprecise but was unable to increase its precision. We find that, although experts are typically successful in using information retrieved from memory to improve the text, novices tend to fail to use retrieved information effectively.

*Text search* is a process in which the reviser scans the text to get a better understanding of a text problem. We observed that experienced writers sharpen their representation of a text problem by rereading with a focused goal in mind. Rereading with a focused goal helps the writer both to specify the problem further and find all related instances of that problem. Writers engaging in this re-representation of the text create goals that respond to both global and local features of the text. Some of the goals we saw experienced writers create before searching the text include the following:

> Pinpoint the location of contradictory assertions.
> Check for missing or redundant information.
> Evaluate for organization and coherence.
> Locate arguments that may offend the audience.
> Check for the consistency of subheadings and other internal structural markers.
> Check for variety of sentence openers and sentence structures.
> Check for the frequency with which a particular phrase, word, or concept has been used.

We find that expert writers often employ a text search strategy to determine the location, frequency, and scope of problems to be found in the text. However, many times experienced writers search not for errors of commission but rather for what is missing. They look consciously for gaps, missing information, and places where examples, analogies, or metaphors are needed.

For many experienced writers, search is a powerful strategy for discovery and subsequent invention. As indicated by our model of reading to evaluate (see Figure 4), a wide range of possible outputs is associated with the various levels of the comprehension process. Words often suggest alternative words, and schemas alternative schemas. In evaluating text the reader is stimulated to think of new and better ways of saying the same ideas.

Moreover, many re-representations involve the coordination of memory and text search. For example, revisers are sometimes alerted to contradictory assertions when something they are reading does not fit with what they remember about the preceding text. In this situation they initiate a search of the text for that earlier information.

### Strategies for modifying text: rewriting and revising

We observed two distinct strategies that lead to modifying the text: rewriting and revising. Our characterizations of rewriting and revising strategies grow out of analyzing how writers carry out the task they define for themselves. For the most part, our writers chose one of these revision paths and stuck with it. By "path" we mean a consistent set of revising strategies, whether by design or default, that describes the majority of the writer's responses to text problems. As one can imagine, elements of both strategies appeared to various degrees in the protocols of both expert and novice writers.

**Rewriting: redrafting or paraphrasing.** Rewriting is a strategy used by revisers who are not necessarily trying to save the original text, but are trying to preserve the meaning. Rewriting generally takes one of two shapes: redrafting or paraphrasing.

When revisers *redraft* a text, they often extract the text's gist and then abandon the existing text and start over – sometimes reformulating the top-level goals and modifying text plans; for example, "What I intended was to inform my audience by making three points, but I want the audience to see how these points are shared values, so I need to argue these points more by creating a shared context than by simply listing my points." The writer then recasts the entire argument structure. The redraft strategy is thus a restructuring of the text's purpose or plan. It does not rely on transformations of sentences or clauses to produce new text.

A writer redrafts, for example, when the text is riddled with both high- and low-level problems, inconsistencies that compete for the writer's attention, and so he or she saves effort by *not diagnosing* each problem, but rather by making a whole-text diagnosis such as "This text will not accomplish my goal for the reader. I need to rewrite the whole thing."

*Paraphrasing*, the second rewrite strategy we observed, is invoked when the writer's goal is to save the text's meaning but to express the meaning in different words, using a different surface structure. Novices are more likely to paraphrase than to redraft, partly because the implicit test of paraphrase is a comparison between it and the integrity of the gist and not a check against a plan.

Writers usually paraphrase the text by extracting the sentence-by-sentence gist and then recasting the sentences. A writer who chooses to paraphrase and rewrite often does so in a linear manner. This strategy is accompanied by a considerable amount of rereading of the text produced up to the last change. Like redrafting, paraphrasing uses little if any specific diagnostic information but relies mainly on making detections and seeing the gist.

We observed that experts often use a "density of text problems" heuristic to prompt a redraft revision strategy. By "density of text problems," we mean the frequency and diversity of text problems. Using a density heuristic tells the writer to attend to the frequency and type of text problems before taking action. This decision procedure is useful because it allows the expert to (1) coordinate the solution of separate text problems to produce a coherent revision and (2) select efficient revision strategies. Furthermore, it provides the writer with criteria for deciding whether to accept the text's surface structure or to reject it and start over. We have found that experts using such a heuristic have the advantage of making decisions that are better informed by the requirements of the task. For example, when one of our professional writers noticed that the tone of the opening paragraph of the letter was wrong for the intended audience, her reaction was to scan the text to see how many times a word or phrase offended the audience. She then used the density guideline "I can't simply change a word here and there, because the whole tone is offensive. I'll have to rewrite the whole thing."

Another situation that prompts a rewrite strategy is one in which writers run into a range of problems that would take considerable effort to fix one at a time with the help of diagnosis. Experienced writers in this situation may say to themselves, "I see too many different problems here and I'll simply need to rewrite." There are many reasons people choose to rewrite rather than repair the existing text. Below are a few:

1. When writing for discovery, the writer often finds that, by rewriting, he or she is freed from the text's influence on the production of new ideas or ways of presenting ideas.
2. The writer may not have an adequate strategy for fixing the text problem.
3. The writer may be unable to integrate the text's gist, or there may be several competing gists that may cause the writer difficulty.

Although rewriting can be a powerful strategy, we have observed that it creates several problems:

1. It can be an inefficient strategy for novices because they frequently do not have sufficient criteria for deciding when to accept their rewriting and therefore do not know when to stop generating new versions. Because it requires so much trial and error, it usually takes longer than a focused solution.

2. Sometimes rewriting is very frustrating. When the writer is not especially fluent, even the rewriting of a sentence can be cumbersome. When novice writers get bogged down in a particular sentence part, it is difficult for them to see the context in which the sentence functions.
3. Sometimes the text is a powerful constraining stimulus, one that discourages invention and encourages a myopic perspective of the text. When the novice writer tries to paraphrase the text, the recasting of the old meaning interferes with producing the intended one. The novice's attention to the existing text limits the alternatives considered. In trying to recast the same poorly formed syntactic and semantic aspects of a text, it becomes difficult to decide whether the new sentence fits the context better than the old.

We found a special class of writers, both expert and novice, whose choice of goals distinguishes them from the rewriters and the revisers: the *deleters*. Deleters systematically excise text problems rather than invent, restructure, and use procedures for remedying text difficulties. Unlike rewriters, deleters change the surface structure of the text by removing problematic words, phrases, or sentences and, in so doing, often eliminate much of the propositional content of the text. Deletion is the quickest way to modify text, but if driven without clear goals, it can make the text worse. We found that, although both expert and novice writers could be seen as deleters, they seemed to delete with different goals in mind. Novices tended to delete what they thought was "bad" about the text and generally had little more to say. Expert deleters tended to make grammatical or syntactic comments about what they deleted. The novices we observed tended to behave as sentence-level editors and consequently ignored most of the rhetorical problems in the text. When the text needs little improvement, however, deletion is an efficient strategy.

**Revising.** The second major path we saw both expert and novice writers choose is that of making diagnoses and then selecting a repair procedure – a path we call revise. Our model presents revise in a special sense: *Revise* refers to the process of deciding that one will use diagnostic information to fix text problems. Writers usually revise when they believe that much of the text can be saved. This does not mean, however, that revisers do not often diagnose gaps in text that call for elaboration, examples, and details.

We can see how experts and novices differ in the problems they diagnose and in the procedures they use for improving text by looking at their problems and solutions paths diagrammatically via a means–ends table. We are suggesting that the output of revising can be viewed as a matrix of problems and solutions.

### Means–ends tables of revisers

Means–ends analysis was described by psychologists Newell and Simon (1972) as a general problem-solving procedure in which symptoms of problems were

Table 5. *Means–ends table of novice reviser*

| ENDS | | construct sentences: new material | old material | combine sentences | segment sentences | delete | improve wording | fix grammar | fix spelling |
|---|---|---|---|---|---|---|---|---|---|
| **GLOBAL** | Text goal not met | ■ | | | | ■ | | | |
| | audience problem | ■ | | | | | ■ | | |
| | faulty emphasis | ■ | | | | ■ | | | |
| | faulty transition | ■ | | | | ■ | | | |
| **LOCAL** | awkward | | ■ | ■ | | | | | |
| | choppy | | | ■ | | | | | |
| | wordy | | | | | ■ | ■ | | |
| | redundant | | | | | ■ | | | |
| | word choice | | | | | | ■ | ■ | |
| | grammar | | | | | | | ■ | |
| | parallelism | | | | ■ | | | | |
| | subject–pronoun agreement | | | | | | | ■ | |
| | spelling fault | | | | | | | | ■ |

matched to strategies for solving them. For any reviser, we can construct a means–ends description of the problems represented and the strategies taken to solve the problems. Means–ends tables for individual revisers then are not theories, but unambiguous descriptions of the problems the reviser defines and the actions he or she uses to correct them.

Tables 5 and 6 are two sample means–ends tables, one of a novice and the other an expert. In the left column are the ends, or the problems the reviser flagged. (Novice revisers did not always use these diagnostic categories in naming the text problems; they were reliably inferred by two separate coders.) Along the top of the table are the means or the strategies the reviser used to solve the problems on the left. We can see that, for this novice, the detection of global problems is quite limited. More importantly, the novice seems to adhere to the same strategies for remedying a range of text problems, with deleting, improving wording, and constructing new material the most frequent means of solving text problems. Furthermore, notice that the novice is typically working with text units no larger than two sentences.

Compare this table with that of an expert reviser. Notice the elaboration of the

Table 6. *Means–ends table of expert reviser*

| ENDS | | construct sentences: new material | old material | modify paragraph | invent paragraph | delete | delay action | search for information | combine sentences | segment sentences | reorder words | use infinitives | fix spelling | improve wording | insert qualifier | choose precise word | choose synonym | fix grammar |
|---|---|---|---|---|---|---|---|---|---|---|---|---|---|---|---|---|---|---|
| GLOBAL | text goal not met | ■ | | | | | | | | | | | | | | | | |
| | missing information | | | | ■ | | | ■ | | | | | | | | | | |
| | audience problem | | | ■ | ■ | ■ | ■ | | | | | | | | | | | |
| | paragraph problem | | | ■ | ■ | | | | | | | | | | | | | |
| | missing transition | ■ | ■ | | ■ | | | | | | | | | | | | | |
| | missing example | ■ | | | | | | ■ | | | | | | | | | | |
| | faulty emphasis | | | | ■ | | | | | | | | | | | | | |
| | faulty transition | | ■ | | | | | | | | | | | | | | | |
| LOCAL | wordy | | | | | ■ | | | | | | | | | | | | |
| | awkward | | | | | | | | ■ | ■ | | | | ■ | | | | |
| | choppy | | | | | | | | ■ | | | | | | | | | |
| | diction | | | | | | | | | | | | | ■ | | | | |
| | *ambiguity | | | | | | | | | | | | | | | | ■ | |
| | *redundancy | | | | | ■ | | | | | | | | | | | | |
| | grammar | | | | | | | | | | | | | | | | | ■ |
| | *subject-<br>pronoun<br>agreement | | | | | | | | | | | | | | | | | |
| | *dangling<br>modifier | | | | | | | | | | ■ | | | | | | | |
| | *parallelism | | | | | | | | | | ■ | | | | | | | |
| | *split infinitive | | | | | | | | | | | ■ | | | | | | |
| | spelling | | | | | | | | | | | | ■ | | | | | |

local and global ends. We see a broader range of global problems attended to, including gaps in text content that call for inventing paragraphs, examples, and transitions. The expert's means of solving these difficulties are also more fully elaborated and more concentrated on paragraphs than are those of the novice. The expert is also a better manager of the revising process. Notice how this expert chooses to delay action and to search for information as a problem-solving activity for global difficulties.

We observed experts using what we call a "precedence guideline" of handling more important problems before spending time on minor ones. When rereading their text to see if, for example, transitions are logical, they find a disorganized paragraph, they will stop looking at the transitional phrases and concentrate on revising the disorganized paragraph. This inventory-making skill places the expert writer in a position to decide whether to rewrite or revise the text – a useful advantage.

When we look at the "local" part of the expert's means–ends table, we again see that it is more developed than that of the novice and contains embedded categories. The expert notices specific subsets of problems within larger categories, distinguishing between ambiguity and redundancy, for example. The expert also has a wider range of procedures for dealing with local problems. Notice in the "Means" column how specific the procedures become: use infinitives, insert qualifier, choose synonym.

Revisers who have a single means of solving all text problems – we call them deleters – have the sparest of all possible means–ends tables. Their "cut and slash" method, as one might expect, does not always produce the best revisions.

### Major revision paths

Although the rewrite and revise paths are handled quite differently by experts and novices, we cannot argue that one path is generally superior to the other. We found that expert performance is marked by the ability to make strategic decisions about which path to choose given the rhetorical situation, the quality of the text produced so far, and the pragmatic constraints under which the revision activity takes place. We observed that novices tend to choose one path and stick with it, whereas experts sometimes switch paths when necessary. For example, two of our experts took a diagnosis–revise path first and then decided the text was too flawed to fix and rewrote it.

We found that writers often choose a revision path on economic grounds; that is, they choose the path they think will enable them to meet their goals with the least effort. Our data suggest that the perceived effort required by revising depends on at least two factors:

> The perceived quality of the text, that is, the kind, number, and scope of its problems.
> The writer's perception of his or her competence to fix text problems.

The perceived effort required by rewriting, however, depends mainly on the writer's sense of fluency in generating new text. Although novices have difficulty with either revising or rewriting, they have relatively less difficulty with rewriting and hence often choose the rewriting path. In contrast, experts, because they have facility in both rewriting and revising, can switch readily from one to the other.

We noted that some of our experts characteristically rewrote the text, whereas others always revised. When we evaluated the final products, the expert rewriters and revisers did equally well, although they produced quite different kinds of texts; our interrater reliability on this evaluation was 81%. Experts, then, whether rewriters or revisers, recognize available options and invoke strategies that are best suited to the problems encountered in their current situation.

Overall, our research suggests that we may have the most impact on the revising process of inexperienced writers if we find ways to give them a bigger repertory of options – options that will give them flexibility and increase their problem-solving power.

### Summary

In this chapter we presented a new conceptual integration and elaboration of the cognitive processes involved in revision in a process model. Our major findings, organized around the central subprocesses, were the following:

**Task definition.** Owing to the ill-defined nature of writing tasks, differences in task definition contribute importantly to the differences in performance between expert and novice revisers. One important aspect of the difference in definition is that experts see revision as a whole-text task, whereas students see it largely as a sentence-level task. Experts perform better than novices not just because certain of their subskills are better than those of novices, but also and more importantly because they are performing a better task – that is, one better suited to improving text.

**Evaluation.** One part of the revision model is a new model of evaluation – one that is different from dissonance models, applying to the evaluation of *plans* as well as text. Since revision can be carried on in the absence of text, it cannot depend entirely on the comparison of text and intention. Our model differs in this respect from the models of Sommers, of Bridwell, and of Scardamalia and Bereiter.

**Problem representation.** Problem representation constitutes a continuum from ill-defined to well-defined. *Detections*, which fall on the ill-defined end, contain little information; *diagnoses*, however, are based on concept recognition – they categorize the problem and give one access to appropriate procedures.

**Detection.** Novices persistently fail to perceive text problems that experts detect easily. Experts consistently outperform novices in the detection of both local and global text problems.

**Diagnosis:** Diagnoses vary in quality. The diagnoses of experts are more global, elaborate, integrated, and procedural than those of novices.

**Strategy selection:** Strategy selection in revision involves strategies for managing the revising process – *ignore*, *delay*, and *search* – as well as for modifying text – *rewrite* or *revise*. Experts tend to make the choice among these options more effectively than do novices. The *means–end repertory* of expert revisers is more fully elaborated and finely partitioned than that of novices. Most strikingly, it includes more goals concerning global text problems, and it contains *means* absent from novice repertories for solving these problems.

### Appendix A: Instructions for revision task

Here is a copy of a letter written by the Director of Women's Athletics at Illinois Central College, to Jane Fisk, Director of Women's Athletics here at CMU. The letter is in response to a recent article in *Focus*, CMU's faculty newspaper, on women's athletics at CMU. The author, who is an old friend of Jane Fisk's, congratulates her on her field hockey team's performance, discusses the *Focus* article, and gives Jane suggestions for writing a brief, one-page handout for freshman women on athletics at CMU. Jane decided to take her up on her suggestion. She wants to stick as closely to Janet's discussion (in the marked section of the letter) as possible. However, the PR person for the Physical Education Department has forcefully suggested that it needs some work on both the writing and the overall presentation.

#### *Directions*

Your job is to read the letter and revise the marked-off section so that it can stand on its own as a one-page handout. It will be titled "Misconceptions and Facts about Women's Sports at CMU" (the title the author of the letter suggested) and placed in all freshman women's mailboxes.

In this task, you are to stick to the prose just as much as you can, while editing it to improve it. The typist will be given the letter, with your changes marked on it, along with any additional sheets of paper you happen to use. *Be sure to mark clearly in the letter where any additional words, phrases, sentences, etc., belong so the typist knows where to insert them when making a final copy*. Also, when you are revising, *do not erase* any changes you make; instead, whenever you wish to get rid of text, simply draw a line through it.

*Remember*: You are *revising* a one-page handout for freshman women. Stick to the prose as much as possible – don't rewrite, just *revise*.

### Appendix B: Questions subjects frequently ask about talk-aloud protocols of the writing and revision process

#### *What is a talk-aloud protocol?*

A protocol is a sequential recording of a person's attempt to perform a task. Developed early in this century, protocol analysis is a powerful tool in educational research. In particular, the information captured in "talk-aloud" protocols enables the educational researcher to construct detailed models of human thinking processes and in some cases to simulate these processes in a computer program. In short, protocols give the research a "window" through which to look at otherwise invisible mental processes that occur from moment to moment. We are concerned in this short explanation with talking-aloud protocols of writers revising a text.

### How is a talking-aloud protocol made?

The procedure is really very simple. The researcher will ask you to talk aloud while you are revising or rewriting a particular document. You are to say out loud what you are thinking. You are not to worry about speaking correctly, stopping in the middle of thoughts or sentences, and so on, but you should try to verbalize as *continually* as you can during the entire time you are at work. Pauses in your talk will naturally occur, but try to avoid them. If the researcher feels you are not talking often enough, he or she may prompt you.

### Should I try to explain how my writing processes work or how I would usually do this task?

Subjects who ask this question are usually trying to do the researcher's work themselves at the same time they are revising or rewriting. You are not to describe what you "would" do, but *only what you are actually thinking about at the time you are working*. In fact, you are *not* expected to "analyze" your writing habits or creative processes at all. You are not being asked to "introspect," or to give an explanation or interpretation of your writing. You need only say what is on your mind at the moment. *Concentrate on the task you have been given, and simply say aloud whatever occurs to you.*

### How can a protocol capture my thinking processes if I can't say aloud everything I am thinking?

Of course, you will not be able to say *everything* you are thinking when you are completing even a simple writing or revision task. A portion of your thinking is lost and falls between the cracks. But almost everything you *do say* is valuable to the researcher. The amount of information retrieved from the talk-aloud method probably exceeds the amount to be gained by any other research method currently employed for the study of how people write and revise. Moreover, your transcribed protocol is not the only piece of data studied by the researcher; your finished or revised text is also studied and compared with the talk-aloud transcript. By itself, your finished text tells the researcher very little about the *processes* you used to create the text. However, when your finished text is "matched" with the protocol transcript, the researcher has a more detailed picture of how your writing and revising unfolded. Again, *concentrate on the task and on whatever you are conscious of as you work. Say aloud everything that comes to mind.*

*Doesn't talking aloud interfere with my thinking, so that I am not thinking and working as I normally would?*

This question is often asked, and rightly so. It's a very important question for researchers to deal with. At the present time, no one knows for certain if talking aloud does interfere with your thinking during problem solving. A lot of research is presently being conducted to find out. So far, researchers have been unable to find any strong evidence that talking aloud interferes with thinking. Some research has even shown that, with very little practice, you can solve the same problem in the same amount of time whether you are talking aloud or not. Talking aloud can also improve decision making, and many people talk to themselves when they write anyway. The first few minutes of a protocol may feel awkward, but with a little practice this feeling will disappear and you will feel more comfortable.

*Should I write and talk at the same time, or only before or after I write something down?*

You should *talk as continuously as possible*, whether you are writing or not. Sometimes you will find yourself only able to say exactly what you are writing on paper. This is perfectly fine, so long as you don't pause too long between words. If you do, the experimenter will prompt you.

*Should I talk aloud even if I am just rereading what I've written?*

Yes, you should. Avoid the temptation to mumble if, and when, you reread your text. Even if you are skimming rapidly, and not rereading sentences in their entirety, talk aloud and make sure your voice is audible and clear.

### Sample protocol

The experimenter will now play a tape recording of a person talking aloud as he works. The tape illustrates the concerns raised above. In particular, notice how the writer-subject concentrates on the task: For the most part he talks *while* he both reads and writes, though the experimenter has to prompt him a few times to keep talking. In the first sample segment, the *bracketed* parts indicate what the writer-subject is actually putting on paper as he talks. The directions he is reading are italicized:

Um – ok – my task is to – let's see you want me to read the directions – OK. *Directions: Your task is to describe the drawing you are given so accurately that someone could reproduce it only from your written account. Remember, however, that efficiency is as important as accuracy.* OK – I get it – this isn't easy because it says *accurately* – how accurately? – and *efficiently* – the detail that's tough – OK – I guess I'll get started and make an outline – no, wait a minute – *reproduce* they say – does that mean it just has to have the same parts, but not look the same – completely the same? – says *so accurately that* – uh – *could reproduce it simply from your written account–*. (Experimenter: Please keep talking, OK?) Yeah, OK – I just don't quite understand what these instructions are trying – it seems there's probably a hidden problem in here – I guess we'll– the first thing is to just list all the parts – OK, here's a castle, kind of a snake, a star–(Experimenter: You're falling silent; please keep talking.) I keep thinking about the assumptions in the directions and it's like – it looks like– I wonder if I could sneak some pictures into my writing – so the guy, the reader who's doing– uh, no, that would be cheating I guess – how about if I call this shape like an open book? Yeah, it does look like a book, or the corner of a room – and then describe each of the walls as pages in turn – yeah, that's a snap – just start off writing for now and go back later to see– [Envision an open book. In this drawing the left portion of the book– ] No, scratch that – of the [open book looks like a rectangle, but the top and bottom lines of it slant inward, toward the middle of the paper– ] Uh, just to get this exact, uh – left to right – OK [left to right]. Is this confusing? I don't think I like talking about the middle of the paper–

Here is more of the same writer-subject's protocol, a little later on. In this segment, the italicized parts of the protocol indicate when the writer-subject is *reading or rereading his text.* The *bracketed* text here indicates when the writer is revising parts of his text and adding new parts.

Well now what a job – that does it for paragraph one I think – it's not very good I think but at least it's exact. They have to get the biggest most general things first so they'll know where to put others. This – all this left and right seems hard but– It seems like this needs to be changed here– (Experimenter: You're falling silent again; please keep talking.) I'll read to see how this sounds – it sounds too complicated, anyway, well, let's see: *Envision an open book – in this drawing the left portion of the open book looks like a rectangle but the top and bottom lines of it slant inward, toward the middle of the paper from right to left–* OK, OK, that's clear enough, not perfect, but– [The right portion looks like a trapezoid.] Maybe can't say that – can't say trapezoid because some people may not know what that is exactly and this has to be very simple so a child can do it – OK so [like a square but its top and bottom lines are also slanted inward toward the center of the page from right to left]. Well that's wordy but I don't have to worry about the term now– [the slants from the rectangle meet with the slants of the square in the center of the page at a vertical line– ] No, change that– [meet with the slants from the square in the center of the page at a vertical line – this vertical line is the rectangle's right side and the trapezoid's– ] Uh, nope, trapezoid again, have to change that to square – so [this vertical line is the rectangle's right side and the . . . the square's left side]. There, I think that's a lot better, a lot – so now I'm ready to describe the left inside cover of this book – or so-called book – I think I'll reread this from the start again–

## Appendix C: Stimulus text to be revised

December 2, 1980

Jane Fisk
Director, Women's Athletics
Dept. of Physical Education
Carnegie-Mellon University
Schenley Park
Pittsburgh, PA 15213

Dear Jane,

Congratulations to you and the field hockey team on this season's performance!

I was quite pleased to see that piece in the recent *Focus* (Vol. 10, No. 3, November 1980) on the situation for women athletes at CMU. It doesn't say everything that probably need to be said on the subject, but it's a beginning! I think you're right about student pressure being needed to create change. For myself, I have found that the only way to get a large, active group to lobby for more funding is to recruit more women for the teams. That may seem like getting the cart before the horse, but I think it wouldn't be so difficult to attract more women if a little more PR was done.

Most women are reluctant enough to participate in sports, let alone busy CMU students. I've found that many women seem to have a lot of misconceptions about the time required, necessary ability, etc. Our department found it very useful to make a brief handout giving the reasons women should get involved – I think it was titled "Misconceptions and Facts about Women's Sports at Illinois Central College." It was especially effective with the incoming freshmen, and a comparatively inexpensive method of recruitment. We used all the handouts and I seem to have misplaced the original, but the ideas we included were roughly the following: [BEGIN TO REVISE HERE]

Many naive women students possess the assumption that it is necessary that they be superlative athletes in order to successfully be a member of a varsity team. They fail to realize that schools like Illinois Center (CMU) are Division 3 AIAW schools – that is, schools that do not offer athletic scholarships. Therefore, many of the teams are less competitive than many students expect. In sports like fencing for a long time many of our varsity team members had no previous experience anyway. Even some students without background if they have good coordination have learned so much in their first semester that they even surpassed other with a background in athletics in high school.

I don't want to infer that the only chance women get for participating in sports is on varsity teams. Intra-mural sports are not quite the same as varsity sports, in which the rules are better, equipment is better, and with the techniques of the players being more developed.

Irregardless, IM sports may be the choice for many women – they can be just as much fun and take less time.

Perhaps a more influenctial aspect in freshman students' reluctance to participate in sports is one's fear of the time commitment. Many new students, worried about the academic demands of college and inexperienced at organizing their time, feel that participating in sports is another pressure they don't need. It is hard for them to see that the benefits of sports, are worth the time invested. However, being involved in sports *demands* that the student develop their ability to organize their time. Its structure encourages the student to plan their time. And being part of a varsity team, very fine friendships are a further dividend for the student athlete.

Students also gain many personal benefits from an involvement in sports. They develop cardiorespiratory endurance and freshman athletes avoid that common enduring affliction – freshman-year weight gain. Students also learn to interact with people, cooperation, punctuality, responsibility, how to win and lose correctly, and how to treat your opponents. All these abilities are important in the working world – which is why potential employers are impressed with a candidate who has experience in athletics.

There is, however, one comment which I frequently hear and which is more convincing than all these arguments, and that's a comment I hear time and time again from women who've started sports late in their college career – "Oh, I wish I'd started earlier!"

These arguments tend to make a very convincing little handout: we had about 25% more freshmen sign up for teams the year we used one than had signed up the previous year. By the way, you should remember to list the sports women can participated in at CMU. [END REVISION HERE]

I hope this method of recruitment works as well for you as it has for us. I'll send you a copy of the handout if the original turns up. Good luck, and best wishes for your teams' continued success.

Warmly,

Janet Grotzinger
Director, Women's Athletics

## Notes

**1.** We include this collapsed category of fix/eliminate to account for several observations that made it impossible, in some cases, to ascertain whether the fixing of a text problem was planned or coincidental with another activity. For example, some writers fixed problems by using a rewrite strategy, thus apparently never focusing on the text problem as the target to fix. At other times, writers eliminated some problems in the process of deliberately remedying others.

**2.** Four judges independently ranked the revisions for overall quality from 1 for *worst* to 14 for *best*. The average pairwise rank correlation between judges was 0.812. The average rank assigned to novices was 6.07 and that to experts, 8.93. The difference in ranked quality between experts and novices was significant at the .05 level by the Mann–Whitney test.

## References

Bartlett, E. J. (1981). *Learning to write: Some cognitive and linguistic components*. Washington, DC: Center for Applied Linguistics.

Beach, R. (1976). Self-evaluation strategies of extensive revisers and nonrevisers. *College composition and communication, 27*, 160–4.

Bereiter, C., & Scardamalia, M. (1981). From conversation to composition: The role of instruction in a developmental process. In R. Glaser (Ed.), *Advances in instructional psychology* (Vol. 2, pp. 3–25). Hillsdale, NJ: Erlbaum.

Bracewell, R. J., Scardamalia, M., and Bereiter, C. (1978). The development of audience awareness in writing. *Resources in Education*, pp. 154–433.

Bracewell, R. J. (1983). Investigating the control of writing skills. In P. Mosenthal, L. Tamor, & S. Walmsley (Eds.), *Research on writing: Principles and methods*. New York: Longman.

Bridwell, L. S. (1980). Revising strategies in twelfth grade students: Transactional writing. *Research in the Teaching of English, 14*(3), 107–22.

Cooper, M., & Holzman, M. (1983). Talking about protocols. *College Composition and Communication, 34*, 284–93.

Cooper, M., & Holzman, M. (1985). Counterstatement reply. *College Composition and Communication, 36*, 97–100.

Emig, J. (1971). *The composing process of twelfth graders*. Urbana, IL: National Council of Teachers of English.

Ericsson, K. A., and Simon, H. A. (1984). *Protocol analysis: Verbal reports as data.* Cambridge, MA: MIT Press, Bradford Books.

Faigley, L., & Witte, S. (1981). Analyzing revision. *College Composition and Communication, 32,* 400–14.

Flavell, J. H. (1977). *Cognitive development.* Englewood Cliffs, NJ: Prentice-Hall.

Flower, L., & Hayes, J. R. (1981a). A cognitive process theory of writing. *College Composition and Communication, 32,* 365–87.

Flower, L., & Hayes, J. R. (1981b). The pregnant pause: An inquiry into the nature of planning. *Research in the Teaching of English, 15*(3), 229–43.

Flower, L., & Hayes, J. R. (1981c). Plans that guide the cognitive process of composing. In C. Frederiksen, M. Whiteman, & J. Dominic (Eds.), *Writing and the nature, development and teaching of written communication* (Vol. 2, pp. 39–58). Hillsdale, NJ: Erlbaum.

Flower, L., Carey, L., Hayes, J. R. (1984). Diagnosis in revision: the expert's option (Communication Design Center Tech. Rep.). Pittsburgh, PA: Carnegie-Mellon University.

Flower, L., Hayes, J. R., Carey, L., Schriver, K., & Stratman, J. (1986). Detection, diagnosis, and revision. *College Composition and Communication, 37,* 16–55.

Hairston, M. (1981). Not all errors are created equal: Nonacademic readers in the professions respond to lapses in usage. *College English, 43*(8), 794–806.

Murray, D. M. (1978). Internal revision: a process of discovery. In Charles R. Cooper & Lee Odell (Eds.), *Research on composing: Points of departure.* Urbana, IL: National Council of Teachers of English.

Newell, A., & Simon, H. A. (1972). *Human problem solving.* Englewood Cliffs, NJ: Prentice-Hall.

Nold, E. (1982). Revising. In C. Frederiksen, M. Whiteman, & J. Dominic (Eds.), *Writing: The nature, development and teaching of written communication.* Hillsdale, NJ: Erlbaum.

Pianko, S. (1979). Description of the composing process of college freshman writers. *Research in the Teaching of English, 13,* 5–22.

Rose, M. (1980). Rigid rules, inflexible plans, and the stifling of language: A cognitivist analysis of writer's block. *College Composition and Communication, 31*(4), 389–401.

Scardamalia, M., & Bereiter, C. (1983). The development of evaluative, diagnostic and remedial capabilities in children's composing. In M. Martlew (Ed.), *The psychology of written language: A developmental approach.* New York: Wiley.

Schriver, K. (1984). *Revising computer documentation for comprehension: Ten exercises in protocol-aided revision.* (Tech. Rep. No. 14). Pittsburgh, PA: Carnegie-Mellon University, Communication Design Center.

Sommers, N. (1980). Revision strategies of student writers and experienced writers. *College Composition and Communication, 31,* 378–87.

Stallard, C. (1974). An analysis of the writing behavior of good student writers. *Research in the Teaching of English, 8,* 206–18.

Suppes, P. (1974). The place of theory in educational research. *Educational Researcher, 3*(6), 3.

Thibadeau, R., Just, M., & Carpenter, P. (1982). A model of the time course and content of reading. *Cognitive Science, 6,* 157–203.

# 6    Second-language acquisition: an experiential approach

*Evelyn Hatch and Barbara Hawkins*

A discussion of second-language teaching and learning necessarily involves one's point of view as to how language development occurs. The position taken in this chapter is that language grows out of experience. For many people, this may seem quite obvious, because most learning comes about by means of interaction with life experiences. For others, it may seem quite inconsistent with much of the linguistic investigation that posits the existence of a "language acquisition device" (LAD) in the brain as the underlying mechanism of language development, needing only minimal experience for maximum language development. Still others, weary of the many variations of the nature–nurture argument and believing that these questions can never be resolved, view such statements as useless. Nevertheless, in order to understand the work we have done, the theoretical background should be clear. Otherwise, research such as that on language switching and mixing, teacher talk to second-language (L2) learners, the study of pragmatic coding in L2 talk, and descriptions of language play of bilingual children all seem like so many disconnected studies of L2 phenomena unrelated to any theory.

Our position that interaction is the main experience guiding language development becomes more concrete if we consider the task of second- or foreign-language teachers. As second-foreign-language teachers, we are constantly faced with the question of how to help our students become competent in the second language, of how to proceed with instruction such that it enhances L2 development. Do we begin with the syntax of the language, making it the central focus of our instruction and thereby giving it primacy in terms of language development? Do we begin with experience, with the idea that giving meaning to our experiences is the driving force behind language development? There are, of course, many other places where we might choose to begin. However, it is one's point of view as to how language development occurs that guides both teaching and research practice.

In this chapter, we opt for beginning with experience, believing that all of the

Portions of this chapter are based on a paper presented by the first author at the thirteenth University of Wisconsin–Milwaukee Symposium, 1984.

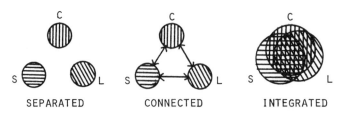

Figure 1. Three views of the internal mental systems of cognition, social knowledge, and language.

subsystems of language develop as we make meanings clear to ourselves and others. To clarify why we believe this to be the case, we begin by discussing basic assumptions regarding the scope of research on language development. Changes in the scope of this research have shaped both research and teaching practices. They have also caused us to change the direction of our search for a theory of L2 acquisition, a theory that must account for the observed facts of L2 use revealed in acquisition data. That is to say, the starting point for theory building is actual L2 data, since these are the data we hope to explain. To trace our ongoing search for an adequate theory, we begin by posing the following questions:

> Given that there exist internal mental systems that encompass language, cognition, and social meanings,

> (1) what is the nature of the relation among these systems, and
> (2) how does language, and second language in particular, develop as a result of this relation?

## Separateness of internal mental systems

No one denies that language acquisition, comprehension, and production are mental processes. Nor do we imagine that anyone would deny that cognitive and social knowledge involve internal, mental processes. Since mental processes are not easily accessible to study, we may make whatever hypotheses we wish, and some may, quite rightly or wrongly, make more sense to us than others. The more we learn about neuroanatomy, the more convincing some arguments may become.

Lewis and Cherry (1977) outlined three basic notions of the relation of social (S), cognitive (C), and linguistic (L) knowledge in the internal system, which can be diagrammed as shown in Figure 1. The first diagram shows three separate internal systems. One need not consider social or cognitive systems when building hypotheses about the nature of the language faculty. In this view, sociolinguistics would not be the study of an interconnected system handling social and language knowledge, but rather the discovery of a set of modification rules that apply to the language system alone. Psycholinguists would not study an interconnected social, cognitive, and language system, but rather devise sets of predictions about language and language performance given certain hypotheses about cognitive processing. Although the separation of systems is important to linguists who wish to narrow the scope of inquiry in order to make precise statements regarding the phonology or syntax of language, the separation, we believe, makes it impossible to account for language learner data.

The separate-systems outlook, however, underlies much of the descriptive work done in the late 1960s and early 1970s in which samples of child language data were reduced to formal syntactic rules, which were checked against the remaining data for their predictive power. These studies involved both first-language (L1) learners (see Bellugi & Brown's descriptions of the language of Adam, Eve, and Sarah, 1964) and our own research on L2 learners (see Huang & Hatch's analysis of the English of a Taiwanese child, 1978, and Ravem's rules for the emerging English of a Norwegian child, 1978). Although these descriptions of data are important in establishing the linguistic structures learners use at different points in language development, they give us little information, if indeed any, as to why these particular forms appear. Preliminary attempts to link the appearance of forms with social interaction failed. Significant correlations were not obtained when the frequency of structures in adult talk were compared with the appearance of forms in child data. Since, in this research tradition, language is being investigated separately from anything else, the only solution is to claim that an internal, innate system accounts for regularities that are found in the data across learners.

In the second diagram of Figure 1, the three systems are still seen to be separate systems, but each has some connection with the other systems. Some would claim causal direction for these connections. For example, claims have been made that language cannot develop unless the appropriate cognitive structures are already in place. Other theorists have argued that, once language structures are in place, they govern the cognitive system or even the social system. However, whatever the direction of causal claims, there is always evidence to support claims that parts of each system can still develop in the absence of one of the other two. (See Yamada, 1981, for a case study of a severely retarded woman with well-developed syntactic skills, and Blank, Gessner, & Esposito, 1979, for a case study of a child with no apparent social skills but well-developed syntax.)

Research within the form–function school fits this view of connections between linguistic and cognitive knowledge. For example, while using a separate-systems approach, one could describe negatives in the data of L2 learners separate from other systems. The outcome of the research would be a set of stages in the development of the negative system. Alternatively, in a connected approach, one could examine the functions of negation (to negate, deny, etc.) and the relation of these functions to the appearance of negative forms in the data. In L1 research, it has often been the case that the acquisition of cognitive function appears before the acquisition of linguistic form, so a unidirection claim is often made (cognitive → linguistic) of function before form.

In past efforts, we have also used this approach in attempting to understand the data of L2 learners. The interaction of linguistic forms and cognitive functions was clearly spelled out by Gough (1975) in her analysis of form and function in the acquisition of the English verb ending *ing* (progressive) by an Iranian child. The form, perhaps because of its saliency, was acquired long before the child distinguished its function from that of other verb forms. This has led to less unidirectional claims regarding the emergence of form and function. However, the research tradition of considering cognitive function while investigating linguistic form is important and continues in the pragmatic form–function analyses being done on L2 data of guest workers in Europe (see Dittmar, 1984; Perdue, 1984) and on the "fossilized" language data of adult L2 learners in the United States (Andersen, 1983, 1984; Schumann, 1983; and their students).

The connection between the circles for linguistic and social knowledge is exemplified by research on the language of caretakers and children during their *social interaction*. The study of "motherese" – the language used by caretakers with child learners – and the study of "foreigner talk" – the language addressed to L2 learners by native speakers – showed the ways in which "teachers" simplify language and cognitive tasks for the learner. However, from the earliest studies where frequencies of question forms in the input match the order of appearance of those forms in the output (Hatch & Gough, 1976) through the many following studies we have summarized elsewhere (Hatch, 1983), the emphasis was on matching forms in input and output. The claims were still centered on *language* rather than on the *interaction* that produced these forms. Long's (1980) turn to the consideration of interaction (rather than the form of simplified language) changed the direction of our search toward a more interactive point of view.

An interactive relation resulting in the integrated system, depicted in the third diagram of Figure 1, is the one that now seems most plausible to us. It allows one to consider which parts of the systems build on those of other systems. The construction of a piece of one system may offer a scaffolding for parts of other systems. For example, intonation seems to have a very large role in play, humor, joke telling, and verbal "fights." Small children seem very attuned to the intonation of jokes. (They laugh at the appropriate time even though they do not understand the joke.) It is as if they had developed a suprasegmental "envelope" for jokes and need learn only the story that goes into the joke. In this sense, the intonation system of the language acts as a scaffolding on which the other parts of the system can build. Young's (1974) two kindergarten L2 subjects acquired this suprasegmental envelope (accelerating rate, rising volume and pitch) necessary for verbal threats. In fights, they used high-frequency chunks (e.g., "No way," "I can beat you up") and filled the rest of the sequence with nonsense. In the following, the children are playing on swings:

L1 child:    I can beat your brother up. I can beat him up.

L2 child:    [gradual build in volume over talk turn] You can beat him up huh I can beat

Figure 2 (Left).  Separate view of second-language addition.
Figure 3 (Right).  First language as a sieve through which second language is seen and measured.


him to my party 'n you can beat my brother 'n he beat you up (noises) it.
I CAN BEAT YOU UP!

Intonation thus provides a scaffolding on which to build the structures needed for such discourse. (This fits well with the neurolinguistic studies of Wapner, Hamby, & Gardner, 1981, in which patients with certain types of lesions show deficits in both expressive intonation and the recognition of humor, jokes, teasing, etc.)

Using the integrated system figure, one can also account for the exceptional cases of Yamada (1981) and Blank et al. (1979). That is, in normal circumstances, the total system evolves through interaction. In abnormal cases, it is possible to develop parts of the total system without interaction with some of the subsystems. The figure also shows that parts of the system do not overlap. So it is always possible to take care of objections that some sets of procedures must be language specific.

It is not just that there is tremendous borrowing among systems (i.e., procedures that work well for one system can easily be used by the others). In addition, one system may form a "framework" to which another might attach its material. To continue the "building" metaphor, there may be a few general, powerful "basics" for building of knowledge structures. There must also be infinite possibilities for variation around these basic procedures. The result would be that some learners construct a more adequate and/or efficient system than others. Each person builds a total system, however, that is both shared and unique (since it must result from an interpretation of both shared and unique experiences).

What happens when a second language is added or when two languages are acquired simultaneously? For researchers who view language and social knowledge as separate, only one new circle need be added, that of the second language (Figure 2). The languages themselves are also seen to be distinct and separate.

Second-language teaching materials, too, were and still are available that consider the second language to be a separate, autonomous system of syntactic structures where social and cognitive content is not consulted. In such materials, the second language is categorized into basic sentence patterns. These patterns are arranged in some order of complexity, and each pattern is practiced and drilled in isolation and then added to the repertoire of structures already mastered. The materials and methods, like the research findings, assume that the learner is acquiring a set of syntactic building blocks that will gradually come together and enable the learner to communicate with others about his or her experiences.

At the same time, researchers have used descriptions of the first language to predict where learners might encounter problems because of the differences in language systems. In some models of bilingualism, however, it is assumed that the two languages overlap or are more tightly linked. The first language is seen as a sort of sieve through which the second language is processed (Figure 3). The position held by many applied linguists, particularly those interested in contrastive analysis, is well summarized by Trubetzkoy (1969): "The sounds of the foreign language receive an incorrect phonological interpretation since they are strained through the 'phonological sieve' of one's own mother tongue" (p. 52). In contrastive studies, to discover the "sieve," the syntactic, phonological, lexical, or morphological systems of one language were compared with those of the first language. These descriptions of correspondences between the two systems led to predictions of difficulty in L2 learning (see the Stockwell, Bowen, & Martin, 1965, hierarchy of difficulty). Textbooks based on contrastive analysis follow these predictions by giving special focus and additional practice time to the areas of predicted difficulty. The analysis, obviously, does not include possible connections with nonlanguage components of difficulty.

From a contrastive analysis point of view, the ultimate goal is separation of the two languages. Separate language systems are clearly promoted as superior to overlapped systems. Although the first language might promote acquisition via transfer and/or hinder acquisition via interference, the ideal is two clearly separated systems.

Ervin and Osgood (1954) proposed a coordinate–compound bilingual dichotomy that has since been used to suggest that successful language learning is characterized by two separated language systems. Kolers (1968) used a "water tap" analogy to clarify the differences in compound and coordinate bilinguals. In compound bilinguals, there would be two water taps, one for each language, which tapped the same central lexical supply center. In contrast, coordinate bilinguals would have two separate water systems. Lambert (1969), Baetens Beardsmore (1974), and Genesee and his associates (1978) emphasized the importance of the environment in determining the type of bilingualism acquired. The best way to secure the development of separated systems, according to these researchers, was to be sure that learning took place in two separate social environments. Separate systems were more likely if a child learned English in America and French in France or, perhaps less successfully, learned one language at home and another at school or heard one language consistently from one parent (or grandparent) and a second language from the other. This led to a "one person–one language" prin-

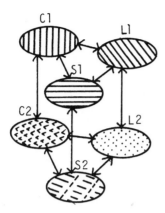

Figure 4. Connected view of second-language addition.

ciple as the best course to take in promoting bilingualism for children in bilingual families. It also led to the advocacy of alternate days or half-day L1, half-day L2 formats for bilingual education programs. When teachers switch back and forth between the two languages, it is very easy for the child simply to "tune out" the new language. When the discourse is in one language, the learner must attend in order to interact. Less successful separation of systems was assumed to occur when the learner was faced with two language systems within the same environment and from the same speakers. Although social environment seems to be an important distinction in this view of L2 learning, the connection between social and linguistic knowledge is not explicit. There has been no attempt to show how social interaction promoted or hindered the development of a separate L2 system. This view also assumes that the cognitive processes that are related to language development do not change when a second language is added, and therefore the role of cognition was not considered.

The connected figure (the six-circle diagram in Figure 4) applied to two languages would allow us to look across a variety of contrasts to discover, for example, how differences in social knowledge can offer better explanations of some L2 phenomena than can differences in L1–L2 linguistic structure.

Figure 4 allows us to consider contrasts in cognitive organization in which learners categorize information in ways used in the first language and then display that information inappropriately in the second language. Teachers who find that their foreign students write grammatically correct English but do not "think logically" are commenting on what constitutes "logical" cognitive organization in two different systems. With this figure in mind, one can look for the effect of each separate system on all others. Again, language-teaching materials are available that reflect a "separate-but-connected" model of internal systems. Communicative approaches and notional-functional approaches present materials that connect

Figure 5 (Left).  Integrated view of second-language addition, Stage 1.
Figure 6 (Right).  Integrated view of second-language addition, Stage 2.

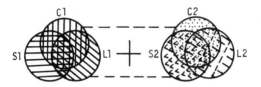

Figure 7.  Integrated view of second-language addition, Stage 3.

language forms with their social functions. For example, the function of a particular grammatical form is taught at the same time as the form itself, assuming that
the learner will be better able to learn the second language if he or she knows the
relation between form and function.

Certainly, this view is an improvement over the separate-systems outlook. However, if we have already opted for an integrated framework in L1 acquisition, how
can we justify returning to the connected framework when considering bilingual
performance?

The integrated framework presents us with problems because it is difficult to
see how the learner can disentangle systems that have already been unified. Perhaps there are stages or variations, during the first of which the learner simply uses
his or her unified L1 system as the basis for tagging on new information, the second language (Figure 5). In this stage, the learner would use the L1 system, plug-
ging into it whatever seems to overlap with it in the second language. In a second
variation (Figure 6), the learner may work out a system in which the second language is a product of its own unified system yet overlaps and interacts with the L1
system. In Figure 7, the learner fully realizes the separateness of the two unified
systems (i.e., the separateness of the L1 unified system and the L2 unified system)
with loose connections between the two, and the result is the ideal promoted by
the literature on compound versus coordinate system.

There are few examples of teaching materials that take an interactive approach
aimed at achieving a unified system. One example might be the Brattleboro experiential materials (Michael & Clark, 1983); others can be found in Hatch, Flashner, & Hunt (1986) and in Brown & Yule (1984). These L2 teaching materials
encourage the student to adopt a "language researcher" attitude with respect to the

second language. This means that the student is encouraged to learn through interaction how native speakers of the second language use the language to communicate. Consider the following anecdote, which exemplifies this teaching-learning technique:

> While living in Spain, an English-speaking friend and I noticed that many times, after we had been talking at length with Spaniards, they would say *Pues nada*. At first, we felt a little insulted, since translated, it meant "Well, nothing," as if what we had been saying was worth nothing. Due primarily to our aggravation, which slowly turned into curiosity, we decided we were going to figure out what it meant. We therefore began taking mental notes of the times we heard it and reported back to each other our findings. We finally narrowed it down to the fact that it was used whenever there was a lengthy pause in a conversation. Having realized this, we decided that the next time we were out with Spaniards, we would say it whenever such a pause occurred. When we did, the mystery unraveled itself, for everytime we used it, without fail, a new topic of conversation was begun. *Pues nada* was a way of closing one topic and moving on to another. (K. Hribar, personal communication, 1984)

In this example, we see the learners acting as researchers, trying to understand new information presented to them in the second language. They measured the language they were experiencing against what they already knew from their first language. When they could not find a match, they sought further experience of the language. They then tested what they had observed and finally figured out the language they had heard. In doing so, they employed social knowledge of conversational scripts, cognitive processes to investigate the lexicon and environment, and language to express themselves.

Although we believe in a reciprocally and interactively built system that becomes integrated, no one can give a definitive answer as to how the system functions internally. All of us have our own aesthetics as to what is a pleasing hypothesis. Although the clear crisp lines of syntactic analysis detached from context may be appealing, we cannot believe in a model that sees L2 acquisition simply as a matter of building syntactic systems separate from all else. Nor do we believe that language, when it is considered alone, is a monolithic, autonomous system. The various subsystems of language may be more related to subsystems of the social system or other cognitive subsystems than to one another. How they all interrelate nobody knows; nevertheless, we believe in a messy, interrelated picture rather than one that is neat and clean, not because of aesthetics, but because nothing else seems viable.

### Language development in relation to internal mental systems and external experience

Regardless of one's claims about the separateness of the model of internal mental systems, the next consideration is that of the relation of external experience to the internal mental system. Let us consider the four classic claims: a contagion relation, a causal relation, a triggering relation, and an interactive relation.

A contagion relation would claim that one "contracts" language based on degree of exposure to it. That is, if one is around language, one catches it, just like the flu. In some ways, the contagion claim makes sense, but unfortunately not everyone exposed to a second language catches it. In addition, it is not a direct copy of the experience that is being created, but a system of abstract knowledge structures. The contagion claim obviously is not valid.

Nor is the causal claim one we want to make. The strict behaviorist school of language teaching reflects this point of view. It is not the case that, just because a learner has opportunities to use particular language forms, he or she will acquire the structure (anymore than one could say that social knowledge is acquired just because the learner has opportunities to display social interaction forms). The acquisition of all mental systems is an internal neurological matter.

The third position, triggering, is held by many linguists. This view is that some outside influence is necessary to "trigger" what is already there in the internal system (as an acorn is already an oak tree and needs only a shower or two to set it on its way). That is, a "universal grammar" (UG) is already in place along with an internal markedness theory, which only needs experience to be set off. Some development does take place; that is, the complete language system is not already present ready to be set off. So experience is seen to be necessary, although it plays an almost irrelevant role. Any experience would seem to "do"; the amount of experience is not specified, but appears to be minimal.

If the system of universal grammar is sufficiently rich, then limited evidence will suffice for the development of rich and complex systems in the mind, and a small change in parameters may lead to what appears to be a radical change in the resulting system . . . . Endowed with this system and exposed to limited experience, the mind develops grammar that consists of a rich and highly articulated system of rules, not grounded in experience in the sense of inductive justification, but only in that experience has fixed the parameters of a complex schematization with a number of options. (Chomsky, 1980, pp. 66–7)

The fourth position, that of an interactive relation between the internal mental systems and external experience, claims that the total communication system must evolve from the interpretation of our experiences for ourselves and others. As experience gives us new data, each new problem, new form, and new function acts as a catalyst for cognitive responses that get these experiences mapped into or onto old knowledge structures through very small changes. This is, of course, far afield from the "triggering" position discussed earlier. Surely it is not just one bolt from the blue that sets the acquisition process in motion, but rather a continuous interaction of the external and the internal. Anyone who has worked with longitudinal data knows that the huge leaps predicted by a UG model do not happen. Instead, thousands of infinitesimal additions occur, and the systems are reorganized over and over as new additions accrue. Quantum leaps do not appear in the data. As Lindblom (n.d.) says, we should not underestimate the structure-forming power of thousands of small changes. Those changes take place because experience is fed into self-organizing internal processes.

It might be argued that the experiences that are being fed to the internal system are always social and cognitive and that the learning of language would therefore always be *incidental* to learning about something else. Of course, much language is acquired in this way. Indeed, a variety of teaching methods explicitly recommend this procedure (e.g., versions of immersion, English for Specific Purposes, adjunct programs in which students learn a language by studying subject matter in that language). However, *intentional* language learning is also amply evidenced both in L2 data and in these teaching programs. Diary study data show child learners intentionally eliciting L2 information. For example, at 36 months, the child Louie (the French–German bilingual child studied by Ronjat, 1913) elicited vocabulary: "Mama, purée de pommes de terre, wie heisst?" After the mother named a dish "Gefullte Tomaten," he asked his father, "Comment tu dis, toi?" to get "tomates farcies." Five-year-old Antti, a Finnish-speaking child studied by Lennakyla (1980), asked for parallels and for definitions: "Mita hurry up tarkottaa?" (What does "hurry up" mean?) These children comment on their hypotheses about the language they are learning. For example, Kenyeres (1938) reports that gender fascinated Eva, a 6-year-old Hungarian child learning French as a second language. She wanted very much to have a semantic rule to determine gender. She began by using her own logical classes: "la fleur, le jardin, no la jardin" because the garden was the mother of the flower; *chaise* became feminine and "table" masculine because the table was the papa of the chairs. She next argued that all things good and beautiful must be feminine. She tried out a phonological rule for gender (refusing to say *la dame* or *le monsieur* because she did not like the vowel euphony) and discarded it quickly. She became angry when she learned that *oiseau* had only one gender, and she wanted *le* and *la* for her dolls. Like many other learners faced with a language that includes grammatical gender, her struggle included both intentional and incidental learning. The Hribar anecdote given earlier further illustrates the intentional nature of strategies used outside the classroom by successful language learners. Certainly, intentional language instruction is the focus in most language classrooms, although, even there, much incidental learning takes place as students work through a variety of social or cognitive tasks. Intentional learning may be more efficient than incidental learning, but both are important to our understanding of the acquisition process.

In a very brief way, we have answered the two questions put forth at the beginning of this chapter. We believe that the internal mental systems of language, cognition, and social meanings are interactively built and that language develops as a result of the external experience that continually feeds the internal mental systems.

Having stated our position, we now proceed to offer a framework, including a model, that has as its goal an understanding of language, language acquisition, and language use.

## A model of internal, integrated mental systems

The model we present here is neither completely articulated nor original. Rather, we have combined our version of ideas proposed by Schank and Abelson (1977) and others with our version of Kempen and Hoenkamp's (1981) incremental procedural grammar (IPG). Since we have adapted their ideas, the descriptions that will be given should not be considered to be faithful representations of their work.

Let us assume that, in learning, the acquirer builds a "knowledge structure" (using Schank's terminology) that serves to organize the events of his or her world such that they become understandable. The question is how this "knowledge structure" is built, changed, and added to. Schank and Abelson have outlined a procedure involving plans, goals, and scripts. A script is "a structure that describes appropriate sequences of events in a particular context" (p. 41). As such, it is the interconnected whole of its parts and is capable of handling standardized, everyday situations. If, for example, one goes to the grocery store, one expects food to be available for purchase; moreover, one expects to go through standardized procedures to get the food one wants. If we were to list the events involved in a "going to the grocery store" script, our list would include at least the following:

1. Go into the store.
2. Get a grocery cart if the amount of food to be purchased requires it.
3. Select the food you want to buy.
4. Take the food to the checkout counter, where it will be bagged and its cost determined.
5. Pay for the food.
6. Take the food out of the store.

In reality, the script is much more detailed. It would also include information ranging from what to do when you cannot find specific items you want to buy, to what to do if you do not have enough money, to the language attached to each event of the script. Suppose, however, a friend told you that he had gone to the grocery store and seen the latest Meryl Streep movie. Chances are very likely that you might have a few questions to ask him, since viewing movies does not fit into the standard grocery store script. Keeping this example in mind, let us look at some of the processing that has occurred that allows you to know that it is time to ask some questions.

The first point is that you are already familiar with the grocery store script. How did you come to know this script? Schank and Abelson would argue that scripts begin as plans, or "sequences of actions that are intended to achieve a goal" (p.

72). They are based on expectations you have because your experiences have given you these expectations. That is, in trying to understand your experiences of life, your internal mental systems attempt to see the connections between events that make up your experience. Some events occur so frequently and become so routinized that they produce definite expectations as to what is happening when they occur. These routinized events then become scripts. It is for this reason that Schank and Abelson claim that scripts come from plans. Plans are made up of general information about how actors achieve goals. For example, if you have as a *goal* to go to school, you may know generally that you should register in a particular school. This, then, represents the *plan* (registration) to achieve the *goal* (going to school). You assume that there will be someone at the school whom you should contact for this purpose. Specifically, however, you have no script for this procedure; you have only general knowledge about how registration is to be carried out. You would simply go to the school with the plan of registering for classes and "play it by ear." If you continue on at the school and register every semester successively for eight semesters, however, the general plan you used in the beginning will most likely become a script. By then you will know the routine well enough to have definite expectations of what will happen and will have questions if those things do not happen.

Returning to the grocery store script, we came to understand the script in the first place because of our experiences. At one time, it was not a script; that is, it developed into a script over repeated instances of the experience, perhaps when we went as children to the grocery store with our parents. If we reconsider the example of our friend who had seen a movie at the grocery store, we question his statement because it does not fit the script as we know it. If we then consider what happens when we assess a script about the grocery store when we are, say, in the countryside in Egypt, we are in trouble. Our expectations will not be met. At this point, we face a decision. We can reject the total experience. We can begin a new script, rejecting our old one. Or we can hold everything in abeyance, hoping that perhaps the next time the event will match our script. In any case, we will want to understand the new information; that is, we will want to connect the event with our own previous experience.

An important facet of scripts and script building is the language attached to the scripts. The following anecdote recalled by one of the authors (B. H.) illustrates how language can be integrated into the script:

> When I was a child of about 5 or 6, my father, who was taking care of my younger sisters and me one day, sent me to the small, local grocery store to buy some ketchup. He gave me some money and told me what to do. I followed his directions, went to the store, picked out a bottle of ketchup, paid the man at the cash register, and came home. When I got home, I found out that, somehow, I had made a mistake. My father didn't want ketchup after all. He wanted hamburger buns, "the things you put ketchup on when you have hamburgers." He told me to go back to the store and exchange the ketchup for hamburger buns. I ran all the

way back to the store. When I got there, however, I didn't go inside. Instead, I lingered outside, trying to figure out what I was going to tell "the man" – the cashier. I didn't know what to say to him. I thought he would be angry with me, and even though my father didn't seem to think there would be a problem, I wasn't at all sure that he would take back the ketchup. Also, what would happen if the hamburger buns cost more (or less) than the ketchup? My grocery store script at that point had no part for returning or exchanging goods already purchased. After several minutes of indecision, I ran back home with the unwanted bottle of ketchup. My father, of course, was dismayed. I burst into tears, telling him that I didn't do as he asked because I didn't know what to say to "the man." At that point, my father sat me down and told me exactly what to say to him. He then role-played the situation with me, making sure I waited until he (taking the part of "the man") wasn't too busy (i.e., "Don't interrupt"), said "Excuse me," explained the problem clearly, and showed him the receipt. He then acted out several things "the man" might say or do. At the end, he made sure I said "Thank you." Feeling better, I ran back to the store for the third time. I was nervous, of course, but did everything my father had told me to do. I was amazed at how nice "the man" was, and even more amazed that I was able to bring home the hamburger buns – at last.

I am sure that my father would not remember this incident, but for me it was traumatic enough to stand out in my memory. The point here is that it was traumatic only because I didn't know the "return or exchange" events of the grocery store script. Even when told to act out that part of the script, I failed at first because I didn't know what to say. I knew I couldn't walk into the store, put back the bottle of ketchup, pick up a package of hamburger buns, and walk out, without saying anything.

For anyone who has experience with children and/or L2 learners, this example of not knowing what to say in certain situations will be familiar. Recall the many times children have said to you, "But what do I say?" – when they do not know how to handle someone who is picking on them at school, when they have to ask the teacher for help at school, when they want to ask someone out on their first date, when they want to refuse a date, and so on. Likewise, L2 learners frequently ask questions such as, "What do you say when you're being introduced?" or "How do you sign business or personal letters?" Second-language learners (if they are adults, at least) know that there probably is something that they should say, if only because the scripts in their native languages have ritualized what is to be said in these situations. Even as adults operating in our first language we are often in a position of not knowing what to say – the first time in a computer store, dealing with the IRS, buying a home for the first time. The difference is that we have the advantage of having plans at a more general level – a script, actually, of what to say when you don't know what to say.

Interwoven with script building, then, is language-building work. In order to do this language-building work, new elements must be recognized *within* experiences. This means that language is learned as a way of structuring experience as that experience takes place. In interactions, for example, the discourse frames, the scripts for interactions develop and the language appropriate for that development builds precisely on this interaction.

However, in order to do this language-building work, new elements that are needed to carry out goals must be recognized as options within experiences. The cognitive system must be alerted or activated to deal with the "new" and, eventually, to find the best way to accommodate the new into the internal system.

In L2 learning, not only must the learner recognize the new and discover how it fits into previous knowledge structures, but he or she must also discover where and how far the "new" can be generalized across scripts. Zernik (1984) provides an example. Assume an L2 learner hears a new term, "rip-off," during a conversation in which a friend complains, "Your mechanic ripped me off." The "car mechanic" experience is called up. Since the search shows no easy explanation of the terms in that experience, the learner shifts to the next highest level, the "service encounter" memory organization packet ("mop"; see Schank, 1982, for an in-depth explanation of "mops"). Some few cases of "rip-off" are found at the service level, perhaps in the restaurant or the dentist or any of the other "service encounter mops." Within "service" there are a series of normal actions such as arrange-service, do-service, pay-for-service, evaluate-service. In addition, there are cases of deviation from the norm such as service-not-done, bad-service, high-price, free-service, excellent-service. In trying to guess the meaning of "rip-off," the learner is guided by intonation and other nonverbal clues to select from the negative examples that diverge from the normal. This narrows the scope to service-not-done, bad-service, and high-price. In this model, then, the learner would search for a known phrase that might cover these meanings – for example, "cheat" – and test the scope and generalizability of "rip-off" to those of "cheat." When divergences between "rip-off" and "cheat" are found, these are identified and incorporated into the new knowledge structure.

To change the knowledge structure, then, estimates of differences (how the new differs and the extent of the difference) are made. To do this, the learner must accurately abstract the "new" from the context and recognize it as a new alternative for achieving a communicative goal. There is no way to predict the size of the "new" – that is, we cannot say what the unit extracted will be until we locate the "new." In language, it might be a single sound unit, a bound morpheme, a word, a phrase, a clause, a topic, or whatever. Learners frequently extract the new and then err in using that unit either because they fail to transfer it to appropriate new contexts or because they fail to break the unit down into smaller units via analysis.

For example, Shapira's (1976) adult subject, Zoila, abstracted the unit "pick you up" from discourse in which someone offered to pick her up at a set time. She never broke this unit down into smaller units, using it as a verb with various results – correctly, as in "I pickyaup 3:00, okay?" and incorrectly, as in "She's a little angry but I think so is because the other sister no come here mm for ehh pickyaup her." (Notice a second unanalyzed chunk, "I think so," in this example.) Gough's L2 learner was more successful in breaking up such chunks. The child, Homer, extracted large units from language addressed to him, incorporating these in his responses:

Mark:    Come here.

Homer:    No come here.

Mark:    Don't do that.

Homer:    Okay don't do that.

(Gough, 1975, p. 34)

The incorporated parts were then gradually analyzed and either dropped or replaced in the response. In some cases, one can trace the analysis, the breaking up of chunks in the data. For example, Homer's wh-questions evolved from a unit question plus a unit response through several alternatives until the wh-question was produced correctly:

1. Juxtapose related units of social discourse (question and response pattern) to create wh-pattern:

   Question + response = Homer's wh-pattern
   What is this this is truck?

2. Delete identical segments:

   Delete "is this" = What is this airplane?
   Delete "this is" = What this is tunnel?
   Delete "this" = What is this is car?

3. Delete identical element + noun phrase:

   = What is this? What is this is? What this is?

Similar examples of the early use of chunks and the subsequent analysis of these chunks are found in L1 data. Peters (1983) cites an example from S. Shoen in which Christine, a 4-year-old, has been told that she must behave if she wants S to read to her. A few minutes later, the following exchange was noted:

C:    Steven, I am /heyv/.

S:    What? You hate? What do you hate?

C:    /heyv/ I am /heyv/.

S:    You hate? You hate me? The music? What?

C:    No, I am /heyv/ /heyv/.

S:    I don't know what you are talking about.

And a moment later:

C:    I /heyv/.

S:    You hate me?

C:    [shakes head no]

S:    Who do you hate?

A bit later, Christine tries again:

C:   I am behaving.

(Peters, 1983, p. 43)

Clearly, the internal mechanisms of the brain must allow the learner to abstract units from the incoming data and later to segment them in some analytic way. Failure to break down units is, of course, much more obvious in the data than failure to generalize segments across new situations. Kellerman's (1978) work shows how conservative L2 adults are in extending the range of meanings of lexical items in experimental situations. Examples are less readily available in natural data. Examples in which extensions are made inappropriately do occur. Often the unit is not analyzed and, in addition, is transferred to an inappropriate context in its chunk form. For example, an Italian professor visiting our university, on leaving a party, said to his hostess, "Well, see ya at the pole." This was a leave-taking formula used by two professors in an adjoining office at the university who always met later at a flagpole to share a ride home. The chunk was abstracted and correctly identified as a leave-taking marker, which then was extended, inappropriately, to other contexts. Jisa and Scarcella (1981) also note inappropriate extension of conversation routines to written discourse by adult L2 learners (e.g., "But ten years ago *you know* we still a developing nation").

The recognition of difference and estimate of degree of difference will depend on several factors (see diagram). The frequency and scope of forms and their perceptual saliency (i.e., how naturally accessible they are in experience) are as important in this regard as are the contrasts between forms and functions of first and second languages.

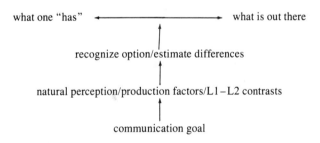

This puts "markedness" into an external rather than an internal position (contrary to UG markedness theory). *Markedness* here is considered a cover term for external phenomena. Forms that have high frequency, have wide scope, or mark important pragmatic distinctions should be learned early because they are more accessible in experience than those less obvious in interactions. Those with high perceptual saliency, which differ most drastically from one another, should be best able to activate the cognitive system. Once the cognitive system is on the alert to differences and assesses them accurately (or inaccurately), it must build a new structure, or adapt an old structure, or decide that the problem is not severe enough to warrant building anything. (Note that the use of the term *building* is metaphoric: No building may be going on.)

*Contrastive analysis* also plays an important role in this model. In broad terms, L1 knowledge structures constitute much of what one has in the initial stages of L2 learning. For some learners, it may continue to be the base on which the second language is "built." For other learners, this may not be efficient so that, once a foundation of L2 scripts is built, the new language builds on these knowledge structures rather than on those of the first language.

If we take our model a step farther, we might ask more specifically how the grammar of the language works. In this chapter we present one proposal among several that allow for parallel processing. We are not especially committed to the details of this grammar but selected it as an illustration because it allows for parallel processing and, in addition, gives us a way to unite script theory with grammar through a "conceptualizer." In IPG (Kempen & Hoenkamp, 1981), sentences are not built in a single sentence-producing machine of phrase structure and transformational rules. Rather, it has three parts: a *conceptualizer*, which we will claim activates a script and then begins to present a fragment of the script, the meanings of which are to be expressed in utterances; a *formulator*, which lexicalizes these fragments and begins to build phrasal structures for them; and an *articulator*, which is responsible for the saying of utterances. (Note that the terminology used here is metaphoric. We do not claim that the conceptualizer, formulator, and articulator are actual entities within the brain. Rather, they are ways of representing processes we believe are integral to understanding how the grammar of the language works. Furthermore, we separate the cognitive, social, and language aspects into three processes only for ease of discussion. In fact, we believe that the processes are tightly integrated, to the extent that they cannot be truly separated.)

The conceptualizer presents activated conceptual fragments to the formulator team, which is charged with building a pragmatic and syntactic structure. In service encounters, formulas (e.g., "Can I help you?" "That'll be xxx") are already part of the script. To use Berko Gleason and Weintraub's (1976) child language example, "trick or treat" and "thank you" are protocols attached to the Hallowe'en script. School games already have language (e.g., "my turn," "no way," "me first") attached to them. In larger scripts, such as conversations, the opening, pre-closing, and closing expressions are part of the script. In addition, it seems unlikely that communicator markers such as continuers ("and then," "I see"), concord markers ("for sure," "I know whatcha mean"), affect expressions ("Are you kidding?" "Come on"), clarification requests ("I don't get it," "What was that?"), misplacement markers ("Where was I?" "Oh, I meant to tell you"), summary phrases ("In other words," "so"), prediction, comparison, and inference markers ("What would happen if," "So . . . ," "How x was he?"), probe markers ("What happened then?" "How did x happen?"), challenge markers ("Prove it!"

"How come?") are generated by looking up individual lexical items and building phrase structures around them. Rather, they are part of the language available ready-made to the formulator. When the fragment sent to the formulator is not already developed, more work must be done. Imagine a team of formulator specialists selecting a key element from a fragment and beginning a search for the best lexical candidate. Other experts begin working up candidate syntacticization for the lexical items to show the relations among the conceptual units. The formulating teams may even work out possible organization for several synonyms (or the same material in the second language) and hold these in abeyance pending the success or failure of the favored choices. These "experts" also check for pragmatic intent (e.g., deciding what is new vs. old information; whether agent, patient, instrumental, or other pragmatic functions are to be emphasized). The formulator team is made up of procedure "experts," who specialize in one type of assembly work:

For example, procedure NP knows how to build noun phrases; procedure PP can deliver prep phrases; procedure SUBJECT is responsible for the shape of subject phrases in main and subordinate clauses. Like the procedure or routine of ordinary computer programs, syntactic procedures are permitted to call on each other for subprocedures ("subroutines"). Procedure S, for instance, may decide to delegate a portion of its sentence formation to SUBJECT and OBJECT as subprocedures. OBJECT need not necessarily wait for SUBJECT to finish; they can get started simultaneously and run in parallel. (Kempen & Hoenkamp, 1981, p. 11)

Each conceptual fragment is handled piecemeal; NP experts may work simultaneously with S experts on some conceptual fragments. At the same time, other conceptual fragments are being set up by other specialists. The formulated structures are sent on to the articulator. In the output, each formulated package (whether only a single lexical item, a phrase, a clause, or a lexicalized sentence) is queued in the order received. Decisions are made about ordering according to the pragmatic properties of the package, its destination markers, source, and content. The ordering should work to unite the pragmatic and syntactic organization.

If the formulator is working on several conceptual fragments simultaneously and sending output to the articulator, one might wonder where choices are made regarding morphophonemic markers and phonological choices. We believe that this work is done at the articulator planning level (although IPG does not). Placing these together makes sense if we want to handle the adult L2 learner's recognized difficulty in acquiring a native-like accent and correct use of bound morphology (i.e., such morphology as verb endings, noun plurals, and noun possessives). (Placing them in the articulation, motor preplan level also agrees with Kean's, 1981, belief that it is the phonological component where certain "clitics" fall out as a group in Broca's aphasia.) Although we do not wish to develop a new topic here, the articulator becomes central to the explanation of the optimal age hypothesis for L2 acquisition since the data on which it is based are primarily phonological and morphophonemic. It is also central to the research of the 1970s on "natural orders of acquisition" in L2 research (see Bailey, Madden, & Krashen, 1978; Dulay & Burt, 1978).

This presentation of a three-level process (conceptualizer, formulator, articulator) is still very simplified and incomplete. However, it can be linked to our view of the integrated nature of cognitive, social, and language knowledge. The knowledge regarding scripts is basically social knowledge but with much language attached to it. The processes needed to search, sort, and retrieve this information are cognitive processes handled by the conceptualizer. Pragmatic decisions are both social and cognitive. That is, identifying and locating objects depend on what is important to speakers and to their listeners in a social sense. Decision making, of course, is a cognitive process, but for pragmatic decisions, the sorting has to be in terms of near/far, old/new, in-/out-of-focus, which are social discourse functions that must be realized in language. The formulator, then, is doing primarily cognitive and language work while keeping social and pragmatic information on tap. The articulator is mainly language oriented, but certainly its work also involves cognitive processes. The model, then, does not clearly separate social, cognitive, and language work. Rather, the work at each stage requires an interaction among all three in one unified process.

It should be clear from this description that there is nothing in the model that parallels exactly the parameters of UG. The "computational" language rules of transformational grammar are taken care of, in part, by the teams of experts in the formulator and, in part, by the articulator. Although they can be roughly equated in this way, there is no claim that we are biologically preprogrammed with a separate computational LAD that sets parameters for language development early on in life. Rather, we assume that an integrated language–social–cognitive system is formed and continually changes as a result of internal conceptual mechanisms interacting reciprocally with external stimuli.

Furthermore, we have included incremental grammar rather than a sentence grammar in the model because it has definite advantages over a simpler sentence grammar. It allows us to account for slips of the tongue, for repairs, for language switching and mixing within turns at talk, as well as for hesitation phenomena in which failures occur in procedures or as word searches have to be reinitiated, and for the one-phrase- or one-clause-at-a-time character of extemporaneous talk. The model does not require "complete-sentence" generation, nor does it require that we go back to a beginning S-node and run through phrase structure rules and transformational rules again when trouble occurs.

By combining the Schank and Abelson and IPG models into one, we can better understand the learner's approaches to language learning outside the classroom. The strategy is to select a script (e.g., "the bus ride script" from the travel script), observe it in detail, and capture the high-frequency phrases and lexical entries for knowledge structures in that script. While trying out these words and lexicalized phrases (supplementing them with many nonverbal cues), the learner can begin to improve production, selecting from the script whatever is most salient, formulating as much as possible (usually only short phrases in the beginning), and articulating that output as well as possible. As Lindblom (n.d.) suggests in his "self-organizing" model of phonetics, this should give the learner enough syllables to begin organizing the phonemic system. (Given the already in-place L1 system, those with greatest social and perceptual benefit per articulatory cost should be produced first.)

As the learner begins work on other scripts (e.g., service scripts such as bargaining at the vegetable market or less observable service scripts such as getting the plumbing fixed), the formulator has more and more information as to what kinds of team experts will be needed and how they can best carry out their piecemeal work. The articulator also begins to refine the output. If the model is correct, the early stages of L2 acquisition should be rich in chunks, high-frequency vocabulary tied to scripts, and short phrases linearly arranged to show pragmatic intent. As the formulator has more and more material to work with, simple clauses (Pawley & Syder's, 1977, one-clause-at-a-time hypothesis) finally supplement the one-phrase-at-a-time and lexicalized sentence (chunk) output, and lexicon is generalized more appropriately across scripts. The problem is to get the conceptual information and lexical choices into the pragmatic and syntactic frames that develop. Often, it is difficult to get both out of the articulator at the same time. That is, "empty boxes" appear. Even native speakers begin "If –" and can't find the material that has to go into the clause, or we begin a relative clause with "That's –" without the lexical material required. So then the articulator picks up a "backup box," usually a less complex phrase. False starts and repairs of this sort occur in L1 data as well as L2 data. However, in L2 data, we also find that, on occasion, the material in the "backup box" is in the first language (or in the closest or last-learned language for multilinguals).

Given the complexity of the task, the learner who already has well-developed scripts, a rich lexicon, and automatic control of the morphology and sound systems of the first language may well try to generalize as much of this system as possible in facing an L2 task. Generalization may, in fact, work quite well for some tasks. For example, adult learners know the overall structure of stories – the script of storytelling appears to be fairly universal in all languages (for descriptions of narrative discourse, see the *Journal of Pragmatics*, December 1982 special issue on stories). If the learner can call up the universal components of the narrative, establish the characters in the story, and list the events in the order in which they occur, the result may be communicatively quite effective. Minimal syntactic elaboration is needed from the formulator. Even problems with pragmatic coding may go unnoticed. If the overall script structure is adequate, communication can take place despite such problems. The formulator can use a mixture of chunked stereotyped phrases or develop a minimal phrasal elaboration.

Nevertheless, the story will be comprehensible to most listeners. In the following example, the plus sign symbolizes a pause:

L:    I'm very ah, nervous, anda excite.

NS:   How come?

L:    Ah, about + seven month ago + I wait the ah + Washington Boulevard.

NS:   Umm.

L:    Then + I uh by bus + + anda + people + four people + come to beside for me. "Give me a money!" It's a little knife.

NS:   Ohh!

L:    Then + I can't + I don't like by bus. I'm very scared. "Give me a money!" "I cannot money." "You get out here!"

NS:   Ummm.

L:    Check the notes + outside. Nobody help me.

NS:   Oh!

L:    Nobody.

NS:   This was seven months ago?

L:    Eight + about seven months + eight months ago.

(Kuwahata, 1984, data appendix)

Looking at this example in a print medium, we see many errors that presumably could make the story difficult to understand. However, the listener clearly understood the story. The transfer of an L1 narrative frame for the "robbery script" worked. The listener recognized the robbery script from the elements given, pulled up a richly embellished script for the robbery, and placed the details given by the speaker into that framework. In other genres, where generalization of a frame from the first to the second language might not work or where more cues would be needed before the listener could call up his or her own matching script, the communication might not be so successful. The following examples of L2 complaint data illustrate just such an instance (the data were collected in response to a prompt indicating an inordinate wait – three hours – in a doctor's office for a scheduled appointment):

NNS1:   Thank you for calling me in a few hours!

NNS2:   I have been waiting for three hours. Everytime you just tell that I can see the doctor in a few minutes. Is the time scale of you different from mine? – Or is your watch manufactured on the moon?

NNS3:   I have waited for two hours. It's beyond my endurance.

NNS4:   I've been waiting here too long. What's going on here?

(Hawkins, 1985, p. 3)

If we examine these data, we realize that the generalization of the discourse frame for complaints from the first to the second language did not work well, even though there may not have been any syntactic errors. The overall result is that the complaints seem very abrupt at best, and rude at worst. In terms of achieving the goal of complaints – a change in the addressee's behavior – the complaints do not appear to be optimally successful. Instead, they are likely to arouse excessive antagonism. Appropriate phrasing that might ameliorate the confrontation involved in complaining are not used here.

The degree of transferability and the amount of planning required from the formulator vary from context to context. On-line talk, however, gives the formulator much less time to do its work, and so the output of unplanned, spontaneous talk is less tightly organized (see discussions of the unplanned to planned continuum in Givon, 1979; Ochs, 1979; Tannen, 1983). Since so much of our work in L2 acquisition has had the syntactic system as its major focus, we want to reinforce our point that the formulator's work in on-line, spontaneous talk is mainly clausal or phrasal in its organization. Consider, for example, Brown and Yule's (1983, p. 18) "rainbow" example. The written version is highly planned, shows dense syntax, and is richly lexicalized in comparison with the one-clause-at-a-time, unplanned spontaneous talk version of the same topic.

Normally after + very heavy rain + or something like that + and + you're driving along the road + and + far away + you see + well + er + a series + of + stripes + + formed like a bow + an arch + + very very far away + ah + seven colors but + + I guess you hardly ever see seven it's just a + a series of + colors + which + they seem to be separate but if you try to look for the separate /kəz/ – colors they always seem + very hard + to separate + if you see what I mean + + (Postgraduate student speaking informally)

And then, in the blowing clouds, she saw a band of faint iridescence colouring in faint shadows a portion of the hill. And forgetting, startled, she looked for the hovering colour and saw a rainbow forming itself. In one place it gleamed fiercely, and, her heart anguished with hope, she sought the shadow of iris where the bow should be. Steadily the colour gathered, mysteriously, from nowhere, it took presence upon itself, there was a faint, vast rainbow. (D. H. Lawrence, *The rainbow*, chap. 16)

Written language does release us from the stream-of-speech mode, and syntactic organization can take on a more major role. This can be accomplished either by giving the formulator more time to do the work, or perhaps by adding an *editor* to the model. An editor would allow us to revise, reorganize, and package ideas in discourse that is highly planned. For the learner who has acquired a foreign language in an environment where few opportunities for interaction with native speakers exist, the type of syntactic structures and lexicon are determined by experience with written text. If one learns a foreign language via reading, the types of experience are quite different from those noted above. One would hope that even the learner who might be able to interact only with written text knows that it will not mirror oral interaction. Language textbooks, even though they include dialogues and drills, often fail to mirror authentic oral interaction. Instead, even in oral exercises, such as sentence-combining drills, the emphasis is on syntactic form. This results in students' practicing language that is seldom, if ever, used by native speakers. For example, when was the last time you heard the following sentences?

> The man who bought the house is my father.
> The man is wearing a green hat.
> ⟹ The man wearing a green hat who bought the house is my father.

Before we look at evidence supporting the framework we have proposed, there is a fundamental question to be discussed. Although our framework conflicts with the strong view of UG regarding innateness, it is clear that any framework must include some such notion. As Marshall (1980) states, "No animal can learn what its central nervous system (and gross anatomy) does not permit it to learn" (p. 112). The question is not whether learning of second (or first) languages presupposes innate mental abilities. It does. Rather, the question concerns the scope of the innateness claim. It might be noticed that our discussion has not been free of many of the lexical trappings of innateness claims. We have promulgated the "little man in the head" fallacy in describing teams of experts that are involved in piecemeal assembly of that communication system. Where do these "little men" come from and are they any different from "black boxes" filled with innate structures? In the model we have proposed, we do assume there is something there (rather than assume a tabula rasa) but the "something there" develops as the system reorganizes itself via thousands of infinitesimal changes in response to the environment, albeit in overlap with cognitive and social systems. In contrast, advocates of UG attempt to specify a strong, universal component with parameters that, once set, determine subsequent language development. This would be the biological component, special genetically determined faculties for language that differ in kind from those of general learning. To date we have no neat and comprehensive set of principles of UG, principles that might comprise the strong innateness component. However, L2 researchers (see Flynn, 1983, 1984; Hilles, 1985; White, 1983, 1984) are aware of UG claims regarding parameter setting and language acquisition and are beginning to investigate the predictions of the model with L2 data.

Not only is the scope of our innateness claim different, but also we find it strange to suppose that general learning processes would be shut off from language learning. In addition, in our model, the scope of "language" differs from that in other models. Advocates of UG are concerned with the acquisition of "language" in the technical sense of "language" as a set of sentences. As McCawley (1983) points out with, as he says, malicious intent, when one is reading studies that treat the acquisition of language in the technical sense,

it is not obvious that the topic has any relation to the learning of a language in the ordinary sense. It is not clear that an adult, let alone a child, knows a language in the technical sense of the mathematical models literature, that is knows which strings of words are and which ones are not members of a set that can be taken to constitute "language." (p. 170)

Regardless of our differing beliefs regarding the scope of the innateness claims

Table 1. *Language subsystems used to structure communication*

| Communication need | Language subsystem |
|---|---|
| How to interact | Conversation, text structure |
| How to organize | Discourse scripts, text types |
| How to identify concepts | Lexicon, lexical rules |
| How to highlight or emote | Suprasegmentals, word order |
| How to make relations clear | Pragmatics, syntax |
| How to be explicit and accurate | Morphosyntax, phonology |

and the scope of "language" we wish to examine, there is obviously much to do if we are to understand the variability found in L1 and L2 acquisition.

### Evidence for the framework

Now that we have outlined the kind of model needed to account for the development of communication via language, let us look at the language subsystems used to structure experience as that experience takes place (Table 1). If some of these subsystems have prominence, that prominence is related to the way the subsystems contribute to making experiences comprehensible. The subsystems clearly overlap with one another, so that intentional use of one subsystem provokes incidental learning of others. To understand what this might mean, let us turn to examples in the data, first with regard to interaction via conversational structure:

"F" is sitting in her seat holding a rubber toy which is tied to the side of the chair. Mother has her back to "F" as she reaches for a dish. "F" squeaks a rubber toy making noise. As a "consequence," "F" kicks her feet and squeals with apparent delight. Mother turns toward "F," smiling and vocalizing. "F" quiets, eyes fixed on Mother. Mother touches "F's" face. "F" vocalizes and moves her hands toward mother. Mother sits in front and listens. Mother pauses, "F" vocalizes. Mother touches "F" and vocalizes to her. "F" vocalizes. (Freedle & Lewis, 1977, p. 158)

Freedle and Lewis (1977) claim that such conversational interactions convey meaning (albeit ambiguous meaning) and provide a "how to interact" base on which a communication system of language and gesture builds.

As Richards and Schmidt (1983) show, "instructional sequences in turn taking and conversational openings and closings continue over time":

Woman:   Hi.

Boy:   Hi.

Woman:   Hi, Annie.

Mother:   Annie, don't you hear someone say hello to you?

Woman:   Oh, that's okay, she smiled hello.

Mother:   You know you're supposed to greet someone, don't you?

Annie:    Hello. [Hangs head]

(Richards & Schmidt, 1983, p. 128)

Parents insist (see Greif & Berko Gleason, 1980) that children say "thank you" and "bye-bye" as part of "how to interact" instruction. Second-language children, too, are directly instructed, even by playmates, on appropriate conversation moves. For example, during a telephone conversation, Heidi instructs Nora on appropriate openings, which include self-identification:

Nora:     [Lifts phone] Hello – come to my house, please.

Heidi:    Who are you?

Nora:     Nora!

Heidi:    Nora, you've got to say, "What are you doing?"

Nora:     What are you doing?

Heidi:    Making cookies. What are YOU doing?

Nora:     Making cookies too.

Heidi:    Ok, 'bye. [Hangs up phone]

Nora:     Bye. [Hangs up]
          [To herself] Mama, who are you telling? Mama, what are you doing? What are you doing? What are you doing? I knowed it, I knowed it!

(Wong Fillmore, 1976, p. 684)

Clearly, the exchange gives the child instruction in openings but at the same time provides incidental learning practice with syntax, suprasegmentals, and the invitation-giving script. Wong Fillmore suggests that learners discover that questions such as "What are you doing?" not only function overtly by asking for information, but also perform the social function of providing a polite way of easing into a conversation. The exchange requires contrastive stress on the pronoun as part of a polite reply – "Making cookies. What are *you* doing?" – and thus offers an opportunity for incidental learning of the use of the suprasegmental system in this regard. As Schegloff (1979) and others have pointed out, "What are you doing?" is also a preface to invitation giving in American English. Therefore, yet another piece of incidental learning may have taken place.

Let us consider what happens when a child L2 learner already knows about turn taking in conversation and that responses must be relevant to the ongoing talk. Itoh's data (Itoh & Hatch, 1978) on Takahiro, a 2½-year-old Japanese child learning English, show his earliest interactions with his aunt. His strategy for contributing to the conversation (even though he understood no English) was to repeat what he heard. To make it more relevant, he changed the intonation so that a question and answer sequence of paired parts resulted:

Aunt:     [Parking cars and airplanes] Make it one at a time.

Child:    One at a time?

Aunt:     Park everything.

Child:  /evrisin/?

Aunt:  Park them.

Child:  Park them?

Aunt:  Does it fly?

Child:  Fly.

(Itoh & Hatch, 1978)

Within such interactions, toys are named and manipulated during play, thus allowing for the development of these lexical items, an example of the reciprocal nature of conversational and lexical subsystems. That is, the communication needs are both how to interact and identification of objects.

Much of the early talk of caretaker and child centers around the here and now of object identification and description ("how to identify" concepts such as numeracy, colors, possession, and place) and action and causation labels. In making relationships clear and being explicit and accurate about these concepts, we find the beginnings of syntax. The early emergence of "this + noun" ("this baby"), "this + color" ("this red"), "this my," "*wh* + noun" ("where dolly?"), and "noun + adjective" ("car all gone") is easily attributed to the here and now nature of early conversational interactions. Since the rules of conversational cooperation are invoked in such exchanges, the caretaker does not nominate topics the child learner cannot be expected to identify. The here and now talk, then, is a result of the selection of topics in which the goals are identifiable (and relevant responses can be made by the child). Given such topics, the interactions focus the child's attention on what is "new" in the here and now – what is noticeable and worthy of comment. For example, Sachs and Truswell (1978) have suggested that *wh*-games ("Where's your tummy?" "Where's your nose?") help infants determine that simple variations in form signal differences in meaning. It also sets the stage, so to speak, for discovering *where* new information is likely to appear (at the end of utterances). At the same time, the child's perceptual system is activated by what is new and noticeable as well. As Greenfield and Smith (1976) have shown, here and now interactions allow for labeling of the new.

The data showing a cooperative building of syntax through question prompts has an obvious (though unintended) instructional look:

Brenda:  [Looking at a picture] Cook say

R:  What'd the cook say?

Brenda:  Something.

Brenda:  Kimby.

R:  What about Kimby?

Brenda:  Close.

R:  Closed? What did she close, hmmm?

(Scollon, 1979, p. 83)

Scollon and others have suggested, on the basis of a considerable number of examples such as these, that grammatical organization grows out of learning to participate in such conversations. Such question prompts could help to establish the expected word order of the second language.

Child L2 data yield similar examples:

Juan:       Teacher lookit [holds up a quarter].

NS:         Mmhmmm. A quarter.

Juan:       Quarter.

NS:         For what?

Juan:       For Monday [the day milk money is due].

NS:         On Monday? For what?

Juan:       For milk.

(Young, 1974, data appendix)

Takahiro:   /flo/.

NS:         Flower. Green flower.

Takahiro:   Green flower.

NS:         Oh, what color is this?

Takahiro:   Green, green flower.

(Itoh & Hatch, 1978, p. 82)

Here and now talk makes up much of the earliest talk in interactions of child L2 learners and adults. Although the adult may pose more questions during these interactions, the here and now quality of talk also shows itself in L1 child–L2 child interactions, even in classroom settings.

In the following excerpt from Wong Fillmore's data, the L1 child, Kevin, limits his talk to the learner, Alej, to the here and now. His talk, however, differs markedly when he addresses the adult observer:

Kevin:      Hey, Alej, Alej, lookit, lookit. [Shows playdough object to Alej]

Alej:       Hey, gimme see!

Adult:      You guys really do like this playdough stuff, don't you? Don't you you ever get tired of it?

Kevin:      Huh-uh.

Adult:      Why do you like it so much?

Kevin:      I like squashing this stuff. I wish I could take some of this home. I've got one of those playdough factories? – but I lost the playdough. I want to bring some of this home with me. You can get some of this for my birthday. It's on the twentieth.

Alej:       Eh – escuela, playdough!

Kevin:      Alej, Alej, I'm gonna make a Santa Claus hat. Ho-ho-ho-Merry Christmas! Ho-ho-ho!

| | |
|---|---|
| Alej: | Lookit, lookit. |
| Kevin: | Alej, Alej! [Holds up playdough triangle] Ho-ho-ho! |
| Alej: | [Looks at Kevin's work and starts shaping similar piece] Wait a minute. |
| Kevin: | See, I'm making a round thing, and then, I'm making a picture on it. Watch this, watch this. |

(Wong Fillmore, 1976, p. 694)

Objects present in the here and now can, however, touch off talk about objects not in the environment:

| | |
|---|---|
| Juan: | [Drawing picture] I have a /dɪs/ dog. |
| NS: | You don't have no dog. |
| Juan: | You no have a no dog. |
| NS: | Yes I do. |
| Juan: | Nuh-uh. Lemme see. |
| Enrique: | What color /dæ/? |
| Juan: | I have a /dɪs/ dog. |
| Enrique: | Uh-uh you /do:/ got ANY dog. I got /dæ/ dog. |

(Young, 1974, data appendix)

As this verbal duel continues, the two L2 learners continue to talk about the *concept* of ownership with the *linguistic structures* of "have" and "got." The goal of the children, however, is a social one, the assertion of power in a verbal duel script. To carry out the duel, they work at, in an incidental learning fashion, the expression of ownership concepts in a subject–verb–object linguistic structure.

Of course, the language of young children is not limited to the here and now. At about 15 months, the caretaker begins to lead the child into nonliteral fantasy play. These sequences allow the child to practice scripts. For example, the earliest fantasy play involves the themes of making dinner, going to the doctor, going shopping, birthday cake, driving the car. At this stage, the mother makes fantasy comments (e.g., "Oh, this is good" as she sips imaginary coffee from a toy cup, or "Is the dolly tired?" giving animate qualities to an inanimate object). By the time the child is 24 months, the mother requests that he or she create an element in the fantasy (e.g., "Where is Big Bird going?" asked as the child moves a toy figure, or "What'll we put in the pan?" asked while the mother points to a toy frying pan). The mother directs much of the fantasy play at the 20-month stage, but by 38 months, the child is nominating and carrying out much of the work of fantasy play. Although Kavanaugh, Wellington, and Cerbone (1983) suggest that fantasy play gives the child opportunities to know how things feel and how objects work, it also gives exposure to temporal ordering for narration, in the planning of activities through talk, and much practice (e.g., with play phones) using conversation structure. Once again, then, we see that a "teacher" leads the child learner through verbalization of goals, plans, and scripts. The child is urged to play the roles of family members (including pets) and relevant outsiders in fantasy script play.

Let us backtrack once again and look at teasing sequences. Observing a 2-year-old named Beth, Miller (1982) traces the development of the ability to respond appropriately to and initiate teasing sequences. Although the mother used teasing for other purposes, such interactions focus on ownership rights that are linguistically marked. Most interesting, they give experience in emphatic stress, rapid delivery rate, and singsong intonation. In the first three samples, Beth (25 months) displayed none of these except rate. Once she began to use singsong intonation, she overextended it to other contexts. She used the intonation with formulaic utterances (e.g., "yeayeayea") directed at no one in particular as she reveled in her own physical abilities. (Actually, self-displays are not so different from asserting one's rights in "this is play" teasing sequences.) Less frequently, Beth used this intonation for defiance or as she seized possession of some object. At 28 months, Beth was beginning to narrow down the contexts in which she used this intonation. In the final data collection period, Beth used dispute tactics with her mother, including emphatic stress and rapid delivery, appropriate voice quality (giggles and laughter to show the "this is play" quality of the teasing), seized possession of disputed objects, and made fighting gestures. Again, much reciprocal language learning and script learning (in this case, the fantasy "fight script") work was taking place.

Young children are also taught games that have specific rules. They may require the child to stand in a circle, to throw or pass objects, to jump up and run around chairs, and so forth. Stereotypic language accompanies much of this play. When the phrase is particularly pleasing to the child, endless repetitions ensue:

Enrique:    Fall down!

NS:         Okay-dokey.

Enrique:    What you say?

NS:         What?

Enrique:    You say "okay-dokey" xxxx "okay-dokey"?

NS:         Okay-dokey, yeh.

Enrique:    Okay-dokey. Hey, I did it. Okay-dokey. [Continues saying "okay-dokey," changing stress]

NS:         [Disgusted] Oooh, you made a boo-boo!

Enrique:    I made a boo-boo.

NS:         Boo-boo lookit.

Enrique:    So what? All up! Boo-boo yep. Boo-boo. Everybody do boo-boo. I did wrong [laugh].

(Young, 1974, data appendix)

As Wong Fillmore has shown, opportunities to acquire stereotypic chunks (prefabricated language) abound in the classroom. She claims that a wide variety of structures are learned as chunk formulas initially during these classroom interactions. The child learns that the appropriate way of "doing" a classroom "experience" is to use these utterances. The utterances allow the child an admission ticket to "doing" an interaction, and the interaction gives the child practice with the utterances. Each builds on the other.

The five children in the Wong Fillmore study acquired a large number of formulaic utterances to carry out classroom functions:

*Interactional*
Attention caller: Hey, stupid! Oh, teacher.
Name exchanges: What'cha name? My name is X.
Greetings and leave takings: Hi. Take care!
Politeness routines: How are you? 'Scuse me.
Language management: I don't speak English.
Conversation management: You know what? Guess what!
Comments: All right! Beautiful! All right, you guys!

*Questions*
What is X? You wanna X? Can I X?

*Responses*
I know. I do. I don't care! I donno.

*Commands and requests*
Watch! Take it easy. No fighting now. Wait for me. Knock it off!

*Presentatives*
Here you go! This go here/there. You go like this. There goes X.

*Play management*
You be the X. I won it. Your turn. Me first.

*Storytelling routines*
Once upon a time. One day the [noun] was [verb]ing.

*Explanations*
Because, that's why. That's why.

*Wannas and wannits*
I wanna do it. Gimme. I wanna take X home.

Children's use of formulaic expressions gives them an entrée to further experience, an opportunity that adult L2 learners often cannot as successfully employ. In addition, when adults try out formulas, they are not often so lavishly praised as are child learners:

Observer: Do you guys want to play doctor?

Juan: I wanna be the doctor.

Carlos: [on phone] Allo doctor, I'm sick.

Juan: Come.

Carlos: OK, I be right there.

Juan: 'Bye.

Carlos: [Hangs up phone and pretends to knock at door]

Juan: Come in.

Carlos: [Turns to observer with a proud grin] Hey, he knows a lotta English!

Heidi:      Here, you take this car. [Playing service station]

Nora:       You no do dese. I be! ( = I'll be the attendant)

Heidi:      She talks good now, huh? She knows everything now.
                                            (Wong Fillmore, 1976, pp. 687–8)

Interactions among child learners also feature a great deal of language play – that is, in which verbal expressions are the object of the play. The "boo-boo" and "okay-dokey" excerpt from Young's data is a short example of child language play. Language play, however, also gives the child incidental practice in phonologically difficult sequences. The diary studies, for example, show children "practicing" words with similar sounds in their bedtime monologues. Eva, a Hungarian child learning French (Kenyeres, 1938), loved the French *ui* sound and practiced it with delight. She also practiced the uvular *r* sound in words that she claimed disgusted her. Wes, the adult learner in Schmidt's (1983) observational study, also played with difficult *r/l* sounds in words like "Marilyn Monroe." Language sound play is part of having fun, but it also gives learners practice with difficult sounds. In the following example, the young children get special practice on the difficult fricative /f/ (J = Mother, K = 3.1-year-old child, C = 18-month-old child):

K:          I said Fredded Wheat.

J:          You said what? [Pretends surprise]

K:          I said, I said Fredded Wheat.

C:          [Laughs]

J:          You think that's funny, Christopher, too?

K:          Mommy, could I have uh Fredded Wheat?

C & J:      [Laughter]

J:          I think it's in the buboard (cupboard), don't you?

K:          [Laughs]

J:          Let's get the yox (box) out and fee (see) if we have any Fredded Wheat.

K:          What socks out?

J:          The yox of cereal.

K:          Yox of cereal.

C:          Yox oo cereal.

K:          Yox of cereal.

C:          Yox of cereal.

K:          Mommy, can I pour the yox, the yix into my bowl?

J:          Oh, I fink fo.

K:          [Laughs]

C:          Fo.

J:          I fink fo.

K:          I fink fo. Fie fo fum. I smell a fum.

J, K, and C:   [Laughter]

(Gough, 1984, p. 7)

Playing the game requires playing with language. Second-language learners are equally adept at the rules of the game and enter it quite willingly. In Peck's (1978) data, the language play at times included simple sound repetition (e.g., NS: /nə/. Angel: /nə/). Sometimes it consisted of prosodic shift (e.g., NS: I will *do* it. Angel: I *will* do it.) Sometimes it included a free-wheeling variation on sounds, as in the modification of the word "pieces" (used during the working of a puzzle) into the Pepsi-Cola song. In the following excerpt Angel and Joe are working a jigsaw puzzle:

A:   (frustrated) Oooh!

J:   Oooh!

A:   Only one piece.

J:   Only one /piš/ /piš/ /piš/ /piš/ //I can't stop//.

A:   //This a old// piece. Piece.

J:   /piš/ /piš/ You like /pišəš/?

A:   No, I like pieces.

J:   What? Whatta you mean – you like /pišəž/ //I like// /pišəz/.

A:   //pizza// I like pieces, pizzas.

J:   /pɛpsis/?

A:   [Singsong] Pepsi-Coli – yeah.

J:   /pɛpši koliš/ [*Laugh*] /pɛpši koliš/ /pɛpši/ cola!

(Peck, 1978, p. 396)

In these examples, we have tried to show how the communication goal drives the learner to discover options available (in conversation or text structure, scripts or text types, lexicon, suprasegmentals, word order, pragmatics and syntax, and morphosyntax and phonology) to meet communicative needs. The examples have been almost exclusively from child L2 data. However, adult L2 data, even that collected in language classrooms, is very similar. Faerch (in press) gives teacher–student interaction examples in which teachers in the classroom help students by providing a scaffold for their utterances. The first example shows the teacher–student cooperation in paraphrasing the expression "thick bull's-eye glasses":

T:   What does it mean when she says she wore thick bull's eye glasses – that

S:   Her glasses were thick.

T:   Like

S:   The glasses

T:   The eyes of a

S:   Bull.

In the second, the teacher reads a sentence aloud and then nominates a student. The student offers a few words and stops, and the teacher offers missing words or nominates another student to cooperate in the task:

T:     og tog den ene af pindene og slog James pa ryggen ('and took one of the sticks and beat James on the back')

S1:    and – took one of the – er sticks.

T:     ja og slog – er James pa ryggen – ('yes, and beat James on the back')

S1:    er det kan je ikke huske – ('I can't remember')

T:     Jette (S2's name)

S2:    beat

T:     er beat Peter pa ryggen ('on the back'; Peter with English pronunciation)

S1:    on his back

Such examples are not far from those of Scollon, of Young, and of Itoh and Hatch cited earlier.

However, adults are expected to demonstrate written as well as oral language skills. As we move away from talk data, we encounter interactions that require the work of an *editor* (or, at least, much more work from the formulator). Even children, once in school, are soon required to interact with written text. We often assume that for the L2 child this is just a matter of acquiring basic decoding skills or basic handwriting skills, that everything else remains the same. Obviously, this is not the case. The language of talk and the language of written text are different, and the cognitive tasks involved are also different.

To show that, once again, interaction enables learners to acquire literacy skills, let us turn to a slightly more advanced academic setting. In talking with teachers, it is clear that it is not only theoreticians who see linguistic, social, and cognitive knowledge as separate rather than interrelated. This is especially true once literacy is included in the picture. Teachers often make statements that show they believe that cognitive and linguistic systems are separate or that one is a prerequisite of the other. That is, teachers may say, "If I could start all over again, I'd teach kids how to think before teaching them to write" (quotation from Falkof & Moss, 1984). This statement reflects a belief that there is a one-way relation between critical thinking (cognition) and writing (language). Reading theorists (see Smith, 1973) claim that the skilled reader attacks the text using well-developed critical thinking skills, another one-way relation. And teacher trainers (see Krashen, 1981) claim that excellence in writing depends on well-developed reading habits, another unidirectional relation from cognition to reading to writing. In each case, one skill area is seen to be a prerequisite of another, and the end result is a La Ronde model.

Language curriculum specialists, too, claim prerequisites – namely, that basic language skills are prerequisites of the use of the skills for higher-order cognitive processes. The various forms of the "threshold hypothesis" show basic language

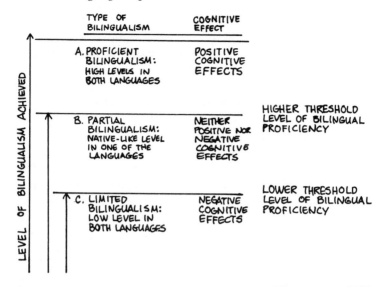

Figure 8. "Threshold hypothesis" associated with different types of bilingualism. (Adapted from Toukomaa & Skutnabb-Kangas, 1977, p. 29.)

skills as prerequisites of the use of language for higher-order problem solving (Figure 8). Until basic skills (threshold-level skills) are acquired, the language requires so much attention that the learner is unable to use it for academic purposes. Since semiautomatic control of the basic level is needed before higher-order work can be done, the threshold skills are considered to be prerequisite – again a one-way relation between language and cognition. Even within language, methodologists have long argued that basic language skills (those associated with beginning instruction below the threshold level) are also unidirectional. One skill area is seen as a prerequisite of (or, at least, corequisite with) the other as follows:

Listening → speaking → reading → writing

Our view of these relations is that they are neither linear nor completely hierarchical. That is, we believe that learning is reciprocal, that each skill area continues to develop reciprocally with the others. Rather than try to refute each of these one-way relationship claims, we shall consider one area, that of cognitive skills, social knowledge, and writing, the case of the teacher who wants to teach students to think before teaching them to write. Our claim is that writing abilities, critical thinking skills, and social knowledge are reciprocally developed and become more and more interrelated over time.

As composition experts (from Rohman, 1965, to de Beaugrande, 1983) have shown, cognitive support activities make writing easier. In turn, the composing process promotes conceptual processes. As de Beaugrande suggests, *prewriting* promotes ideation by relaxing the demands for cohesion of the written text. Writers can make notes, visualize, gather new information, and discuss and explore their ideas without producing continuous text. In our terms, this means that the conceptualizer is allowed full reign. The formulator is busy with the largest units of organization, paying little attention to the editor functions needed for a more final product. The cognitive tasks required of the conceptualizer in accessing information and of the formulator in organizing that information within a rhetorical text framework and of both in considering alternative ways of presenting information are precisely the "higher-order" cognitive skills needed for academic achievement. *Outlining*, another prewriting task, requires us to *organize* our ideas in a rhetorical frame that we consider logical, to *search* and *organize* support for ideas, to *sort* ideas to show focus, and to construct the conceptual framework for the text. During the composing process, that framework (accomplished by the conceptualizer and formulator) is reworked (a formulator and/or editor function) to fit the emerging text. In *speedwriting* activities, students write whatever occurs to them at top speed. This provokes *search*, *retrieval*, and *listing out* of ideas found by the cognitive search procedures of the conceptualizer. The complex cognitive procedures – the sorting, arranging, consolidating, and rearranging – are part of working on the text. The development of these cognitive procedures and the development of composing talents are reciprocal.

The sorting and reorganizing are done differently across languages. That is, written text is organized in slightly different ways in different languages. What constitutes a logical arrangement in one language may neither be valued nor appear logical in another language. This is true of text organization (the text script), of pragmatic coding, and of syntax. Maccoun (1983), in her work on text organization, found this to be particularly true of L2 students' comprehension of argumentative text. Her university-level students claimed that it was strange that anyone would use a rhetorical organization in which the arguments of the other side were presented. They were especially puzzled and often misread the author's intent when the argument of the other side was presented first. Researchers (see Scarcella, 1984) note, however, that native English speakers have difficulty understanding the logic of text scripts in certain other languages. For example, in an Arabic script, argumentation would be achieved through presentation (Koch, 1983). An arguer presents truths by stating them, repeating them, rephrasing them, calling attention to them again and again. Koch notes the Arabic saying, "Even a donkey will be convinced by enough repetition", but it is the elegance of the repetition that is essence, the proof of the argument. The point here is that English and Arabic argumentation scripts differ. The rules that direct the cognitive processes of selecting, sorting, and organizing material in the two languages are different; it is not just the language used to express the final product that differs.

Pragmatic organization (the way speakers and writers package their information so that listeners or readers know what is referred to, where items are located in time and space, what information is old or new, etc.) also differs across languages. For example, writers are often confused about how to refer pragmatically to time – should they use the time of writing as their reference point or the time of the reader? Notice, in the following excerpt from a letter sent to a group of teachers that "tomorrow" had already arrived by the time the readers received the letter:

> Dear Rater,
>
> My sincere thanks for your cooperation in scoring these additional essays. I know you have a lot to do today, and I hope it is not as hot there tomorrow as it is here today . . . .

Similarly, writers must decide whether to locate people in reference to their own location or to that of the reader. The "come"–"go" distinction is a reflection of this. The pragmatics of "come"–"go" are not simple, nor is the "come"–"go" distinction easy for learners to acquire. Niimura (1985), for example, shows how an adult Japanese learner of English becomes confused about the way this perspective should be expressed:

> Tomo:  ah, I came stay before New York City.
> ('Ah, I first went to New York City')
> ah, I came here Los Angeles alright.
> ('Ah, I came here from New York City')
>
> (Niimura, 1985, data appendix)

Japanese, like English, has a "come"–"go" distinction, and the speaker's perspective plays a role in determining which form will be used. The preferred choice does not match that of English even though both "come" and "go" are possible in each language depending on the location of the speaker. Although we can say "I first came to New York" if we locate ourselves as in the United States, it is much more likely that an American from Japan located in Los Angeles would use "went to New York." In Japanese, the speaker could also use "come"–"go" but would more likely select "came to New York." (One explanation offered for this is the relative size of America and the distance from Los Angeles to New York; in Japan distances are not that great.) So even though the learner may expect to find such a distinction (since it exists in the first language), the correspondence between the languages as to when and how the split is to be accomplished is related to pragmatic and cognitive levels.

The differences that occur in relating pragmatics to syntax are even more obvious. For example, in English, perhaps the most common structure is subject–verb–object. In many other languages the structure is a topic plus comment. In English, we can say, "I like rice" using subject–verb–object syntax. We could say, "Rice, I like it" a topic plus comment structure, but such structures are very rare. If the L2 learner organizes his or her ideas in a topic–comment format, the outcome will not be "English." In the following example from a Chinese student, notice the use of "topics" at the beginning of each sentence.

> How to use variable English sentence to express myself exactly, that is the main

> problem I faced when I just picked up my pencil to write my first assignment. . . .
> For more complex feeling, I had trouble to write it down clearly and exactly.

Learners are unlikely to find helpful explanations of such differences in their language textbooks. Nor can explanations be easily formulated by naive native speakers. To discover what works and what does not requires a great deal of effort for L2 learners. For many (even for native speakers), the effort outweighs the benefits. For "good language learners," however, it is a matter of constantly hypothesizing and testing (i.e., researching) ways to improve communication during interactions.

As these examples of pragmatics show, social knowledge also has an important part in the writing process. As Rubin (1980) has pointed out, one reason written language is different from oral language is that the communicative media differ. Writers must be aware of the reader, since they are trying to communicate their experience to the reader. Readers require written signals to compensate for the inability to interact orally with the writer if they are to interact successfully with the text. Writers, keeping the reader in mind, try to be as precise as possible (i.e., precision of time and person references, rhetorical organization, topic demarcations, punctuation, and lexical choices). All of this implies that writers realize that they are interacting with a reader, and their cognitive, social, and language efforts must be called on to accommodate that interaction. For example, revision is largely, after all, the process of making every effort to be sure the text will be clear to the reader. For this reason writers often ask others to read what they have written before they formally finish the writing task. As they revise, they call into action their social knowledge, which allows them to consider the reader, the cognitive skills with which to analyze possible problems in the text, and the language skills with which to make the text's meaning clear. Again, it is the three skills operating reciprocally with one another that help writers make their experiences clear. For L2 learners the writing process becomes one of making their experiences clear in written form in the second language to a new reader – a native speaker of the second language.

## Conclusion

In arguing for the reciprocal nature of learning in this discussion of the composing process, we have talked about the link between linguistic and cognitive processes. In our earlier discussion of scripts, we talked about the link between social and linguistic knowledge. In proposing a model that draws on scripts and an incremental procedural-based grammar, we have tried to make specific the type of language production mechanism that would code our experiences in talk and print. The data we have presented from both L1 and L2 studies show the interactive nature of the learning process. Learning is guided via interaction with a "teacher" (though the teacher may at times be oneself) in an associated set of experiences.

The experiences gained from these interactions serve many functions related to language: They set preferred structures of discourse scripts, of lexical boundaries and categorization, highlight important information through suprasegmental and pragmatic organization, clarify syntactic organization, and give data on accuracy at the morphophonemic and phonological levels as well.

These experiences differ for children and adults and for instructed and uninstructed learners. In instructional sequences, more intentional learning may be possible. However, in all cases, the interactions provide massive possibilities for incidental learning.

At the beginning of this chapter, we said that research and teaching practices involve one's point of view – one's theory of language acquisition. That theory, too, reciprocally evolves with our experience in teaching and research. If our *goal* is to understand the learning process and the *way* teaching can affect that process, we do not begin with theorizing. Rather, we begin with our own experience as language learners, language teachers, and language researchers. Our experience in teacher-training programs and as readers of other people's research is part of that experience as well. As we form hypotheses, we test them against what we meet in our interactions with other learners and teachers. We modify our ideas, decide to broaden or constrict the scope, perhaps according to temperament but also according to the scope of the questions we pose. Gradually, after many attempts, we form a script – this time a "theory script." As we do our research and teaching or talk with others about our work, we call up that script. We hope that those with whom we talk access a similar script so that what we talk about makes sense to them. This chapter, then, has been an attempt to make clear the components of that script. The components are not sets of actions, nor are they fully developed as yet. Over time, we expect to revise components to provide a better match of data, theory, and teaching practice.

## References

Andersen, R. (1983). Transfer to somewhere. In S. Gass & L. Selinker (Eds.), *Language transfer in language learning* (pp. 177–201). Rowley, MA: Newbury House.

Andersen, R. (1984). What's gender good for, anyway? In R. Andersen (Ed.), *Second language: A cross-linguistic perspective* (pp. 77–99). Rowley, MA: Newbury House.

Baetens-Beardsmore, H. (1974). Development of the compound-coordinate distinction in bilingualism. *Lingua, 33,* 123–7.

Bailey, N., Madden, C., & Krashen, S. (1978). Is there a natural sequence in adult second language learning? In E. Hatch (Ed.), *Second language acquisition: A book of readings* (pp. 362–70). Rowley, MA: Newbury House.

Bellugi, U., & Brown, R. (1964). The acquisition of language. *Monographs of the Society for Research in Child Development, 29* (1, Whole No. 92).

Berko Gleason, J., & Weintraub, S. (1976). The acquisition of routines in child language. *Language in Society, 5,* 137–51.

Blank, M., Gessner, M., & Esposito, A. (1979). Language without communication: A case study. *Journal of Child Language*, 2, 329–52.

Brown, G., & Yule, G. (1983). *Discourse analysis*. Cambridge University Press.

Brown, G., & Yule, G. (1984). *Teaching language comprehension*. Cambridge University Press.

Chomsky, N. (1980). *Rules and representations*. New York: Columbia University Press.

de Beaugrande, R. (1983). *Text production: Toward a science of composition*. Norwood, NJ: Ablex.

Dittmar, N. (1984). Semantic features of the pidginized learner varieties of German. In R. Andersen (Ed.), *Second language: A cross-linguistic perspective* (pp. 243–70). Rowley, MA: Newbury House.

Dulay, H., & Burt, M. (1978). Natural sequences in child second language acquisition. In E. Hatch (Ed.), *Second language acquisition: A book of readings* (pp. 347–361). Rowley, MA: Newbury House.

Ervin, S., & Osgood, C. (1954). Second language learning and bilingualism. *Journal of Abnormal and Social Psychology*, 49, 139–46.

Faerch, C. (in press). Meta talk in foreign language classroom discourse. *Studies in Second Language Acquisition*.

Falkof, L., & Moss, J. (1984). When teachers tackle thinking skills. *Educational Leadership*, 42(3), 4–10.

Flynn, S. (1983). Similarities and differences between first and second language acquisition: Setting the parameters of Universal Grammar. In D. R. Rogers & J. A. Sloboda (Eds.), *Acquisition of symbolic skills* (pp. 484–500). New York: Plenum.

Flynn, S. (1984). A universal in L2 acquisition based on a PBD typology. In F. Eckman, L. Bell, & D. Nelson (Eds.), *Universals of second language acquisition* (pp. 75–87). Rowley, MA: Newbury House.

Freedle, R., & Lewis, M. (1977). Prelinguistic conversations. In M. Lewis & L. Rosenblum (Eds.), *Interaction, conversation, and development of language* (pp. 157–86). New York: Wiley.

Genesee, F., Hamers, J., Lambert, W., Mononen, L., Seitz, M., & Starck, R. (1978). Language processing in bilinguals. *Brain and Language*, 5, 1–12.

Givon, T. (1979). From discourse to syntax. In T. Givon (Ed.), *Syntax and semantics: Vol 12. Discourse and syntax* (pp. 81–114). New York: Academic Press.

Gough, J. (1975). *Comparative studies in second language learning*, Vol. 26. CAL-ERIC/CLL Series on Languages and Linguistics. Washington, DC.

Gough, J. (1984). *Adult–child language play: A naturalistic study*. Unpublished doctoral qualifying paper, University of California, Los Angeles.

Greenfield, P., & Smith, J. (1976). *The structure of communication in early language development*. New York: Academic Press.

Greif, E., & Berko Gleason, J. (1980). Hi, thanks and goodbye: More routine information. *Language in Society*, 9, 159–66.

Hatch, E. (1983). *Psycholinguistics: A second language perspective*. Rowley, MA: Newbury House.

Hatch, E., Flashner, V., & Hunt, L. (1986). The experience model and language teaching. In R. Day (Ed.), *Talking to learn* (pp. 5–22). Rowley, MA: Newbury House.

Hatch, E., & Gough, J. W. (1976). Explaining sequence and variation in second language acquisition [special issue]. *Language Learning*, 4, 39–57.

Hawkins, B. (1985, February). *Learning to complain through experience*. Paper presented at the Second Language Research Forum, University of California, Los Angeles.

Hilles, S. (1985, February). *Interlanguage and the pro-drop parameter*. Paper presented at the Second Language Research Forum, University of California, Los Angeles.

Huang, J., & Hatch, E. (1978). A Chinese child's acquisition of syntax. In E. Hatch (Ed.), *Second language acquisition: A book of readings* (pp. 118–31). Rowley, MA: Newbury House.

Itoh, H., & Hatch, E. (1978). Second language acquisition: A case study. In E. Hatch (Ed.), *Second language acquisition: A book of readings* (pp. 76–90). Rowley, MA: Newbury House.

Jisa, H., & Scarcella, R. (1981). *Discourse markers in adult second language performance*. Paper presented at CATESOL conference, Los Angeles.

Kavanaugh, R., Wellington, S., & Cerbone, M. (1983). Mothers' use of fantasy in speech to young children. *Journal of Child Language*, *10*, 45–55.

Kellerman, E. (1978). Giving learners a break. *Working Papers on Bilingualism*, *15*, 59–92.

Kempen, G., & Hoenkamp, E. (1981). *A procedural grammar for sentence production* (Internal Rep. 81) Nijmegen, The Netherlands: Katholieke Universiteit, Vakgroep psychologische functieleer, Psychologisch laboratorium.

Kenyeres, A. (1938). Comment une petite Hongroise apprend le francais. *Archives de psychologie*, *26*, 321–66.

Koch, B. J. (1983). Presentation as proof: The language of Arabic rhetoric. *Anthropological Linguistics*, *25*, 47–57.

Kolers, P. (1968, March). Bilingualism and information processing. *Scientific American*, pp. 78–86.

Krashen, S. (1981). *Second language acquisition and second language learning*. Oxford: Pergamon Press.

Kuwahata, M. (1984). *The negation system in the interlanguage of a Japanese speaker*. Unpublished master's thesis, University of California, Los Angeles.

Lennakyla, P. (1980). Hi Superman: What is most functional English for a Finnish five-year-old? *Journal of Pragmatics*, *4*, 367–92.

Lewis, M., & Cherry, L. (1977). Social behavior and language acquisition. In M. Lewis & L. Rosenblum (Eds.), *Interaction, conversation & development of language* (pp. 227–46). New York: Wiley.

Lindblom, B. (n.d.). *Can the models of evolutionary biology be applied to phonetic problems?* Unpublished paper, Stockholm University, Linguistics Department, Sweden.

Long, M. H. (1980). *Input, interaction, and second language acquisition*. Unpublished dissertation, University of California, Los Angeles.

Maccoun, W. (1983). *On the acquisition of argumentative discourse from the comprehension point of view*. Unpublished master's thesis, University of Los Angeles, California.

Marshall, J. C. (1980). Biology of language acquisition. In D. Caplan (Ed.), *Biological studies of mental processes* (pp. 106–48). Cambridge, MA: MIT Press.

McCawley, J. D. (1983). Towards plausibility in theories of language acquisition. *Communication and Cognition*, *16*, 169–83.

Michael, J., & Clark, R. C. (1983). *Experiential language teaching techniques: Resource Handbook 3*. Brattleboro, VT: Pro Lingua Associates.

Miller, P. (1982). Teasing sequences. *Bulletin of Cross-cultural Human Cognition & Development*, *6* (University of California, San Diego).

Niimura, T. (1985). *The English interlanguage of a native Japanese speaker: Temporality and transfer*. Unpublished master's thesis, University of California, Los Angeles.

Ochs, E. (1979). Planned and unplanned discourse. In T. Givon (Ed.), *Syntax and semantics: Vol. 12. Discourse and syntax* (pp. 51–80). New York: Academic Press.

Pawley, A., & Syder, F. (1977). *The one clause at a time hypothesis*. Unpublished paper, University of Auckland, New Zealand, Linguistics Department.

Peck, S. (1978). Child–child discourse in second language acquisition. In E. Hatch, *Second language acquisition: A book of readings* (pp. 383–400). Rowley, MA: Newbury House.

Perdue, C. (1984). *Second language acquisition by adult immigrants: A field manual*. Rowley, MA: Newbury House.

Peters, A. (1983). *The units of language acquisition*. Cambridge University Press.

Ravem, R. (1978). Two Norwegian children's acquisition of syntax. In E. Hatch (Ed.), *Second language acquisition: A book of readings* (pp. 148–54). Rowley, MA: Newbury House.

Richards, J., & Schmidt, R. (1983). Conversational analysis. In J. Richards & R. Schmidt (Eds.), *Language and communication* (pp. 117–55). New York: Longman.

Rohman, G. (1965). Prewriting: The stage of discovery in the writing process. *College Composition and Communication, 16*, 106–12.

Ronjat, J. (1913). *Le développement du langage observé chez un enfant bilingue*. Paris: Campion.

Rubin, A. (1980). A theoretical taxonomy of the differences between oral and written language. In R. J. Spiro, C. B. Bertram, & W. F. Brewer (Eds.), *Theoretical issues in reading comprehension: Perspectives from cognitive psychology, artificial intelligence and education* (pp. 411–38). Hillsdale, NJ: Erlbaum.

Sachs, J., & Truswell, L. (1978). Comprehension of two-word instructions by children at the one-word stage. *Journal of Child Language, 5*, 17–24.

Schank, R. (1982). Reminding and memory organization: An introduction to MOPs. In W. G. Lehnert & M. H. Ringle (Eds.), *Strategies for natural language processing* (pp. 455–93). Hillsdale, NJ: Erlbaum.

Schank, R., & Abelson, R. (1977). *Scripts, plans, goals and understanding: An inquiry into human knowledge structures*. Hillsdale, NJ: Erlbaum.

Scarcella, R. (1984). *The development of cohesion in the writing of native and nonnative English speakers*. Unpublished Ph.D. dissertation, University of Southern California, Los Angeles.

Schegloff, E. (1979). Identification and recognition in telephone conversation openings. In G. Psathas (Ed.), *Everyday language: Ethnomethodological approaches* (pp. 23–78). New York: Irvington.

Schmidt, R. W. (1983). Interaction, acculturation, and the acquisition of communicative competence. In N. Wolfson & E. Judd (Eds.), *Sociolinguistics and language acquisition* (pp. 137–74). Rowley, MA: Newbury House.

Schumann, J. (1983, November). *The expression of temporality in basilang speech*. Paper presented at the Second Language Research Forum, University of Southern California, Los Angeles.

Scollon, R. (1979). A real early stage: An unzippered condensation of a dissertation on child language. In E. Ochs & B. Schieffelin (Eds.), *Developmental pragmatics* (pp. 215–27). New York: Academic Press.

Shapira, R. (1976). *A study of acquisition of ten syntactic structures and grammatical morphology by an adult second language learner*. Unpublished master's thesis, University of California, Los Angeles.

Smith, F. (1973). *Psycholinguistics and reading*. New York: Holt, Rinehart & Winston.

Stockwell, R., Bowen, J. D., & Martin, J. W. (1965). *The grammatical structures of English and Spanish*. University of Chicago Press.

Tannen, D. (1983). *Spoken and written language*. Norwood, NJ: Ablex.

Toukomaa, P., & Skutnabb-Kangas, T. (1977). *The intensive teaching of the mother tongue to migrant children of preschool age and children in the lower level of comprehensive school* (Research Rep. No. 26). Tampere: University of Tampere, Department of Sociology & Social Psychology, Finland.

Trubetzkoy, N. (1969). *Principles of phonology* (C. Baltaxe, Trans.). Los Angeles & Berkeley: University of California Press.

Wapner, W., Hamby, S., & Gardner, H. (1981). The role of the right hemisphere in the apprehension of complex linguistic materials. *Brain and Language, 14*, 15–33.

White, L. (1983). The pro drop parameter in adult second language acquisition. In F. Eckman, E. Moravcsik, & J. Wirth (Eds.), *Proceedings of 12th Annual University of Wisconsin-Milwaukee Symposium on Markedness*. New York: Plenum Press.

White, L. (1984). *Universal Grammar as a source of explanation in second language acquisition*. Paper presented at the 13th Annual University of Wisconsin-Milwaukee Symposium, Milwaukee.

Wong Fillmore, L. (1976). *The second time around: Cognitive and social strategies in second language acquisition*. Unpublished dissertation, Stanford University, Stanford, CA.

Yamada, J. (1981). *On the independence of language and cognition: Evidence from a hyperlinguistic retarded adolescent*. Paper presented at the International Congress of Child Language, University of British Columbia, Vancouver.

Young, D. (1974). *The acquisition of English syntax by three Spanish-speaking children*. Unpublished master's thesis, University of California, Los Angeles.

Zernik, U. (1984). *Rina: A program that learns English as a second language*. Paper presented at the Southern California Conference on Artificial Intelligence, University of California, Los Angeles.

# 7 Bilingualism and cognitive development: three perspectives

*Kenji Hakuta, Bernardo M. Ferdman,*
*and Rafael M. Diaz*

The problem of researching the relation between bilingualism and cognitive development at once raises two thorny definitional issues. What do we mean by bilingualism, and what is it that develops in cognitive development? Much of the confusion in this area can be attributed to the lack of theoretical specificity in defining the intersection point of these component concepts. Our primary emphasis in this chapter is on the definition of bilingualism, with a secondary emphasis on cognitive development. The reason for the asymmetry is to be consistent with the traditional assumption that bilingualism is the independent treatment variable and cognitive growth is the dependent outcome variable, even though, as we shall see, very few studies actually address the cause–effect issue. The major goal of this chapter is to demonstrate the great range of social and theoretical contexts in which the question has historically been asked and to argue for the importance of integrating the many disciplinary levels and perspectives that bear on the problem.

## Defining the component concepts

The concept of bilingualism has been used in various ways by scholars and lay persons alike. It has been viewed as an individual-level mental concept – a characteristic of individuals who possess or who use two linguistic systems. It has also been viewed as a social psychological concept, still a characteristic of individuals, but of individuals who organize the social world in terms of the different groups and social situations associated with the two languages in which they interact. Bilingualism has also been used as a societal construct to describe the interactions between social groups and societal institutions, as well as among groups, in which the group and institutional boundaries correspond to linguistic boundaries. These different starting points for the definition of bilingualism have resulted in discrepancies in the kinds of statements that have been made about bilingualism and its relation with cognitive development.

The preparation of this chapter was supported in part by National Institute of Education Contract 400-85-1010 for the Center for Language, Education and Research.

284

When bilingualism is defined in the first way, as a characteristic of an individual who possesses two linguistic systems – we call it *cognitive bilingualism* – one tends toward statements about the packaging problem of fitting two linguistic systems in the mind of an individual. It is a cognitive puzzle on the relation between language and thought and how these systems are represented neurologically and conceptually. Variables of obvious importance in cognitive bilingualism are the extent to which the individual has mastery of the two languages and the cognitive functions in which the languages are engaged.

Bilingualism defined in the second way, as a characteristic of the social condition and affect of the individual – we call it *social psychological bilingualism* – tends toward social psychological accounts of the packaging of value systems within an individual. These emphasize not so much the linguistic aspects of bilinguals as the social correlates of the two languages. In this sense of the definition, the grammatical qualities of languages hardly matter. What really matters is the symbolism about group affiliation that the languages convey to the individual.

Bilingualism defined in the third way, as a characteristic of a societal unit – we call it *societal bilingualism* – is concerned with between-group interactions in which the two languages serve as a symbol over which interaction occurs. This perspective is not so concerned with individual differences within groups. As in the social psychological view of bilingualism, the extent of the vitality of the two languages – vitality in the sense of the extent to which the grammar and form of the languages are maintained – is not so important in this view, though it can be made to be important depending on social conditions. What matters in this perspective is that language in some way signals membership in a group and serves to maintain the group's cohesiveness and identity.

At the same time that there have been different levels of conceptualization of bilingualism, different theories of cognitive development have preoccupied psychologists of different generations. The earliest systematic attempts to document the relation were made at the beginning of the twentieth century. At that time, the primary definition of what we now call cognitive development was a psychometric one, based on the differential performance of individuals within a defined population on IQ tests. Subsequently, learning theory, skill theory, Piagetian operational thought, Chomskyan rationalism, and Vygotsky's views of mind and society offered additional conceptions of what develops in cognitive development.

Although a review of the various theories of cognitive development is far beyond the scope of this chapter, it would be important to consider the dimensions of theories that would or would not predict effects of bilingualism on cognitive development. One might think of bilingualism as an environmental "treatment," to be compared with the alternative treatment of monolingualism.

As a first approximation toward appreciating the range of cognitive theories available, one can begin with commonly used typologies, particularly as relevant to bilingualism. These include nativism versus empiricism, modularity versus commonality of functions, and context and cultural sensitivity versus independence.

With regard to the nativistic–empiricist dimension, any theory of cognitive development that subscribes to primarily innate factors, with respect to both the qualitative aspects of cognition and differences among individuals, would not predict bilingualism to have any effect on the course of cognitive growth. This would include a Chomskyan orientation that attributes the characteristics of our linguistic and other cognitive knowledge to our genetic makeup. It would also include a hereditarian interpretation of individual differences in intelligence, such as that espoused by Jensen (1980). In contrast, theories that emphasize the role of learning and the environment would easily accommodate influences of bilingualism on development. These would include traditional learning theory and skill theory, as well as Piagetian constructivism.

The second dimension of cognitive theories – modularity versus commonality of structures – will predict, given some effect of the bilingual treatment on cognitive development, how it would generalize to other domains of cognitive functioning. For example, Chomsky and Fodor's extreme modular approach (see Piatelli-Palmarini, 1980), in which cognitive functions including language are considered to be analogous to structurally autonomous organs of the mind, would find minimal compatibility with broad-sweeping effects of bilingualism. The effects would be confined to the specific aspects of cognitive functioning that are influenced by the bilingual environment. For example, if bilingualism were to be defined strictly as a linguistic treatment rather than a social or societal one, the effects would be confined to linguistic aspects of cognitive functioning. In contrast, learning theory as well as theories of general intelligence and Piagetian operational theory would expect generalized effects since all cognitive functioning share a common source and are interrelated. However, it should be noted that Piagetian theory, though a theory of general intelligence, is characterized by its ascription of a marginal role for language in structuring intelligence.

The third dimension of cognitive theories, the cultural or context sensitivity of theories, holds the strongest promise for relating cognitive development with the social psychological and societal levels of bilingualism. The theory best noted for its emphasis on culture is Vygotsky's (1962), in which specific cognitive functions might exist in rudimentary form as part of the child's genetic endowment, but the majority of the variance in cognitive growth can be explained by the ways in which society amplifies and interrelates these capacities. In contrast, both Chomskyan and Piagetian views on the role of culture are limited.

In this chapter, we make two general points centering on the definitional considerations of bilingualism described above. First, we point to the importance of drawing clear distinctions among the definitions of bilingualism. Failure to do so can lead to misunderstandings about the role of bilingualism in cognitive development. Second, even though these various perspectives can and should be distinguished, attention should also be paid to the interactions of variables across levels. Indeed, the question of bilingual cognitive development highlights the importance of maintaining multiple perspectives and cutting across levels of analysis in social science.

We make these points using the following structure. The first section takes a historical perspective in examining changes in the way bilingualism has been thought to influence intelligence in children. The section illustrates the importance of maintaining clear distinctions among definitions of bilingualism, while at the same time pointing to the importance of the historical context of research. Then, we follow with a discussion of bilingualism and cognitive development as seen from each of the three levels discussed above – cognitive, social psychological, and societal. Obviously, the cognitive perspective has the most to say with regard to cognitive development, but the latter perspectives are important to the extent that social psychological and societal factors influence the degree of bilingualism that might be attained by the population of interest. In the concluding section, we trace the implications of this multilevel analysis of the problem toward a greater understanding of language, mind, and society, drawing from our own research efforts.

### Some history

If one were to look at the literature on bilingualism and intelligence over its long history, it would at first seem that the early literature showed that bilingualism had negative consequences, whereas the more recent literature, improving on the earlier methodologies, showed the opposite, that bilingualism could have a positive influence on cognitive development. Consider the contrast to be found in following two accounts of the relation between bilingualism and intelligence. Conclusions from the early literature can be summarized by the following statement that appeared in George Thompson's (1952) American textbook on child psychology:

There can be no doubt that the child reared in a bilingual environment is handicapped in his language growth. One can debate the issue as to whether speech facility in two languages is worth the consequent retardation in the common language of the realm. (p. 367)

A rather brighter portrait is drawn by Elizabeth Peal and Wallace Lambert (1962) in reporting a study of bilingual children in Montreal. They describe their typical subject as

a youngster whose wider experiences in two cultures have given him advantages which a monolingual does not enjoy. Intellectually his experience with two language systems seems to have left him with a mental flexibility, a superiority in concept formation, a more diversified set of mental abilities . . . . In contrast, the monolingual appears to have a more unitary structure of intelligence which he must use for all types of intellectual tasks. (p. 20)

These statements and their inherent contradictions can be interpreted as a dramatic example of misunderstandings that resulted from failure to distinguish between different levels of definition of bilingualism.

Clearly, if the goal of a study were to establish whether the extent of bilingualism in children had an effect on individual-level cognitive development, one should define bilingualism in terms of their abilities in the two languages. What one should *not* do is to use a societal definition of bilingualism. Yet the earlier literature primarily used a societal definition – bilinguals consisted of newly arrived immigrants to the United States – whereas the more recent literature has tended to use a cognitive definition. In part, this discrepancy in definitions and findings can be attributed to improvements in methodological controls. For example, the more recent studies attempt to control for the socioeconomic status (SES) of the comparison groups, whereas the older studies did not. However, a historical perspective enables us to appreciate why the earlier literature used the societal definition and essentially ignored what are now considered obvious confounds, such as SES.

In order to comprehend the early literature and what the debate was all about, one must view them against the backdrop of the concerns of Americans at the turn of the century (see Gould 1981; Hakuta 1986). At that time, there raged a social debate over the quality of the new immigrant groups from southern and eastern Europe, a fear that was expressed forcefully by Francis Walker, president of MIT and a prominent spokesperson for immigration restriction:

These immigrants are beaten men from beaten races, representing the worst failures in the struggle for existence. Europe is allowing its slums and its most stagnant reservoirs of degraded peasantry to be drained off upon our soil. (Quoted in Ayres, 1909, p. 103)

The various measures of intelligence, particularly in the tradition of Goddard's translation of Binet's IQ test, came to play a major role in this debate, for the immigrants' performance on these tests seemed to confirm the worst fears of restrictionists like Walker.

In explaining the poor performance of the new immigrants on intelligence tests, the battle line was drawn between those who believed in genetic versus those who believed in experiential explanations. Researchers in those days – including luminaries in the field such as Lewis Terman, Florence Goodenough, and George Stoddard – debated whether bilingualism was or was not a handicap in the measurement of intelligence.

The hereditarians, who believed that IQ test performance was attributable largely to genetic factors, accounted for the poor test performance of the new immigrants – those primarily from southern and eastern Europe – in terms of selective migration. The data were considered to support the general fear about the quality of the new immigrants. The strongest data in support of the hereditarian position were the results of the testing of U.S. Army recruits in World War I, conducted by Robert Yerkes and synthesized and popularized by Carl C. Brigham (1922). The most compelling bit of evidence, in the eyes of hereditarians, was the decreasing intelligence test scores as a function of recency of immigration. Brigham's explanation was as follows:

Migrations of the Alpine and Mediterranean races have increased to such an extent in the last thirty or forty years that this blood now constitutes 70% or 75% of the total immigration. The representatives of the Alpine and Mediterranean races in our immigration are intellectually inferior to the representatives of the Nordic race which formerly made up about 50% of our immigration. (p. 197)

The alternative explanation, of course, was that those who had immigrated most recently had learned less English and that inadequate proficiency in English resulted in poor test performance. This possibility of a language handicap in test taking was recognized by proponents of the hereditarian position, such as Lewis Terman (1918). He and his students began a full-scale assault of the possibility that the bilinguals might be taking the tests under a language handicap and attempted to show that the differences existed even despite it (Young, 1922). Such heroics notwithstanding, however, it became clear that the recent immigrants – the bilinguals – were operating under a handicap. For example, Terman's own student Darsie (1926) showed that bilinguals performed particularly poorly on the subtests of the Binet scale that required language.

Despite evidence of this sort, the hereditarians did not change their position on the genetic quality of the new immigrants. Florence Goodenough (1926), for example, turned the argument around and wrote that "those nationality groups whose average intellectual ability is inferior do not readily learn the new language" (p. 393).

In contrast to the hereditarians, psychologists who emphasized the environmental factors associated with intelligence test scores, spearheaded by George Stoddard and Beth Wellman of the Iowa Child Welfare Research Station, were trying to explain the poor performance of immigrants using experiential factors (Stoddard & Wellman, 1934). Rather than question the validity of the IQ tests for this particular population, they arrived at the conclusion that bilingualism – an experiential factor – must cause some kind of mental confusion, resulting in the poor development of verbal skills.

Madorah Smith, who received her doctorate at Iowa, figures prominently in this history. For her dissertation, she had pioneered a method of analyzing free speech utterances of young monolingual children to obtain quantitative indices of language development. Later, she moved to Hawaii, where she began applying her method to the speech of bilingual children from a wide variety of language backgrounds (Smith, 1939). A comparison of these statistics with her Iowa samples showed that bilinguals were inferior to the monolinguals, leading her to the conclusion that "an important factor in the retardation in speech found in the preschool population is the attempt to make use of two languages" (p. 253). (There are many alternative explanations of her data, a discussion of which can be found in Hakuta, 1986.)

The twists and turns of this research area can be recapitulated as follows. The backdrop of the initial research was concern with the new immigrants, who performed poorly on tests of intelligence. The hereditarians argued that this poor performance reflected inferior genetic stock and attempted to argue against a language handicap in test taking. The evidence mounted, however, that bilinguals were operating under a handicap. The hereditarians then interpreted this handicap to be the result of innately inferior intelligence. In contrast, the environmentalists took the language handicap of bilinguals to be the result of experience, the most salient experience to them being exposure to two languages.

What is remarkable about this debate is that the language handicap of bilingualism, initially construed as a test-taking factor associated with a group trait – namely, foreignness and recency of immigration – soon became an alleged characteristic of a supposed mental state – in our terminology, cognitive bilingualism.

How were these early studies of bilingualism and intelligence conducted? They were primarily comparisons of two groups of students, one labeled "bilingual" and the other "monolingual," on the various tests of intelligence (including the Stanford–Binet) that were becoming increasingly popular in those days. And how was bilingualism defined? Societally. For example, studies were conducted in which children were classified as bilingual if they had a foreign last name. What was relevant for these researchers was that bilinguals were from certain ethnic backgrounds and were recent immigrants to the United States. We do not know whether the bilinguals in these studies were actually cognitively bilingual or only societally bilingual. It is quite possible that children participating in some of these studies actually were proficient only in their native, non-English language. What these studies suggest to us is that societal bilingualism, being a label in this historical context for individuals who are low on the societal totem pole, can be detrimental to performance on tests of intelligence that are used as the basis for predicting success in the educational system. What they do not suggest is that cognitive bilingualism could be detrimental to the mental development of children, since the extent to which they were cognitively bilingual is uncertain.

Indeed, as we argue in the following section, if we adopt a cognitive definition of bilingualism, as recent studies of bilingualism and cognitive development have done, there emerges a relatively consistent picture of a positive relation. In these studies where bilingualism is defined cognitively rather than societally, the criterion has often been to include only those children who are equally proficient in the two languages.

In general, this shift in definition of bilingualism from a societal to a cognitive one has gone hand in hand with a shift in the type of subject population studied. Earlier studies tended to look at immigrants and minorities in the process of language shift from their native language to English. The more recent studies, though not all, have tended to look at subjects who live in societal circumstances where equal proficiency in two languages is possible and advantageous, such as in Canada, and who tend to come from middle-class populations. Thus, in order to appreciate the full range of studies conducted on the topic of bilingualism and cognitive development, it will become necessary to delve into the societal correlates of different types of bilingualism. First, however, we turn to a fuller consideration of the cognitive perspective.

### Cognitive-level bilingualism

In this section, we review two types of studies conducted strictly at the cognitive level of bilingualism, where subjects are defined in terms of their relative abilities in the two languages rather than on a social or societal basis. The first type of study looks at cognitive performance in balanced bilingual children; the second type relates children's degree of bilingualism to cognitive ability. The section concludes by documenting the present search for a model at the cognitive level that explains how bilingualism might affect the development of children's intelligence.

The concept of the "balanced" bilingual child was conceived by Peal and Lambert (1962) in an attempt to distinguish "pseudobilinguals" from truly bilingual children. In our terminology, they shifted the definition of bilingualism from a societal to a cognitive one. Peal and Lambert were responding to the long history of bilingual research, just described, that failed (from the cognitive perspective) to take into account the actual language proficiency of bilingual samples. In their famous monograph, the investigators argued that, in order to understand the effects of bilingualism on children's intelligence, the first thing that is needed is truly bilingual subjects or, in their new term, a sample of "balanced" bilingual children. Furthermore, they argued that previous negative findings could be attributed to careless sampling procedures, under which subjects' bilingual proficiency was questionable. Several formal definitions of balanced bilingualism have been formulated through the years, some more rigid than others. For the purpose of the present review, we assume the idealization that a balanced bilingual child is a child who can function, age appropriately, in his or her two languages.

When Peal and Lambert compared their sample of French–English balanced bilingual fourth graders with a group of comparable monolinguals on a battery of intelligence tests, the results were surprisingly in favor of the bilingual children. The study had a significant impact on the field, on two different counts. First, the positive findings questioned the validity of a long string of studies that had employed the societal definition of bilingualism and had concluded that bilingualism had a negative influence on a child's language and cognitive development. Second, the study was perceived as a methodological breakthrough. Peal and Lambert's research paradigm (i.e., a comparison of balanced bilinguals with monolinguals, controlling for SES, parental education, years of schooling, and other relevant variables) promised to be a sure way to document empirically what linguists' case studies (e.g., Leopold, 1949; Ronjat, 1913) had been claiming for years. The new paradigm, as evidenced by the studies reviewed below, fulfilled its promise.

In a detailed account of his daughter Hildegard's bilingual upbringing, Leopold

(1949) not only reported adequate language development and minimal confusion between the child's two languages, but also suggested that bilingualism seemed to be an advantage in his daughter's mental development. Leopold noted Hildegard's special objective awareness of language, proposing that bilingual children, forced to make an early separation of word and referent, would develop an early awareness of the abstract and symbolic nature of language. According to Leopold, such awareness would free the child's thinking from the concreteness and "tyranny" of words. At present, such objective awareness of language is commonly referred to as "metalinguistic awareness."

A large number of studies have shown that, when compared with monolinguals, balanced bilingual children show definite advantages in measures of metalinguistic awareness. Ianco-Worrall (1972) showed that children raised bilingually outranked monolinguals in the capacity to compare words along semantic rather than phonetic dimensions. Cummins (1978) found that Irish–English and Ukranian–English bilingual children outperformed monolinguals on several measures of metalinguistic awareness, including the capacity to evaluate tautological and contradictory sentences. More recently, in a study of Spanish–English bilingual children in El Salvador, Galambos (1982) found that bilinguals had a stronger "syntactic orientation" than both English and Spanish monolingual children when judging grammatical and ungrammatical sentences in both languages. Syntactic orientation was defined as the ability "to note errors in constructions, to use syntactic strategies in the correction of these constructions, and to offer syntactically rather than semantically oriented explanations for the ungrammaticality noted" (p. 2).

A study done with Hebrew–English balanced bilingual children (Ben-Zeev, 1977) clearly shows bilinguals' awareness of linguistic rules and structure. The investigator gave children a "symbol substitution" task, measuring children's ability to substitute words in a sentence according to the experimenter's instructions. For example, the children were asked to substitute the word "I" for the word "spaghetti." The children were given correct scores when they were able to say sentences like "Spaghetti am cold" rather than "Spaghetti is cold" or a similar sentence that, although grammatically correct, violated the rules of the game. Basically, in the symbol substitution task, the children were asked to violate the rules of grammar, and hence the task demonstrated their control over the somewhat automatic production of correct sentences. Needless to say, this task required an unusual awareness of and attention to linguistic features and detail. Through their performance on this and other related tasks, the balanced bilingual children showed a greater objective awareness of language than their monolingual peers.

Bialystok (1984; Bialystok & Ryan, 1985) increased the sophistication of the conceptualization of metalinguistic awareness by arguing that the skill consists of two components: access to the knowledge about language, and the ability to control linguistic processes and apply them to a problem situation. She argued that bilingualism would influence the latter, but not the former. To support her point, she demonstrated that bilingual children were superior to monolingual controls specifically on items with anomalous meanings that were nevertheless grammatically correct. Bialystok argued that these items recruited controlled processing of linguistic knowledge, since the subject has to overlook the meaning and focus on the grammatical form. Bialystok further related her findings to the attainment of biliteracy, since of the different groups of bilinguals that she tested, the strongest effect was observed among students who had developed the ability to read in both languages. Presumably, the positive effects of bilingualism are most likely to occur in situations where the use of both languages in the literate, decontextualized functions (Snow, in press) is emphasized.

The paradigm comparing balanced bilingual to monolingual children has also been used to assess bilingual advantage on measures other than metalinguistic awareness. Balanced bilingual children outperform their monolingual peers on measures of concept formation (Bain, 1974; Liedtke & Nelson, 1968), divergent thinking skills and creativity (Torrance, Wu, Gowan, & Alliotti, 1970), and field independence and Piagetian conservation concepts (Duncan & De Avila, 1979) as well as in their capacity to use language to monitor cognitive performance (Bain & Yu, 1980). With unusual consistency, the findings suggest that bilingualism has a positive effect on a child's developing intelligence.

Despite consistent positive findings, the methodology adopted in the studies of balanced bilingual children has been criticized (see Diaz, 1985a; Hakuta & Diaz, 1985; MacNab, 1979). The foremost criticism is that bilingual and monolingual groups are not comparable groups. Children are not randomly assigned to bilingual or monolingual upbringings and, more often than not, childhood bilingualism co-occurs with variations in a wide range of socioeconomic, cultural, educational, and ethnic variables. Regardless of experimenters' efforts to match the groups on relevant variables, good experimental science tells us that cognitive differences between bilinguals and monolinguals could ultimately be explained by differences other than proficiency in a second language. A second criticism of this line of research concerns its exclusive focus on balanced bilingual children. These children are not representative of the majority of children who are exposed to two languages at an early age or who are educated bilingually. The findings, therefore, cannot be generalized to most populations of interest. Finally, the conclusion that bilingualism has a positive effect on children's cognitive development has been criticized because of its gross inference regarding causality. The finding that balanced bilinguals outperform their monolingual peers can also be interpreted in the reverse way: that only the most intelligent children become truly balanced bilinguals. Research comparing balanced bilinguals and monolinguals cannot distinguish between these two alternative explanations. Of course, a third explanation is that other factors are related to both balanced bilingualism and cognitive ability.

### Degree of bilingualism and cognitive ability

A second group of studies, more modest in number than the studies just reviewed, have attempted to deal with current methodological criticisms by studying the effects of bilingualism using a "within-bilingual" design. The effort is directed at relating, within a group of bilingual children, the degree of a child's bilingualism to his or her cognitive abilities. The claim is that, by using a within-bilingual design, a study not only will avoid the bilingual–monolingual comparison, but also will necessarily include children who are nonbalanced bilinguals. In addition, the inclusion of a longitudinal component in some of these studies has allowed for some analysis of the direction of causality between bilingualism and cognitive variables.

In one of the first attempts to use a within-bilingual design for assessing the cognitive effects of childhood bilingualism, Duncan and De Avila (1979) studied children from four Hispanic populations who differed in their relative abilities in English and Spanish. On the basis of their scores on the Language Assessment Scale, the children were assigned to one of five language proficiency groups: proficient bilinguals, partial bilinguals, monolinguals, limited bilinguals, and late language learners, where proficient bilinguals had the highest scores and late language learners the lowest scores in both languages. Subjects were given several tests of cognitive ability, including two measures of field independence and a measure of Piagetian conservation concepts.

Duncan and De Avila reported two major findings. First, proficient bilinguals ranked higher than any other proficiency group on all cognitive measures; second, no differences were found between partial bilinguals, limited bilinguals, and monolinguals on the same measures. Specifically, the data ranked the five proficiency groups in the following order: (1) proficient bilinguals; (2) partial bilinguals, monolinguals, and limited bilinguals; and (3) late language learners.

The investigators pointed out that the lack of a significant difference between partial bilingual, limited bilingual, and monolingual groups brings into question the "usual view of limited-English speaking children as being intellectually inferior to their monolingual peers" (p. 16). In addition, supporting Cummins's (1976) threshold hypothesis, they concluded that, after a certain threshold of proficiency in the two languages, bilingualism is clearly related to positive cognitive gains.

A major problem in interpreting Duncan and De Avila's (1979) data is that the observed rank ordering of proficiency groups could be attributed simply to group differences in intellectual ability or IQ rather than to differences in degree of bilingualism. Since the authors did not control for group differences in a measure of basic ability, it is possible that the proficient bilinguals and the late language learners represent the opposite tails of the IQ distribution. This IQ or basic ability confound, to which within-bilingual designs are vulnerable, was dealt with by Hakuta and Diaz (1985), Diaz and Padilla (1985), and Diaz (1985a) by the use of multiple regression techniques, as explained in the remainder of this section.

The multiple regression approach advocated by the present authors proposes that the effects of bilingualism on cognitive ability can be assessed by estimating the variance explained by second-language proficiency, once the variance explained by first-language ability and other relevant variables (such as age and SES) is partialed out from the analysis. Specifically, the following hierarchical regression equation is proposed for the analysis of the data (the two steps in the regression are separated by a slash),

Cognitive ability = first-language proficiency + age + SES / + second-language proficiency

where the outcome variable is any measure of cognitive ability appropriate for the age of the sample, the measure of first-language proficiency is considered a measure of "basic ability," and the measure of second-language proficiency is entered last in the equation. The claim is that any changes in the variance explained ($R^2$) by the inclusion of second-language proficiency as the last variable in the equation is a good estimate of the effects of bilingualism on a child's cognitive ability.

Three recent studies have taken the multiple regression approach (Diaz, 1985a; Diaz & Padilla, 1985; Hakuta & Diaz, 1985) to examine the effects of bilingualism in preschoolers, kindergarten children, and first-grade children who were, at the time, attending bilingual education programs. The measures of cognitive ability included measures of analogical reasoning, metalinguistic awareness, and visual–spatial skills for kindergarten and first-grade children and measures of classification, story sequencing, and block designs for preschoolers. Overall, the multiple regression analyses indicated significant contributions of second-language proficiency to most of the cognitive abilities measured. As reported by Hakuta and Diaz (1985) and Diaz (1985a) the findings were particularly strong for the effects of bilingualism on the Raven's Progressive Matrices, a commonly used measure of nonverbal intelligence.

Hakuta and Diaz (1985) and Diaz (1985a) reported several analyses of direction of causality between bilingualism and cognitive abilities. The analyses were done on short-term longitudinal data with measures of language proficiency and cognitive ability at two points in time. Even though causality cannot be appropriately determined from correlational data, longitudinal designs allow for an examination of the direction of causality between two sets of variables. Using both multiple regression and path analyses techniques, the authors reported stronger relations between language variables at Time 1 and cognitive variables at Time 2 than vice versa. Recognizing the limitations of their correlational data, the authors argued that, if bilingualism and intelligence are causally related, bilingualism is most likely the causal factor.

Two additional findings, reported in Diaz (1985a), are worth noting. First, in contrast to Cummins's (1976) threshold hypothesis, which predicts positive effects of bilingualism at high levels of second-language attainment, these data suggest that degree of bilingualism may have a stronger effect on cognitive abilities for children who are at the beginning stages of second-language learning. When Diaz (1985a) examined the regression equations for groups of relative high and low second-language proficiency separately, the variance explained by degree of bilingualism was significant and substantial for the low group on most cognitive measures but was weak and nonsignificant for the high group on the same measures. These findings suggest that some effects of bilingualism might occur as a result of the initial struggles and experiences of the beginning second-language learner. This does not rule out the possibility that there are additional effects at the high threshold level.

A second important finding is that groups of high and low second-language proficiency are significantly different on measures of SES, suggesting an SES–bilingualism confound even within a somewhat homogeneous group of Spanish-dominant children who are learning English in the context of bilingual education programs. It is for this reason that SES should be controlled for in the hierarchical regression equation. We address the problem of how to interpret this confound in the section on societal bilingualism.

## A review of explanatory hypotheses

The positive relation between cognitive bilingualism and children's other cognitive abilities is well replicated. Beyond the issue of causality, a major gap in our knowledge is the lack of an explanation for this positive relation. That is, if bilingualism affects children's intelligence, how does it do so? As Diaz (1985b) has suggested, "The gap in our knowledge is due in part to the fact that research has focused mostly on outcome rather than process variables" (p. 19). Such a focus on outcome variables does not clarify such issues as whether bilinguals solve cognitive tasks differently from monolinguals or whether the positive effects are explained by a higher rate of cognitive development fostered by the bilingual experience. Nonetheless, regardless of the scarcity of process data, several hypotheses have been formulated to explain the positive results.

**The code-switching hypothesis.** Code switching refers to the observation that bilinguals can move from one language to the other with relative ease. As an explanatory hypothesis, code switching was proposed first by Peal and Lambert (1962) when explaining their pioneer findings. The investigators believed that the possibility of switching linguistic codes while performing cognitive tasks gave bilingual children a flexibility that monolingual children did not enjoy. In their own words:

[the] hypothesis is that bilinguals may have developed more flexibility in thinking . . . . [B]ilinguals typically acquire experience in switching from one language to another, pos-

sibly trying to solve a problem while thinking in one language and then, when blocked, switching to the other. This habit, if it were developed, could help them in their performance on tests requiring symbolic reorganization since they demand a readiness to drop one hypothesis or concept and try another. (p. 14)

More often than not, errors in cognitive and academic tasks are caused by children's perseveration on the wrong hypothesis. Bilingual code switching might, indeed, facilitate the development of a more flexible "mental set" to approach cognitive tasks (Duncan & De Avila, 1979). Furthermore, when a bilingual child is frustrated or blocked when performing a task verbally, he or she has the option of switching to the second language, starting the problem once again with a fresh and different perspective.

**The objectification hypothesis.** In a large number of studies, bilingual children have shown a special objective awareness of language. The second hypothesis claims that bilinguals' objectification of language is conducive to higher levels of abstract and symbolic thinking.

As suggested by Leopold (1949), bilingual children have two words for each referent and, early on, are forced to realize the conventional nature of language. The separation of word from referent is seen as one of the major milestones in the development of symbolic thinking. Furthermore, as Vygotsky (1962) suggested, since bilinguals could express the same thought in different languages, a bilingual child tends to "see his language as one particular system among many, to view its phenomena under more general categories, and this leads to an awareness of his linguistic operations" (p. 110). In other words, according to this view, learning more than one language leads not only to knowledge of a second language but to a knowledge of "language." Through this objectification process, the hypothesis suggests, children are able to bring their concepts to a higher level of symbolism and abstraction.

**The verbal mediation hypothesis.** Cognitive development in the preschool years is heavily influenced by children's increasing reliance on language as a tool of thought (Luria, 1961; Vygotsky, 1962). The use of language for self-regulatory functions, commonly referred to as "private speech," appears shortly after the onset of social speech and gradually becomes subvocal to constitute inner speech or verbal thinking. The internalization of private speech forms the basis for the capacity to use covert verbal mediation. The origins, development, and internalization of private speech have been documented elsewhere (see, e.g., Frauenglass & Diaz, 1985; Zivin, 1979).

Several investigators (Bain & Yu, 1980; Diaz, 1983; Diaz & Padilla, 1985) have suggested that the unique linguistic experience of bilingualism and the accompanying awareness of language might lead to an increasing reliance on verbal mediation in cognitive tasks. In fact, bilingual advantage on some nonverbal measures (e.g., the Raven's test) has been explained in terms of bilinguals' increasing reliance on covert verbal or linguistic strategies when solving the tasks (Hakuta & Diaz, 1985). It is possible, as the hypothesis suggests, that the bilingual experience and the resulting metalinguistic awareness foster a more efficient and precocious use of language as a tool of thought. Bilinguals' improved performance on so many different tasks could be explained by this efficient reliance on self-regulatory language.

### Evaluating and integrating the models

No single study has tested a model of the process by which bilingualism might affect a child's cognitive development. Nonetheless, the data from several studies can be pooled and integrated, first, to examine the validity of the hypotheses reviewed above and, second, to outline some empirical constraints on the development of an explanatory model of the relation between bilingualism and cognitive ability.

In a study of the self-regulatory private speech of bilingual preschoolers, Diaz and Padilla (1985) reported two major findings that shed light on the verbal mediation and code-switching hypotheses. First, the study reported a positive relation between degree of bilingualism and production of task-relevant private speech utterances. Children in this sample with a relatively higher degree of bilingualism not only emitted more self-regulatory utterances than the other children but also used a higher number of task-relevant language functions such as labeling and description of materials, transitional utterances, guiding, and planning statements. This first finding gives some support to the hypothesis that bilingualism fosters an increased and more efficient reliance on language in cognitive tasks.

The study also examined the patterns of language switching in the private speech protocols. If the code-switching hypothesis were correct, three observations would be expected: (1) Within a given task bilingual children should switch or use more than one language, (2) the incidence of language switching should increase with tasks of increasing difficulty, and (3) the frequency of language switching should be positively related to children's performance on the tasks. The findings, however, supported none of the three predictions. The observed frequency of language switching in private speech was minimal (less than 2%), even for those children who could easily switch languages in social situations. The findings suggest that, at least in bilingual preschoolers, language switching is a social and not an intrapersonal cognitive phenomenon.

To summarize the preceding discussion and review, a process model should take into account the following research findings:

1. Bilinguals show consistent advantages in metalinguistic awareness and in the use of language as a tool of thought.

2. There is no evidence for the suggestion that bilinguals switch languages spontaneously while performing cognitive tasks.
3. If bilingualism affects a child's cognitive development, the effects can occur at
   the beginning stages of second-language learning as well as at the more advanced
   stages of balanced bilingualism.
4. Bilingual environments in which the languages are used for functions that require
   controlled cognitive processing lead to stronger effects on metalinguistic awareness.
5. The positive effects are found in bilingual additive situations (i.e., contexts
   where the second language is acquired without loss of the mother tongue) that
   involve a somewhat systematic use of the two languages.

Taking into consideration present findings on bilingual cognitive development,
we offer the following integrative hypothesis: The systematic exposure to two languages found in bilingual additive situations will give children a unique advantage
in the objectification of language. Such objectification of language, in turn, will
foster an increased and more efficient use of language for self-regulatory functions. These effects will be more pronounced in contexts where the decontextualized functions of language engaged in information-processing tasks, rather than
conversational functions of language, are emphasized.

### Cognitive bilingualism in perspective

To obtain clear answers to cognitive questions, studies must be designed with a
cognitive perspective on bilingualism in mind. However, a selective focus on individual cognitive effects, when properly studied, is made at the expense of losing
contact with social psychological and societal aspects of bilingualism. Remember
that what properly designed cognitive studies attempt to do is to control for societal background characteristics such that the "pure" effects of bilingualism can be
discerned. Searching for such controls may be a futile and unrealistic endeavor.

Researchers concerned with the cognitive effects of bilingualism have often
made methodological points regarding the proper design of studies to answer such
questions. McLaughlin (1984) describes the ideal study as one that would include
the random assignment of children to bilingual and monolingual groups, as well
as longitudinal testing and control of relevant variables, such as intelligence. In
the same book in which McLaughlin's chapter appears, *Early bilingualism and
child development*, Lebrun and Paradis (1984) title their introduction "To be or not
to be an early bilingual?"

Although such experiments and such questions are important to pursue, one
must question their ecological validity. To whom would the findings of a study
with random assignment be applied? To randomly assigned children? A focus on
the social psychological and societal aspects of bilingualism highlights the way in
which bilingualism is distributed in the population in a nonrandom fashion. For
many children, it is not a matter of individual preference whether "to be or not to

be an early bilingual," and in any case, it is not a decision made by families and children on purely cognitive grounds. Moreover, the presence of two languages in an individual's environment may affect a variety of other variables that in turn may be responsible for any cognitive effects. McLaughlin (1984) does point out that the family environments of children raised monolingually are probably different from those of children raised bilingually, and that therefore it is impossible to separate the environmental effects on linguistic and cognitive variables from those of bilingualism itself. MacNab (1979) makes similar points in discussing the limitations of many of the cognitively oriented studies in this area.

In this section, we reviewed constraints on models of the relation between bilingualism and cognitive development and proposed an integrative hypothesis. This is not sufficient, however, because so far we have treated individual-level cognitive bilingualism as the independent variable and have not paid attention to factors associated with the social environment in which bilingual children develop. A more complete model must consider the context of bilingual cognitive development. In the following section, we consider perspectives that take into account the social psychological and societal correlates of bilingualism and then discuss their implications for our models of the relation between bilingualism and cognitive development.

## Social psychological and societal bilingualism

The issues of language and cognition aside, bilingualism has captured the interest of social scientists precisely because of its correlation with social psychological and societal phenomena of interest to them. Ethnographers such as John Gumperz (1982) take interest because of the roles that language plays in regulating social order by serving as a symbol of group identification and societal status. Sociologists such as Joshua Fishman (1971) take interest because language is correlated with the traditional institutional categories of the sociologist, such as the domains of society where language can be used. These other perspectives on bilingualism are important for the student of bilingualism and cognition because they grapple with the question of the determinants of the distribution of bilingualism. Even though we may establish that certain types of cognitive bilingualism are related to mental development, these types of cognitive bilingualism are not characteristics randomly distributed in the population. Bilingualism is rooted in a set of social conditions that lead particular individuals to particular outcomes.

Aside from trying to arrive at a "pure" assessment of the relation between bilingualism and cognition, then, we must consider the conditions under which various types of bilingualism might obtain and how these might be related to the cognitive models elaborated in the previous section. Investigations of the cognitive effects of bilingualism must be accompanied by an investigation of the parameters within which bilingualism occurs. Fishman (1977) makes this point quite well:

My own socio-historical perspective leads me to doubt that answers . . . can be found by better controlled experiments, which in essence, cannot explain shifts in social climate that take place across a decade or more. I would predict that every conceivable relationship between intelligence and bilingualism *could* obtain, and that our task is not so much the determination of whether there is a relationship between the two but of *when* (i.e., in which socio-pedagogical contexts) *which kind* of relationship (positive, negative, strong, weak, independent or not) obtains. (p. 38; emphasis in original)

In one of the early attempts to account for the contradictory findings on the effects of bilingualism, Lambert (1975) proposed a distinction between additive and subtractive bilingualism. The distinction between these terms hinges on the context in which bilingualism develops and thus effectively integrates a social psychological perspective into the question of the effects of bilingualism. The concepts were developed to explain the divergent findings of studies that looked at immigrant or minority children from those looking at majority children in immersion programs. Additive bilingualism is said to occur when an individual acquires a second language at the same time that all abilities in the first language are maintained. In such situations, there is no threat of loss of the first language. This is the type of bilingualism most often seen in situations where children of the dominant ethnolinguistic group in a society learn the minority language at school, such as the case of Anglophones learning French in Canada. It can also be found in situations where the maintenance of language minority children's first language, although societally subordinate, is strongly promoted at school.

Subtractive bilingualism (also termed replacive bilingualism) refers to situations in which the group shifts in the direction of the second language while losing its ethnic language. The language situation of immigrant children is characterized by this type of bilingualism, in which they never fully develop their abilities in their home language while they are instructed at school in a new language, that of the host culture. In this subtractive situation, it is likely that children will be less proficient in each of the two languages than would monoglot native speakers (Cummins, 1984a).

Rather than describing the characteristics of the individual, these terms are better seen as describing the social milieu in which an individual develops his or her language abilities. The effects of each of these types of bilingualism cannot be understood in isolation from an analysis of the environment of the individual. Additive bilingualism occurs when the society values both languages and sees acquisition of the second language as a positive aspect of the child's development. This type of bilingualism occurs in situations where the linguistic and cultural systems represented by the two languages exist in a complementary fashion. In contrast, subtractive bilingualism exists where these two systems are in competition or conflict. Schooling for ethnolinguistic minorities in a society may be available only in a language different from the home language. The society may not value the minority's language, and upward mobility may be possible only when the majority language is acquired. Such acquisition may be associated with a loss of the original home language. More significantly, a social milieu of subtractive bilingualism is likely to be associated with quite different characteristics in terms of home support for language development than an additive situation. In sum, these variant social conditions are seen as leading to different types of individual-level cognitive bilingualism.

Cummins (1976, 1981, 1984a) developed the threshold hypothesis cited earlier in order to explain why these different situations might influence bilingual children's cognitive development. This view explains the effects found in additive and subtractive situations in linguistic and cognitive terms by seeing the development of children's level of proficiency in each language as a variable mediating the cognitive consequences of bilingualism. Different types of social environment in which children acquire language lead to different types of cognitive bilingualism, which in turn affect cognitive development by resulting in different levels of proficiency in each language. What is important about Cummins's theoretical framework is that it explicitly recognizes the way in which linguistic and cognitive development must be understood as occurring within a sociocultural context. It is the differences among these types of societal bilingualism that lead to the variety of cognitive findings.

Also important to know are the conditions that lead to each of these types. By considering bilingualism, or, more precisely, degree and/or type of bilingualism, as a dependent variable, one can ask what social conditions lead to different characterizations of bilingual proficiency, at both the group and the individual level. We first discuss individual-level social psychological variables accounting for bilingualism. Then we discuss group-level factors. In both cases, however, we attempt to look for precursors to individual degree of bilingualism.

### Social psychological perspectives

Robert Gardner (1983) addresses this question from the perspective of social psychological variables at the individual level. Subjects in his research come mostly from the English-speaking parts of Canada and thus are primarily speakers of the majority language learning a second language in a social milieu where there is little contact between the two language groups. Gardner has used primarily paper-and-pencil attitude measures and correlates them with various measures of second-language acquisition.

Gardner accounts for the findings of his many studies through a socioeducational model (based in part on Carroll, 1962, and Lambert, 1967) that emphasizes four elements involved in second-language acquisition: the social milieu of learning, individual difference variables (including attitudes, motivation, and language aptitude), the contexts for language acquisition, and outcomes.

Gardner hypothesizes that the cultural beliefs developed in a particular social milieu influence the development of attitude variables, which include integrative-ness – referring to positive affect toward the other language community – and attitudes toward the learning situation – referring to the individual's evaluative feelings about the learning context. These two types of attitudes, in turn, influence the individual's motivation. The *integrative motive* is the composite of these three variables. This notion of an integrative motive was developed from Lambert's (1967) distinction between an instrumental orientation toward learning a second language – when the language is being learned primarily for utilitarian reasons – and an integrative orientation – when the language is acquired because the individual wants to learn more about the language group or even join it.

Another hypothesis of the model is that motivation and language aptitude, two individual difference variables, interact with the context of language acquisition – formal or informal – to influence the development of language proficiency and the outcomes of second-language acquisition, which include both linguistic and nonlinguistic effects. In formal acquisition contexts, such as classrooms, both aptitude and motivation are seen as being important, whereas in informal contexts, motivation becomes predominant because it affects whether the learner will take advantage of the available opportunities. The outcomes need not be just linguistic – that is, language knowledge and skills – but can also be nonlinguistic – for example, the degree to which the individual wishes to learn more of the language, and his or her attitudes toward the second-language community.

Gardner's model is important because it clearly links cognitive variables to social ones such as attitudes. It addresses some of the complexity inherent in the development of bilingualism by viewing second-language learning as a dynamic process affected by a variety of factors acting on each other.

Unfortunately, however, much of the research supporting Gardner's model has been done only in situations in which language majority children are studying a second language in school. In these contexts, the model has received a good deal of empirical support. As Gardner (1983) points out, little work has been done linking the social milieu to the individual difference variables. Although acknowledged within the model, this connection is left in a general and unelaborated state. When bilingualism is seen from a societal perspective, this is a crucial link to elucidate theoretically in our view. Because Gardner's model has not been tested in situations involving a variety of intergroup conditions, we do not know in what range of contexts it will be valid. An example of its limitations as a tool for understanding the situation of language minority children is that Gardner's model says nothing about the role of the individual's first language. Clearly, this takes on different importance in situations of language minority children learning the dominant language than in situations where majority children are learning a foreign language.

Fred Genesee (1984; Genesee, Rogers, & Holobow, 1983), in attempting to expand Gardner's model to bilingual, cross-cultural contexts by including intergroup factors in the model, has examined the role of the second-language learner's perceptions of motivational support by the target language group. He defines this more explicitly as the "learner's beliefs or expectations that his/her motives for learning a second language are supported by the target language group" (Genesee, 1984, p. 347). Genesee et al. (1983) studied English Canadians learning French. They found that motivational support predicted second-language learning independently of self-motivation. In other words, those students who thought that French Canadians wanted them to learn French showed greater French proficiency and expressed more willingness to interact with French Canadians than did other students.

In a different context, such as that of Spanish-speaking minority children learning English in the United States, motivational support may have a different quality. It may represent a more negative force; for example, those who feel that Anglos' attitudes toward Hispanics are uninfluenced by their English proficiency may not learn English as well as those who do not hold this belief. This raises a number of complexities, however, that will be more fully addressed in our discussion of Howard Giles's work below.

An important issue in applying Gardner's theory to different language-learning situations is that of variance on the variables included in the model. Gardner (1979) found, for example, that there were higher correlations between language achievement and both motivation and language aptitude in monolingual than in bilingual communities. This led him to suggest that the second-language-learning process may differ in these two types of communities or for language majority and minority group members. This may be the case, for example, if there is much more room for variability on the variables in the model for language majority members than for language minority members, in particular in situations where clear social policies exist that shape the educational environments of children who do not come from homes where the dominant language is spoken.

In spite of its limitations as a complete model for understanding what leads to different types of bilingualism, Gardner's theory is useful for understanding how particular contexts may influence the way children learn at the individual level. The theory clearly brings in social causes for cognitive effects and can serve as a link with more macrolevel theories. Indeed, one way in which the model can be elaborated is in terms of the way various cultural beliefs may come about and influence attitudes and motivations.

So far, we have looked at theories that address, from the perspective of the individual, how various social contexts might lead to different levels of bilingual proficiency. We can elevate the question of social context to the level of groups by exploring how the pattern of intergroup relations and individuals' beliefs about them and about their own social identity can affect language acquisition and proficiency as well as cognitive performance. At this point, we bring in theoretical perspectives that include concepts of the individual as a group member and consider how these might shed light on the development of different types of bilingualism.

## Societal perspectives

When we use such concepts as "ethnolinguistic vitality" (Giles, Bourhis, & Taylor, 1977) and "diglossia" (Ferguson, 1959; Fishman, 1971) as they relate to bilingualism, we are no longer speaking of individual-level variation, but rather bilingualism found in the group as a whole. Earlier, we described one particularly useful societal concept – the distinction between additive and subtractive bilingualism proposed by Lambert (1975) – used in accounting for different findings among the studies of bilingualism and intelligence. What leads to these different situations is best analyzed from the societal level, since the concept is most meaningful in terms of group, rather than individual, bilingualism.

The dynamics of societies in which bilingualism exists is usefully described by theories that have been developed to discuss interethnic relations. One of the most frequent situations in which bilingualism has been described is that of language minorities learning the language of the dominant societal group. Christina Bratt Paulston (1980; Paulston & Paulston, 1980) has effectively applied Schermerhorn's (1970) group conflict theory to this kind of bilingualism. She describes the societal conditions that are likely to lead to group bilingualism – in particular the role of different types of interethnic contact – and the role that language plays in the maintenance of boundaries among ethnic groups.

Paulston's analysis highlights the role of power in a society and of the possibilities available to ethnic minorities to become integrated into the dominant group. She points out, for example, that in the United States, when job opportunities have been available that require learning English, minority groups have done so. When these opportunities have not been available, members of these groups have been less likely to learn English. Maintenance of the mother tongue is also seen as being dependent on its role for the group, and this in turn is affected by the group's relationship to other groups in the society. For example, the dominant group may expect assimilation of the subordinate groups. The latter groups may differ as to whether they agree with this goal. In the case of conflict, maintenance of the mother tongue then becomes a symbolic way of resisting assimilation and maintaining a distinctive identity.

Important here is how the contact originated – for example, whether the minority group in question is an indigenous or an immigrant group. Under conditions of interethnic contact, dominant groups, whether subordinate or superordinate, are likely to maintain their mother tongue (Lieberson, Dalto, & Johnston, 1975), whether or not they learn a new one. Among subordinate groups, however, indigenous peoples are more likely than immigrants to resist a rapid shift in mother tongue. Examples of such groups in the United States are Puerto Ricans, Chicanos, and native Americans, all living in areas annexed or colonized by the United States. Lieberson et al. (1975) show how these and other indigenous groups, such as French-speaking whites in Louisiana, evidence a much slower rate of language shift than immigrant populations. Paulston attributes this to the degree of resistance to assimilation.

Thus, from this perspective, language is an important symbol in the intergroup dynamics within a society. Paulston examines this issue from a sociological perspective, considering groups as the units of analysis. Also important is a consideration of individuals within these groups. Giles and his colleagues have proposed an intergroup theory of second-language acquisition that accounts for the development of proficiency in the dominant language by members of ethnolinguistic minorities, using as explanatory constructs social psychological concepts derived from ethnolinguistic identity theory (Ball, Giles, & Hewstone, 1984; Giles et al., 1977; Giles & Byrne, 1982; Giles & Johnson, 1981) and from social identity theory (Tajfel, 1978; Tajfel & Turner, 1986). This theoretical perspective is useful for understanding the intergroup factors that may affect individual language behavior and outcomes.

The basis for the intergroup model of second-language acquisition is ethnolinguistic identity theory (Ball et al., 1984; Giles & Johnson, 1981). This theory makes predictions about the conditions under which individuals will perceive language as an important aspect of their social identity and will attempt to attain "positive psycholinguistic differentiation from outgroups" (Ball et al., 1984, p. 674). Individuals' group memberships form an important part of their social identity, which can be positive or negative depending on how one perceives one's own group status relative to that of other groups (Tajfel & Turner, 1986). In this view, people are motivated to develop a positive social identity by comparing themselves favorably to outgroups. In many cases, language can become a salient dimension for comparison and thus a source of either favorable or unfavorable social identity.

When individuals experience a "negative ethnic identity," they may respond with various intergroup strategies designed to recover a positive sense of their social self (Ball et al., 1984; Tajfel, 1981; Tajfel & Turner, 1986). These include individual mobility (trying to "pass," which can result linguistically in a loss of ingroup speech markers), social creativity (the redefinition of ingroup–outgroup comparisons, which can result in the upgrading of the status of an ingroup language or dialect or the creation of new ones), and social competition (which can result in overt intergroup conflict). Each of the strategies used by members of a subordinate group in a community or society may be countered by members of the dominant group; for example, new ingroup linguistic markers could be invented to keep the outgroup out (see Giles & Johnson 1981).

The theory proposes that to the extent that language is a salient dimension for intergroup comparisons, which is most likely in interethnic contexts, it will be a focus of the intergroup strategies used by individuals. In these situations "accentuation or attenuation of ingroup speech markers" (Ball et al., 1984, p. 674) would be expected. Ball et al. (1984, pp. 674–5) give five conditions under which people will attempt to distinguish themselves from outgroups on the basis of language:

1. When, as members of a group, they identify language as an important dimension of the group's identity
2. When they regard their group's relative status as changeable and attribute the cause of their relative social status to advantages taken unfairly by the outgroup
3. When they perceive their ingroup's ethnolinguistic vitality to be high
4. When they perceive intergroup boundaries to be firm
5. When they identify with few other social groups and/or with ones that offer only unfavorable social comparisons

The reverse of these conditions is proposed to lead to attempts to become assimilated into the outgroup and to attrition of the ingroup language.

Ball et al. (1984) use these propositions to construct a model that predicts when members of a subordinate group will acquire native-like proficiency in the dominant language. They distinguish between subgroups of the language minority to whom the above propositions do and do not apply. For the first group, who are predicted to experience fear of assimilation and to avoid informal learning contexts, the model predicts that intelligence and aptitude are important predictors of proficiency. In contrast, for the second group, who have integrative motivation and do seek out informal learning contexts, proficiency is predicted to be more related to factors such as anxiety in situations of second-language use. Clearly, the behavior of the outgroup in reaction to the changes in language proficiency among minority group members becomes important in predicting subsequent perceptions and interactions, although this factor does not play a key role in the model.

Ball et al. also attempt to account for the large group of "intermediates," those individuals who do not fit clearly into either of the above subgroups. They use mathematical catastrophe theory to develop a cusp model of second-language acquisition that predicts motivation primarily from the perceived vitality of the learner's first language and the perceived firmness of the intergroup boundaries between the language groups. Individuals who consider their own language to be low in vitality will exhibit motivation to learn the outgroup language as a monotonic function of the perceived mutability of the intergroup boundary.

When the group language vitality is perceived to be high, however, a different relation is predicted. For high and low perceived boundary firmness, the lowest and highest motivation levels, respectively, are predicted. For intermediate firmness, however, a bimodal distribution is predicted – in other words, learners are predicted to polarize in terms of their motivation, so that some will have quite integrative motives and others will not be very willing learners and will fear loss of identity. This situation is one in which learners do not consider their own language to be in any danger of loss and thus must assess likely reactions to their acquisition of the outgroup language. If the intergroup boundaries are perceived to be permeable, but not easily so, learners could go either way, as it were. They could decide that the outgroup will not accept them anyway, so that there is no reason to bother with the second language, or they could decide that, with some effort, intergroup barriers could be overcome, and therefore it is worth "investing" in second-language learning.

Three features of the work of Giles and his colleagues make it important in the context of this chapter. First, in considering the social psychological variables that affect whether particular individuals will acquire a second language and the level of proficiency with which they will do so, Giles and his co-workers explicitly recognize the extent to which language serves as a marker of group membership and social identity. Their model focuses on the functions of language in its important symbolic and practical role in the formation and maintenance of ethnic identity.

Second, the model attempts to account for individual behavior *within* an ethnic group. The theory successfully integrates group- and intergroup-level concepts with an analysis of the social psychological variables likely to affect an individual's behavior. The question asked by Giles and Johnson (1981) is, "Who in an ethnic group uses which language strategies, when and why?" (p. 214). In terms of attempting to account for cognitive data, conceptualized and measured at the level of the individual, it is important to make such a theoretical link between sociological models that make predictions for whole groups or subgroups and purely individual-level accounts that do not consider the importance of language in the context of society and intergroup relations. In this model the individual is primarily a group member.

Third, the model developed by Giles and Byrne (1982) and Ball et al. (1984) is formulated in such a way that it is testable in a broad range of situations. Its basic concepts are applicable to a variety of ethnic groups and to different types of "language," including dialects. In a sense, this aspect of the model is also a shortcoming in the current context, because what Giles and his colleagues are attempting to describe is not a process of acquiring language proficiency in the way we described it earlier. Rather, they describe the way in which language acquisition and use may be one of the means by which group members seek to enhance their social identity. This process then can be seen to have important effects on the ultimate level of proficiency in one or both languages. Nevertheless, the model is useful because it is a tool for understanding both within-group variance and between-group differences.

What are the model's implications for the present discussion? The intergroup theory of second-language acquisition is a dynamic model that effectively links individual-, group-, and intergroup-level factors in predicting individual bilingualism. Although it does so only in situations of language minority individuals acquiring the dominant language in their community, the theory serves as an example of the way various levels of analysis can be combined within one predictive framework. The theory also helps to highlight how bilingualism reflects more than cognitive capacities and consists of more than a cognitive phenomenon. Its development is a function of intergroup situations, which themselves can vary even within a group.

The model is not without shortcomings for our purposes, however. The major weakness is that perceptions of the group's linguistic vitality are not linked to the individual or the group's actual language proficiency. Moreover, the model does not distinguish between dialect differences or ethnic language markers and language proficiency in the terms we discussed earlier. When one is attempting to link intergroup variables that predict bilingualism to its cognitive effects, the cognitive functions of what is learned become much more important.

Not much consideration is given, either, to what happens to the learner's first language, for example, as a result of experiences with the second language and the second-language group. In terms of accounting for cognitive effects of bilingualism, the use and maintenance of the first language and what factors may predict this are quite important. As it currently stands, the Ball et al. model includes first-language proficiency only as it relates to the perceived vitality of the first language. It would also be useful to know how various conditions of second-language acquisition affect learning of the first language. This is especially important in dealing with children, who are at a stage of acquisition in *both* languages.

Despite the shortcomings, as well as the desirability of further empirical illumination of the complexities addressed by the intergroup theories, the student of bilingualism and cognitive development should pay serious attention to the social psychological and societal perspectives. The models explored here begin to help us better understand the larger shifts that have occurred in research in the course of history and to gain a handle on macrolevel determinants of the types of cognitive bilingualism evidenced in different subject populations.

## Research directions

It should be evident from the discussion in this chapter that the study of the relation of bilingualism and cognitive development is in many ways a vortex of classic questions about the nature of language, mind, and society. A complete understanding of the problem must come through a multilayered analysis that considers historical, linguistic, cognitive, social psychological, and sociological perspectives.

In an area as complicated as this one, it is easy to lose sight of the forest for the trees. Each level of analysis has its own set of puzzles that are inherently interesting. Thus, it would be useful to summarize the set of tension points in the area of bilingualism and cognitive development that any reasonably complete model should address.

The first point has to do with the degree of bilingualism of the individuals who are labeled "bilingual." Our historical analysis revealed that different conclusions could be made depending on who constituted the subject population. Nonbalanced bilinguals did not fare as well as monolingual counterparts. In contrast, balanced bilinguals were superior to monolinguals. Although considerable additional research has to be conducted in this area, for example, to determine whether the initial phases or the more developed phases of bilingualism have an impact on cognitive development, it is clear that degree of bilingualism must be included in any model purporting to account for the relation between bilingualism and cognition.

Second, in any description of bilingualism, one must distinguish among the functions to which the languages of the bilingual are put to use. Particularly interesting is the distinction between decontextualized language (used for academic and cognitively demanding tasks) and contextualized language (used for social interactional tasks) skills (e.g., Cummins, 1984b; Snow, in press). Presumably, the development of a second language that can be used for decontextualized skills should be distinguished from a second language developed primarily for conversational uses. Similarly, the dichotomy can also be applied to maintenance of the native language. Our discussion of possible explanatory cognitive developmental models suggested that an important link may be the extent to which bilingualism develops an objective awareness of language, followed by the efficient use of language for self-regulatory functions, including academic tasks. One might then speculate that bilingualism in which the use of language for cognitive functions is emphasized (i.e., decontextualized language skills) would lead to more cognitive effects than that developed with an emphasis on contextualized use.

The third point is that the functions of language use can be related to different variables, as suggested by Gardner's (1979, 1983) research. His social psychological approach revealed that aptitude and basic intelligence predicted language performance in formal contexts, whereas attitudes and motivational variables predicted the use of language in informal settings. It seems reasonable to hypothesize that language use in the informal context would tend to be of the contextualized variety, whereas the formal context would call for greater recruitment of decontextualized language. If so, one might speculate that attitudinal and social psychological factors, since they are more directly related to contextualized language, would have a less direct bearing on cognitive development than would basic aptitude factors that are related to decontextualized language skills.

A fourth point is the importance of what happens to the native language in the process of second-language acquisition – whether it is maintained or devitalized. At the individual level, this question is equivalent to the question of the degree of bilingualism mentioned earlier. Depending on the extent to which the native language is maintained or developed, individuals may become balanced or unbalanced bilinguals. At the group level, the vitality of the native language in the group as a whole when in contact with another language determines whether the bilingualism is additive or subtractive (Lambert, 1975). In general, positive effects of bilingualism are reported in additive settings (which usually consist of language majority children learning the minority language) and negative effects in subtractive ones (consisting mainly of minority children learning the majority language at the expense of their mother tongue). This variable presents an interesting question for future research with respect to the factor of individual degree of bilingualism. Presumably, one could compare subjects who are equivalent in their linguistic proficiencies in two languages but differ in the social circumstances that led them to these proficiencies.

A fifth point is the need to understand bilingualism and cognitive development in the context of intergroup relations. Language and bilingualism can serve as the societal symbols around which ethnic politics are enacted, both at the individual and group levels. Work in this area has suggested the importance of the role of language as a marker of group membership. Even in cases in which the use of language for symbolic purposes has no direct bearing on the cognitive development of bilingual children, it is important to the extent that language politics affect the types of social and educational environments in which children develop or fail to develop their two languages. A salient example here is the policy of bilingual education in the United States, in which the debate over the feasibility of the program is clearly an argument over control of the educational system (Paulston, 1980). Such societal processes affect the ways in which group members perceive their own language, the way in which deviation of an individual group member from group norms is perceived by other members of the group, and the extent to which the group maintains its bilingualism or shifts toward monolingualism. These, in turn, will influence the extent to which individual children maintain or lose their native language while acquiring English.

These tension points are not meant to be presented as orthogonal factors. Indeed, the challenge they pose for the researcher is that they are highly interrelated. For example, balanced bilingualism is generally found in majority groups who hold considerable political power and who have access to school resources that make possible the rapid development of decontextualized uses of both languages. And generally, minority groups have difficulty gaining access to the educational system in such a way that their native-language development can be fostered, which would result in an additive bilingual setting that would in turn produce balanced bilingual children.

What should be clear from this broad picture of the major tension points in the literature on bilingualism and cognitive development is that the seemingly straightforward question concerning the effect of bilingualism on cognitive development actually raises questions of considerable complexity. For example, how is bilingualism accompanied by the full decontextualized functions of both languages different from bilingualism in which only the oral and contextualized uses of the native language are maintained? In turn, how are these differences related to social psychological variables and the societal institutions that support them? One can also ask questions about the interactions among levels of analysis in order to identify the appropriate loci for theorizing. For example, *within* bilingual environments defined as additive or subtractive, how is the individual child's level of maintenance of the native language related to cognitive development?

The complexity of such questions is a mixed blessing. On the one hand, it may lead to frustration with a problem that eludes simple empirical formulations. On the other hand, because of the juxtaposition of the variety of issues that have dominated the study of language, mind, and society, there is fertile ground for the desegregation of specializations and subsequent enrichment of each (Hakuta, in press). In our own research in New Haven, we have experienced both aspects of this blessing, and it would seem fit to conclude the chapter with an account of our experience in order to illustrate the intricate dimensions of the problem and to point out directions for future research.

### The case of New Haven

We began our research with the Puerto Rican Spanish–English bilingual students in New Haven with the specific motivation of conducting a pure assessment of cognitive bilingualism, uncontaminated by extraneous societal factors associated with bilingualism (Hakuta & Diaz, 1985). Specifically, we reasoned that the assessment of variation *within* a group of students becoming bilingual would provide a more uncontaminated evaluation than the traditional comparisons of bilinguals and monolinguals.

We found our ideal subject population in the bilingual education program in the New Haven public schools. This program, like most bilingual programs currently implemented in the United States, is a transitional program the goal of which is to move students into English-only mainstream classes as quickly as possible. Once the students are out of the program, they no longer receive instruction in Spanish, but while they are in the program, their native language is well supported through instruction in the basic skills. Thus, as the students go through the program, they add the second language, English, while maintaining Spanish. We reasoned that the situation, minimally, simulates additive bilingualism.

Indeed, within the group, as we described in the cognitive section of this chapter, degree of bilingualism correlated significantly with performance on both verbal and nonverbal measures of cognitive performance, thereby supporting the findings of previous studies that used between-group comparisons. Furthermore, there were some indications that the direction of causality went from bilingualism to cognitive ability rather than in the other direction.

In the strictly cognitive domain, then, we found reason to develop explicit models explaining why bilingualism might have positive effects on cognitive performance. One of us (Diaz) independently pursued research to test several alternative hypotheses, as described above. At this purely cognitive level, there are several directions for future research that would clarify, develop, and test a model explaining how bilingualism might affect children's cognitive development.

One suggestion derives from the observation that the effects of bilingualism are likely to occur even during the initial period when children are exposed to the second language, at least in an additive context. If true, this calls for a detailed ethnographic description of the processes and events (at both the social and intrapersonal levels) that characterize the beginning stages of second-language learning.

Another direction comes from the observation that, in speaking of cognitive development, we are dealing with a complex relation between different kinds of knowledge and acquired skills. For example, metalinguistic awareness is a multidimensional construct for which we will require a more detailed description (Bialystok & Ryan, 1985), especially as it relates to the bilingual experience.

Finally, the integrative hypothesis entertained at the end of the cognitive section assumed that the objectification of language is a function of its systematic use in a social situation including the engagement of language for problem solving. This claim should be made in the context of a theory that specifies the relation between interpersonal and intrapersonal variables. For example, how are the uses of language in the social exchange incorporated into the child's own system of self-regulation? In this context, Soviet developmental theory, as represented in the work of Luria (1961) and Vygotsky (1962), can provide a useful framework.

In our New Haven sample, the attempt to evaluate the effects of pure cognitive-level bilingualism rapidly led us to consider the societal aspects of bilingualism as well (Ferdman & Hakuta, 1985a, 1985b). We undertook the study of societal-level bilingualism in New Haven in part because we were frequently asked why we did not compare our sample of students in the bilingual program with other Hispanic students who were not in the program. We did not do so because we knew from the characteristics of the bilingual program and from our informal observations of the community in general that the program drew from a different segment of the Hispanic community than did the regular mainstream program. That is, we strongly suspected the existence of demographic differences within the Hispanic community between those in bilingual and those in mainstream programs. We saw no reason to compare these groups on our cognitive measures because, even if differences emerged, we would not be able to interpret them in terms of cognitive hypotheses.

Nevertheless, we were moved to describe our subject population in terms of their group characteristics. How they differed from the rest of the Puerto Rican community in New Haven became the question of interest. We felt that such a demographic picture would set the limits on the generalizability of our cognitive study. In order to gain an understanding of the social psychological and societal factors related to bilingualism in New Haven, we thus conducted a large-scale survey of the home backgrounds of all elementary school Hispanic children in the

New Haven public schools. In cooperation with the school system, we sent out questionnaires to the parents (heads of household) of all Hispanic students in the schools that covered their backgrounds and their home environment, focusing on language.

Within our New Haven population, we found clear home background differences between students in the bilingual program (i.e., those who were subjects in our studies) and those in the English-only, mainstream classes. The program status of the children was associated (in the predictable directions) with a series of social and demographic variables. These included the parent's birthplace, length of residence in the U.S. mainland, whether the parent was educated primarily on the mainland or in Puerto Rico, the parent's employment status, the frequency of moves in the past 5 years, plans for a future move, and where that move would take the family. Also varying as a function of program status were language variables: the language in which the questionnaire was filled out, the parent's self-reported English proficiency, the language used by adults and children at home, the number of English and Spanish books and periodicals in the home, the parent's assessment of the child's ability in English compared with that in Spanish, and the parent's judgment of the extent of the child's difficulties in Spanish. In general, the demographic survey suggested that, in the community of Puerto Ricans in New Haven, the bilingual program – in which we had obtained our cognitive results – recruited students from the lower end of the socioeconomic scale (in terms of employment, parent education, and residential mobility). Their homes were also the ones most strongly oriented toward Spanish.

The survey also revealed that the bilingualism in the community as a whole can be characterized as subtractive. Indicators of English and Spanish in the home were negatively related with one another. Furthermore, length of residence on the mainland was positively associated with English and negatively with Spanish. However, there were strong indications that the use of Spanish in the home continues to be maintained by a large proportion of the entire Puerto Rican community. For example, 88% of all students reportedly use some Spanish at home. Even among parents born on the mainland, two-thirds reported both English and Spanish use by children at home. Thus, the case can be made that there is some maintenance of Spanish in this community, even among long-term residents.

However, in thinking about these indications of Spanish maintenance together with an overall subtractive situation, we have found the distinction between contextualized and decontextualized language use to be helpful. Some support for this distinction can be found in our data. Parents' level of education was a good predictor of their self-reported proficiency in English (controlling for whether they were educated on the mainland or in Puerto Rico). We take this to be an indication that at least part of the variation in level of English has to do with "aptitude" or academic-type language. For Spanish, however, we do not have the same indication. We found that level of education was correlated with both the number of English and Spanish books in the home and the number of English periodicals, but not with the number of Spanish periodicals. The implication is that at least some of the Spanish use, that related to which newspapers are read, for example, may have to do, not with variation in academic language, but rather with the extent of social identification with Puerto Rican culture.

A slightly more detailed look into choice of newspapers is in order here to illustrate the importance of social psychological dimensions within the societal context. Two newspapers are commonly read in this community: *El Vocero*, a Puerto Rican Spanish-language daily available in New Haven, and *The New Haven Register*, the local English paper. We found that which paper respondents reported reading was clearly related to English proficiency. On average, the higher their self-reported English proficiency, the more likely they were to read the *Register* rather than *El Vocero*.

However, English proficiency was by no means the only determinant of choice of newspaper. How can we account for individual variation within particular levels of English proficiency? Why do some people read only the English paper, whereas others read both the English and Spanish, and others only the Spanish? This may have to do with the kinds of variables contained in social psychological models: for example, orientation toward Puerto Rico versus the mainland. We explored this possibility by analyzing responses on the questionnaire to the question of whether the respondents planned to move back to Puerto Rico.

At the low levels of English proficiency, whether respondents planned to move back to Puerto Rico or not was not related to newspaper choice. At an intermediate level, however, it made a large difference. In this group, 62% of those who said they would move to Puerto Rico read *El Vocero*. Only 31% of those who planned to stay in New Haven read *El Vocero*. Thus, within a given proficiency level of English, the individual social psychological orientation seems to have made a difference in the choice of newspaper.

If our cognitive, social psychological, and societal analysis of the New Haven situation is correct, the following overall picture might be drawn. The Puerto Rican community can be characterized as losing Spanish for decontextualized, academic functions, while maintaining Spanish for use in face-to-face communicative situations. It would appear that level of maintenance of Spanish for conversational use would be related to the social psychological functions of language, including the establishment of individual social identity, long-term plans about where to take up residence, and attitudes toward one's own group. Loss of the decontextualized functions, however, may be more related to group- and societal-level functions, including the availability of programs to maintain Spanish in the public schools. Currently, for example, Spanish is not offered in the public schools in the elementary grade levels, even though the students maintain spoken Spanish at home.

The bilingual education program seems to afford some level of maintenance of the native language while students are in it. Students in the program are in a temporary milieu of additive bilingualism, at least until they are placed in mainstream classrooms. They learn to use Spanish for decontextualized tasks in addition to contextualized ones. There is evidence that, while the students are in this environment, bilingualism has some positive effects on their cognitive ability. However, it is not clear how long these effects might last, since the children's Spanish undergoes attrition as soon as they leave the program.

As we came to an understanding of the bilingual population that we had originally defined in strictly cognitive terms (i.e., in terms of their degree of bilingualism), we became increasingly aware that we were describing only one part of the relation between bilingualism and cognitive development. We had been whittling down the concept of bilingualism using purely cognitive criteria, attempting to remove as much of the societal context as possible. However, social psychological and societal concerns began creeping in even as we tried to define a supposedly individual cognitive variable, such as degree of bilingualism.

The proper understanding of cognitive development in bilingual children can be obtained only through a thorough knowledge of the way language proficiencies in both languages interact with the variables that cut across cognitive, social psychological, societal, and even historical levels of analysis. In that sense, the study of bilingualism and cognitive development is a microcosm of issues that pervade our attempts to understand the relation between mind, language, and society.

### References

Ayres, L. P. (1909). *Laggards in our schools*. New York: Russell Sage Foundation.

Bain, B. (1974). Bilingualism and cognition: Toward a general theory. In S. T. Carey (Ed.), *Bilingualism, biculturalism, and education: Proceedings from the Conference at College Universitaire Saint Jean* (pp. 119–28). Edmonton: University of Alberta.

Bain, B., & Yu, A. (1980). Cognitive consequences of raising children bilingually: 'One parent, one language.' *Canadian Journal of Psychology, 34*, 304–13.

Ball, P., Giles, H., & Hewstone, M. (1984). Second language acquisition: The intergroup theory with catastrophic dimensions. In H. Tajfel (Ed.), *The social dimension: European developments in social psychology* (pp. 668–94). Cambridge University Press.

Ben-Zeev, S. (1977). The influence of bilingualism on cognitive strategy and cognitive development. *Child Development, 48*, 1009–18.

Bialystok, E. (1984, November). *Influences of bilingualism on metalinguistic development*. Paper presented at the National Reading Conference Meeting, St. Petersburg, FL.

Bialystok, E., & Ryan, E. B. (1985). Towards a definition of metalinguistic skill. *Merrill-Palmer Quarterly, 31*, 229–51.

Brigham, C. C. (1922). *A study of American intelligence*. Princeton, NJ: Princeton University Press.

Carroll, J. B. (1962). The prediction of success in intensive foreign language training. In R. Glaser (Ed.), *Training research and education* (pp. 87–136). Pittsburgh, PA: Pittsburgh Press.

Cummins, J. (1976). The influence of bilingualism on cognitive growth: A synthesis of research findings and explanatory hypothesis. *Working Papers on Bilingualism, 9*, 1–43.

Cummins, J. (1978). Metalinguistic development of children in bilingual education programs: Data from Irish and Canadian Ukrainian–English programs. In M. Paradis (Ed.), *The Fourth Lacus Forum 1977* (pp. 127–38). Columbia, SC: Hornbeam Press.

Cummins, J. (1981). The role of primary language development in promoting educational success for language minority students. In California State Department of Education, *Schooling and language minority students: A theoretical framework* (pp. 3–49). Los Angeles: California State University, Evaluation, Dissemination and Assessment Center.

Cummins, J. (1984a). *Bilingualism and special education: Issues in assessment and pedagogy*. San Diego: College-Hill Press.

Cummins, J. (1984b). Linguistic interdependence among Japanese and Vietnamese immigrant children. In C. Rivera (Ed.), *The measurement of communicative proficiency: Models and applications* (pp. 32–65). Washington, DC: Center for Applied Linguistics.

Darsie, M. L. (1926). The mental capacity of American-born Japanese children. *Comparative Psychology Monographs, 3*(15), 1–89.

Diaz, R. M. (1983). Thought and two languages: The impact of bilingualism on cognitive development. *Review of Research in Education, 10*, 23–54.

Diaz, R. M. (1985a). Bilingual cognitive development: Addressing three gaps in current research. *Child Development, 56*, 1376–88.

Diaz, R. M. (1985b). The intellectual power of bilingualism. *Quarterly Newsletter of the Laboratory of Comparative Human Cognition, 7*, 16–22.

Diaz, R. M., & Padilla, K. (1985, April). *The self-regulatory speech of bilingual preschoolers*. Paper presented at the 1985 meetings of the Society for Research in Child Development, Toronto.

Duncan, S. E., & De Avila, E. A. (1979). Bilingualism and cognition: Some recent findings. *NABE Journal, 4*, 15–50.

Ferdman, B. M., & Hakuta, K. (1985a, April). *A population perspective on bilingualism in Puerto Rican children*. Paper presented at the 1985 meetings of the Society for Research in Child Development, Toronto.

Ferdman, B. M., & Hakuta, K. (1985b, August). *Group and individual bilingualism in an ethnic minority*. Paper presented at the American Psychological Association, Los Angeles.

Ferguson, C. A. (1959). Diglossia. *Word, 15*, 325–40.

Fishman, J. A. (1971). Societal bilingualism: Stable and transitional. In J. A. Fishman, R. L. Cooper, & R. Ma (Eds.), *Bilingualism in the barrio* (pp. 539–55). Bloomington: Indiana University Press, 1971.

Fishman, J. A. (1977). The social science perspective. In *Bilingual education – Current perspectives: Vol. 1. Social science* (pp. 1–49). Arlington, VA: Center for Applied Linguistics.

Frauenglass, M., & Diaz, R. M. (1985). Self-regulatory functions of children's private speech: A critical analysis of recent challenges to Vygotsky's theory. *Developmental Psychology, 21*, 357–64.

Galambos, S. (1982, October). *The development of metalinguistic awareness in bilingual and monolingual children*. Paper presented at the Seventh Annual Boston University Conference on Language Development, Boston.

Gardner, R. C. (1979). Social psychological aspects of second language acquisition. In H.

Giles & R. St. Clair (Eds.), *Language and social psychology* (pp. 193–220). Oxford: Blackwell.

Gardner, R. C. (1983). Learning another language: A true social psychological experiment. *Journal of Language and Social Psychology*, *2*, 219–39.

Genesee, F. (1984). Beyond bilingualism: Social psychological studies of French immersion programs in Canada. *Canadian Journal of Behavioral Science*, *16*, 338–52.

Genesee, F., Rogers, P., & Holobow, N. (1983). The social psychology of second language learning: Another point of view. *Language Learning*, *33*, 209–24.

Giles, H., Bourhis, R. Y., & Taylor, D. M. (1977). Towards a theory of language in ethnic group relations. In H. Giles (Ed.), *Language, ethnicity and intergroup relations* (pp. 387–444). New York: Academic Press.

Giles, H., & Byrne, J. L. (1982). An intergroup approach to second language acquisition. *Journal of Multilingual and Multicultural Development*, *3*, 17–40.

Giles, H., & Johnson, P. (1981). The role of language in ethnic group relations. In J. C. Turner & H. Giles (Eds.), *Intergroup behavior* (pp. 199–241). Oxford: Blackwell.

Goodenough, F. (1926). Racial differences in the intelligence of school children. *Journal of Experimental Psychology*, *9*, 388–97.

Gould, S. J. (1981). *The mismeasure of man*. New York: Norton.

Gumperz, J. J. (1982). *Discourse strategies*. Cambridge University Press.

Hakuta, K. (1986). *Mirror of language: The debate on bilingualism*. New York: Basic Books.

Hakuta, K. (in press). Why bilinguals? In F. Kessel (Ed.), *The development of language and language researchers (essays presented to Roger Brown)*. Hillsdale, NJ: Erlbaum.

Hakuta, K., & Diaz, R. M. (1985). The relationship between bilingualism and cognitive ability: A critical discussion and some new longitudinal data. In K. E. Nelson (Ed.), *Children's language* (Vol. 5, pp. 319–44). Hillsdale, NJ: Erlbaum.

Ianco-Worrall, A. (1972). Bilingualism and cognitive development. *Child Development*, *43*, 1390–1400.

Jensen, A. R. (1980). *Bias in mental testing*. New York: Free Press.

Lambert, W. E. (1967). A social psychology of bilingualism. *Journal of Social Issues*, *23*, 91–109.

Lambert, W. E. (1975). Culture and language as factors in learning and education. In A. Wolfgang (Ed.), *Education of immigrant students* (pp. 55–83). Toronto: Ontario Institute for Studies in Education.

Lebrun, Y., & Paradis, M. (1984). To be or not to be an early bilingual? In M. Paradis & Y. Lebrun (Eds.), *Early bilingualism and child development* (pp. 9–18). Lisse, The Netherlands: Swets & Zeitlinger.

Leopold, W. F. (1949). *Speech development of a bilingual child: A linguist's record: Vol. 3. Grammar and general problems*. Evanston, IL: Northwestern University Press.

Lieberson, S., Dalto, G., & Johnston, M. E. (1975). The course of mother-tongue diversity in nations. *American Journal of Sociology*, *81*, 34–61.

Liedtke, W. W., & Nelson, L. D. (1968). Concept formation and bilingualism. *Alberta Journal of Educational Research*, *14*, 225–32.

Luria, A. R. (1961). *The role of speech in the regulation of normal and abnormal behavior*. Elmsford, NY: Pergamon.

MacNab, G. L. (1979). Cognition and bilingualism: A reanalysis of studies. *Linguistics*, *17*, 231–55.

McLaughlin, B. (1984). Early bilingualism: Methodological and theoretical issues. In M.

Paradis & Y. Lebrun (Eds.), *Early bilingualism and child development* (pp. 19–45). Lisse, The Netherlands: Swets & Zeitlinger.

Paulston, C. B. (1980). *Bilingual education: Theories and issues*. Rowley, MA: Newbury House.

Paulston, C. B., & Paulston, R. G. (1980). Language and ethnic boundaries. *Language Sciences*, *2*, 69–101.

Peal, E., & Lambert, W. E. (1962). The relation of bilingualism to intelligence. *Psychological Monographs*, *76*(27, Whole No. 546).

Piattelli-Palmarini, M. (Ed.). (1980). *Language and learning: The debate between Jean Piaget and Noam Chomsky*. Cambridge, MA: Harvard University Press.

Ronjat, J. (1913). *Le développement du langage observé chez un enfant bilingue*. Paris: Champion.

Schermerhorn, R. A. (1970). *Comparative ethnic relations: A framework for theory and research*. New York: Random House.

Smith, M. E. (1939). Some light on the problem of bilingualism as found from a study of the progress in mastery of English among pre-school children of non-American ancestry in Hawaii. *Genetic Psychology Monographs*, *21*, 119–284.

Snow, C. E. (in press). Beyond conversation: Second language learners' acquisition of description and explanation. In J. Lantolf & R. DiPietro (Eds.), *Second language acquisition in the classroom setting*. Norwood, NJ: Ablex.

Stoddard, G. D., & Wellman, B. L. (1934). *Child psychology*. New York: Macmillan.

Tajfel, H. (1978). *Differentiation between social groups: Studies in the social psychology of intergroup relations*. European Monographs in Social Psychology, No. 14. New York: Academic Press.

Tajfel, H. (1981). *Human groups and social categories: Studies in social psychology*. Cambridge University Press.

Tajfel, H., & Turner, J. C. (1986). An integrative theory of intergroup conflict. In S. Worchel & W. G. Houston (Eds.), *Psychology of intergroup relations* (2d ed., pp. 7–24). Chicago: Nelson-Hall.

Terman, L. M. (1918). The vocabulary test as a measure of intelligence. *Journal of Educational Psychology*, *9*, 452–9.

Thompson, G. G. (1952). *Child psychology*. Boston: Houghton Mifflin.

Torrance, E. P., Wu, J. J., Gowan, J. C., & Alliotti, N. (1970). Creating functioning of monolingual and bilingual children in Singapore. *Journal of Educational Psychology*, *61*, 72–5.

Vygotsky, L. S. (1962). *Thought and language*. Cambridge, MA: MIT Press.

Young, K. (1922, July). *Mental differences in certain immigrant groups*. University of Oregon Publication, Vol. 1, No. 11. Eugene, OR: The University Press.

Zivin, G. (1979). *The development of self-regulation through private speech*. New York: Wiley.

# Index